GRAND SLAM BASEBALL

The Lore & Legends
of America's Game

Contributing Writers: Paul Adomites, Bruce Markusen, Matthew Silverman, Jon Springer, Marty Strasen, Jodi Webb, Saul Wisnia.

Cover Illustrator: Peter Siu

Contributing Illustrator: Elizabeth Traynor

The quotation on page 301 is reprinted by permission of *The Complete Pitcher, Inc.*

Contents

America's Grandest Game

Hey, baseball fans! Welcome to *Armchair Reader™: Grand Slam Baseball.*

Baseball has had a long and colorful history, with fascinating personalities, long-standing traditions, spirited rivalries, and generation after generation of devoted fans.

Through the years, baseball has remained steeped in tradition and true to its original principles. This is what impressed us the most as we compiled the stories and fascinating facts for *Armchair Reader™: Grand Slam Baseball.* Sure, the uniforms and equipment have changed, and the players now earn a lot more money, but baseball today retains much of its vintage style.

It still has six outs per inning, nine innings per game. Take ball four and walk to first base, hit it fair over the fence and trot around the bases. The positions are all the same, and even many of the teams are the same. The Pirates still play in Pittsburgh; the Cubs still suit up in Chicago; and even though they moved from Brooklyn to Los Angeles, the Dodgers still boast the same name. This uniformity and consistency is one of baseball's greatest traits. Throughout all the challenges (the Black Sox scandal, the Great Depression, segregation, World Wars I and II, the strikes of 1981 and 1994, the controversy of steroid use), the essence of the game has endured.

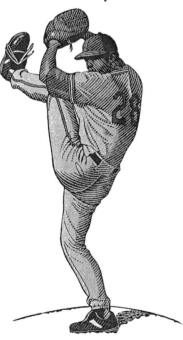

In *Armchair Reader™: Grand Slam Baseball,* we pay tribute to the game's rich traditions. Through stories, stats, anecdotes, quotations, and unusual and little-known facts, baseball comes alive. We examine the great moments, the unique and colorful personalities, the tension of the game, the joy of victory, and the heartbreak of loss. Although it's impossible to cover every topic in one book, we hope you'll find this to be one of the most entertaining compendiums on baseball you've ever read.

Here are just a few of the many great stories you'll find inside:

Players other than Jackie Robinson who broke the color line

The history of baseball cards, Little League, and team mascots

The nasty antics of baseball's bad boys

Tips from the pros about pitching, hitting, and fielding

The best—and quirkiest—ballparks, and what makes them so special

I hope that after you've savored the stories, been fascinated by the facts, and learned about the greats of yesterday and today, you'll come to the same conclusion that we did: America's favorite pastime is still the same grand game it has always been—only maybe now it's even better.

So sit back in your armchair (or wherever you might be most comfortable), and enjoy.

The Publisher

P.S. If you have any thoughts, questions, or ideas, or are interested in any of our other great Armchair Readers™, please contact us at: www.armchairreader.com.

Bill Veeck: The Grand Hustler

One man seemed to have the magic touch when it came to boosting attendance, and doing it fast. That man was Bill Veeck, and he kept fans in stitches with gimmicks and goofiness for years.

Bill Veeck was literally born into baseball. His father was president of the Chicago Cubs, hired by owner William Wrigley. The junior Veeck grew up in the ballpark, working as everything from a soda-pop vendor and ticket taker to groundskeeper (he claimed to have planted the ivy on the outfield walls of Wrigley Field), moving up to club treasurer while he took night courses in business, accounting, and engineering.

A Man of the People

In 1941, he bought the American Association Milwaukee Brewers. Veeck was just 27 years old, but he was already exploding with ideas. He never announced his promotions ahead of time, so folks would show up at the park with no idea what to expect. What they got were giveaways such as live lobsters, buckets of nails, or hosiery. They got fireworks, live bands, and ballet. Anything could happen, and the fans loved it.

Veeck was unlike any other owner. While the other big-league moguls still wore steamed shirts and stickpins, Veeck never—ever—wore a tie. He much preferred the company of the bleacher fans to that of millionaires and movie stars. He spent his time during the games out in the stands, chatting with the fans, joining them for a beer, talking baseball. He asked the fans what they wanted, and he listened to their answers.

Taking Chances

As owner of the Cleveland Indians, Veeck had his greatest success. He integrated the American League by signing Larry Doby in 1947. (Veeck allegedly received 20,000 pieces of hate mail about the signing and replied to each one by hand.) When he persuaded living legend Satchel Paige to join his team in '48, many called it a ridiculous publicity stunt. But it turned out to be anything but when Paige (at age 42, the oldest rookie in major-league history), went 6–1 in 72.2 innings, recorded an ERA of 2.48, and threw three complete games and two shutouts in his seven starts. The Indians won the pennant and the World Series in 1948, and fans came out in record numbers.

Make 'em Laugh

Veeck bought the St. Louis Browns in 1951, and that year he engineered a stunt designed to send the fans home chuckling and the baseball powers huffing and puffing in dismay. The fans were to help celebrate the 50th anniversary of the American League; everyone received a slice of birthday cake as they entered the gate. Between games of the doubleheader, a fake birthday cake was rolled onto the field, and out of it jumped 3′7″ Eddie Gaedel, wearing a Browns uniform with number ⅛ on the back. His job was to crouch down and ensure he'd get a walk. He did, and the fans went crazy.

The Fans Have Their Say

Another memorable Veeck promotion was "Grandstand Managers' Night" on August 24, 1951, in which more than 1,000 St. Louis Browns fans decided on the game strategy while manager Zack Taylor sat alongside the dugout, propped up his feet, and drank an orange soda while he counted the fans' votes. The fans were given signs that said "YES" and "NO." Before the game, they held up these cards to select the Browns' starting lineup. During the game, they used these cards to vote on such questions as "Infield In?" or "Bunt?" The lineup choice was probably the fans' best decision. They replaced the regular starting catcher and first baseman with bench-sitters Sherm Lollar and Hank "Bow Wow" Arft. Each wound up with two RBI; Lollar had a homer and a double. The Browns, who had lost four of their previous five games, snapped the streak with a 5–3 crowd-managed win. Then they lost their next five.

In 1959, Veeck bought the Chicago White Sox and continued his fun-filled promotions. He created the exploding scoreboard that set off fireworks when a Sox player homered. And it was Veeck's idea to have Harry Caray lead the crowd in singing "Take Me Out to the Ball Game" during the seventh-inning stretch, a tradition that moved with Harry from Sox Park to Wrigley Field in 1982.

Versatile Veeck

Any attempt to categorize Bill Veeck will inevitably result in slamming into a few walls of contradictions. Was he simply a ruthless (self) promoter who delighted in blowing the buttons off stuffed shirts? Was he truly the fans' owner, the man who cared for them more than anything? Was he merely a hustler, a Barnum, primarily a con-man? Was he a savvy baseball intellect, or was he just lucky?

The answer to the final question is probably easiest. From 1947 through 1964, the New York Yankees were toppled from their habitual perch atop the American League just three times—twice by a team Veeck owned (1948 Indians, 1959 White Sox) and once by a team he had built (1954 Indians). If Veeck didn't always know how to make money running a team, he knew how to make money selling it. Every deal he made showed substantial profits. He set attendance records in Cleveland and Chicago, and he quintupled attendance in St. Louis.

Even when Bill Veeck made a mistake, he turned it into good publicity (or at least a good laugh). But perhaps the trait that most clearly defined the huge and paradoxical style of Bill Veeck was his sheer lust for life. Despite living in severe pain (he was said to have had 36 different operations), he never let it hold him back. After he died, one of his obituaries noted that if a life is measured not by how long it is, but by how full it is, "the old rapscallion [Veeck] must have turned over the odometer a few times."

Fast Facts

- *They say baseball stats run in cycles. If so, none does more than basestealing. Of the top 13 seasons for steals, six happened in the 1880s and five happened in the 1980s.*

- *In 1999, Fernando Tatis, playing for the St. Louis Cardinals, became the only player to hit two grand slams in the same inning.*

- *The first major-leaguer to hit a home run with the lights on was Babe Herman of the Reds in July 1935.*

- *Major-league umpire Cal Hubbard is the only person in both the football and baseball Halls of Fame.*

- *Pitcher Phil Niekro holds the record for having the most wins without ever appearing in a World Series (318). He played 24 seasons, mostly with the Braves.*

- *The list of batters with hitting streaks of 30 or more games includes some dynamite batters: Joe DiMaggio, Pete Rose, George Brett, Tris Speaker, Rogers Hornsby, Stan Musial, and Albert Pujols. However, only two players have done it twice: Cobb and Sisler.*

- *Eddie Mathews is the only person to play for the same franchise in three cities: Boston, Milwaukee, and Atlanta.*

- *Chuck Finley of the Indians and Angels is the only pitcher to strike out four batters in one inning more than once. He did it three times from 1999–2000.*

- *In 1882, Paul Hines became the first ballplayer to wear sunglasses on the field. They weren't corrective; he just didn't like having the sun in his eyes.*

Magical Moments

With luck and force of will, Johnny Vander Meer made lightning strike twice.

The Setting: Ebbets Field, Brooklyn; June 15, 1938
The Magic: Johnny Vander Meer reaches the stars with his unprecedented second consecutive no-hitter.

It's a record that is highly unlikely to be tied and almost certain never to be broken: no-hitters in back-to-back pitching outings. Cincinnati Red Johnny Vander Meer was just 23 years old when he faced the Boston Bees on June 11 and nailed a 3–0 victory without allowing a hit. It was the 48th no-hitter since the National League had been founded in 1876. Four days later he faced the Brooklyn Dodgers in Ebbets Field. The game was already historic—it was the first night game ever played there. Some will claim that the poor lighting had as much to do with Vandy's success as his furious fastball. Vander Meer was a notoriously hard-throwing wild lefty. Sometimes the ball went where it was supposed to, and plenty of times it didn't.

In his first no-hitter, on June 11, Vander Meer had walked just three. Things were different the night of June 15. He had already given free passes to five Dodgers when the ninth inning started. One out came quickly. Then the torture began. He walked Babe Phelps, Cookie Lavagetto, and Dolph Camilli in succession to load the bases. A ground ball forced one man out at home. The next batter was the veteran Leo Durocher. On a 2–2 count, Durocher tagged a Texas Leaguer into center that Harry Craft nabbed at the knees. Thanks to his own skill and the help of his teammates, Vandy had claimed a new spot in the record books—one that will probably never be matched.

Best Breaking Pitches

The ball went thataway.

Bert Blyleven's Curve

Blyleven's big, looping bender was a textbook picture of how much a ball could break. No one of his time threw a better one. And with superb control, he rang up a lot of strikeouts and few walks. Of course, when his bender hung, it cost him in home runs. In 1986, pitching for the Twins, he set the record by allowing 50 taters. Then to prove it was no fluke, he gave up 46 the next year.

Steve Carlton's Slider

Among lefties, only Warren Spahn won more games. Among all pitchers, only Nolan Ryan, Roger Clemens, and Randy Johnson have fanned more. Carlton was a good pitcher until he learned his remarkable slider—then he became a great one. He won four Cy Youngs, something nobody else had ever done. In 1972, he won 27 games for a Phils team that won only 59—the highest percentage of games won by one man in the 20th century.

Carl Hubbell's Screwball

The screwball is thrown by twisting the arm the opposite direction from the curve. Proof that Hubbell threw a zillion of them is that his arm was permanently twisted. But he dominated the NL in an era when big hitters were the rule. On July 2, 1933, he pitched an 18-inning shutout, striking out 12 and allowing no walks. In the 1934 All-Star Game, he set down Babe Ruth, Lou Gehrig, Jimmie Foxx, Al Simmons, and Joe Cronin on consecutive strikeouts.

Sandy Koufax's Curve

Koufax was the archetypal wild left-hander until a patient catcher told him to relax and rely on his curveball more. That curve became one of the deadliest weapons in Sandy's pitching arsenal. In his last five seasons (1962–66), he led the league in ERA every year; in wins, strikeouts, and shutouts three times; and in complete games twice. But an arthritic arm ended his career prematurely.

Christy Mathewson's Fadeaway

A hero of the 1900s and '10s, Bucknell-educated Matty had one especially nasty pitch: the fadeaway, with its brutal opposite-direction break. (Today it would be known as a screwball.) He threw it rarely, perhaps a dozen times a game. He took it easy on most hitters; it was only "in the pinch" when he had to bear down.

Bruce Sutter's Splitter

The split-fingered fastball, gripped like a forkball but thrown so hard it could sink devilishly, was known as "the pitch of the 1970s," and Sutter's was probably the best one out there. He learned it after arm surgery threatened his career in 1973. Sutter used the nasty pitch (sometimes called the splitter because of its resemblance to a spitball) to lead the National League in saves five of six years with the Cubs and Cards.

Ed Walsh's Spitter

Before 1920, the spitball wasn't dirty, sneaky, or illegal. It was simply a potent tool in the hands of a master like Ed Walsh. Walsh learned it from Elmer Stricklett, who learned it from George Hildebrand, a minor-league teammate. Walsh could throw it a lot without tiring himself out. In 1908, he set the American League record by pitching 464 innings. He won 40 games that year, too.

Hoyt Wilhelm's Knuckler

Wilhelm didn't make it to the majors until 1952, when he was almost 30 years old, but with that wildly dancing knuckleball of his, he stuck around past his 48th birthday. In Baltimore, they had the catcher wear an oversized glove to snag the thing. Wilhelm won more games in relief than any other pitcher ever.

Barry Zito's Curve

It has the classic "12-to-6" downward break, with little or no sideways movement. Batters who try to hit it often perform curious contortions. Those who don't even try often look positively demoralized by it. Zito's judicious use of the curve helped him win a Cy Young Award in only his second full season in the bigs (2002).

All-Time Great

Babe Ruth

Not just the greatest ballplayer (hitter and pitcher) of all time, but a unique American icon.

Born: February 6, 1895; Baltimore, MD
MLB Career: Boston Red Sox, 1914–19; New York Yankees, 1920–34; Boston Braves, 1935
Hall of Fame Resume: 714 homers (third) * In the top three lifetime in runs, home runs, home run percentage, RBI, on-base percentage, walks, and walk percentage
Inside Pitch: When Babe Ruth died, he owned 56 major-league records plus ten more AL marks—including the best winning percentage for a pitcher, lifetime, *against* the New York Yankees.

No one in baseball history has matched the achievements of the most well-rounded player of all time: George Herman "Babe" Ruth, pitcher and slugger extraordinaire.

A kid of the streets who learned to play ball while he was an "inmate" at St. Mary's Industrial School for Boys, 19-year-old George made the majors with the Boston Red Sox in 1914. Starting the next year, he went 78–40 with an ERA under 2.30 in helping the club to three World Series titles over four seasons. The left-hander completed a Series-record 29 consecutive scoreless innings in 1918, yet he was such a successful hitter that manager Ed Barrow began giving him outfield assignments on non-pitching days. The 6'2" giant liked the arrangement, and when he was allowed to roam the out-field almost exclusively in 1919, he hit an ML-record 29 home runs.

Theatrical producer and Red Sox owner Harry Frazee was not impressed. Needing money for his latest show and believing the uninhibited Ruth and his exorbitant $10,000 salary were to blame for a sixth-place slide in 1919, Frazee sold Babe to the New York Yankees in January 1920 for $125,000—plus a $300,000 loan on Fenway Park. Babe put his stamp of approval on the stupidest move in baseball history with a record-shattering 54 homers that year—more homers than 14 of 16 major-league teams compiled—and the spark was lit. Fans wanted excitement after the hard realities of World War I and the Black Sox scandal, and Ruth supplied it—showing that one swing could accomplish what had previously taken a series of bunts, steals, and slides.

He was the quintessential hero of the Roaring '20s, a ham for the cameras who enjoyed having every move followed and could back up his bravado. Dominating as no player before or since, he averaged 47 home runs and 133 RBI during the decade when just four other players hit as many as 40 homers even once. Over his career, Ruth would lead the Yankees to seven pennants and four World Series championships (hitting 15 homers in Series play), despite regular indulgences in women, booze, and food. He drew suspensions from his managers and screams of delight from kids—and it was the kids who seemed to matter to him most.

Even when his 94–46 pitching mark is not factored in, Ruth's records are remarkable. He slugged .849 in a single season (1920) and averaged a .690 slugging and .474 on-base percentage over his career. When the .342 lifetime hitter retired, his 714 home runs were about twice as many as his nearest competitor. That career total and Babe's season high of 60 homers in 1927 have both since been topped, but his impact on the game remains undisputed. He was baseball's most beloved performer—and its finest.

⚾ ⚾ ⚾

"Ruth made a grave mistake when he gave up pitching. Working once a week, he might have lasted a long time and become a great star."

—Tris Speaker on Babe Ruth's switch to the outfield, 1919

⚾ ⚾ ⚾

"Every big-leaguer and his wife should teach their children to pray: 'God bless Mommy, God bless Daddy, and God bless Babe Ruth.'"

—Ruth teammate Waite Hoyt, *Baseball as I Have Known It*

Fans or Fanatics?

*Whether or not the actual etymology of the word "fan" is "fanatic,"
when fans are at their most fanatic, they get in the way
of the game on the field. The earliest example on record of fans
interfering with the game happened when professional
baseball was barely a year old.*

The Stockings Get Tangled

June 14, 1870. The Cincinnati Red Stockings (the sport's first all-professional team) came to Brooklyn with 84 consecutive wins under their belt. When the Brooklyn Atlantics managed to force the matchup into extra innings, fans really got into the game. The Red Stockings scored two in the 11th to take the lead, but in the bottom of the inning, with a man on third, Joe Start of the Atlantics drove a ball into right, where it rolled into the overflow crowd standing there. Cincinnati right fielder Cal McVey tried to make a play on it, but tangled with a fan, and Start ended up on third. Before long the Atlantics had tied, then won, the game, and the longest winning streak in history was (at least partially) ended by a fan.

Snowball Fight!

April 11, 1907. It was Opening Day for the New York Giants against the Philadelphia Phillies. There was snow in New York, and when the game proved lacking in action, the fans got restless. They began throwing snowballs at each other, then at the players and umps. The general tone of merriment was too much for the highly serious umpire Bill Klem, who brought the proceedings to a halt and awarded the forfeit to the Phils.

The Royal Rooters

October 15, 1912. They were the most famous fans in the game: the "Royal Rooters" of Boston, led by politico "Honey Fitz" Fitzgerald (President Kennedy's grandfather) and saloon owner "Nuf Ced" (because he always had the last word) McGreevey. The Royal Rooters marched together, traveled together, and sang songs and taunted the opposition together. And they always—*always*—sat together, in the same block of seats at Fenway Park. Except in Game 7 of the 1912 World Series. With the Red Sox up three games to two (Game 2 had ended in a tie), a Boston ticket clerk mistakenly sold the seats that belonged to the Royal Rooters. When the group arrived at the ballpark and found that they had no seats, they didn't handle it well. Just as the game was about to start, they broke through an outfield fence, disrupting fans and players, then marched around the field in a riotous scene. By the time the police restored order and the game was able to begin, the Boston pitcher's arm had cooled off. He allowed five first-inning runs, a deficit the Sox were unable to make up. So the Rooters had effectively forced another Series game—something they had not intended, seats or no seats. The Rooters were so miffed that they refused to go to Game 8, although they were right there celebrating with everyone when Boston won the championship.

A Medwick Salad
October 9, 1934. It was a wild scene in Detroit. The Cardinals jumped out to an early lead in Game 7 of the World Series, and in the sixth inning Card Joe Medwick tripled in a run to make the score 8–0. When Medwick slid hard into Tiger third baseman Marv Owen, they got into a scuffle. And when Medwick took his position in left field for the next inning, the irate fans let him have it. With lunch. The array of fruits and vegetables tossed at Medwick included bananas, apples, cabbage, soda bottles, oranges, and more. Finally, Commissioner Landis had Medwick removed from the game for his own safety, and the game continued without further incident. St. Louis won 11–0.

Ten-Cent Beer Night
June 4, 1974. In theory, it was a great idea. Offering ten-cent beers brought more than 25,000 fans into Cleveland's Municipal Stadium for the Indians-Rangers game. (The average attendance the previous season was 8,000.) However, the more these fans drank, the rowdier they became, and by the ninth inning things got ugly. Some fans started streaking; others yelled obscenities and

threw things onto the playing field. In the end, the field was littered with debris, and hundreds of fans had charged the field—some yielding weapons. When umpire Nestor Chylak realized things were truly out of control, he forfeited the game to Texas.

A 12-Year-Old Magician

October 9, 1996. It was the first game of the American League Championship Series. At Yankee Stadium in the last of the eighth, the Yanks were trailing the Orioles by a run. When Derek Jeter slapped a looping line drive toward the right-field fence, Oriole Tony Tarasco moved back to the wall and waited for the ball to come down . . . but it never did. Later, Tarasco likened it to "a magic trick. Because the ball just disappeared out of midair." Was it magic? No, but the ball did disappear—off the glove of 12-year-old Jeffrey Maier, who reached out for it and knocked it into the stands. (He lost it into the crowd, but the damage was done.) The umpire totally missed the play and awarded Jeter a homer, when he should have been out for fan interference. The Yanks tied the score, then won the game in the 11th, and Maier became a New York sensation.

Broken-Hearted Bartman

October 14, 2003. A Chicago fan did something similar at a Cub game in 2003, but instead of being celebrated as a hero, he was nearly chased out of town. The Cubs were within five outs of their first World Series appearance since 1945, leading the upstart Florida Marlins 3–0 in Game 6 of the NLCS. With one out and a Marlin on second, Luis Castillo slapped a pop-up down the left-field line. As the ball drifted into foul territory with Moises Alou in hot pursuit, fan Steve Bartman deflected the ball, blocking it from Alou's reach. The Cubs frantically yelled for fan interference, but the umpire didn't bite. The Marlins went on to score eight times that inning, tying the Series at three games apiece, and then won the league title the next night. Bartman said that he didn't see Alou coming and just tried to catch the ball. He later apologized "from the bottom of this Cub fan's broken heart."

Chatter

"The first rule for sports announcers might well hold true for the patrons in the park: Follow the ball. But this rule should be broken, or modified, to suit the occasion."

—Hall of Fame broadcaster Red Barber,
explaining how to watch a baseball game

"I knew I was good enough to play in the big leagues. I just knew it."

—Negro Leaguer Judy Johnson,
Our Game: An American Baseball History

"[Harry Wright] eats baseball, breathes baseball, thinks baseball, dreams baseball, and incorporates baseball in his prayers."

—*Cincinnati Enquirer*, 1869

"You gotta be a man to play baseball for a living, but you gotta have a lot of little boy in you, too."

—Roy Campanella

"Never change a decision, never stop to talk to a man. Make 'em play ball and keep their mouths shut, and…people will be on your side and you'll be called the king of umpires."

—Player and manager-turned-umpire Bob Ferguson, circa 1890

"Best one-legged player I ever saw."

—Casey Stengel on oft-injured Mickey Mantle,
Baseball Digest, November 1995

"A hot dog at the ballpark is better than steak at the Ritz."

—Humphrey Bogart, in a film ad for organized baseball

An Ambassador and a Gentleman

When we think of baseball legends, we usually place them into one category: player, manager, or pioneer. But there are some icons who defy typecasting, and Buck O'Neil—one of baseball's greatest ambassadors—was one of them.

Buck O'Neil was a solid player in the Negro Leagues, with a career batting average of .288. The first baseman was a strong clutch hitter and had a league-leading .353 average in 1946; the next year he hit .358. He went on barnstorming tours with teammate Satchel Paige, played in the 1942 Black World Series, and was named to the East-West All-Star Game (the Negro Leagues' celebrated all-star game) in 1942, '43, and '49.

Yet there was so much more to Buck O'Neil than what he accomplished as a player. In 1948, he became manager of the Kansas City Monarchs. He won four Negro League pennants, led his clubs to two appearances in the Black World Series, and guided his teams to a perfect record of 4–0 in the East-West Game.

The Negro Leagues began to dissolve in the 1950s, and O'Neil segued into a career with the major leagues. Joining the Chicago Cubs as a scout, O'Neil played crucial roles in signing Hall of Famers Lou Brock and Ernie Banks and quality major-leaguers like Joe Carter and Oscar Gamble. O'Neil also became the first African-American coach in major-league history, joining the Cubs' "College of Coaches" (which unsuccessfully employed a group of managers rather than just one) in the early 1960s.

O'Neil's contributions to baseball reached far off the field. After leaving scouting and coaching, O'Neil probably did more than anyone else to promote the legacy of the Negro Leagues. Whether charming audiences on Ken Burns' *Baseball* documentary or appearing on David Letterman's talk show, or through his work as a voting member of the Hall of Fame's Veterans Committee, O'Neil always did his best to praise the abilities and personalities of other Negro League stars. Ever modest about himself, he said that Oscar

Charleston was the equal of Ty Cobb and praised Satchel Paige for bringing out the best in everyone—even the opposition.

O'Neil's storytelling greatly enhanced the public's knowledge and familiarity with the Negro Leagues, which had been largely overlooked until the 1990s. In 2000, O'Neil visited the Hall of Fame and discussed the ability that black players showed when they barnstormed against white teams featuring major-leaguers. "They [the major-leaguers] were just out there for a payday, but we wanted to prove a point that they weren't superior," O'Neil told the Cooperstown audience. "So we would stretch that single into a double, that double into a triple, that triple into a home run. This was Negro Leagues baseball, this was the baseball Jackie Robinson brought to the major leagues." O'Neil emerged as an unofficial ambassador for the sport, exposing younger generations to the rich culture of the Negro Leagues.

Even in Buck's final summer, he persisted in advancing the awareness of black baseball. He continued his work as the chair of the Negro Leagues Museum, which he had started through tireless promotional and fundraising efforts. At the Hall of Fame induction ceremony in July 2006, O'Neil stole the show with a humorous, lively, and uplifting speech. Then in August, he achieved an unusual place in baseball history when he became the oldest man—at 94 years of age—to take the plate in a professional game.

Unfortunately, the one thing O'Neil was not able to accomplish during his life was induction into Cooperstown. In 2006, he fell one vote short, which shocked his fans and supporters and certainly caused O'Neil a deeper disappointment than he ever let on. He passed away on October 6, 2006, at the age of 94.

In considering someone's candidacy for the Hall of Fame, most people feel it is not enough merely to focus on what one did as a player. Rather, the accomplishments of an entire *career* must be taken into consideration. In the case of O'Neil, his efforts as a manager, scout, coach, and ambassador raise his status, making him one of the most diverse and respected figures in baseball history. And it's the entirety of those accomplishments that should one day earn Buck O'Neil what he deserves—election and induction into baseball's Hall of Fame.

Billy Sunday

He was speedy on the field, but his real power was in the pulpit.

As a ballplayer, Billy Sunday was good enough while playing in Marshalltown, Iowa, to impress the legendary Cap Anson, former Marshalltown native and future Hall of Famer. Anson signed him and brought him up to play for his White Stockings in 1883. Billy was not a superlative hitter, but he was fast—very fast. He was once timed circling the bases in 14 seconds flat. And he used that speed to swipe bases: In one of his eight big-league seasons he stole 71; in another, 84.

But what Sunday did off the field made him a legend far beyond what his baseball skills would indicate. In 1887, while sitting on a Chicago street corner, a little drunk, Sunday was attracted by the familiar religious songs sung by a traveling missionary troupe. That experience led him to the Pacific Garden Mission, where he had a religious experience and quit drinking. Over time he was fully converted, and three years later he left baseball to become a preacher, turning his back on nearly $500 a month to work for less than $80.

And what a preacher he became. Full of fire and brimstone, he bounced around the stage—one observer claimed Sunday covered a mile on foot at each sermon. Onstage, he raced around—sometimes pretending to slide into home plate—danced, and even broke chairs to emphasize a dramatic point, often regarding the evils of liquor. His audiences ate it up.

Using baseball as a central metaphor, Sunday preached to countless willing listeners; some say more than a hundred million throughout his career. From small towns in Iowa and Illinois to, later, Philadelphia, Boston, and Carnegie Hall in New York City, Billy Sunday became the most successful evangelist the United States had ever known.

◖◗ ◖◗ ◖◗

"Good-bye, boys, I am done with this kind of living."

—Billy Sunday upon quitting baseball to go into preaching

Fast Facts

- In 1981, Rollie Fingers of the Milwaukee Brewers became the first relief pitcher to win the American League Most Valuable Player Award. He also won the Cy Young Award that same year. Relief pitcher Jim Konstanty of Philadelphia won the 1950 National League MVP Award.

- The first "Babe" in baseball was Babe Adams, who pitched from 1906 to 1926.

- The reserve clause meant that for nearly 100 years players were unable to change teams.

- Until 1975, rules required that all major-league baseballs be covered in horsehide. As horsehide became more expensive, it was also okay for balls to be covered in cowhide.

- On May 30, 1946, Bama Rowell was the first player to smash the Bulova clock at Ebbets Field, which some have said was the inspiration for the scoreboard scene in the movie The Natural.

- The first All-Star Game broadcast on television took place on July 11, 1950.

- In 2006, when Diamondback rookie Carlos Quentin hit a home run off Astro relief pitcher Chad Qualls, it was the first time in major-league history that a "Q"-surnamed batter hit a home run off a "Q"-surnamed pitcher.

- The 1945 Washington Senators failed to hit a single ball over the fence in their home park, Griffith Stadium. Of the team's 27 home runs that season, 26 came on the road, and one was Joe Kuhel's inside-the-park shot.

Going, Going...Gone!

The batter squares up, the pitcher unloads, the bat whips around in a clean arc—and you witness the most celebrated daily accomplishment in baseball. About 5,400 home runs are hit in the majors in a typical year, but that doesn't diminish the allure of the four-bagger. Here are some special long-ball facts and stats.

Most Home Runs in One Month

AL	Rudy York, Detroit	August 1937	18
NL	Sammy Sosa, Chicago	June 1998	20

Most in One Month by a Left-Handed Batter

AL	Babe Ruth, New York	September 1927	17
NL	Barry Bonds, San Francisco	May 2001	17

Most in One Month by a Switch-Hitter

AL	Mickey Mantle, New York	May 1956	16
NL	Ken Caminiti, San Diego	August 1996	14

Most Home Runs, Season, by a Leadoff Hitter Leading Off a Game

AL	Alfonso Soriano	New York, 2003	13
NL	Bobby Bonds	San Francisco, 1973	11

Most Home Runs, Season, by a Pinch Hitter

AL	Joe Cronin	Boston, 1943	5
NL	Dave Hansen	Los Angeles, 2000	7
	Craig Wilson	Pittsburgh, 2001	7

Most Home Runs, Season, by a Pitcher

AL	Wes Ferrell	Cleveland, 1931	9
NL	Don Newcombe	Brooklyn, 1955	7
	Don Drysdale	Brooklyn, 1958	7
	Don Drysdale	Los Angeles, 1965	7
	Mike Hampton	Colorado, 2001	7

Players Who Hit Four in One Game

Bobby Lowe	Boston NL	May 30, 1894	⅄
Ed Delahanty	Philadelphia NL	July 13, 1896	
Lou Gehrig	New York AL	June 3, 1932	
Chuck Klein	Philadelphia NL	July 10, 1936	
Pat Seerey	Chicago AL	July 18, 1948	
Gil Hodges	Brooklyn NL	August 31, 1950	
Joe Adcock	Milwaukee NL	July 31, 1954	
Rocky Colavito	Cleveland AL	June 10, 1959	X
Willie Mays	San Francisco NL	April 30, 1961	
Mike Schmidt	Philadelphia NL	April 17, 1976	
Bob Horner	Atlanta NL	July 6, 1986	
Mark Whiten	St. Louis NL	September 7, 1993	
Mike Cameron	Seattle AL	May 2, 2002	
Shawn Green	Los Angeles NL	May 23, 2002	
Carlos Delgado	Toronto AL	September 25, 2003	

NOTE: Only Klein, Seerey, and Schmidt hit their final homer in extra innings. Lowe, Gehrig, Colavito, Schmidt, Cameron, and Delgado all did it in four consecutive at-bats.

Number of Times Home Runs Were Hit from Both Sides of the Plate in One Game, Lifetime

Eddie Murray	Baltimore AL, Los Angeles NL, Cleveland AL	11
Chili Davis	San Francisco NL, California AL, Minnesota AL, Kansas City AL	11
Mickey Mantle	New York AL	10

Career Inside-the-Park Home Runs

AL	Ty Cobb	Detroit/Philadelphia	46	⅄
NL	Tommy Leach	Louisville/Pittsburgh/Chicago	49	
ML	Sam Crawford	Cincinnati/Detroit	51	⅄

Most Home Runs, Season

AL	Roger Maris	New York, 1961	61
NL	Barry Bonds	San Francisco, 2001	73

Lifetime Home Run Leaders, by Number of Letters in Last Name

Letters	Homers	Player
3	511	Mel Ott
4	714	Babe Ruth
5	755	Hank Aaron
6	536	Mickey Mantle
7	583	Mark McGwire
8	586	Frank Robinson
9	573	Harmon Killebrew
10	335	Darryl Strawberry
11	452	Carl Yastrzemski
12	84	Red Schoendienst
13	98	Todd Hollandsworth

Most Home Runs in One World Series, by Number of Games Played

Games	Player	Team, Year	Homers
4	Lou Gehrig	New York AL, 1928	4
5	Donn Clendenon	New York NL, 1969	3
6	Reggie Jackson	New York AL, 1977	5
7	Hank Bauer	New York AL, 1958	4
	Barry Bonds	San Francisco NL, 2002	4
	Babe Ruth	New York AL, 1926	4
	Duke Snider	Brooklyn NL, 1952	4
	Duke Snider	Brooklyn NL, 1955	4
	Gene Tenace	Oakland AL, 1972	4
8	Patsy Dougherty	Boston AL, 1903	2

Most Consecutive Games with at Least One Home Run

AL	Ken Griffey, Jr.	Seattle, July 20–28, 1993	8
AL	Don Mattingly	New York, July 8–18, 1987	8
NL	Dale Long	Pittsburgh, May 19–28, 1956	8

Can of Corn

"Washington—first in war, first in peace, last in the American League."

—Charles Dryden, on the lowly Senators

"Is that the best game you ever pitched?"

—Question posed by an anonymous reporter to Don Larsen following his perfect World Series game in 1956

"I believe in rules. I also believe I have a right to test the rules by seeing how far they can be bent."

—Leo Durocher, *Nice Guys Finish Last*

"We had a lot of triple-threat guys—slip, fumble, and fall."

—Pittsburgh catcher Joe Garagiola on the awful Pirate teams of the early 1950s

"It was a cross between a screwball and a changeup. It was a screw-up."

—Cubs reliever Bob Patterson on a lousy pitch hit by Cincinnati's Barry Larkin off him for a game-winning homer, from *The Wall Street Journal*, quoted in *Parade*, December 29, 1996

"Well, you can't win them all."

—Connie Mack on his 1916 A's, who went 36–117

"The saddest words of all to a pitcher are three: 'Take him out.'"

—Christy Mathewson, *Pitching in a Pinch*

Helmets Head On

For some players, wearing a helmet only at the plate is not enough.

Since 1971, major-league batters have been required to wear helmets, but most fielders still opt for a soft cap. However, there have been a few players over the years who have wanted to protect their head at bat or in the field.

1953 Pittsburgh Pirates: During the 1953 season, the Pirates took the field wearing rather primitive fiberglass "miner's caps" at the mandate of general manager Branch Rickey, who owned stock in the company that produced the helmets. Though partially motivated by a desire to make money for his company, Rickey also understood the benefit of keeping his players healthy. Under Rickey's orders, the Pirate players had to wear the helmets both at bat and in the field. Even manager Fred Haney joined the helmet-wearing brigade, apparently to protect himself from banging his head against the top of the dugout when leaving it to visit the mound. The helmets became a permanent feature for Pirate hitters, but the fielders figured their chances of getting beaned in the head were so small, it wasn't worth putting up with the awkward, heavy headgear.

Richie Allen: Often a verbal target of fans in Philadelphia, Allen one day found himself bombarded by hundreds of pennies thrown by fans in the left-field stands at Connie Mack Stadium. The demonstration of violence convinced Allen to wear a helmet for the rest of his career, whether playing in left field or at first base. Even after being traded by Philadelphia, Allen continued the practice while playing in St. Louis, Los Angeles, Chicago, and Oakland.

George "Boomer" Scott: Like Allen, Scott began wearing a helmet in the field because of unruly fan reaction, but his decision came in response to actions of the road fans (who often threw things at him), not the hometown faithful at Fenway Park. The clunky helmet belied Scott's fielding grace; "Boomer" won eight Gold Gloves for the Red Sox and the Brewers.

Joe Ferguson: Primarily a catcher during his major-league career, Ferguson also played in right field from time to time. The time-sharing plan began early in his career with the Dodgers, who already had a fine defensive catcher in Steve Yeager but wanted to make room for the power-hitting Ferguson in their batting order. When the 200-pound Ferguson took to the outfield—a position he hated to play—he made sure to take his hard hat with him. This may have been due to his lack of confidence in catching the ball. Ferguson once lost two fly balls in the sun during the same game, making his head an easy target for a baseball dropping out of the sky. While Ferguson's fielding prowess in right field sometimes made his managers nervous, he didn't lack for ability in throwing the ball. Playing for the Dodgers during the 1974 World Series, Ferguson unleashed a 290-foot throw from right field to the catcher, taking a potential run off the board for the Oakland A's.

Dave Parker: It's easy to understand why "The Cobra" decided to start wearing a helmet in right field. On July 20, 1980, during the first game of a doubleheader against the Dodgers at Pittsburgh's Three Rivers Stadium, one particularly nasty hometown fan fired a nine-volt transistor battery at the beleaguered Parker, who had come under criticism for playing poorly while saddled with an injured knee. The battery barely missed Parker's head, whizzing by his ear before landing on the artificial turf. Stunned by the near miss, Parker walked off and didn't return to the outfield for the rest of the doubleheader. Amazingly, the battery episode wasn't the first time that Parker had found himself in the line of fan fire. Earlier in the 1980 season, another idiotic fan had hurled a bag of nuts and bolts in Parker's direction. (It also missed.)

John Olerud: While attending Washington State University in 1989, Olerud suffered a brain hemorrhage and an aneurysm during a morning workout. Though he recovered, doctors advised him to wear a protective batting helmet while playing first base or pitching (he was a two-position player in college). This would protect against line drives and collisions with baserunners that might result in contact with the skull.

Who Does What?

*You don't put on a show without an army of support personnel,
and you don't field a baseball team without plenty of help, either.
Here's a guide to the often-unseen worker bees of baseball.*

Major-league baseball teams have much in common with other
corporate entities, with departments such as finance/administra-
tion, human resources, information technology, and sales/market-
ing. Here are the other jobs, those more directly related to
baseball. Note: Many of these are now actually departments,
staffed by anywhere from a handful to several dozen employees.

General manager has the ultimate responsibility for the on-field
activities of the team, including obtaining, signing, and trading
players; hiring the manager and minor-league managers and
coaches; and doing it while staying within the budget established
by upper management.

Manager determines who will play and pitch, the batting order,
in-game substitutions, and pregame strategy.

Bench coach aids the manager, mostly during the game, and can
take over if the manager gets ejected.

Third-base coach transmits signals from the bench to batters and
runners, often letting them know whether or not they should
attempt to score.

First-base coach uses verbal and manual signals to keep runners
aware of the count, outs, etc., and guide them in baserunning.

Bullpen coach supervises relief pitchers.

Batboy or batgirl sees that bats, balls, and helmets are in their
correct places.

Hitting and pitching coaches work with players on those skills.

Equipment manager has the responsibility for all equipment, including clubhouse and training-room facilities.

Traveling secretary makes arrangements for planes, buses, and hotels while their team is on the road.

Head athletic trainer oversees players' workouts and is the first line of diagnosis and injury care. This is the only person in the dugout who must have college training.

Director of player development/scouting finds players, then tracks them throughout the farm system.

Special assistant for international scouting is a job new to many teams; this person must do scouting work abroad.

Park operations supervises a ballpark's physical plant, including the building itself, the grounds, lighting, and heating.

Groundskeeper oversees the field's maintenance and repair.

Corporate sales works to sell tickets to businesses.

Spring training operations handles the ballpark and the other details for spring training.

Minor-league field coordinator supervises minor-league physical plants and operations.

Broadcasting department is responsible for production and sales of radio, television, and other media.

Team videographer shoots every game to provide the database that coaches and players rely on to improve performance.

Greatest Teams of All Time

1885–88 St. Louis Browns

Record: 95–40 (1887)
Manager: (and first baseman) Charlie Comiskey
Hall of Famers: Comiskey
The Season: The third of their four consecutive American Association flags; they won by 14 games.
The Legacy: After the season, Comiskey had the owner sell off most of the stars.

With a haughty, flamboyant owner and a sometimes ragtag collection of players, the 1885 St. Louis Browns seemed an unlikely club to win four straight pennants. But they had a nucleus of superstars—plus a drive to win inspired by a no-nonsense manager—that helped them establish the viability of the American Association and earn a spot among the top teams of all time.

Their owner was German-born Chris Von der Ahe, who was easy to ridicule, easy to hate, but was still an intuitive entrepreneurial genius who boosted the Browns to success. First baseman and manager Charlie Comiskey believed in aggressive baseball and in total support from his players.

In 1885, the Browns won their league by 16 games without one batter in the top ten in batting average, on-base percentage, slugging average, total bases, home runs, or hits. Their secret was the remarkable pitching of Bob Caruthers and Dave Foutz. Between them, they hurled 890 innings with a 2.33 ERA and a 73–27 record. Caruthers had a deceptive delivery and a strong sense of a batter's weakness; Foutz was known for his calm demeanor.

That fall, they took on the Chicago White Stockings, led by Cap Anson, in the second-ever World Series. Most folks saw it as just another postseason exhibition series, not the major event it has since become. After a Game 1 tie and a Game 2 forfeit to Chicago, the teams split the next four games and agreed that Game 7 would be a "winner-take-all" match. The Browns prevailed 13–4.

The next year, the Browns won the AA by 12 games. Their two best hitters were Caruthers (the pitcher), who batted .334, and notoriously bad baserunner and fielder Tip O'Neill. The enterprising Von der Ahe decided to promote the "World's Championship Series" into a major spectacle. His ploy worked, people took note, and the fans were treated to the first great World Series finish.

That '86 Series was won by the Browns in six games against the White Stockings. They scored three times in the last of the eighth to tie the final game. In the bottom of the tenth, St. Louis outfielder Curt Welch stormed across the plate with the winning run on a wild pitch, an event that went down in history as "the $15,000 slide," even though some accounts indicate he didn't slide, and the dollar amount was overstated, too. (Von der Ahe took half of the Series receipts; the players each got about $600.) But most historians agree that that dramatic play was the high point of the AA's existence.

The Browns copped the 1887 pennant in easy fashion, winning by 14 games. It was Tip O'Neill's year. Because of a rule change that counted walks as hits, he batted .492 (.435 if you exclude the walks). He also led the league in hits, runs, doubles, triples, home runs, total bases, and slugging average—the only player ever to dominate a major league so completely. New pitcher Silver King was the top hurler, winning 32 games. For some reason, the success of the 1886 World Series format was lost on the moguls of baseball, and they experimented with a new way to determine the champion: a 15-game, 10-city, 17-day tour. It was a mess. The Browns lost eight of their first 11 games, ending their Series chances.

After three straight pennants and two World Series titles, the Browns looked solid for 1888, but strong-willed Comiskey felt he was losing control of his star players. So Von der Ahe put them up for sale. Before long, he had peddled or sold Caruthers, Foutz, Welch, star catcher Doc Bushong, and infielder Bill Gleason.

But the decimated Browns won again in '88. King pitched in nearly half of his team's 137 games, totalling 585 innings with 45 wins and an ERA of 1.64—about half the league figure. O'Neill supplied the offense, once again winning the batting title and finishing second in on-base percentage and third in slugging. St. Louis, though, fell to the New York Giants in the World Series, six games to four.

High Hopes, Bad Deals

Baseball's worst trades show the risk inherent in all swaps.

Just as bad guy Biff Tannen from the movie *Back to the Future* cleans up at the racetrack by using a futuristic sports almanac, today's baseball general managers undoubtedly wish they could make trades while armed with the still unknown statistics of every major-leaguer through 2050. Since in reality their profession is more Wall Street than Hollywood, GMs know that any swap they make has the potential to backfire—and earn its spot among the worst deals of all time.

Listed below are some of the most one-sided swaps in baseball history. In each, future superstars (noted in bold) with great years ahead of them were dealt for players beyond their prime or on the fast track to mediocrity. Often, GMs and owners had to live with the ramifications—and reminders from fans—for decades. All you have to do is read about them.

The Trade: Brooklyn Grooms send **OF Wee Willie Keeler** and **1B Dan Brouthers** to Baltimore Orioles for 3B Billy Shindle and OF George Treadway.
The Date: January 1, 1894
The Fallout: Keeler (.371) and Brouthers (.347) shined for the Orioles in 1894, with Wee Willie eventually batting above .300 for 13 straight seasons after the trade—including .424 with the Orioles in 1897. Shindle, while productive, never went over .300 for the Grooms. Treadway had one good year but was gone from the majors in three.

The Trade: Cincinnati Reds send **P Christy Mathewson** to New York Giants for P Amos Rusie.
The Date: December 15, 1900
The Fallout: Mathewson remains the NL's all-time winner with 373, all but one of which were with the Giants—whom he pitched to five pennants. Rusie had won 246 himself prior to the swap but went just 0–1 with the Reds before retiring.

The Trade: Boston Red Sox send **OF Tris Speaker** to Cleveland Indians for P Sam Jones, 3B Fred Thomas, and $55,000.
The Date: April 12, 1916
The Fallout: This was the first of many disastrous deals made by Boston. Speaker, a .336 hitter and top-notch fielder with the Sox over nine years, lasted another 13 stellar seasons (11 with the Indians) and retired with a lifetime .345 mark and 3,514 hits. Jones helped the Sox to the 1918 World Series title but was a mediocre 64–59 with Boston overall. Thomas, a .225 lifetime hitter, spent just one forgettable year with the Sox.

The Trade: Boston Red Sox send **OF Babe Ruth** to New York Yankees for $425,000 in cash and loans.
The Date: January 3, 1920
The Fallout: The granddaddy of bad swaps shifted baseball's power base from Boston to New York, where Babe hit 659 homers and rewrote the record books while leading the Yanks to seven pennants and four World Series championships in 15 years. The Sox, World Series victors four times from 1912 through 1918, wouldn't win it all again until 2004. Then-Sox owner Harry Frazee is still reviled in New England for this one.

The Trade: Boston Red Sox send **P Red Ruffing** to New York Yankees for OF-1B Cedric Durst and $50,000.
The Date: May 6, 1930
The Fallout: The last in a string of stars sent from cash-poor Boston to New York in one-sided deals, Ruffing rebounded from a 39–96 mark with woeful Sox clubs to a Cooperstown-worthy 231–124 slate with the Yanks—plus a 7–2 mark in ten World Series starts. Durst hit .245 with one homer for Boston during the rest of 1930, his last year in the majors.

The Trade: Chicago Cubs send **OF Lou Brock,** P Jack Spring, and P Paul Toth to St. Louis Cardinals for P Ernie Broglio, P Bobby Shantz, and OF Doug Clemens.
The Date: June 15, 1964
The Fallout: It was essentially a Brock-for-Broglio swap. The

Cubs hoped Ernie (18–8 in 1963) would anchor their staff; instead, he went 7–19 over parts of three years. Brock, a .251 hitter with Chicago, caught fire with the Cards—batting .348 with 33 steals the rest of '64 to help St. Louis win the World Series title. He retired in 1979 with 3,023 hits, a then-record 938 steals, and a .391 average in 21 World Series games.

The Trade: Cincinnati Reds send **OF Frank Robinson** to Baltimore Orioles for P Milt Pappas, P Jack Baldschun, and OF Dick Simpson.
The Date: December 9, 1965
The Fallout: After ten stellar seasons (including 324 home runs), Robinson was deemed "an old 30" by Reds owner Bill DeWitt, architect of the swap. Robinson went on to win the Triple Crown and AL MVP Award in 1966 and led the Orioles to four pennants and two World Series titles through 1971, eventually hitting 586 homers. Pappas won 209 games in his career but went just 30–29 with the Reds. Throw-ins Baldschun and Simpson gave Cincinnati one win and five homers, respectively.

The Trade: Philadelphia Phillies send **P Ferguson Jenkins,** OF Adolfo Phillips, and OF John Herrnstein to Chicago Cubs for P Larry Jackson and P Bob Buhl.
The Date: April 21, 1966
The Fallout: Jenkins, 2–1 in two years with the Phillies, won at least 20 in each of the next six years for Chicago en route to 284 lifetime victories. Phillips (mediocre) and Herrnstein (awful) were soon gone from the scene, while the aging Jackson and Buhl— once very good pitchers—were a combined 47–53 with the Phils.

The Trade: New York Mets send **P Nolan Ryan**, P Don Rose, OF Leroy Stanton, and C Frank Estrada to California Angels for SS Jim Fregosi.
The Date: December 10, 1971
The Fallout: The Mets saw Fregosi, a six-time All-Star shortstop with the Angels, as the long-term key to their third-base woes; instead, he failed to adapt to his new position and hit just .232 in

1972 before he was sent packing in '73. Young fireballer Ryan, 29–38 with New York, was an instant sensation with the Angels—winning 19 with 329 strikeouts in '72 on the way to staggering lifetime marks of 324 wins, seven no-hitters, and a record 5,714 whiffs. Rose, Stanton, and Estrada? Mere footnotes to history.

The Trade: St. Louis Cardinals send **P Steve Carlton** to Philadelphia Phillies for P Rick Wise.
The Date: February 25, 1972
The Fallout: Wise was a dependable pitcher before and after this trade, going 32–28 in 1972–73 and winning 188 games in his career, but he was no Steve Carlton. "Lefty" went an incredible 27–10 for the last-place Phillies of '72 and, all told, won 241 games and four Cy Youngs for the club en route to 329 lifetime victories.

The Trade: Philadelphia Phillies trade **2B Ryne Sandberg** and SS Larry Bowa to Chicago Cubs for SS Ivan DeJesus.
The Date: January 27, 1982
The Fallout: Sandberg played just 13 games for Philadelphia but became a legend with the Cubs, hitting 282 homers and earning nine Gold Gloves over 15 years. The aging Bowa, a perennial All-Star with the Phils, was Ryne's double-play partner for three years with the Cubs, the same amount of time DeJesus—a .250 hitter with zero power and a so-so glove—lasted in Philadelphia.

The Trade: Boston Red Sox send **1B Jeff Bagwell** to Houston Astros for P Larry Andersen.
The Date: August 31, 1990
The Fallout: It wasn't as bad as Ruth for cash, but it was close. The Sox, seeking a reliever for the stretch drive, got 22 solid innings from Andersen and won the 1990 AL East. He then left as a free agent—while Boston-born Bagwell debuted as '91 Rookie of the Year with Houston and through 2005 smashed 449 homers and 488 doubles as the greatest hitter in Astros history. He's not in Cooperstown yet, but he likely will be.

Heaters and Benders

Pitchers have to know how to grip, coax, and finesse the ball into doing what they want it to do. Here's what the pros do to make their fastballs whistle and their benders break.

Four-seam fastball. The four-seamer is the most basic fastball and often the speediest. It's a good one for throwing strikes. The grip for this straight-shooting pitch involves three important points: The fingers must cross all four seams, the fingertips should have contact with the top seam, and the thumb must be under the ball. The fingers should not be too far apart—the farther apart they are, the less speed can be generated—and it's best to keep the grip relaxed, as if holding an egg.

Two-seam fastball. The two-seam fastball is designed to move more than the four-seamer to keep the batter from knocking it too hard. It is held *with* the seams, where the seams are closest together on the ball. When the two-seam fastball is thrown properly, a right-hander's pitch will move in on a right-handed batter; a lefty's will run *away* from a righty batter.

Curveball. This pitch should "break" just before reaching the plate, causing the batter to swing above it. For any breaking ball, the pitcher places an index finger alongside a long seam on the ball, which should be visible on both sides of the fingers. Then the wrist is cocked inward in such a way that when the ball is released it rolls forward over the fingers. This creates a spin, which produces a force that pulls the ball down. In essence, the curveball imparts forward spin on the ball, the opposite of the fastball's backspin.

Slider. Sliders are between fastballs and curves in both speed and movement. A slider is gripped like a two-seam fastball but is held slightly off-center. A good slider will come out of the pitcher's hand off the thumb-side of the index finger. Gripping the outer third of the ball and applying a slight wrist cock makes that easier, though care must be taken not to twist the arm. Faster than a curveball, the slider often tricks batters into expecting a fastball—until the ball breaks.

Changeup. There are several kinds of changeups. To throw a **three-finger changeup,** center the ring, middle, and index fingers on top of the baseball; the thumb and pinky go underneath. Then hurl it the same as a fastball. This is a good pitch for beginners or people with smaller hands. For a **circle changeup,** the pitcher makes a circle or an "okay" sign with the hand, then centers the ball between the middle, ring, and pinky fingers. Using the same arm speed as a fastball, the hurler turns the ball over slightly as though throwing the circle toward the plate. This is good for producing ground balls. The **palmball** grip requires choking the ball deep in the hand, with all four fingers around it and the thumb directly below. Although thrown like a fastball, this pitch moves more slowly and can trick a batter into swinging too soon.

Split-finger fastball or splitter, or forkball. The index and middle fingers are "split" on either side of the ball. It works best if you aim the palm-side of the wrist directly at the target while keeping the index and middle fingers extended upward and the wrist stiff. This pitch is thrown with a fastball motion, but the grip slows the pitch and helps gravity yank the ball downward.

Cutter or cut fastball. This type of fastball has a slight break—less than a slider but more than a fastball. Typically, the feeling of "cutting" the ball comes from releasing the pitch with slight pressure from the tip of the middle finger.

Screwball. A screwball is essentially a backward curveball, thrown by powerfully pronating the forearm (turning the palm downward). The ball's rotation comes from the arm movement, not from the placement of the fingers. This pitch breaks in the opposite direction of a curveball and is often used by right-handed pitchers against left-handed batters.

Fast Facts

- *Yogi Berra holds the record for having the most World Series rings. He acquired ten from 1946 to 1962.*

- *In 2005, three 70-year-olds were active managers at the same time: Frank Robinson of the Nationals, Jack McKeon of the Marlins, and Felipe Alou of the Giants. This was a first in baseball history.*

- *Roger Clemens is the only pitcher who has won the Cy Young Award seven times.*

- *When Babe Ruth retired in 1935 with 714 home runs, only two other players had hit 300 home runs: Lou Gehrig with 378 and Rogers Hornsby with 300. Since then, 105 major-league players have hit 300 home runs or more.*

- *On May 6, 1953, St. Louis Browns hurler Bobo Holloman became the only pitcher in modern times to toss a no-hitter in his first major-league start.*

- *Joe DiMaggio beat out Ted Williams for the American League MVP Award in 1941, even though Williams hit for a .406 average and had one of the best seasons of his career.*

- *On April 23, 1952, Hoyt Wilhelm won his first game and hit his first home run, which became the only home run he ever hit in 1,070 games.*

- *In 1960, Bill Veeck of the White Sox became the first owner to put players' names on the back of their uniforms.*

- *Johnny Mize is the only player in history to have at least 50 home runs and fewer than 50 strikeouts in the same season. He had 51 homers and 42 strikeouts for the 1947 New York Giants.*

The Hardest-Hitting Hydrant

For a few years, Hack Wilson was the most powerful hitter in baseball this side of Babe Ruth. He was elected to the Hall of Fame on the basis of a five-year stretch in which he hit .331 and averaged 142 RBI.

Lewis Robert "Hack" Wilson looked like a fire hydrant made of muscle. He wasn't tall, but he was thick: Only 5'6", with size six shoes, he topped the scales at a rock-solid 190 pounds. Hack was power personified; some said his nickname came from his resemblance to a German wrestler named Hackenschmidt, but it's just as much fun to believe it came from the way he approached his job at the plate.

Wilson was as tough as he was sturdy; no one wanted to scrap with him. He proved he had slugging skills with the Cubs, topping .313 in each of his first four years with them (1926–29), knocking home at least 109 runs, and homering 21 times or better. Hack earned three home run titles in these four years. His 159 RBI in 1929 was the National League's all-time high to that point.

But in 1930, Wilson was positively unstoppable: 56 homers, 190 RBI (since changed to 191), and 423 total bases (then fifth best all time). The homers would remain the NL record until 1998; the RBI are still the most by anyone, ever. Along with all of that, Wilson batted .356, and his .723 slugging percentage was second best in NL history and wouldn't be topped for 64 years. In a year when Bill Terry batted .401, Hack was the league's Most Valuable Player.

Wilson's 1930 manager, Joe McCarthy, knew how to get the most from his happy-go-lucky slugger. But late in the season McCarthy was ousted in favor of the tactless Rogers Hornsby, and under Rajah's constant harping and withering criticism, Hack just couldn't hack it. The big little man just seemed to give up. His batting average dropped nearly 100 points, and his homer total plummeted from 56 to a mere 13. He never batted .300 or hit 25 homers again, and his career was essentially over after just three more seasons.

Bad Breaks and Bum Luck

A great deal of luck is needed to sustain a long major-league career. Sometimes that luck eludes a young superstar.

One of the heartbreaking elements of sport is that a player on his way to greatness can be derailed by something entirely out of his control. Three promising baseball stars who debuted between 1970 and '80 were struck down by illness or injury, leaving their sad and disappointed fans to wonder what might have been.

J. R. Richard

At 6′8″, J. R. Richard possessed the size and talent of an NBA star. He chose baseball instead—a good choice given a right arm that could unleash fastballs at nearly 100 miles per hour and sliders almost as fast. In his major-league debut for the Houston Astros, on September 5, 1971, Richard dominated the potent attack of the San Francisco Giants, striking out 15 batters.

Despite his record-tying debut, Richard's success was not a given. He struggled with his control, three times leading the National League in walks. He also suffered from a lack of stamina, the result of throwing too hard too early in each game. By 1978, Richard had addressed some of those weaknesses. He still walked too many batters, but he led the league in strikeouts, becoming the first right-hander in NL history to reach 300 Ks in a single season. The following year, Richard led all league starters with a tidy 2.71 ERA. Richard's high-powered pitching not only intimidated opposing hitters; it also frightened his own teammates. "I've never taken batting practice against him," Astros first baseman Bob Watson told *The Sporting News*, "and I never would. I have a family to think about."

Richard continued his march toward stardom in 1980. Winning ten of his first 14 decisions, he posted an ERA of 1.90. It seemed as though Richard's career was on a Hall of Fame track. But in early July, Richard started complaining of a tired arm and said he wasn't feeling well. Some critics charged Richard with being lazy and unprofessional. Even some fans and teammates thought he had underlying motives for not wanting to play. But then on July 30, Richard felt so nauseated during a light workout with former teammate Wilbur Howard that he had to lay down on the field. Within moments, he was rushed to the hospital.

Doctors determined that Richard had suffered a blood clot in his pitching shoulder that was blocking the flow of blood in a vessel near his ribs. When the clot moved to Richard's brain, a major stroke ensued. The stroke completely paralyzed the left side of his body.

Richard did his best to recuperate. He ran four miles a day and regained some of the zip on his fastball. In 1982, he attempted a comeback in the minor leagues, but he was hit hard and struggled badly with his control. Richard would never make it back to the major leagues.

Mark "The Bird" Fidrych

While Richard struck an intimidating pose, Mark "The Bird" Fidrych looked more like a character from *Sesame Street*. As a rookie with the Detroit Tigers in 1976, Fidrych brought a whole new attitude to the lagging team. When one of his infielders made a great defensive play, Fidrych openly applauded. After recording the third out of each inning, The Bird didn't walk off the mound—he *ran,* usually in full sprint. He liked to "landscape" the mound with his cleats. And then there was his most distinctive habit: Fidrych actually talked to the baseball. By doing so, he felt he could make his pitches move in the way that he wanted. Although not quite sure what to make of his antics at first, observers and players soon realized that Fidrych was a genuinely joyful (and talented) person, and his goofy style of play won The Bird a large flock of fans.

Showing excellent control of his above-average fastball, the 22-year-old Fidrych won 19 games and sported the American League's best ERA in 1976 (2.34). After Fidrych's amazingly successful debut season (for which he earned the AL's Rookie of the Year Award), the Tigers eagerly awaited his encore. But during a spring training game in 1977, Fidrych hurt his knee chasing a pop-up. He also tore his rotator cuff, but the injury went undiagnosed until 1985. He tried to keep playing, but he never regained the brilliance displayed in his debut year.

Joe Charbonneau

Big, bad Joe Charbonneau was just as colorful as Fidrych but without the down-home innocence. His ride to the majors was rocky. After being signed by the Philadelphia Phillies in 1976, Charbonneau quit playing ball in his second minor-league season because of a dispute with management. He took up slow-pitch softball for a while, before the Phillies gave him another chance. He hit well in the California League, but his habit of barroom brawling led the Phillies to trade him to the Cleveland Indians' organization. After a .352 season at Double-A, Charbonneau finally earned a promotion to the major leagues, where he promptly won the 1980 American League Rookie of the Year Award.

Charbonneau became enormously popular in Cleveland—and not just for his lusty hitting. Nicknamed "Super Joe," Charbonneau emerged as a cult figure because of his unusual habits. He ate cigarettes, opened beer bottles with his eye sockets (and drank the brew through a straw in his nose), and once rid himself of an unwanted tattoo by cutting it out with a razor blade. He even tried to fix his own broken nose by twisting it back into place with pliers. Apparently his penchant for pain rubbed off on his fans: In March 1980, one of them stabbed him with a pen as he waited for the team bus. But Charbonneau's crazy behavior didn't keep him from shining on the field, where he had a .289 batting average and knocked out a team-leading 23 home runs, along with 87 RBI.

However, Charbonneau's reckless ways seemed to foreshadow a short career; the intensity was bound to catch up with him. In 1981, he slumped so badly that the Indians demoted him to the minor leagues (making him the first-ever Rookie of the Year to be playing in the minors the following year). A back injury only made his situation worse, necessitating two operations, neither of which helped. By 1983, Charbonneau was playing minor-league ball for Cleveland's affiliate in Buffalo. Struggling with a .200 batting average, he decided to give the hometown fans an "obscene salute." The gesture angered Indians management, which gave him his release. Only four years after it had begun, the legend of Super Joe had reached its final chapter.

Strongest Sluggers

Baseball's musclemen: They didn't just hit the ball, they hurt it.

Baseball is not a game of brute strength. But muscles don't hurt, especially if they're combined with terrific eyes, sensational reflexes, and superior hand-eye coordination. Having the brains to adapt to different pitchers' styles is helpful, too.

Jimmie Foxx
Foxx earned his nickname, "The Beast." His rippling muscles terrified American League pitchers for years. When he slugged 58 homers in 1932, he became only the third player ever to top 50. Foxx was second in lifetime homers until Willie Mays surpassed him. Jimmie's pokes were often the longest balls ever hit in (or out of) the park.

Josh Gibson
Called the "black Babe Ruth," power-hitting Gibson slammed a number of homers that exceeded 500 feet. The color line kept him from the majors, but Gibson set slugging-distance records that have become legendary. In his Negro League career (1930–46), he was the home run king nine times.

Ryan Howard
In his first 266 games through 2006, Howard, playing for the Philadelphia Phillies, had belted 82 home runs. At the age of 26, he won the Home Run Derby at the All-Star Game and then finished the season with 58 homers. It's said he once hit a 430-foot homer—when he was only 12 years old.

Harmon Killebrew

When Killebrew slugged long home runs, they didn't just go far—they sometimes caused damage. A long ball he hit in 1967 in Minneapolis's Metropolitan Stadium went more than 530 feet and shattered two seats in the process. Eight times he hit more than 40 home runs on his way to a lifetime total of 573, eighth best all time.

Dave Kingman

"King Kong" was not a good hitter, was a poor fielder, and wasn't even considered a nice person. But boy, could he slug the ball. At 6'6", he wound up and sent balls high into the stratosphere. In 1976, playing for the Mets, he hit one out of Wrigley Field, over Waveland Avenue, and off a house on Kenmore Avenue.

Mickey Mantle

No one ever walloped home runs from both sides of the plate like Mantle. He often played in pain, with injuries ranging from childhood osteomyelitis to a knee torn apart in the 1951 World Series. Mantle is given credit for the longest ball ever hit in Yankee Stadium. And a famous photo shows him smiling at the tattered ball he belted out of Washington's Griffith Stadium on April 17, 1953.

Willie McCovey

McCovey didn't have rippling muscles like Jimmie Foxx or Harmon Killebrew, but when he connected, the ball could almost be heard to whimper in pain. Only four men ever hit more homers in the National League than his 521. Not a homer hitter when his career began, he hit full stride from 1963 through 1970, when he hit (in order) 44, 18, 39, 36, 31, 36, 45, and 39.

Mark McGwire

He was called one of the "Bash Brothers" when he played with Jose Canseco for the Oakland A's, but McGwire didn't rewrite the record books until he was traded to St. Louis, where he broke Roger Maris's single-season home run record in 1998 and ended up with 70. He also had four consecutive 50-homer seasons, making him both a strong and consistent slugger.

Babe Ruth

Ruth's prowess as a hitter for distance so far surpassed anyone ever seen before that they had to invent a new word for it: "Ruthian." In his first spring training game in the minor leagues in 1914, Babe cracked the longest ball fans of that town (Fayetteville, North Carolina) had ever seen. His last homer was the longest ball ever hit out of Forbes Field; it cleared the double-deck right-field grandstands. In between, he hit hundreds more.

Willie Stargell

It was a frightening image: Willie Stargell, poised at the plate, absolutely motionless except for his bat as he wristed it in fat circles. The way he flipped it around, it seemed to weigh less than an ounce. That strength and that bat came together to hit homers completely out of Dodger Stadium; he's the only person to do it twice, in 1969 and '73. Stargell also smashed more out of Forbes and Three Rivers than anybody else.

⚾ ⚾ ⚾

Baseball Commissioner Ford Frick ordered an asterisk to qualify Roger Maris's record 61 home runs. It was to indicate that Maris had broken Babe Ruth's record over a 162-game span instead of the 154-game schedule that Ruth played. As Maris later said, "They acted as though I was doing something wrong, poisoning the record books or something."

⚾ ⚾ ⚾

"People ask me how I'd like to be remembered. I tell them I'd like to be remembered as the guy who hit the line drive over Bobby Richardson's head."

—Willie McCovey, who ended the seventh game of the 1962 World Series with a vicious liner caught by Yankee second baseman Richardson with runners at second and third in a 1–0 New York win, *Baseball Anecdotes*

Greatest Games of All Time

September 23, 1908

Cubs 1, Giants 1

The Setting: Polo Grounds, New York

The Drama: In the last week of a red-hot pennant race, this game between the top contenders had one of the strangest endings ever.

The 1908 National League season was the culmination of a thrilling start to the 20th century. The Pirates (who had won the pennant in 1901, '02, and '03) were tangled in a bristling pennant race with the Giants (who had won in 1904 and '05) and the Cubs (winners in '06 and '07). The entire season turned on one bizarre play in one game—a play that unfortunately labeled a smart ball-player, Fred Merkle, a "bonehead" for the rest of his life.

The day before, the Cubs had knotted the race even tighter by beating the Giants in both games of a doubleheader. New York desperately wanted to win at home. Legendary pitcher Christy Mathewson started for New York; Jack "The Giant Killer" Pfiester was Chicago's starter. Mathewson allowed only five hits for the contest. The Giants scored their lone tally in the sixth on a single, an error, a sacrifice, and a single. The sky was darkening when the Giants came to bat in the last of the ninth. The score was 1–1.

With one out, Giants third sacker Art Devlin singled off Pfi-ester. Next up, Moose McCormick figured if he pulled the ball to the right side, Devlin could advance to second. He was half right, because second baseman Johnny Evers flagged down McCormick's hard grounder and forced Devlin.

Batting next was Fred Merkle. Merkle was playing because regular first baseman Fred Tenney was out with a sore back. It was the only game Tenney failed to start at first that entire season for John McGraw's men. Nineteen-year-old Merkle rose to the occasion, rifling a single over first baseman Frank Chance's head down the right-field foul line. McCormick hustled into third. When

Giants shortstop Al Bridwell followed with a liner into right-center, McCormick trotted across the plate, and the sellout mob at the Polo Grounds went roaring home. Some even carried Mathewson on their shoulders as they celebrated on the field.

The problem was, Merkle (apparently) never touched second. A couple weeks earlier, the Cubs had been involved in a similar situation in Pittsburgh. A Pirate single drove in the apparent winning run in the last of the tenth, and the Pirate runner on first failed to step on second. Keen-eyed Johnny Evers appeared with the ball, stepped on the base, and announced the third out, which meant the run couldn't count. Umpire Hank O'Day (the only ump) muttered something to the effect that no one ever bothered to enforce that rule, which was true, even though the books stated it clearly. The Cubs protested to no avail.

When the same thing happened in New York, O'Day was the umpire again. Even though the fans were pouring onto the field and the place was bedlam, O'Day headed toward second to see if Merkle touched the sack. After a scrap to get the ball away from at least one Giant and several fans (some maintain to this day that the real ball never reached second), Evers once again appeared on second with a ball and announced the runner was out.

This time O'Day was on the spot, and he ruled in favor of Evers, although not until after he left the field. He chose the wisdom of avoiding a riot. After meeting with National League president Harry Pulliam that night, he stated that the runner was out, and because of the thousands of fans on the field and impending darkness, the game was to be declared a 1–1 tie.

The papers of the day were full of charges and countercharges. Mathewson assured everyone that he had grabbed Merkle by the arm and made certain the youngster had touched second. But the league upheld O'Day's tardy decision, and the game entered the record books as a tie. And ever since then, the rule that you must touch the next base has been dutifully enforced.

Because of that tie, the Cubs and Giants finished the pennant race in a dead heat. The game was replayed after all the other games had been played, and the Giants and Mathewson lost to the Cubs and Pfiester 4–2.

Magical Moments

Big talent, in a new kind of package.

Setting: Ebbets Field, Brooklyn; April 15, 1947
The Magic: Baseball's color line is finally shattered as Jackie Robinson makes his big-league debut in front of 26,623 fans.

Of all the historic events in baseball, this is one that most transcended sports history and became American history. When Jackie Robinson stepped onto the field, the game was forever changed. Yet Robinson's groundbreaking appearance as the first 20th-century African-American in the previously all-white professional leagues received little fanfare the day it happened. The crowd, though predominantly black, didn't roar, and most major newspapers did not carry this story on their front pages. It seems that many in the baseball world treated this as any other opening day—even though it was anything but.

Jackie's wife, Rachel, was both nervous and excited as she watched from the stands, cradling five-month-old Jackie Jr. While Robinson had the support of some teammates, most notably Pee Wee Reese, others had actively campaigned against him. But Dodgers general manager Branch Rickey, baseball commissioner Happy Chandler, and Dodgers manager Leo Durocher had all worked to ensure that this milestone event would take place.

Robinson went 0–3 that day, hitting into a rally-killing double play, but also scoring the winning run later when his speed forced an error. (The Dodgers won 5–3.) It wasn't pressure or nerves that kept him hitless, he said—it was the talent of pitcher Johnny Sain.

Robinson went on to hit .297, steal 29 bases, and score 125 runs that season, and he was named Rookie of the Year. His team won the pennant and returned to the World Series for only the second time in 27 years.

On that spring day in 1947, Jackie Robinson opened the door, but of course many more had to follow for the "experiment" to truly be a success. It didn't take long for Robinson to make his mark and for baseball to throw off the stigma of segregation, helping it to truly become "America's game."

All-Star Quiz

1) Which two Hall of Famers form the top home run teammate tandem in major-league history?

A: Hank Aaron and Eddie Mathews (863 home runs as teammates)

2) Which members of the Hall were born on Christmas Day?

A: Pud Galvin and Nellie Fox

3) Which two Mobile, Alabama–born Hall of Famers both wore No. 44?

A: Hank Aaron and Willie McCovey

4) Which Hall of Fame outfielder was drafted in three pro sports?

A: Dave Winfield (by the San Diego Padres, the NFL's Minnesota Vikings, and the NBA's Atlanta Hawks and the ABA's Utah Stars)

5) Who in the Hall named his son after his Hall of Fame double-play partner?

A: Luis Aparicio named his son Nelson after White Sox teammate Nellie Fox

6) Who was the second African-American elected to the Hall?

A: Roy Campanella

7) Who was the youngest player elected to the Hall of Fame?

A: Sandy Koufax, 36

8) Who was the first Hispanic player elected to the Hall of Fame?

A: Roberto Clemente in 1973

9) Who was the only member of the inaugural Hall of Fame class to receive more votes than Babe Ruth?

A: Ty Cobb

10) Who is the only Hall of Famer to have played for the Devil Rays?

A: Wade Boggs

Baseball Lingo

Sprechen sie baseball?

Accordion act: To choke, often as a team. **Origin:** Descriptive of the bellows of the instrument, which collapse.

Apple: A generic term for a baseball. Other food-related words for baseballs include onion, bun, and egg. **Origin:** Descriptive.

Backdoor: A pitch, often a slider or curveball, that curves from outside the batter to inside. **Origin:** Descriptive.

Banana stick: A bat of inferior quality. **Origin:** Descriptive of weak or wobbly wood.

Bingle: A single. **Origin:** A combination of the exclamation "bingo!" and single.

Broadway: A pitch in the middle of the plate. **Origin:** A wide street often in the center of a town.

Cadillac: To showboat; also, a home run hitter. **Origin:** Ralph Kiner's remark: "Home run hitters drive Cadillacs."

Crooked number: A score greater than one, usually in one inning. **Origin:** Describes the shape of any number but one.

Dying quail: A batted fly ball that drops in front of a fielder, seemingly suddenly. **Origin:** Hunting.

Eephus: A slow, high-arching pitch delivered usually to disturb a batter's timing. **Origin:** Rip Sewell's name for such a delivery.

Fan: To strike out swinging. Also, a baseball supporter. **Origins:** A swinging strikeout fans the air. Also, a variation on the word "fanatic" or the British term "fancy," meaning "admire."

Gardener: An outfielder. **Origin:** Descriptive of someone who works in an open field. A center fielder is often called the middle gardener.

Glass arm: A pitcher susceptible to injury. **Origin:** Descriptive of fragility.

Hoover: A good infielder. **Origin:** The vacuum cleaner brand.

Makeup: A player's overall attitude and aptitude. **Origin:** Baseball scouting term.

Moxie: Vigor, pep. **Origin:** Descriptive qualities of the acquired taste of a New England soft drink endorsed by Ted Williams.

On deck: The next batter in the lineup. **Origin:** Nautical, probably from the expression of preparedness, "all hands on deck."

Punch-and-Judy hitter: A batter with little power who frequently slaps the ball for singles. **Origin:** Refers to the "Punch and Judy" puppet show; in this case "punch" is descriptive of how such a hitter meets the ball.

Red: A fastball. A batter "looking dead red" is expecting a fastball. **Origin:** Descriptive. Red symbolizes heat.

Sayonara home run: A home run that ends a game. **Origin:** Japanese word meaning "good-bye."

Small ball: A strategy where a team plays to manufacture runs using sacrifice bunts, steals, and other plays that generally don't require extra-base hits. **Origin:** Play on the term "long ball," or home run.

Through the wickets: A ball that goes between the legs of a fielder for an error. **Origin:** Cricket, in which the batsman stands on guard in front of a set of three upright stumps called a wicket.

Which Came First, the Chicken or the Crazy Crab?

Mascot alert! The unforgettable and the regrettable.

Baseball teams have employed mascots as good luck charms and used illustrated characters to promote themselves for as long as the game has been played. But the furry and feathery variety dancing atop dugout roofs today can trace their heritage to a San Diego radio station promotion in 1974. It was then that KGB radio convinced a college student, Ted Giannoulas, to dress up as a chicken and distribute eggs to children at the San Diego Zoo. Encouraged by the success of the stunt, Giannoulas began appearing in costume at Padres games that year and in short stead became the biggest baseball star hatched in San Diego since Ted Williams. By the end of the 1970s, the Chicken's success had prompted other teams, including the Pittsburgh Pirates (the Pirate Parrot), Philadelphia Phillies (the Phillie Phanatic), Montreal Expos (Youppi), and St. Louis Cardinals (Fredbird) to introduce their own characters. In the 1990s, a second wave of mascots arrived as part of an effort to market the game to children: In 2006, every team except the Dodgers, Cubs, and Yankees employed at least one mascot.

The San Diego Chicken: Despite never having been an "official" Padres character—the Swinging Friar has served that role since the team's founding in 1969—the Chicken has become a traveling attraction. It is famed for physical comedy routines that include presenting an eye chart to umpires in a mock challenge to calls that don't go in the Padres favor and, with the help of a participating catcher, re-creating the Pete Rose–Ray Fosse All-Star Game collision, complete with slow-motion replay.

The Phillie Phanatic: Against the better judgment of team owner Bill Giles, the Phillies introduced this wide-bodied, long-snouted creature in 1978. It won cheers in a city otherwise famous for its hair-trigger boo reflex. Originally embodied by Dave Raymond, a Phillies mailroom clerk, the Phanatic was at his best when making a straight man of whichever Phillie opponent *least* wanted to be part of the act. Dodgers manager Tommy Lasorda, with his low tolerance for on-field antics, was a favorite foil.

Mr. Met: The original live-action costumed mascot, the baseball-domed Mr. Met first appeared on the cover of a 1963 yearbook and debuted live with the opening of Shea Stadium in 1964. His cheery gait and smiling eyes delight children but hide a mischievous nature, perhaps suggesting that the disappearance of his one-time companion, Lady Met, is a mystery best left unsolved. Though entering his late 40s, Mr. Met is still one of the most visible and active Mets. His schedule of party and event appearances, merchandise tie-ins, and TV commercial spots rivals the team's most marketable stars.

Youppi: The fluffy orange giant, whose name means "Hooray" in French and whose uniform number was !, became the first two-sport anthropomorphized character. He served the Montreal Expos from 1979 until they carelessly left him behind when they moved to Washington, D.C., in 2005. Their loss was the Montreal Canadiens' gain: Youppi bolted to the NHL, signing a reported six-figure deal with the Canadiens.

The Pirate Parrot: Kevin Koch, the actor behind the green mask of the Pittsburgh Pirates' mascot for its first six years, went undercover in more ways than one: He made a drug deal while wearing a hidden transmitter to help the FBI secure evidence in its investi-

gation of drug use among ballplayers. The dealer, whom Koch reportedly introduced to some Pirates players, later pleaded guilty to 20 counts of selling cocaine during the 1985 Pittsburgh drug trials.

Dandy: A pin-striped bird with a mustache resembling relief pitcher Sparky Lyle's, Dandy was the official mascot of the Yankees from 1982 to 1985—a fact the team's own stuffed shirts, including owner George Steinbrenner, profess not to recall. Ultimately, a cuddly mascot had difficulty finding a home within the Yankees' stodgy corporate image. Dandy rarely made an appearance beyond the upper reaches of Yankee Stadium.

Crazy Crab: Intentionally hideous, Crazy Crab was unveiled as a subversive "anti-mascot" in 1984 by the San Francisco Giants, who encouraged fans to boo the bug-eyed, belligerent crustacean and whose scoreboard admonitions—PLEASE DO NOT THROW THINGS AT THE CRAZY CRAB—practically begged fans to do just that. After a season of fan abuse, both physical (bottles and garbage hurled from the stands) and verbal (booing, hissing, and epithets), the Crazy Crab was retired. In 2006, sparked in part by a fan petition, Crazy Crab appeared during an '80s throwback promotion. The Crab, true to his sullen nature, attacked Stomper, the mascot of the visiting Oakland A's.

Mettle: Ignoring the fact that they had a perfectly acceptable mascot in Mr. Met, in 1979 the New York Mets unveiled a live mule as their new mascot. Mettle, like the team that year, often left a mess on the field, and he was quietly sent out to pasture after a single season, the worst at the gate in Met history.

◎ ◎ ◎

Baseball team names often change, sometimes because the club moves to a new location, or sometimes just because. A few National League teams with creative names prior to 1900 were the Indianapolis Blues, the Buffalo Bisons, the Troy Trojans, the Worcester Ruby Legs, the Detroit Wolverines, the Kansas City Cowboys, and the Cleveland Spiders.

Fast Facts

- Brooks Robinson hit into triple plays on four occasions, a major-league record. The first was on June 2, 1958.

- The average lifespan of a major-league baseball is seven pitches.

- The cork center was added to the official baseball in 1910. Before that, the core of a baseball was made of rubber. The cork center made for a much "livelier" ball, resulting in an explosion of offense. In the 1911 season alone, the number of .300 hitters tripled.

- On July 4, 1939, Lou Gehrig was the first major-league player to have his number (4) retired.

- Ray Oyler played 111 games at shortstop for the 1968 Detroit Tigers and made only eight errors. Good thing, because he batted just .135.

- On May 23, 1901, Nap Lajoie was the first player in baseball history to be intentionally walked with the bases loaded.

- The strangest combined no-hitter happened on June 23, 1917, when Babe Ruth was the starting pitcher for the Boston Red Sox. He walked the first hitter and was tossed from the game when he vociferously argued the call. Ernie Shore then came in as the relief pitcher, and after the runner was caught stealing, he retired the next 26 batters.

- Numbers on uniforms did not become mandatory until the 1930s.

- Jeff King is the only player to hit two home runs in a single inning in back-to-back seasons. He did it for the Pittsburgh Pirates in 1995 and 1996.

League of Dreams

Little League baseball has produced a parade of stars, but it's the everyday heroes that make it a success.

For Nolan Ryan, Little League was the first stop on his way to the Hall of Fame and an important one on the journey through fatherhood. The latter, its founders might say, is precisely what Little League baseball was engineered to be.

Youth baseball leagues were formed in the United States as early as the 1880s. In 1938, Carl E. Stotz started a league for children in Williamsport, Pennsylvania, and devised rules and field dimensions for what would become, officially, Little League baseball. The next year, the first three teams—Lycoming Dairy, Lundy Lumber, and Jumbo Pretzel—took the field, with the parents who organized them forming the first Little League board of directors.

By 1946 there were 12 similar leagues, all in Pennsylvania. Three years later there were more than 300 such leagues throughout the United States, and in 1951 Little League took hold in Canada. The league has now spread worldwide. Little League baseball is the world's largest organized youth sports program, with nearly 200,000 teams in more than 80 countries. Williamsport, though, has remained central. The Little League World Series (LLWS)—a truly international event—is played there each year, and its final hit the national television airwaves as early as 1963.

Of these hundreds of thousands of teams, only 16 compete for the title of Little League World Series champion. To make it to the finals in Williamsport, teams of 11- and 12-year-olds must advance through the International Tournament—a process that requires more games worldwide than six full major-league seasons!

Eight teams from the United States battle for the U.S. championship as eight teams from other countries fight for the international crown in a ten-day tournament that culminates with the top international team and the winning U.S. squad battling for the LLWS title. Fans from all over the world pack hotels throughout central Pennsylvania each summer for the event. In 2004, the 32-game World Series drew 349,379 fans.

The format of the event has been tweaked through the years. And as the young players have gotten better, the dimensions of the park have grown. From 1947 through '58, the final was played at Original Field, where the outfield fences were all less than 200 feet from home plate. Beginning in '96, a 205-foot blast was required to clear the fences in all fields. As of 2006, those fences stood at 225 feet.

Through all its growth, some things have remained pleasantly constant. For example, the World Series champions get invited to the White House. And Little League's founding goal remains this: to teach children the fundamental principles of sportsmanship, fair play, and teamwork, just as Stotz envisioned nearly 70 years ago.

That those principles can help talented young players advance their baseball careers is a bonus Stotz may or may not have foreseen. Nolan Ryan's first organized sports experience was in Little League. "The first field in Alvin [Texas] was cleared and built by my dad and the other fathers of the kids in the program. I played Little League from the time I was nine years old until I was 13. Some of my fondest memories of baseball come from those years."

Little League remains a big deal in towns all over America. Ryan knows. Not only did he pitch a Little League no-hitter long before he threw seven of them in the majors, but he also helped coach his own sons' Little League teams. Less famous mothers and fathers do the same for their less famous sons and daughters on diamonds around the world.

Ryan, of course, graduated from Little League ball to the Hall of Fame, as did George Brett, Steve Carlton, Rollie Fingers, Catfish Hunter, Jim Palmer, Mike Schmidt, Tom Seaver, Don Sutton, Carl Yastrzemski, and Robin Yount. None of those greats ever played in the famed Little League World Series, but all were boosted by their organized baseball experience as youngsters, as were countless other major-league stars.

Only a small fraction of Little League players go on to the ranks of professional baseball, of course. But where would one be without dreams? And Little League baseball is about so much more than reaching the majors.

Little League/Major League Notables

Boog Powell
Little League: Powered Lakeland, Florida, to the 1954 World Series.
Major Leagues: Won the 1970 American League MVP Award and led Baltimore to four World Series trips in six years.

Lloyd McClendon
Little League: Socked five home runs in five consecutive at-bats for Gary, Indiana, in the 1971 World Series.
Major Leagues: Served as a valuable utility man for the Reds, Cubs, and Pirates from 1987 to '94 before graduating to a managing career with Pittsburgh.

Dwight Gooden
Little League: Served as the ace of a powerhouse Belmont Heights team in Tampa, Florida, that reached the 1979 World Series.
Major Leagues: Captured NL Rookie of the Year and Cy Young awards, and pitched the Mets to a 1986 World Series title as one of the most dominant pitchers of his day.

Derek Bell
Little League: Took the same Belmont Heights team Gooden starred in to back-to-back World Series in 1980 and '81, reaching the finals both years.
Major Leagues: The first big-leaguer to play in two Little League World Series won a title with Toronto in '92 and hit .276 over 11 seasons.

Gary Sheffield
Little League: Teamed with Bell in 1980 as stars of the United States team that fell to Taiwan in the World Series championship game.
Major Leagues: Has slugged more than 450 career home runs, has twice batted .330, and helped the Marlins claim the 1997 World Series championship.

Shake, Rattle & Play Ball!

The real drama at the 1989 World Series had nothing to do with baseball.

It measured 6.9 on the Richter Scale (7.1 surface-wave magnitude), claimed more than 60 lives, and injured thousands. Technically, the earthquake that rocked San Francisco at 5:04 P.M. on October 17, 1989, was the Loma Prieta Earthquake. But it's known as the World Series Earthquake.

The Oakland A's and San Francisco Giants, Bay Area neighbors, were squaring off for the ultimate prize. While people in the region were affected by the quake no matter what they were doing, the nation experienced the tragedy through the eyes of World Series television cameras. ABC Sports play-by-play man Al Michaels was reading taped highlights during the Game 3 pregame show when millions across the country heard him utter the words, "I'll tell you what—we're having an earth—..."

Screens went black. When backup power was restored, the images were powerful. Among them: chunks of concrete falling from an upper deck section of Candlestick Park; Commissioner Fay Vincent looking dazed after nearly being knocked out of his seat near the Giants' dugout; players from both teams leading their wives and children onto the field, away from the stadium's walls.

Though the old stadium shook, the walls held, and no one inside was seriously hurt. Some players clung to their families on the field, thankful for their safety. Others remained lighthearted, not knowing the severity of the damage outside the stadium. It was only on their way home that many people learned they had just survived the area's strongest quake since the 8.3 monster of 1906.

The Series resumed ten days later with a tribute to those who had lost their lives. A moment of silence was observed at 5:04 P.M., followed by the singing of "San Francisco," an unoffical city anthem. The ceremonial first pitch was thrown by representatives of public safety and volunteer organizations who responded to the disaster. Oakland then completed a bittersweet sweep on a stage that wound up being far more about life than baseball.

The Ol' Perfessor

*Casey Stengel spent 55 years as a player and manager with a style,
a sense of humor, and a language uniquely his own.
As he might have put it: "There comes a time in everyone's life,
and I've had plenty of them."*

Charles Dillon Stengel was born in Kansas City in 1890 and made his major-league debut with the Brooklyn Dodgers in 1912. A fair hitter and outfielder, Stengel played 14 seasons, mostly with the Dodgers and New York Giants, where he worked under legendary managers Wilbert Robinson and John McGraw. He gained a reputation as a clown, which was cemented in 1918 when, as a member of the Pittsburgh Pirates, he gave booing fans at Ebbets Field the bird, literally—he removed his cap and out flew a sparrow. "The higher-ups complained that I wasn't showing a serious attitude by hiding a sparrow in my cap," he later said, "but I said any day I get three hits, I am showing a more serious attitude than a lot of players with no sparrows in their hats."

"The Ol' Perfessor" piloted some of the best and worst teams of his time, amassing a 1,905–1,842 record over 25 seasons. After managing the talent-poor Dodgers (1934–36) and Boston Braves (1938–43), his break came when he was unexpectely named

---

Classic Stengelese

Stengel called rookies "green peas." A good fielder was a "plumber," and a tough ballplayer was someone who could "squeeze your earbrows off."

"Good pitching will always stop good hitting and vice versa."

"I don't know if he throws a spitball, but he sure spits on the ball."

"Being with a woman all night never hurt no professional baseball player. It's staying up all night looking for a woman that does him in."

---

manager of the New York Yankees in 1949. His appointment was unpopular with fans and the press, who couldn't believe the stodgy franchise would hire such a joker, but Casey had the last laugh: His Yankees would win ten pennants and seven World Series titles over the next 12 years.

As a manager, Stengel proved to have a keen eye for talent, often using positional platoons and his bullpen brilliantly. ("The secret of managing is to keep the guys who hate you away from the guys who are undecided," he said.) His skill with language—stream-of-consciousness ramblings peppered with large amounts of humor and nuggets of truth and practicality— was known as "Stengelese." He was a master of the malaprop and the mixed metaphor, and with his humor and ability to turn a phrase he engaged writers, deflected attention from his players, and sparked interest in his clubs. These were key advantages throughout his career, especially when managing the dismal expansion New York Mets, whom he led from their founding in 1962 until a hip injury midway through the 1965 season ended his professional career at age 75. He was inducted into the Hall of Fame a year later.

"Can't anybody here play this game?"

—Manager Casey Stengel on his 1962 Mets team,
which went 40–120

"Ruth, Gehrig, Huggins, somebody get that ball back to the infield!"

—Casey Stengel, reacting to a Yankee outfielder fumbling for a ball among the center-field monuments at Yankee Stadium

All-Time Great

Walter Johnson

His slingshot motion gave him a wicked fastball, but it was easy on his arm so he lasted a long time.

Born: November 6, 1887; Humboldt, KS
MLB Career: Washington Senators, 1907–27
Hall of Fame Resume: Retired as the all-time strikeout king * His 110 career shutouts are 20 more than second best * Pitched more than 300 innings nine years in a row * Led league in complete games six times * Averaged nearly 30 wins a season over a five-year period (1912–16)
Inside Pitch: Johnson also holds the record for shutouts lost (65), with 26 of them being 1–0.

The Cy Young Award is given annually to the best pitcher in each league, which is ironic considering it isn't even named for the finest pitcher of all time. Sure, Young had more wins than any major-leaguer, with 511. But while Cy's time was winding down around 1910, another hurler was just getting started with the Washington Senators. And before he was through 21 years later, Walter Perry Johnson would be heralded as one of the game's grandest gentlemen—and the greatest pitcher of them all.

The quiet and ruggedly handsome son of Kansas farmers, Johnson was discovered playing for a semipro team in Idaho and was dispatched on a train to Washington—and the major leagues. A long-limbed right-hander with an easygoing sidearm motion, the 19-year-old could throw a blazing fastball but struggled to learn on the job, going 32–48 his first three years with teams that never rose above seventh place.

More comfortable with his role as Washington's ace by 1910, Johnson had his first spectacular season with a 25–17 record, 1.36 ERA, and 313 strikeouts for the seventh-place Senators. In a pattern that would repeat itself many times, the man nicknamed

"Big Train" was a frequent victim of nonsupport from his light-hitting mates; he would eventually lock up a record 64 contests decided by a 1–0 score—winning 38.

The Senators showed dramatic improvement over the next few years, and Johnson anchored second-place finishes in 1912 and '13 with records of 33–12 and 36–7. The latter may have been the finest performance ever by a major-league hurler, as it included such glittering numbers as a 1.14 ERA, 11 shutouts, and five one-hitters. Those who claim Sandy Koufax's 1962–66 binge was the finest five-year stretch in history should view Johnson's work from 1912 to '16: a 149–70 record, an ERA below 1.90 each season, 1,202 strikeouts, and just 326 walks over 1,794 innings. Eventually, he would pace the AL 12 times in strikeouts, six times in wins, and five times in ERA.

Washington slipped back to the second division as the years wore on; from 1914 to '23, Johnson finished with a winning record only four times. He still put together six straight 20-win campaigns, and then, in 1924, enjoyed the most satisfying year of his career—leading the league with a 23–7 record, 2.72 ERA, 158 strikeouts, and six shutouts, and winning the seventh game of the only victorious World Series in Senators history.

Three more seasons and another World Series appearance remained before a broken leg derailed Johnson's career, but by then he had racked up 417 wins (second only to Young), a 2.17 ERA, and 3,509 strikeouts (a record that held for more than 50 years). Shutouts? The charter Hall of Famer had a record 110 of them, 34 more than a guy named Young.

◖◗ ◖◗ ◖◗

"Can I throw harder than Joe Wood? Listen, my friend, there's no man alive who can throw harder than Smokey Joe Wood."

—Walter Johnson

◖◗ ◖◗ ◖◗

"I am sure that I speak for all when I say that he has been a wholesome influence on clean living and clean sport."

—President Calvin Coolidge on Walter Johnson

Disorder in the Court!

Hear Ye! Hear Ye! Kangaroo court is now in session.

The sight of George "Boomer" Scott in a black robe and white wig in the Milwaukee clubhouse in the 1970s could only mean one thing: kangaroo court. Frank Robinson, who later became Major League Baseball's "director of discipline," trained for that job wearing a mophead for a wig in Baltimore's kangaroo court in the 1960s. Such courts in baseball date back to the late 19th century, but the purpose today remains the same: Promote camaraderie, punish stupidity.

The kangaroo court was a fun way for a team to "punish" a player for doing something stupid either on or off the field. It allowed teammates to become more aware of things they were doing wrong, in a way that promoted camaraderie. The "judge" was usually someone with seniority—or an especially good sense of humor. (Don Baylor and Steve Reed excelled in the role.) The fines imposed were collected and used for a party or given to charity at the end of the season.

Mishaps on the field—throwing to the wrong base, multiple whiffs, missing signs, forgetting the number of outs—ranked high on the list of offenses. Off the field there were even more ways to get on the court's bad side: making out in public, wearing a hideous outfit (and in the heyday of the kangaroo court in the 1970s, there were lots of questionable clothing decisions), or fraternizing with the "enemy." No one, from batboys to team owners, was safe from the court's watchful eye and imposition of justice.

Kangaroo courts have become rare these days, though they do happen occasionally. Players today are more of a collection of independents, and they tend to be friendlier with the opposition, eliminating one of the major infractions. Some players are just too touchy for the ribbing that goes along with the fines. Many young players aren't even aware of the lore of the kangaroo court. But for those who took part, the court was about more than pointing out mistakes—it was a way to bring their team together (and have a lot of fun in the process!).

Fast Facts

- *Guy Hecker of the 1886 American Association Louisville team is the only pitcher to win a batting title, playing the field when he wasn't pitching. He won 26 games as a pitcher and hit .341.*

- *Of all the records that Babe Ruth and Lou Gehrig set, the rarest is that Babe and Lou are two of only 38 players in history to have stolen home ten times or more in their careers.*

- *Until 1859, umpires were often seated in padded chairs behind home plate.*

- *The batter who struck out the most times in a single season was the Cincinnati Reds' Adam Dunn, who fanned 195 times in 2004. He almost broke his own record in 2006 with 194 strikeouts.*

- *During a spring training game on March 7, 1941, Pee Wee Reese and Joe Medwick of the Brooklyn Dodgers were the first major-league players to wear plastic batting helmets. Although many teams, including the Dodgers, began insisting that all of their players wear batting helmets, they did not become mandatory for all MLB players until 1971.*

- *The first night game in World Series history was Game 4 of the 1971 series, when Pittsburgh hosted Baltimore.*

- *In 1961 and '62, the Chicago Cubs operated without a manager. At the time, decisions were made by a rotating board of "head coaches" known as the "College of Coaches." The Cubs landed in seventh place in '61 and ninth place in '62, so the team scrapped the "college" and went back to having one manager.*

- *Until 1954, players were allowed to leave their gloves on the field while their team batted.*

Greatest Teams of All Time

1902 Pittsburgh Pirates

Record: 103–36
Manager: (and left fielder) Fred Clarke
Hall of Famers: Clarke, Honus Wagner, Jack Chesbro
The Season: They finished 27½ games ahead of the second-place finisher—the largest margin ever.
The Legacy: They won again in 1903 and in 1909. Wagner's offensive decade stands alongside Ruth's and Hornsby's 1920s.

The National League, which had expanded to a bloated 12 teams after the 1892 collapse of the American Association, could see by 1899 that they had problems. The gap between first place and the middle of the pack was often 20 games by June. Not surprisingly, the fans of second-division teams stopped showing up soon afterward. The owners agreed to drop four of the poorest teams: Cleveland, Washington, Baltimore, and Louisville.

However, Louisville owner Barney Dreyfuss didn't like that idea, so he engineered the most amazing trade in baseball history. Dreyfuss obtained half-interest in the Pittsburgh franchise. Pirate ownership paid him $25,000 (to settle debts remaining from the Louisville operation) and sent four Bucs to the as-yet-undissolved Colonels for 14 Louisville players, including stars Claude Ritchey, Tommy Leach, Deacon Phillippe, and Rube Waddell. But the key men were left fielder/manager Fred Clarke and Honus Wagner. Clarke would go on to make the Hall of Fame as a manager; Wagner would become the greatest shortstop of all time.

As of 1902, though, the 28-year-old Wagner didn't even have a regular position. Part of the reason was his sheer abundance of natural talent; he could play anywhere well. Several baseball experts have said he could have been a Hall of Famer at any of four or five positions. In 1902, Wagner played in 136 of the 142 Pirate contests, appearing in the outfield, at shortstop, at first base, and at second. He even hurled five shutout innings—fanning five opponents—in one game.

This was a potent Pirate offense. They outscored the next best team by 142 runs and also led the NL in hits, doubles, triples, batting average, on-base percentage, and slugging average and tied for the league lead in stolen bases. Their 103 wins put them 27½ games ahead of second-place Brooklyn. Their .741 winning percentage was the second highest of the 20th century.

The Buc batting game was built around center fielder Ginger Beaumont (who led the league with a .357 average), .330 hitter Wagner, .316 batsman Clarke, and third baseman Tommy Leach, whose 22 triples tied for the league lead and whose total of six homers led all NL blasters. He finished second to Wagner in RBI. Wagner led the league in runs, doubles, RBI, and slugging average.

As was the custom of the era, only a handful of pitchers supplied nearly all of the Pirate innings. But unlike some other teams, the Pirates didn't rely on one man to carry all (or nearly all) the weight. Four Bucs pitched more than 200 innings; one threw 188. In comparison, four other NL teams had pitchers who threw more than 300 innings. Jack Chesbro led the Pirate staff and the league with 28 wins. Phillippe and Jesse Tannehill each won exactly 20.

Another reason for the success of the 1901, '02, and '03 Pirates (pennant-winners all, and the '03 group played in the first modern World Series) was owner Dreyfuss's personality. While other National League operations were being raided by Ban Johnson's upstart American League, Dreyfuss maintained a carrot-and-stick style of motivation to keep his team together. He treated his players well, but if anyone was rumored to be talking to American League scouts (and Dreyfuss had his spies hard at work), the potential deserter was canned.

Player/manager Clarke was also an inspired leader, as well as a solid hitter and superb fielder. Historian MacLean Kennedy, in his 1928 book *The Great Teams of Baseball,* stated, "Great players are born into the game once a decade, and great leaders come into the game once a decade, but great player/managers are born into the game once in two decades." Kennedy ranked Clarke as one of the best of all time—just like the team he led.

Home Is Where the Hump Is

Ballparks' strange quirks keep fans—and fielders—on their toes.

A ballpark's beauty is in the eye of the ticket holder. Modern stadiums cater to the appetites of the modern fan, offering unobstructed views, ample seats, special club sections, and scoreboards that display images and play music. Ballparks of the past had far fewer—if any—frills and were contoured to their surroundings, creating unique, sometimes quirky features and distinctive environments in which to watch baseball.

Baker Bowl, Philadelphia

Home of the Philadelphia Phillies, 1894–1938

Erected as a wooden park in 1887, it was replaced with concrete and steel after seven years, following a fire. Sections of the stands collapsed in 1903 and 1927, but each time the Phillies moved back in within a few weeks. The stadium was built near a train yard, and the indentation for a tunnel underneath right field led to the park's nickname: "the Hump." The club tried to compensate for the short fence in right (280 feet) with a 40-foot tin fence, and a 15-foot in-play net was added in 1929. No matter—it was still the best hitter's park in the game. The National League batted .352 there in 1930.

Fate: Demolished in 1950.

Griffith Stadium, Washington, D.C.

Home of the Washington Senators, 1911–1960; expansion Senators 1961

The stadium, built in just one month after National Park burned down in March 1911, was one of the most cavernous parks in history. Its 407 feet to the left-field line was deeper than dead-center in 16 parks standing in 2007. Even stranger was the way Washington's structure jutted in to accommodate neighboring houses. The year of their only world championship, 1924, the Senators hit one home run there all season.

Fate: Demolished in 1965.

Polo Grounds, New York

Home of the New York Giants, 1911–1957; New York Yankees, 1913–1922; New York Mets, 1962–1963

This fifth incarnation of the Polo Grounds was erected in concrete and steel after a fire destroyed the previous one in April 1911. The horseshoe-shape ballpark allowed for very short home runs to left and right—279 and 257 feet, respectively—but extended 483 feet to the raised clubhouse in center. Only three major-leaguers ever reached the bleachers in center: Joe Adcock, Lou Brock, and Hank Aaron. Managers could only see the top half of their outfielders since the outfield was sunken for drainage, but it was good enough for groundskeeper Matty Schwab, who was lured to the job because owner Horace Stoneham built him an apartment under the left-field stands in the 1950s.

Fate: Demolished in 1964.

Tiger Stadium, Detroit (formerly Navin Field and Briggs Stadium)

Home of the Detroit Tigers, 1912–1999

Detroit's landmark underwent many changes over the years, but fans were always close to the action (and perhaps a girder). The "Cash Register," a second-deck overhang in right field, caught many balls that outfielders had a bead on, while many other balls cleared the roof altogether. The 125-foot flagpole in center field was the tallest in-play obstacle ever at a major-league park. The same corner previously housed Bennett Park, which opened in 1896 (and closed in 1911). The Tigers moved out in 1999.

Fate: Plans are in the works for all but one section of the stadium (the third-base line lower grandstand) to be dismantled and auctioned off to make way for condominiums and shopping. The actual field may be saved for Little League events.

Ebbets Field, Brooklyn

Home of the Brooklyn Dodgers, 1913–1957

A half-century after the final game was played there, Ebbets Field remains the granddaddy for ballpark nostalgia. Dodgers owner Charlie Ebbets bought up dozens of small parcels in what was known as "Pigtown" and wedged his elegant ballpark near the Gowanus Canal. The wall and scoreboard in right, 318 feet from the plate, had a reported 289 different angles. The scoreboard posted an ad for Schaefer Beer, and the letters "h" (for a hit) or "e" (for an error) lit up in the sign to reflect the action on the field.

Fate: Demolished in 1960, after the Dodgers moved to L.A.

Braves Field, Boston
Home of the Boston Braves, 1915–1952

The first superstadium was built in response to Boston's "Miracle Braves" of 1914. A massive single deck held 40,000 spectators, and its vast dimensions—402 feet down the line in left and 542 to the right-center corner—held in everything. There were no home runs hit over the outer wall for the first decade of the park's existence. The Braves won their only world championship in Boston at Fenway Park in 1914; the Red Sox won the World Series at Braves Field in 1915 and 1916.

Fate: Sold to Boston University in 1952. The core remains today and serves as a football, soccer, and field hockey stadium named Nickerson Field.

Jarry Park, Montreal
Home of the Montreal Expos, 1969–1976

The first major-league foray into Canada stretched a recreational facility from a capacity of 3,000 to 28,000. Construction was still ongoing during the opening month of the inaugural Expos season. A swimming pool remained in right field, with long drives to right getting wet. Montreal surpassed one million fans in each of its first six seasons. The Expos moved into Olympic Stadium the year after the 1976 Montreal Games.

Fate: Part of Jarry's seating remains in Stade Uniprix, an indoor facility used for professional tennis events.

Exhibition Stadium, Toronto
Home of the Toronto Blue Jays, 1977–1989

It was a football stadium—a Canadian Football League Stadium, at that—so fans in the center-field bleachers sat a mile (or rather a kilometer) from home plate. At least the bleachers were covered; the grandstand was not. Astroturf and cozy dimensions kept hitters happy (330 feet down the lines, 400 to center). But the frigid Toronto weather—snow covered the field for the first game in 1977, and high winds caused a game to be canceled in 1984— plus an abundance of birds made Blue Jays fans happy to leave Exhibition for the SkyDome in 1989.

Fate: Demolished in 1999; the site is now a parking lot.

Metrodome, Minneapolis
Home of the Minnesota Twins, 1982–present

You could call it the shortest dome in history (186 feet high) or just the ugliest. The 23-foot-high wall in right covers seats used for football and is called "the Baggy" because of its resemblance to a trash bag. Past manipulation of the air conditioning ducts—and ball flight—helped the team's offense, but a bigger advantage is the way the place traps noise and disrupts opponents. The dome, held in place by air pressure, has twice deflated temporarily.

Fate: Currently hosts the Twins and the NFL's Vikings, though the Twins have plans to move to a new park in 2010.

Minute Maid Park, Houston (formerly Enron Field)
Home of the Houston Astros, 2000–present

Houston has one of the newest yet quirkiest parks in the game. While the "Crawford Boxes"—so dubbed because that's the street they're located on—are ridiculously short in left field, a drive to more distant left-center must pass over a hard-to-see line that determines a home run. "Tal's Hill," named after team president Tal Smith, is downright dangerous, requiring center fielders to race up a 30-degree hill to catch 430-foot pokes. Smith modeled this hill after a slope in old-time Crosley Field in Cincinnati. While Crosley's slope was there of necessity (to bring the field level closer to street level), Tal's Hill was built merely as a quirk. While navigating the hill, outfielders also have to avoid running into the flagpole planted in center field.

Fate: Currently hosts the Astros.

DL? I Don't Think So.

These players overcame physical limitations to make their mark on the game.

Baseball is a meritocracy in which pitchers work to exploit a hitter's weakness, hitters seek vulnerability in fielders, and physical short-comings are routinely punished. Following are profiles of some players who entered the baseball world with their own physical limitations and worked to overcome them in an unforgiving sport.

William Ellsworth "Dummy" Hoy

The day that William Hoy made his major-league debut in 1888, his Washington Nationals teammates arrived to find a handwritten note posted on the clubhouse wall.

"Being totally deaf as you know and some of my teammates being unacquainted with my play, I think it is timely to bring about an understanding between myself, the left fielder, the shortstop and the right fielder," the note began. "The main point is to avoid possible collisions with any of these four who surround me when in the field . . . " Hoy's note went on to explain that, as center fielder, his teammates should listen for him to yell, indicating that he would make the play on a fly ball. "Whenever you don't hear me yell, it is understood I am not after the ball." Though team-mates would describe Hoy's yell as more of a squeak, they under-stood him perfectly.

Rendered deaf and mute as the result of a childhood bout with meningitis, "Dummy" Hoy enjoyed a 14-year career in which he amassed 2,044 hits, 1,426 runs, 40 home runs, 594 stolen bases, 726 RBI, and 273 assists as an outfielder with six teams. As his teammates learned, he was a magnificent fielder and a fine hitter (with a .287 batting average)—one of baseball's first stars to over-come a physical handicap.

On May 16, 1902, Hoy came to bat against Luther "Dummy" Taylor of the Giants in the first matchup in baseball history of a deaf pitcher versus a deaf hitter. The opponents exchanged greet-ings in sign language, then Hoy singled.

Mordecai "Three-Finger" Brown

Mordecai Brown turned childhood tragedy into professional success. Growing up on an Indiana farm, Brown lost his right index finger just below the knuckle when he got his hand caught in a corn grinder. Shortly afterward, with his hand still in a cast, he fell and broke the pinky and middle fingers on the same hand. Those fingers grew bent and misshapen.

Brown's deformed hand was an impediment to gripping a baseball, but through ingenuity and practice he developed a unique grip that produced baffling pitches with incredible movement. Not blessed with great velocity, Brown relied on movement, smarts, and remarkable control: He consistently ranked near the top of his league in fewest walks per innings pitched. "The main objective in pitching is to take the power away from the hitter," he told *The Sporting News*. "Keep him from putting too much wood on the ball."

In an era of low scoring, Brown stood out as a run preventer: His ERA was below 2.00 for five straight seasons beginning in 1906. Over a 14-year Hall of Fame career, he won 239 games and fashioned an ERA of 2.06—sixth best in the history of baseball—and led the Chicago Cubs to two world championships and four National League pennants.

Giants ace Christy Mathewson was one of Brown's toughest opponents. The Hall of Famers faced one another 25 times, with Brown winning 13 of the games, including a stretch of nine victories in a row. After one such game, exasperated Giants manager John McGraw reportedly examined Brown's hand and remarked, "I'm going to have the first finger on the throwing hands of every one of my damned pitchers cut off tomorrow."

Pete Gray

An accidental fall off a wagon when he was six years old cost Pete Gray nearly his entire right arm. Faced with this limitation, he developed a fierce determination to overcome it.

Gray channeled that determination toward a career in baseball. He taught himself to make solid contact swinging a bat with his left arm only, and he used a customized glove, which he would deftly tuck beneath his stub when fielding. He worked his way from semipro ball through the minor leagues, winning over doubters and garnering MVP honors with the Memphis Chicks of the Southern Association in 1944.

The following year, with many of the best major-league players off to war, Gray was signed by the St. Louis Browns, who saw the addition of a disabled player as both a gate attraction and a message to wounded war veterans. Gray understood this and with a grim resolve made the most of the opportunity, hitting .218 and striking out just 11 times over 77 games and 253 plate appearances.

Bert Shepard

Shepard was a left-handed pitcher for the Bisbee Bees in the Texas–Arizona League when he joined the Army to serve in World War II. He flew 20 combat missions in Europe before his plane was shot down over Berlin in May 1944, and when he awoke in a German hospital he found his right leg amputated just below the knee. Needless to say, baseball officials were surprised when Shepard arrived at Washington Senators camp in 1945 anxious to resume his career.

"I had been an athlete all my life," said Shepard, "and I promised myself the day I found my leg was off I would continue to be one."

He made the club as a coach, batting-practice pitcher, and goodwill ambassador, pitching in a series of benefit exhibitions. Shepard's courage and determination were an inspiration to the country at a time when hundreds of young men were returning with injuries like his. On August 4, 1945, when the Red Sox had battered two Washington pitchers for 12 runs in the fourth inning, Shepard entered the game and struck out Catfish Metkovich to end the rally. He followed with five more innings of one-run, three-hit ball in a 15–4 Washington loss. With the Senators in a pennant race, it turned out to be Shepard's one and only appearance in a big-league game, though he continued to pitch in the minors until 1954.

Jim Abbott

"I wanted to be like Nolan Ryan. I didn't want to be like Pete Gray."

Such were the boyhood dreams of Jim Abbott, a Flint, Michigan, native who sought a baseball career despite having a right arm that ended just above the wrist. Abbott didn't want to be accepted into the majors as an oddity, the reason many believe one-armed Gray caught on in the war-depleted summer of 1945. Abbott yearned to succeed on his talent alone, and in the end he would do so—but not without becoming a reluctant hero.

Born in 1967, just as his own hero, Ryan, was breaking in with the Mets, Abbott taught himself to transfer his glove from his left arm to his right by throwing against a brick wall. He later said that his missing hand "wasn't really an issue when I was a kid." By becoming an expert fielder, he kept hitters from using the logical tactic of bunting against him to their advantage. During his college career he racked up a 26–8 record at the University of Michigan, won a gold medal in the 1988 Olympics, and took home the Sullivan Award the year before as the nation's best amateur athlete.

California's first pick in the 1988 draft, Abbott became one of a handful of players in history to completely bypass the minor leagues, then overcame a media circus to go 12–12 as a rookie with the 1989 Angels. More great moments would follow—including a 1993 no-hitter for the Yankees—and it wasn't long before he had gotten his wish. He was simply Jim Abbott—pitcher.

◖ ◖ ◖

"God gave me an unusual arm. I've done well with it, and maybe I can keep doing well with it. I certainly don't see anything to be angry about."

> —Sandy Koufax's response when asked if he was bitter about having arthritis at age 28, *The Baseball Life of Sandy Koufax*

◖ ◖ ◖

"To know for sure, I'd have to throw with a normal hand, and I've never tried it."

> —Mordecai "Three Finger" Brown, when asked if his curveball was aided by the mangled fingers on his pitching hand

Chatter

"Next to religion, baseball has furnished a greater impact on American life than any other institution."

—Herbert Hoover

"Well, Mr. Barrow, Lou Gehrig is badly underpaid."

—Joe DiMaggio's response when Yankee general manager Ed Barrow told Joe that his 1937 contract demand of $45,000 following his rookie season was higher than what Gehrig was making after 15 years

"All I want out of life is that when I walk down the street, people will say, 'There goes the greatest hitter who ever lived.'"

—Red Sox rookie Ted Williams

"I could field the ball all right, but on the throw I couldn't hit the first baseman or anything near him."

—John McGraw on his early days as a 16-year-old minor-leaguer

"A couple of years ago, they told me I was too young to be President and you were too old to be playing baseball. But we fooled them."

—45-year-old John F. Kennedy to 41-year-old Stan Musial at the 1962 All-Star Game

"The only man who could have caught it, hit it."

—Sportswriter Bob Stevens after Willie Mays belted a drive over the center fielder's head

"Throw strikes. The plate don't move."

—Satchel Paige, *Strikeout: A Celebration of the Art of Pitching*

Santa, Baby

The best Christmas gift Babe Ruth gave to kids was himself.

There is a famous photograph that shows Babe Ruth surrounded by what seems like a hundred clamoring children, yet that moon face and huge grin under the straw boater are unmistakable for their goofy brightness. Ruth was in his element, surrounded by his biggest fans and most starstruck admirers, and he was loving every minute of it.

Throughout his career, after ball games and at special appearances, Ruth spent up to several hours at a time signing autographs. He couldn't bear the thought of any tyke going home disappointed. In New York and on the road as well, the Babe frequently visited hospitals to help cheer up sick children. In 1931 alone, he played Santa Claus for hundreds of kids at city hospitals. He also spent a lot of time visiting orphanages—probably because he basically grew up at Saint Mary's Industrial School for Boys, an orphanage in Baltimore.

By 1947, when Ruth could no longer deliver joy to fans with his majestic home runs and, in fact, could barely walk, one thing he still could do was make children happy. That December, the cancer-stricken Ruth painfully pulled on a Santa Claus suit, beard and all, and handed out presents to young victims of polio at the Hotel Astor in New York. As their faces lit up, it was clear their delight gave Babe much joy. Afterward, he pulled down his beard and addressed the cameras and microphones. Though his voice was subdued and raspy, he spoke with the utmost sincerity. "I want to take this opportunity," he said, "to wish all the children—not only in America, but all over the world—a very merry Christmas." Throughout his life, Babe Ruth had played Saint Nick to a lot of kids in a lot of ways, and this year was no different.

⚾ ⚾ ⚾

"Don't quit until every base is uphill."

—Babe Ruth, *The Babe Ruth Story*

Strangest Homers

*Not every home run is a cut-and-dried event;
some are downright weird.*

Sometimes it is obvious that a home run has been hit the second
the ball leaves the bat. Other times fans anxiously wait to see
whether the ball sneaks over the wall or collides with the foul pole
before they are able to celebrate a home run. And then there are
those times when the ball takes an entirely different route and
does something downright strange.

In the Doghouse

One of the oddest homers in history took place at American
League Park, which was the home of the Washington Senators
from 1904 to 1910. In this ballpark there was a doghouse near the
outfield flagpole. The groundskeeper stored the flag inside the
doghouse between games. One afternoon the doghouse door was
left open, and a member of the Senators hit the ball inside of it.
Philadelphia A's center fielder Socks Seybold crawled inside to
retrieve the ball and got stuck, allowing the batter to circle the
bases for an "inside-the-doghouse" home run.

Not a Stolen Base—A Stolen Ball!

That wasn't the first time an open door figured into a homer.
When the Louisville Colonels visited the Pittsburgh Pirates on
May 3, 1899, the Colonels were leading comfortably in the last of
the ninth when the Pirates staged a rally. Jack McCarthy had
already homered when teammate Tom McCreery drove a ball to
the right-field fence. A Pirates employee opened the right-field
gate, picked up the ball, and ran off with it. McCreery circled the
bases, and despite protests from the Louisville players, the umpire
allowed the play to stand. The outcome was a 7–6 Pittsburgh
victory. However, later that season at a league meeting, the game
was thrown out and was replayed. It did not count in the final
National League standings.

Feeling Heat from the Warm-Ups

In 1911, American League President Ban Johnson attempted to speed up games by eliminating warm-up pitches between innings. On June 27, at the Huntington Avenue Baseball Grounds, the A's Stuffy McInnis capitalized on the rule change when he noticed Boston pitcher Ed Karger tossing warm-ups. McInnis drilled a ball that center fielder Tris Speaker refused to chase because he thought it was hit during warm-ups. McInnis touched them all for a home run. Umpire Ben Egan had no choice but to allow the homer to count because Johnson was sitting in the stands.

Oddities at Ebbets

In 1940 at Ebbets Field, Lonnie Frey of the Cincinnati Reds hit a ball to right field. It bounced off the screen and landed on top of the wall that extended between the scoreboard and foul pole. The ball bounced up and down but never fell back to the field of play, allowing Frey to complete an inside-the-park home run. The same fate would ultimately help the Dodgers in 1950, when Pee Wee Reese duplicated the feat in a game that helped Brooklyn clinch the NL pennant.

Another home run occurred at Ebbets Field that seemed to defy the laws of gravity. George Cutshaw, who played for the Dodgers from 1912 to 1917, hit a line drive to the left-field wall. Apparently the ball had a lot of topspin on it; when it hit the wall, the ball rolled up and over the fence for a home run.

It Is! Or Is It?

One of the most memorable homers of George Brett's career was disallowed for a brief period of time. Brett's two-out, two-run, ninth-inning homer off Yankees relief ace Goose Gossage was a majestic drive. The game took place on July 24, 1983, at Yankee Stadium, and the blast gave the Royals a 5–4 lead over the Yanks. But after

Brett circled the bases, New York manager Billy Martin came out of the dugout and asked the home plate umpire to examine Brett's bat. It was determined that the pine tar on Brett's bat exceeded the legal limit of 18 inches. Brett was called out, and the home run was nullified. The umpire was later overruled by American League President Lee MacPhail; the home run counted, and the game was picked up at that point and finished three weeks later.

Just a Hop, Skip, and a Jump

Sometimes the opposition actually helps the hitter. In May 1993, Cleveland's Carlos Martinez hit a fly ball to right field that bounced off Jose Canseco's head and over the fence for a home run. The gift round-tripper gave the Tribe a 7–6 win over the Rangers.

While that was embarrassing for Canseco, it was at least less frustrating than what happened to Dick Cordell during a minor-league game on August 9, 1952. In the seventh inning of a score-less game between Denver and Omaha in the Western League, Cordell ran down a long drive off the bat of Denver's Bill Pinckard. Cordell caught the ball before crashing into the left-field wall. The ball was jarred from his glove on impact, ricocheted off the wall, then bounced off his head and over the fence. After a lengthy discussion, the umpire ruled that Pinckard's drive was indeed a homer. It turned out to be the only run of the game.

Only the Best of Intentions

For Jim Bottomley, one home run wasn't worth all of the grief. Bottomley, who spent 16 seasons in the majors and led the NL with 31 homers in 1928, was once sued after one of his home runs hit a spectator in the face. The suit stated that Bottomley "swung on that ball deliberately and with the intention of creating a situation commonly known as a home run."

During questioning at a deposition, an attorney suggested that a skilled contact hitter could place the ball to whichever part of the field he determined. He then asked Bottomley, "Did you deliberately intend to hit anyone when you batted that ball?"

"No sir," replied Bottomley. "There is no malice in any of my home runs."

Fast Facts

- Although the 1930 Phillies had a .315 team batting average, they finished dead last because of dreadful pitching and defense. The team's ERA was 6.71, worst in baseball history, and the fielders made 239 errors in 154 games.

- Ty Cobb holds the career record for stealing home plate. He did it 54 times.

- Juan Marichal was in the top ten in ERA seven times, in the top four in wins six times, in the top four in fewest walks eight times, in the top five in innings pitched five times, and in the top two in complete games six times. However, only once did he finish in the top ten in Cy Young Award voting, placing eighth in 1971.

- Ted Williams won the American League batting title at age 39 and again at age 40. The last at-bat of Ted's career was a home run on the last day of the 1960 season.

- On October 10, 1920, Bill Wambsganss became the only player in World Series history to complete an unassisted triple play.

- In 1935, Phil Cavarretta set the all-time season records for the most hits, runs, RBI, triples, doubles, and total bases by a teenage major-leaguer.

- The American League's first Most Valuable Player Award was given to St. Louis Browns first baseman George Sisler in 1922. The second was given to Babe Ruth. This award was abandoned in 1929 and replaced in 1931 with the Baseball Writers' Association of America MVP Award.

- George Steinbrenner hired Billy Martin to manage the Yankees five times and fired him an equal number of times.

Greatest Games of All Time

1912 World Series, Game 8

Red Sox 3, Giants 2

The Setting: Fenway Park, Boston

The Drama: Only the second World Series to go the distance featured a final game with heroes, tricksters, and lots of drama.

The 1912 World Series between the Giants and Red Sox was an almost nightmarish drama of emotional swings for fans of both teams. Close plays, backbreaking errors, great pitching, and clutch hitting were the order of the day. And, appropriately enough, the final game was the most sensational of them all.

Both of these powerful teams had scored around 800 runs to lead their respective leagues and had out-homered all of their competition. The Red Sox had led the AL in slugging average; the Giants had topped the NL in batting average. But the pitching matchups promised the most excitement. The Giants featured a lefty/righty duo of Rube Marquard and Christy Mathewson; the Sox countered with Smokey Joe Wood and Hugh Bedient. Wood won Games 1 and 4 but was roughed up in Game 7. Mathewson threw 11 innings in Game 2 (declared a tie because of darkness) and lost Game 5 to Bedient, although he allowed only five hits and no earned runs.

Mathewson and Bedient squared off again in Game 8, the final game. The Giants took the lead when outfielder Red Murray doubled in Josh Devore in the third. In the top of the fifth, Larry Doyle hit a screaming drive deep to right field. Boston right fielder Harry Hooper leaped into the air, snagged the fly, then had it pop out of his mitt. Miraculously, Hooper was able to reach out with his bare hand and grab it before he tumbled into the stands.

The Sox tied it in the bottom of the seventh when Olaf Henriksen, pinch-hitting for Bedient, rapped a double to drive in a run. Sox manager Jake Stahl brought in Wood, who had lasted just one inning the day before. Now the two staff aces were opposing each other. The heat was on.

Neither team could muster offense through the eighth and ninth innings. In the top of the tenth, Murray doubled for the Giants. Next up was Fred Merkle, who singled past second base. Center fielder Tris Speaker bobbled the ball momentarily, and Murray hustled home. Speaker's miscue was amazing in itself; just the day before, the remarkable "Spoke" had performed an unassisted double play—the only time an outfielder has ever done that in a Series.

The last of the tenth was an emotional wringer for both teams. Wood, a good hitter, had injured his hand making the final play at the top of the inning and couldn't bat. So Stahl looked down his bench and found Clyde Engle, a .234 hitter for the season.

Engle lifted a lazy fly ball to center, where reliable Fred Snodgrass camped under it. But when the ball hit his glove, it kept going. Snodgrass instantly landed a place in baseball's pantheon of postseason bumblers, as his error became known as the "$30,000 muff." Engle reached second.

Next up was Hooper, who slugged a shot deep into center. Snodgrass, taking no time to brood over his error, outran the ball to make a spectacular catch of a sure triple, then fired the ball back to the infield—and just barely missed doubling up Engle on his way back to second. Then, most atypically, Mathewson issued a walk to Steve Yerkes. (Christy had walked just 34 men in 310 innings that year.) At the plate was the dangerous Speaker.

One of Mathewson's famous fadeaways fooled Speaker, and Tris could only loft a short foul pop between home and first. But first baseman Merkle froze, and catcher Chief Meyers had to exert a furious dive to try and catch the foul. He came up short, and Speaker had life. Allegedly, someone was shouting "Chief!" for the catcher to make the play. If it was Mathewson, he made the wrong call. If it was the tricky Speaker, he made the right one.

The now-furious Mathewson heaved one that Speaker was able to line into right. Engle scored to tie the game, and the runners moved up on the throw home. After an intentional walk, Larry Gardner poked a fly to right deep enough to score Yerkes with the winning run. It was a dramatic conclusion to a most dramatic Series.

It's Still in the Cards

*After more than a century, card collecting remains
a simple pleasure.*

Long before ESPN and MLB.com provided the opportunity to
keep up-to-the-inning tabs on ballplayers, baseball cards allowed
generations of fans to feel connected with their heroes. And while
big-league salaries may have now reached outrageous levels, for
many devotees of the game, cardboard is still as good as gold.

Trade Cards, Tobacco, and the T-206

Today's cards are aimed primarily at the Little League crowd, but
the first commercial versions (then called "trade cards") in the
1870s were marketed to adults, featuring pictures of top teams on
one side and advertisements on the other. By the 1880s, the game's
rising popularity prompted several tobacco companies to insert
cards into packs of their products, and stars such as King Kelly and
Cap Anson began appearing on their own cards.

The cards considered by many collectors to be the most beauti-
ful ever produced appeared during the 1900–1915 era, featuring
color drawings of players posed or in action. Usually smaller than
today's standard 2½"×3½" cards, they picked up a younger audience when candy companies also began producing them. The
"Mona Lisa of baseball cards"—the T-206 White Borders Honus
Wagner—was introduced during this time. Only about 50 of these
cards were made before a dispute between the tobacco firm and
the Pirates shortstop halted their production. In 2007, one of the
cards reportedly sold to a private collector for $2.35 million.

Kids Get On Board

Back then, of course, nobody was worrying about a card's monetary value. By the 1930s, when Goudey and other gum companies
began producing hundreds of individual player cards each year,
kids began trading the cards—either to complete numbered sets
or to pick up a favorite player. Many kids stuck cards into the
spokes of their bikes to get just the right machine-gun sound.

Baseball's post–World War II boom extended to baseball cards, which reached new heights in popularity during the 1950s. The king now was the Topps Company, which had a virtual monopoly on collecting from 1952 through 1980 and produced as many as 800 new cards each year. Almost every major-leaguer signed an annual deal with Topps; each plastic-wrapped pack available at the corner drugstore contained several cards with players' vital statistics and complete playing records on the back, along with a rectangle of rock-hard pink bubblegum. Cards featured everything from league leaders and All-Stars to fathers and sons, boyhood photos, and even (briefly) umpires.

The Card Collecting Explosion

The Topps monopoly ended in 1981, when two companies (Fleer and Donruss) won the legal right to produce their own sets. Card collecting as a hobby exploded. Kids, faced with numerous choices, bought more cards than ever, and adults who had grown up with Topps paid $10, $20, even $100 to replace the ones they had bought for nickels as youngsters—and that their parents had long since thrown out. In addition to baseball card conventions, fans at one point had some 10,000 card shops in which to seek out treasures. Young collectors now put their top cards in protective cases rather than in their bike spokes, and gum (which damaged cards as well as teeth) faded from the scene.

The sheer glut of cards produced in the late 1980s and early '90s eventually led to a rapid decline in their monetary value, and this, plus fallout from the 1994 players' strike, forced many shops to close their doors. Recently, however, there has been another revival: Topps and numerous rivals now produce a seemingly endless array of specialty cards, including "relic" versions with shavings from actual game-used bats attached and "heritage" versions designed to look like those from the 1950s. Gum has even made a comeback, and the Internet—and especially eBay—has made it easier than ever to find an elusive card. The cards of such Golden Age players as Willie Mays and Mickey Mantle—at least those that have survived in decent condition—are valued in the thousands of dollars. And don't forget that T-206 Wagner!

Magical Moments

Finally, Brooklyn blasts the Bronx Bombers.

The Setting: Yankee Stadium; October 4, 1955

The Magic: On their eighth try, the Dodgers finally win a world championship, and they do it against the hated Yanks!

The Brooklyn Dodgers of the late '40s and early '50s were one of the game's greatest teams, winning pennants in 1949, '52, '53, and '55, and missing out by only one game each in '50 and '51. But the scrappy Brooklynites were consistently stymied in the World Series by the uptown bullies known as the Yankees.

The '55 Dodgers seemed headed for the same fate when they dropped the first two games of the Series in Yankee Stadium. But back home in Ebbets Field for Game 3, young lefty Johnny Podres celebrated his 23rd birthday in fine fashion, nailing an 8–3 Dodger win. They took Games 4 and 5, too. Back in the Bronx, the Yanks blew open Game 6 with a five-run first, and the two teams faced a seventh game for the second time in four years. Dodger manager Walter Alston bypassed his ace pitcher, Don Newcombe (who had zero luck against the Yanks), in favor of Podres for the finale. Gil Hodges knocked in Dodger runs in the fourth and sixth, and Podres bent but didn't break. For the sixth, Alston moved left fielder Junior Gilliam to second base and replaced him in the outfield with speedy Sandy Amoros. The decision paid off immediately. With none out and two on, Yogi Berra drilled a ball down the left-field line that Amoros caught inches from the fence in his right-hand mitt, and his throw in doubled up a Yankee. If he hadn't made the catch, both Yanks would have probably scored, and Berra would have had an extra-base hit. But, instead, the Brooklyn Dodgers captured their only hometown World Series win.

🎾 🎾 🎾

Joe Niekro hit his only major-league homer against his brother, Phil, beating him in a 1976 game. Together, the Niekros won more games (539) than any other pair of pitching brothers.

The Worst of the Worst (Miles out of First)

The teams that are found underneath the bottom of the barrel.

Many arguments have raged about the best baseball team ever. But the worst? Many qualify for the dubious honor of worst team for a single season. Each was terrible in its own way in its own time. Only teams that completed a season schedule are considered here (eliminating several fly-by-night clubs from the 19th century).

1899 Cleveland Spiders
Record: 20–134 (84 games out)
Managers: Lave Cross (8–30); Joe Quinn (12–104)
Nightmare Season: Just three years earlier, the Cleveland Spiders had played in consecutive Temple Cups (the championship series of the day) and boasted Cy Young in his prime as well as a cast of top hitters. With no rules prohibiting multiple team ownership, the best players from Cleveland were shifted to St. Louis in 1899. The result for Cleveland was the most losses in big-league history. The Spiders finished the year going 1–40. They were such a bad draw (fewer than 150 fans per home game!) that ownership forced them to play 112 road games.

1916 Philadelphia Athletics
Record: 36–117 (54½ games out)
Manager: Connie Mack
Nightmare Season: Two years removed from consecutive pennants, Connie Mack's Athletics compiled the worst winning percentage (.235) of the 20th century. Competition from the Federal League, anger at being swept in the 1914 World Series, and dwindling finances led Mack to sell off his best players, leading to 109 losses in 1915 and seven straight last-place finishes. And Mack let his pitchers take the punishment: Despite being the only team in the American League with an ERA above 3.00 in 1916, the A's led the league with 94 complete games.

1935 Boston Braves

Record: 38–115 (61½ games out)
Manager: Bill McKechnie
Nightmare Season: The Red Sox and Braves staged a heated contest for the dubious title of worst team in Boston throughout the 1920s and '30s. With each racking up five 100-loss seasons, neither team was good. But the Braves earned the prize with their doozy of a showing in 1935. After three consecutive .500 or better seasons, the Braves dropped off a cliff. Opponents batted .303, and Boston's 4.93 ERA was the highest in the NL since the offensive explosion of 1930. Aged Babe Ruth was on this team; he quit the game in May.

1941 Philadelphia Phillies

Record: 43–111 (57 games out)
Manager: Doc Prothro
Nightmare Season: The Phillies lost 100 games six times in a seven-season span, with 1941 being the lowest point. Unlike in 1930, when the pitching staff racked up an unfathomable 6.71 ERA at the tiny Baker Bowl in a year the team batted .315, the '41 Phillies at Shibe Park couldn't hit, either. They were last in runs scored and allowed, hit for the lowest batting average yet had the highest batting average against, needed more relief appearances than any other team, and, not surprisingly, had the NL's lowest attendance. The Phils hired a new manager (Hans Lobert) and lost 109 times in '42.

1952 Pittsburgh Pirates

Record: 42–112 (54½ games out)
Manager: Billy Meyer
Nightmare Season: The Pirates have the distinction of being the worst team between America's entry into World War II and baseball's expansion era. And what a bad team it was. The Bucs allowed more walks, hits, and home runs than any other NL team and gave up 134 more runs than anyone else as well. However, thanks to a shortened fence in left field, future Hall of Famer Ralph Kiner tied for the home run crown—his seventh straight year winning or

sharing it. When Kiner asked for a salary increase, owner Branch Rickey famously responded, "We finished last with you, we can finish last without you." After trading him to the Cubs, that's just what the Pirates did...for the next three seasons.

1962 New York Mets
Record: 40–120 (60½ games out)
Manager: Casey Stengel
Nightmare Season: The 1962 Mets are the stars of this dreadful, gloomy list. Oh, they were bad. No one had piled up more losses since 1899. They were outscored by 331 runs. This expansion team lost the first nine games they ever played and had three losing streaks in double digits. But with players like "Marvelous Marv" Throneberry, the Mets lost with panache. New York was so starved for National League baseball that fans ate it up at the Polo Grounds and gleefully followed the team to Shea Stadium. More than 40 years later, books are still published about Casey Stengel's fun, flea-bitten crew.

1962 Chicago Cubs
Record: 59–103 (42½ games out)
Managers: College of Coaches: El Tappe (4–16); Lou Klein (12–18); Charlie Metro (43–69)
Nightmare Season: It's hard to believe that two teams from the same league in the same year could have made it onto this list, but the 1962 Cubs are worthy thanks to the College of Coaches. Owner P. K. Wrigley's bright idea put the sputtering franchise in the hands of the overmatched coaching staff on a rotating basis. Playing their tenth decade as a franchise, the Cubs lost 100 games for the first time, finished seven games behind expansion Houston, and were the only team with a .500 record against the moribund Mets. Three times, the Cubs drew crowds of under 1,000 to Wrigley Field the last week of the season.

1969 San Diego Padres
Record: 52–110 (41 games out)
Manager: Preston Gomez

Nightmare Season: You think the Mets are the only epically bad expansion team? The Padres suffered on the field and at the gate. Just 512,970 fans showed up for their first year of existence. (The Expos, playing at a tiny, frigid facility, drew twice that number that year with the same record.) Even playing at a very pitcher-friendly park, San Diego pitchers struck out the fewest batters in the bigs, while the .225-hitting offense fanned the most times in the NL. The Padres beat out the Expos and the 1977 Blue Jays as the worst first-year team not named the Mets, and they finished last in each of their first six seasons, averaging 101 losses.

1988 Baltimore Orioles

Record: 54–107 (34½ games out)
Managers: Cal Ripken, Sr. (0–6); Frank Robinson (54–101)
Nightmare Season: While there were many terrible seasons between 1970 and 2002, the staggering start and finish of the 1988 Orioles edges out the likes of the 1979 A's, the 1991 Indians, and the 1998 Marlins. The O's began the season with three Ripkens and a record 21 consecutive losses. Cal Sr. was fired six games in. (Cal Jr. and Billy stayed on.) The team managed a 51–69 mark for Frank Robinson between May and mid-September before a dismal 3–17 finish.

2003 Detroit Tigers

Record: 43–119 (47 games out)
Manager: Alan Trammell
Nightmare Season: The Tigers would have made the list anyway for their brutal 53–109 season in 1996, but let's not get greedy. The 2003 Tigers were terrible on an epic scale. Detroit had the most losses in American League history, the third most ever in the major leagues—pitcher Mike Maroth was the first 20-game loser since 1980—and the lowest AL batting average since the 1988 Orioles. Three years later, though, the Tigers took control of the AL Central, making it all the way to the World Series. Revenge is certainly sweet.

Ruth Notables

The numbers prove that Babe Ruth was one of a kind.

• In the American League in 1920, 14.6 percent of all home runs—54 of 369—were hit by Ruth. To match that seasonal percentage today, a slugger would have to belt close to 400 homers.

• After being sold by the Red Sox to New York, Ruth out-homered the entire Boston team in ten of the next 12 seasons.

• From 1920 through 1932, there were only two seasons in which Ruth didn't knock out at least 40 home runs. He had totals as high as 60, 59, and 54 (two times).

• Babe led the American League in dingers 12 times (1918–1921, 1923, 1924, 1926–1931).

• Of Babe's 714 home runs, ten were inside-the-park shots (although not one ever bounced out of the park, even when that was a legal homer). Sixteen were hit in extra innings, and one was as a pinch-hitter.

• Ruth's record of 457 total bases in 1921 has never been equaled.

• Babe's career .690 slugging percentage (total bases divided by at-bats) is the highest ever. The next highest is more than 50 points back (Ted Williams, .634). Ruth led the AL in slugging 13 times.

• Babe batted over .370 six times, with a high of .393 in 1923. His .342 batting average is the tenth best in major-league history.

• Ruth's career record as a pitcher was 94–46 with a 2.28 ERA. He is universally regarded as the greatest hitting pitcher, the best pitching hitter, and because of that parlay, the greatest player *period* in baseball history.

All-Time Great

Ty Cobb

Not just one of the greatest hitters ever, he was also one of the toughest and probably the nastiest.

Born: December 18, 1886; Narrows, GA
MLB Career: Detroit Tigers, 1905–26; Philadelphia A's, 1927–28
Hall of Fame Resume: .367 BA (first) * 4,189 hits (second) * 724 doubles (fourth) * 295 triples (second) * 3,053 singles (second) * 892 steals (fourth) * 2,246 runs (second) * 12 batting titles
Inside Pitch: The famous incident of Cobb challenging Honus Wagner in the 1909 series ("I'm coming down, Krauthead") never happened.

A movie on the life of Babe Ruth drew hordes to the theaters despite being a critical flop a few years back, but when a similar picture on Ty Cobb debuted a while later, it was gone in a matter of weeks. Most folks had little interest in paying tribute to the greatest hitter for average (.367) in major-league history. Nearly 70 years after Cobb's career, the reputation of "The Georgia Peach" apparently hasn't changed much. He might have hit and run better than anyone else in baseball, but he was still one mean SOB.

Cobb's vicious streak seemed at times to engulf him: He used a brutal ferocity to attack the game and beat down opponents. Harassed as a scrawny 18-year-old with the Tigers in 1905, he

quickly added weight and muscle along with a philosophy of playing hard and trusting no one. He never hit below .316 after his rookie season, and with his .350 mark in 1907 (at the age of 20), he became the youngest player in history to win a batting title. He led the American League with 119 RBI, 212 hits, a .468 slugging mark, and 49 stolen bases to boot.

The left-handed hitter with the split-handed grip could bash line drives and bunt with equal skill and take an extra base seemingly at will. In the field, he used his speed and a solid arm to cut down runners, and he registered 20 or more assists on ten occasions.

But what he did best was hit—and run the bases. His 1907 batting title was the first of nine straight and 12 overall (although two of the batting titles are disputed). Cobb led the Tigers to three straight pennants, from 1907 to '09, and remained the key to Detroit's attack for 20 years. Perennially among American League leaders in slugging and steals (he won six stolen base crowns), he was also the team's most reliable RBI man for many years—averaging 106 a season from 1907 to '12 en route to 1,937 for his career. He was rumored to slide with his spikes high, and he liked that intimidating image of himself.

Cobb won the Triple Crown in 1909 with nine homers, 107 RBI, and a .377 average, and two years later he had perhaps his finest season with a career-high .420 average and league-leading totals in hits (248), doubles (47), triples (24), runs (147), RBI (127), and steals (83). In 1915, he set a stolen base record of 96 that held for nearly 50 years, and in 1922 he hit .400 for the third and last time at the age of 35. Serving as player/manager his final six years with the Tigers, he joined Connie Mack's Athletics in 1927 to finish his career. He retired rich from wise investments—but virtually devoid of friends. His major-league records for hits (4,189) and steals (892) have since been topped, but the .367 mark will likely endure—along with the sordid reputation of the man who achieved it.

◉ ◉ ◉

"There probably have been players in the game who had as much natural ability and as good a physique as [Ty] Cobb; there may also have been some—although I doubt it—who could think as fast. But there certainly never was another athlete who combined Cobb's ability and his smartness—or even came close."

—Fred Haney

The Greatest Managers of All Time

They provide the brains behind the brawn. They are the "field generals" who make the tough choices: whom to play and where, when to remove a pitcher or sit a slumping superstar. They also have a fierce intelligence and a drive to win.

Leo Durocher

Brooklyn Dodgers 1939–1946, 1948
New York Giants 1948–1955
Chicago Cubs 1966–1972
Houston Astros 1972–1973
W/L: 2008–1709 (.540)   **Win ranking:** 9th
Pennants: 3   **World Series titles:** 1

He played on the same team as Babe Ruth and was shortstop on the St. Louis Cardinals "Gas House Gang." The title of his autobiography is *Nice Guys Finish Last,* and that pretty much sums up Durocher's style and attitude. The outspoken leader played hunches, took chances, and proved to be right more often than wrong. His 1951 Giants delivered the greatest comeback in major-league history. (See pages 234–235 for the full story.)

Ned Hanlon

Pittsburgh Alleghenys/Pirates 1889–1891
Baltimore Orioles (NL) 1892–1898
Brooklyn Superbas 1899–1905
Cincinnati Reds 1906–1907
W/L: 1313–1164 (.530)   **Win ranking:** 26th
Pennants: 5

With his sensational Baltimore Orioles, Ned Hanlon invented a style of baseball that was scrappy, savage, and creative. Hanlon innovations or improvements included the hit-and-run play and training fielders to back each other up. He was the first manager to hire a full-time groundskeeper to tailor the field to his team's advantage. The "Baltimore Chop" (hitting the ball down in front of home plate so that it bounces up high and allows time for the batter to run to first) was another Hanlon ploy. He was "The Manager of Managers." Among those who learned the craft at his knee were John McGraw, Wilbert Robinson, Hugh Jennings, Kid Gleason, and Miller Huggins. Every one of those men except Gleason won more than 1,000 games; together they combined for more than 7,000.

Joe McCarthy

Chicago Cubs 1926–1930
New York Yankees 1931–1946
Boston Red Sox 1948–1950
W/L: 2125–1333 (.615)   **Win ranking:** 6th
Pennants: 9   **World Series titles:** 7

Teams managed by Joe McCarthy never finished lower than fourth. From 1929 to 1943 his squads finished first or second 14 times. He once said, "So I eat, drink, and sleep baseball 24 hours a day. So what? What's wrong with that?" McCarthy called on his voluminous memory and keen intelligence to put together winners wherever he went. His lifetime winning percentage of .615 is the highest of any manager ever. Joe DiMaggio said, "Never a day went by when you didn't learn something from McCarthy."

John McGraw

Baltimore Orioles (NL) 1899–1900
Baltimore Orioles (AL) 1901–1902
New York Giants 1902–1932
W/L: 2763–1948 (.586)   **Win ranking:** 2nd
Pennants: 10   **World Series titles:** 3

John McGraw was the dominant on-field personality of the game in the early part of the 20th century. When he spoke, people listened. And often he did his speaking with his fists. His style was to demand absolute obedience from his players; they had to trust that his intellect and experience would make the difference between winning and losing. His biggest superstar, Christy Mathewson, said of him, "He doesn't know what fear is." McGraw didn't just take on players and umpires; he did battle with league presidents and team owners as ferociously as his charges took on the opposition. When a particularly savvy move led to a late-season pennant-chasing win in 1921, he told a reporter, "We can win this—if my brains hold out."

Casey Stengel
Brooklyn Dodgers 1934–1936
Boston Braves 1938–1943
New York Yankees 1949–1960
New York Mets 1962–1965
W/L: 1905–1842 (.508)   **Win ranking:** 11th
Record as a Yankee: 1149–696 (.623)
Pennants: 10   **World Series titles:** 7

No genius ever presented himself in a less genius-like way than Casey Stengel. He was a clown on the field, once tipping his cap to the crowd and having a bird fly out from under it. During his 14-year big-league playing career, he was no superstar (despite hitting some big World Series home runs), but he was an excellent student. He played under two of Ned Hanlon's charges: Wilbert Robinson and John McGraw. Under McGraw he learned the art of platooning (assigning two players—usually one right-handed and one left-handed—to the same defensive position). He took over as Yankee manager in 1949 and became the only manager to lead his team to five consecutive World Series. When asked about his smart moves, he responded in a unique form of fractured-syntax double-talk that came to be known as "Stengelese."

Earl Weaver
Baltimore Orioles 1968–1982, 1985–1986
W/L: 1480–1060 (.583)   **Win ranking:** 20th
Pennants: 4   **World Series titles:** 1

Small and pugnacious, Weaver (unlike most other great managers) had no major-league playing experience. But on the field his canny moves and feisty personality set the tone for a fistful of superb Oriole teams. Weaver leads all managers in being ejected from games—nearly 100 times. Once he got tossed while handing the lineup card to the umps before the game even started. And when he got jawing with an umpire over a call he thought was missed, it was a show in itself—the diminutive Weaver would stick his nose in the ump's face, screaming a blue streak. (He learned early on to turn his cap around so the bill wouldn't wind up in the umpire's face when the two went eye-to-eye.) No manager ever had such an impressive start to his career: In his first three full seasons behind the Orioles helm, his charges won 109, 108, and 101 games.

Harry Wright
Boston Red Stockings 1871–1875
Boston Red Caps 1876–1881
Providence Grays 1882–1883
Philadelphia (NL) 1884–1893
W/L: 1225–885 (.581)   **Win ranking:** 34th
League titles: 6

Wright wasn't just a great manager. He was the game's first all-professional-team manager. He came to the United States from England with his father and brother in 1837, at age two. All became excellent cricket players. But Harry and his brother, George (the better player of the two), took a liking to the American game. Harry was just 31 when he founded the Cincinnati Red Stockings. Within three years they were the first team to openly use only paid players, turning baseball into a business. And their team was a juggernaut. In 1869 and 1870, Harry's charges won 130 games in a row. Being a manager in those days was about much more than filling out a lineup card and changing pitchers. Managers had to schedule the games and serve as traveling secretaries and bookkeepers. There was a constant threat from gam-

blers and rowdy behavior, on and off the field. But Wright soared above all that with a total commitment to honesty. In addition, he was a creative thinker, instituting concepts such as hand signals, the hidden-ball trick, and double steals. He was even a fashion innovator: His teams were the first to wear knickers.

Fast Facts

- *During excavation for the building of Oriole Park at Camden Yards, the remains of a saloon were discovered. It turned out that Babe Ruth's father had owned the place.*

- *In 1951, Ned Garver won 20 games for the St. Louis Browns. The rest of the pitching staff won only 32 games collectively. Garver became the only pitcher to win 20 games on a 100-loss team.*

- *Ted Williams won the American League Triple Crown in both 1942 and 1947 but finished second in MVP voting both times.*

- *In 1990, Oakland relief ace Dennis Eckersley had 48 saves and allowed only 45 baserunners.*

- *Outfielder Al Simmons' real name was Aloysius Szymanski.*

- *Mickey Lolich, who pitched for 16 years (13 for the Detroit Tigers), hit his only home run in his first World Series game. It was during Game 2 of the 1968 World Series against the St. Louis Cardinals, the defending world champions. Lolich hit the homer off Nelson Briles in his first at-bat, and the Tigers went on to win the World Series in Game 7.*

- *On June 10, 1944, Joe Nuxhall was just 15 years old when he played his first game for the Cincinnati Reds, making him the youngest player ever in the big leagues.*

- *Ty Cobb hit over .300 in 23 consecutive seasons, the longest such run of any major-leaguer.*

- *Derek Lowe of the 2004 Boston Red Sox is the only major-league pitcher to win the final game of a division series, a league championship series, and the World Series all in the same year.*

A Game of Numbers

On some players, uniform numbers can make a statement.

From Babe Ruth's "3" in the 1930s to Albert Pujols's "5" today, baseball numbers on uniforms have given fans a chance to recognize, cheer on, and—in the case of countless Little Leaguers—imitate their favorite players. At times they have also served as a way for athletes to display their individuality.

Ruth's Yankees wore jerseys that corresponded to their spot in the vaunted New York lineup: Earle Combs "1," Mark Koenig "2," Ruth "3," Lou Gehrig "4," and so on down the line. Giants pitcher Bill Voiselle received special permission from the National League during the 1940s to wear "96"— a tribute to his beloved hometown of Ninety Six, South Carolina.

Just before 3'7" Eddie Gaedel made his surprise pinch-hitting appearance for the hapless St. Louis Browns in 1951, the team's maverick owner, Bill Veeck, gave the crowd a hint of what was coming by printing Eddie's name and number in that day's scorecard: "Gaedel, ⅛." Veeck, in fact, was the man who, while running the White Sox a decade later, became the first big-league boss to add player names atop their uniform numbers. This gave TV viewers a better idea of who they were watching and enabled Chicago outfielder Carlos May to become the first and only major-leaguer to "wear" his birthday: "May 17."

Others making a statement with their backs more recently have included Al Oliver and Rey Ordonez, who presumably wore "0" so that their numbers would more closely match their names, and wacky left-hander Bill "Spaceman" Lee, who took "37" because, when turned upside down, it matched his name minus one "E." Minor-leaguer Johnny Neves, however, had them all topped. In 1951, he wore "7" backward on his Fargo-Moorhead jersey because, of course, his name spelled backward was "seveN." On the creativity scale, that's got to be #1.

All-Time Great

Josh Gibson

This catcher may have been the greatest power hitter of all time.

Born: December 21, 1911; Buena Vista, GA
MLB Career: None. Kept out of the majors by the color line. Played in Negro Leagues 1930–1946.
Hall of Fame Resume: Some say he hit more than 800 home runs in his career, as many as 75 in one season.
Inside Pitch: Although Gibson was hardly talkative, he did have one famous quote: "A homer a day will boost my pay."

The statistics are sketchy, the stories only hearsay from people who have little documentation to prove their points. The Negro Leagues operated under constraints that made keeping close track of player performance an impossible task, but those who watched these banished stars usually agreed on one thing: No one hit a baseball further and with greater frequency than catcher Josh Gibson.

Growing up in Pittsburgh, Gibson began playing semipro ball as a teenager and, as legend has it, was watching the Negro League Homestead Grays in action when he was pulled from the stands and put behind the plate after the Grays catcher hurt his finger. A star on the Grays within a year, the stocky, 6′2″ right-handed batter moved on to the Pittsburgh Crawfords in 1934. There, he played alongside fellow future Hall of Famers Judy Johnson, Oscar Charleston, and James "Cool Papa" Bell in Black Ball's version of "Murderer's Row." On occasion Gibson also formed half of the most intimidating battery in Negro League history along with pitching Hall of Fame legend Satchel Paige.

Fun-loving and popular among his teammates, Gibson—known as "the black Babe Ruth"—drew high praise from players black and white for his abilities. Roy Campanella said Josh was "the greatest ballplayer I ever saw." Walter Johnson claimed he "catches so easy, he might as well be in a rocking chair." Jimmy

Powers of the *New York Daily News* wrote in 1939, "I am positive that if Josh Gibson were white, he would be a major-league star," an argument Gibson supported by blasting three homers off Hall of Fame pitcher Dizzy Dean in two exhibition matchups.

One set of partial Negro League statistics credits Gibson with 146 home runs and a .362 average in 501 games spread over 16 seasons (in Negro League games alone). In reality, he may have slugged as many as 84 homers annually playing in more than 200 contests a year in winter (in the Puerto Rican League), spring, and summer. Sometimes the Crawfords or Homestead Grays (to which Gibson returned for his last five seasons) secured big-league ballparks for their games, and stories abound of Gibson belting homers to the deepest points of Comiskey Park and Yankee Stadium. Hitting home runs farther than 500 feet was not unusual for Gibson.

Pirates owner William Benswanger and Senators boss Clark Griffith both claimed an interest in bringing Josh to the majors, but the man with a reported 850 to 900 home runs was still blasting them for the Grays when Jackie Robinson signed with Brooklyn in 1945. Gibson might still have made the big leagues, but struggles with alcohol and illness shrouded his final years, and he died of a brain hemorrhage at age 35 in January 1947—three months before Robinson's debut with the Dodgers.

⚾ ⚾ ⚾

"If they came to Josh Gibson today and he were 17 years old, they would have a blank spot on the contract and they'd say, 'Fill the amount in.' That's how good Josh Gibson was."

—Junior Gilliam

⚾ ⚾ ⚾

"Josh, I wish you and Satchel [Paige] played with me on the Cardinals. Hell, we'd win the pennant by July 4 and go fishin' until World Series time."

—Dizzy Dean to Negro Leaguer Josh Gibson in 1934

Can of Corn

"I don't know a lot about politics, but I know a lot about baseball."

—Richard Nixon, 1981

"Two hours is about as long as an American can wait for the close of a baseball game—or anything else, for that matter."

—Albert Spalding

"No team ever looked more intense than they did. Getting on the field with them was akin to stepping into a wading pool with Jaws."

—Red Sox pitcher Bill Lee on the Yankees after their record 14½-game comeback in 1978, *The Wrong Stuff*

"After the game, it took me 20 minutes to walk to where he had hit the ball in a split second."

—Yankee ace Lefty Gomez on a homer he allowed to Jimmie Foxx

"Managing is never fun. If you pull off something big, it's expected. If you fail, you're a bum."

—Skipper Paul Richards, *Baseball's Greatest Managers*

"So I swing, and would you believe it's a bases-loaded home run? I really sped around those bases to get back to the dugout and those candy bars in a hurry."

—Ron Santo on hitting while having a diabetic reaction

"In baseball you're with every guy on your club and you're against every player on the other club from the time the game starts until it's over. You've got your whole club with you, too, but you're all alone sometimes where they can't help you."

—Joe Garagiola, *Baseball Is a Funny Game*

Sudden Death

The gifts of even journeymen ballplayers are considerable: speed, strength, eye-hand coordination, mental toughness. Professional players are remarkable human beings, so a death—on the field or off—is inevitably sad and startling.

On the Field
James Creighton, October 14, 1862
The first professional ballplayer to die had been one of the game's greatest and most innovative. Probably the first man to make his living playing ball, Creighton was a brilliant hitter and pitcher who first used the wrist snap to try and get batters out. (Until then the pitcher had been more of a "server," just offering the ball to hit.) He belted a home run on October 14, 1862, at the height of his career. In doing so, his mighty swing caused an internal rupture, and he died several days later from intestinal bleeding. Jim Creighton was only 21 years old.

Ray Chapman, August 16, 1920
The only major-leaguer to die as the result of an on-field injury (there weren't yet major leagues in James Creighton's day) was Cleveland shortstop Ray Chapman. He leaned into a soaring fastball from Yankee Carl Mays, and the ball cracked his left temple. Chapman never regained consciousness. (For more on this story, see page 320.)

In the Air
Roberto Clemente, January 1, 1973
Clemente was a proud man and an outstanding ballplayer. He excelled both on the field and at bat throughout his career with the Pittsburgh Pirates, earning 12 Gold Gloves and four batting titles, as well as the NL MVP Award in 1966. He was also passionate about humanitarian work and was a hero to millions of Latin Americans. In December 1972, an earthquake in Nicaragua had devastated much of the country, and the government's henchmen were pillaging the supplies sent from other nations. They stopped

only when one supply worker shouted, "Touch that, and I'll bring Clemente here and tell him!" Feeling that his presence could help with the delivery of goods to people who needed them most, Clemente, 38, boarded a plane in Puerto Rico on New Year's Eve. He probably didn't know that the plane was in bad shape, the supplies had been poorly loaded, and the pilot was not certified to fly that plane. Soon after takeoff, the plane crashed into the harbor, and no trace was ever found of it or the passengers. Cooperstown waived the five-year waiting period and inducted Clemente into the Hall of Fame that very same year.

Thurman Munson, August 2, 1979

Munson was a seven-time All-Star catcher who provided the rugged alternative to his flashy Yankee teammate Reggie Jackson. Thirty-two-year-old Munson, a married father of three children, had been flying planes for about a year and a half. On a day off he, along with a flight instructor and a friend, went up in his Cessna Citation from the Akron-Canton airport. He was excited that the new twin-engine plane would allow him to travel to see his family more frequently. He was practicing "touch-and-go landings," where the pilot takes off again right away after touching down. After a few successful maneuvers, things started to go wrong, and Munson's plane nosedived 1,000 feet short of the runway. His two passengers survived. Munson, though initially conscious after the crash, did not.

Suicides

Harry Pulliam, July 28, 1909

Pulliam was the 40-year-old president of the National League, a dapper dandy with a charismatic personality. Though successful and charming, he had a nervous nature, and the events of the 1908 season (umpire scandals, gambling and bribery problems, the Merkle incident) left him distraught. He suffered a complete breakdown during a league meeting the following January and returned after a leave of absence six months later. He had been back just a month when he fired a bullet through his head.

Donnie Moore, July 18, 1989
In Game 5 of the 1986 ALCS against the Red Sox, Moore surrendered the pinch-hit homer to Dave Henderson that turned the series around, leading to the Angels' devastating loss. (It would have been their first-ever pennant.) Moore never really recovered. The abuse from fans and the press was bad enough; his own demons seemed worse. Plagued by depression and substance abuse, Moore shot his estranged wife (who survived), then turned the gun on himself.

Other Violent Ends
Ed Delahanty, July 2, 1903
Hall of Famer Delahanty was a superstar—the winner of five slugging titles and the oldest of five pro ball–playing brothers. After a heavy bout of drinking, he was kicked off a train at Niagara Falls for being drunk and threatening other passengers. He began walking over a railroad bridge, and then fell (or jumped or was pushed off) into the Falls. His body was found downriver eight days later.

Don Wilson, January 5, 1975
Wilson, starting pitcher for the Houston Astros, was drunk when he pulled his car into his garage, closed the door, and left the motor running. His death was ruled a suicide, though no one knew for sure. What made this incident especially tragic was that Wilson's five-year-old son, sleeping in his room above the garage, also died from the fumes.

Lyman Bostock, September 23, 1978
Promising young Angels hitter Bostock was generous (giving away part of his salary to charity when he felt he hadn't earned it) and hardworking. After a game in Chicago, Bostock dined with his uncle in nearby Gary, Indiana. As they sat in the car with Barbara Smith, the uncle's adult goddaughter, a man named Leonard Smith pulled alongside them and tried to shoot Smith, who was his estranged wife. But the bullet hit Bostock, who died soon after at the age of 27.

Greatest Teams of All Time

1904–05 New York Giants

Record: 106–47 (1904)
Manager: John McGraw
Hall of Famers: McGraw, Christy Mathewson, Joe McGinnity, Roger Bresnahan
The Season: In 1904, they ran away from the Cubs and the Pirates, ending up with a 13-game lead.
The Legacy: McGraw refused to play a World Series in '04. When the Giants won again in '05, they took on Connie Mack's A's. Mathewson threw three shutouts, McGinnity one, for an easy Series win.

Mathewson and McGraw. Seldom has a great team been defined by two such disparate personalities. On the bench was the short, fiery, hardscrabble manager John McGraw, raised on a baseball diet of rugged, rule-breaking play. On the mound was Christy Mathewson—tall, college educated, genteel, and honest.

Mathewson had already been a 20-game winner in 1901 when McGraw arrived in mid-1902 to take over the Giants' reins. Previous managers had been uncertain whether Mathewson was best as a pitcher or a fielder. McGraw put a quick end to that nonsense. He gave Mathewson 42 starts in 1903; the 22-year-old finished 37 of them and won 30 games. Aided by McGinnity's 31 victories, the Giants, who had been pretty much stumbling around the National League's second division for ten years, shot to second, just 6½ games behind the powerful Pirates.

The next year, they were unstoppable. They put together 106 wins and finished 13 ahead of the Cubs. McGraw dealt for shortstop Bill Dahlen before the season started. In early July, he sent Moose McCormick to Cincinnati for "Turkey Mike" Donlin. The defense was solid. The offense led the league in runs scored without having a single .300 hitter in the lineup.

The key was the masterful pitching of Mathewson and McGinnity—the original "M&M boys." McGinnity started 44 games and finished 38 of them. The year before, Joe had set the modern National League record with 434 innings pitched; in '04, he settled for "only" 408. He collected 35 wins and lost just eight times. He also led the league with nine shutouts and a remarkable 1.61 ERA. Mathewson added 33 wins in 45 decisions with an ERA barely over 2.00. His 368 innings ranked third in the National League. Rounding out the pitching staff were deaf-mute Dummy Taylor, whose 21–15 record was his best season ever, and 23-year-old lefty Hooks Wiltse, who went 13–3. There was no postseason series between the American and National Leagues that year, largely because McGraw felt that all the other teams were "minor league."

Things were different in 1905, as the Giant offense perked up. Donlin hit .356, third in the league, and led the NL in runs scored. With Donlin on base, outfielder Sam Mertes was able to knock in 108 runs, second in the NL. Roger Bresnahan began to display the catching savvy that would eventually earn him a place in the Hall of Fame. And he batted .302, too.

The pitching may have been less spectacular than the 1904 staff, but it was no less effective. Mathewson completely dominated NL batters the way McGinnity had the year before. His 31 wins were eight more than the second-best finisher. He led the league in shutouts, strikeouts, and ERA with a sensational 1.28 figure. Although it would be surpassed later (once by Mathewson himself), at the time it was the lowest ERA for a full season in the 30-year history of the National League.

While McGinnity "fell off" to a 21–15 record and a 2.87 ERA, youngster Red Ames earned 31 starts and finished 22–8. Taylor won 16 games and Wiltse 15. The Giants moved into first place on April 23 and never left. And the two leagues worked out an agreement for a World Series: The Giants would play the AL-champion Philadelphia Athletics.

And there Mathewson put on a clinic, the greatest individual pitching show the World Series would ever see. He started against the A's in Games 1, 3, and 5, shutting them out three times, allowing just 14 hits, striking out 18, and surrendering only one base on balls. McGinnity tossed a five-hit shutout in Game 4. And the Giants won their first world championship.

Blue-Ribbon Ballparks

Great ballyards have as much appeal and personality as the athletes who play in them. Here are some all-time top venues.

Fenway Park, Boston
Year Built: 1912
Who Plays There: Boston Red Sox
Cost to Build: $650,000 ($12.8 million today)
Capacity: 36,108
Outfield Dimensions: L 310, C 389, R 302
Notable Fact: The runs and hits numbers for the scoreboard are 16 inches by 16 inches large and weigh three pounds each.

There's no other place on Earth where the purity of the game and the fan's experience of it is as powerful as in Boston's Fenway Park. It's not just a place where people go to watch baseball; it *is* baseball. It's the oldest ballpark in the bigs, dating back more than 90 years. Maybe it doesn't smell like a new rose, maybe it isn't brand-spanking clean, but here you can feel the history of the game oozing out from between the seats. It hosted the utterly bizarre and wonderful 1912 World Series, it's where Babe Ruth played his first big-league game, and it stood witness to the immortal feats of Ted Williams. Boston's deeply knowledgeable fans will tell you all about it between bites of a Fenway Frank, but only *between* pitches; if you're a Red Sox fan, you stay focused on the game. Fenway's famed "Green Monster," a 37-foot-high wall, stands like a national monument in left field. But now there are seats on top of it.

Petco Park, San Diego
Year Built: 2004
Who Plays There: San Diego Padres
Cost to Build: $450 million
Capacity: 42,445
Outfield Dimensions: L 334, C 396, R 322
Notable Fact: The left-field foul pole is attached to the southeast corner of a former iron and steel foundry built in 1909.

Stucco-walled Petco Park opened to glowing reviews in 2004. Upon entering the ballpark, Padres fans pass a palm court, jacaranda trees, and waterfalls. Once inside, they're treated to views of the city skyline and other sites beyond the outfield fence, including a beach and a park for fans to enjoy. The four-story Western Metal Supply building in the left-field corner now includes the Padres Team Store, a standing room area, luxury suites, a restaurant, and rooftop seating for 800 lucky fans. Need to check some stats from your laptop during the game? No problem: Petco is wired.

AT&T Park, San Francisco
Year Built: 2000
Who Plays There: San Francisco Giants
Cost to Build: $357 million
Capacity: 41,606
Outfield Dimensions: L 339, C 399, R 309
Notable Fact: A giant baseball glove decorates the left-center seats, 501 feet from home plate.

The first privately financed major-league ballpark since Dodger Stadium, AT&T Park has an authentic San Francisco feel: charming and intriguing, yet not too brash or boisterous. Just beyond the right-field fence (or a Barry Bonds home run away) is San Francisco Bay—or McCovey's Cove, as it has come to be called (in honor of Hall of Famer Willie McCovey). You can watch the sailboats pass by between innings, or you can marvel at the nine-foot statue of Giants superstar Willie Mays. An architectural marvel, AT&T Park features a terrific kids' play area with a gigantic Coke bottle that kids can slide down, and the scoreboard has a dozen categories of stats for every hitter and pitcher. The park is always immaculate, and there's a greater variety of first-class food (don't miss the garlic fries!) than you'll find in most other parks.

Ebbets Field, Brooklyn
Year Built: 1913
Who Played There: Brooklyn Dodgers, Brooklyn Eagles (Negro National League)
Cost to Build: $750,000 ($14.3 million today)

Capacity: 31,903
Outfield Dimensions: L 348, C 393, R 297
Notable Fact: Braves batter Bama Rowell rapped a ball off the Bulova clock in the right-field scoreboard in 1946, shattering the glass and providing inspiration for a scene in the 1984 movie *The Natural.*

Built on the site of a former garbage dump, the intimate, unusual, and altogether enjoyable Ebbets Field is what today's retro ballparks are paying homage to. Ebbets hosted the often zany, often brilliant Brooklyn Dodgers and their outrageous fans, including the "Dodger Sym-Phony" and Hilda Chester, who always brought along a pair of cowbells to clank out noisy encouragement to her team. The outfield fences jutted every which way, providing enough angles to tax the talents of any geometrician (or outfielder), while the upper deck hung out over the field. Batters hoped to hit clothier Abe Stark's ad in right field, with its elegantly simple offer: "Hit Sign, Win Suit." The last game played at Ebbets was on September 24, 1957, and the park was demolished in 1960.

Oriole Park at Camden Yards, Baltimore

Year Built: 1992
Who Plays There: Baltimore Orioles
Cost to Build: $110 million
Capacity: 48,290
Outfield Dimensions: L 333, C 400, R 318
Notable Fact: A red seat in left field (Section 86, Row FF, Seat 10) marks the spot where Cal Ripken hit his 278th home run in 1993, breaking Ernie Banks's record for the most home runs hit by a shortstop. Ripken hit the same seat in 1995 during consecutive game number 2,130—the game that tied Lou Gehrig's record.

This is the park that changed everything. It tolled the death knell for the cookie-cutter oval stadiums that had dominated the sports scene for decades. Camden Yards was the first of the magnificent retro ballparks that have now become the standard. Bleacher seats, a picnic area behind part of the center-field fence, and ivy growing on the hitters' backdrop contribute to the park's nostalgic feel. Perhaps most important, Camden Yards is integrated into the urban landscape, not slapped down in the middle of an ocean of parking lots. The park is buffered by the 100-year-old eight-story B&O Warehouse beyond the right-field fence. Inside, Camden Yards boasts comfortable seats, a dual-level bullpen, and fresh flowers along the walkways. The outstanding concessions include freshly squeezed lemonade and ex-Oriole Boog Powell's succulent barbeque.

Wrigley Field, Chicago
Year Built: 1914
Who Plays (Played) There: Federal League Chicago Whales, 1914–1915; Chicago Cubs, 1916–present
Cost to Build: $250,000 ($4.7 million today)
Capacity: 41,118
Outfield Dimensions: L 355, C 400, R 353
Notable Fact: The scoreboard, erected in 1937, is still manually operated and has never been hit by a batted ball.

Nestled into a charming North Side neighborhood, Wrigley Field lives up to its nickname, "The Friendly Confines." Fans—including the infamous Bleacher Bums—are treated to magnificent views of Chicago, ivy-covered walls, and home runs galore, especially when the Windy City gales are blowing out. Best of all, the Wrigley experience connects everyone to what is wonderfully timeless about this sport. Since most of Wrigley's games are played during the day (Wrigley was the last park to add lights, in 1988—40 years after the next-to-last), the idea of ducking out of work early to catch a game is still sinfully, deliciously alive in Chicago. The ballpark seats just 41,118, so some fans prefer to watch from the rooftops and porches of buildings behind the outfield fences.

Yankee Stadium, New York
Year Built: 1923 (renovated 1974–75; reopened 1976)
Who Plays There: New York Yankees
Cost to Build: $2.5 million ($27.6 million today); $48 million for 1974–75 renovation
Capacity: 57,478
Outfield Dimensions: L 318, C 408, R 314

Notable Fact: The outfield fences have been brought in five times to up home run totals.

It was dubbed "The House That Ruth Built," because until the Babe showed up, the Yanks, poorer sisters among New York ballclubs, were able to comfortably share the Polo Grounds with the Giants. Naturally, Ruth christened the place with a home run on Opening Day 1923. This was the first ballpark to be classified a "stadium" because of its size. Over the years, the park has hosted 37 World Series, with the Bronx Bombers prevailing in 26 of them. The stadium's signature features include a short porch in right, "Death Valley" in left center, and monuments of pin-striped legends beyond the outfield fence, including Ruth, Lou Gehrig, Joe DiMaggio, Mickey Mantle, and manager Miller Huggins. But all good things must come to an end: In 2006 the Yankees announced plans to build a new stadium.

PNC Park, Pittsburgh
Year Built: 2001
Who Plays There: Pittsburgh Pirates
Cost to Build: $237 million
Capacity: 38,496
Outfield Dimensions: L 325, C 399, R 320
Notable Fact: The Outback in the Outfield restaurant, overlooking left field, allows fans to watch the game while they dine.

With the emergence of many great new ballparks, discussion rages as to which is the best. Both ESPN and the Web site Ballparks of Baseball named Pittsburgh's PNC Park tops. With only two decks of seats, PNC Park is baseball's second smallest venue (after Fenway Park). The Roberto Clemente Bridge, closed to vehicles on game days, leads pedestrian fans from downtown Pittsburgh to an intimate setting with a panoramic view of the city's skyline. Paying homage to the team's past greats are gigantic statues of Clemente, Willie Stargell, and the team's first superstar, Honus Wagner. The out-of-town scoreboard shows not just the score, but the inning, outs, and men on base for every game being played. PNC's food includes the legendary Primanti's all-on-one sandwich and ex-Pirate Manny Sanguillen's barbeque.

Fast Facts

- When sluggers Hank Greenberg and Ralph Kiner joined the Pirates, the team moved in the left-field fence by 30 feet.

- Baltimore left fielder John Lowenstein had a unique explanation for his hot hitting early in the 1982 season: He spent the time between innings flushing the clubhouse toilet to keep his wrists strong.

- The first World Series was played between Pittsburgh and Boston in 1903 and was a nine-game series. Boston won the series 5–3.

- The shortest home run champion was Hack Wilson, who led the league in home runs in 1926, 1927, 1928, and 1930 for the Chicago Cubs. Although he was only 5'6"with a size six shoe, Wilson weighed 190 pounds, was mostly muscle, and had an 18" neck.

- On April 29, 1953, Joe Adcock became the first major-league player to homer over the center-field wall in New York's Polo Grounds. The home run flew more than 475 feet.

- Gaylord Perry became the first pitcher to win the Cy Young Award in both leagues, with the Cleveland Indians (American League) in 1972 and the San Diego Padres (National League) in 1978.

- On August 5, 1921, the first radio play-by-play of a major-league game was broadcast. The game was Pittsburgh vs. Philadelphia on station KDKA. The Pirates won 8–5.

- First baseman Rip Collins of the Cardinals hated to throw away broken bats. Instead, he brought them home and converted them into a unique picket fence in front of his house.

Enter the Judge

Baseball's dictatorial but effectual commissioner Kenesaw Mountain Landis presided over the game from 1920 through '44. Having served as a judge, Landis had no problem laying down the law.

Judge Kenesaw Mountain Landis operated out of a Chicago office with one word written on the door: BASEBALL. Stubborn and conscientious, the Judge had the final say.

Supreme Power

Serving as Major League Baseball's first commissioner, from 1920 until his death in 1944 at age 78, Landis fought ferociously to protect what he called the "national institution" of baseball. He took office while the game's integrity was under fire (the baseball world was reeling from the Black Sox scandal); he died with its good name restored, and he didn't particularly care whose feelings or finances might be hurt along the way.

When baseball's owners named him commissioner in 1920, Landis demanded "supreme power" over the game. The Judge rapidly established that he wasn't kidding about supreme power. He immediately got on the wrong side of AL president Ban Johnson by ignoring the idea that he was supposed to serve as head of a three-person "commission." The rule of baseball was his and his alone.

At the time of the 1921 World Series, Landis hadn't even been on the job a year. But he had made his presence felt, with suspensions and expulsions of "dirty" players and consolidation of his own power. And the biggest confrontation yet was brewing.

Laying Down the Law

It happened during the final days of the 1921 World Series—the first Series in which Babe Ruth's Yankees appeared. In those days players looked to extend their season and their income by playing postseason games in less-than-major-league locales. They called it "barnstorming," from an old vaudeville term that implied the performers were so eager to strut their stuff they'd even play in a barn during a storm.

The World Series was Landis's special interest. What happened within the leagues was the purview of the league presidents, but the Series was Landis's own. He understood that having an exhibition "Series" after the actual Series diminished the value of the original. There were rules in place that forbade such behavior, but no one was enforcing them. Landis decided to set things straight by telling Babe Ruth himself that he was not allowed to go on a barnstorming tour.

"It seems," Landis said, "I'll have to show somebody who's running this game."

Landis vs. Ruth

The Judge tried to reach Ruth to let him know he was laying down the law. Ruth, ever the big kid, didn't return the Judge's phone calls until after the final game of the Series. ("What has that long-haired old goat got to do with me?" Ruth wanted to know.) Ruth told the Judge he had a contract to play in the barnstorming series, which he couldn't (or wouldn't) break, and he was about to catch a midnight train to Buffalo to start the tour. Landis snarled, "If you do, it will be the sorriest thing you ever do in baseball."

It was the biggest power play in baseball history. The game's superstar versus the game's center of power. Babe had to feel he held the cards; who could stand up to *him*? When asked about Landis's wrath, Ruth replied, "Ah, let the old guy go jump in the lake." But when he ignored Landis's edict and went on the barnstorming trip anyway, the Judge suspended Ruth for six weeks and withheld his share of World Series money. When Babe appealed to the Yankee owners, they backed the commissioner. The Judge had laid down the law, and even the great Babe Ruth had to toe the line. The Judge had indeed proven who was running this game.

⚾ ⚾ ⚾

When Kenesaw Mountain Landis was named commissioner of baseball, comedian Will Rogers concurred. "Might as well give it to the old fella," he opined. "He's at the game every day anyway."

Greatest Games of All Time

1929 World Series, Game 4

Athletics 10, Cubs 8

The Setting: Shibe Park, Philadelphia

The Drama: The most explosive inning in Series history turns the whole thing around for Connie Mack's A's.

By the late 1920s, baseball began to be dominated by big, brawny sluggers, and the 1929 World Series matched two teams of bruisers. The Philadelphia Athletics featured Jimmie Foxx, banger of 33 homers that season, plus Al Simmons, who cracked 34 and drove in 157 runs to lead the league. And these weren't one-dimensional hitters: Foxx batted .354 and Simmons .365, and Al hit 41 doubles, too. Bing Miller and Mickey Cochrane each hit over .330.

The Chicago Cubs countered with some meat of their own. Hack Wilson belted 39 homers, and his 159 RBI led the league. Rogers Hornsby, called by many the greatest right-handed hitter ever, matched Wilson in home runs and chipped in 47 doubles, a .380 batting average, and a league-leading .679 slugging percentage. Joining Wilson in the outfield were Kiki Cuyler, who pounded the ball at a .360 clip and homered 15 times, and Riggs Stephenson, who had two more homers than Kiki and batted two points higher. The three drove in 371 runs and scored 337. It was probably the most potent outfield ever. Thus, it was no surprise when the turning point of the 1929 World Series was an offensive explosion. It just turned out to be one of the most dramatic such detonations in baseball history.

The Series opened in Chicago's Wrigley Field, always a hitter's favorite. But A's manager Connie Mack threw Chicago a curveball before the first game even started. Instead of opening with his ace, Lefty Grove, Connie put Howard Ehmke, a 35-year-old part-timer, in the box. All old Howard did was set a World Series record for strikeouts (13 batters) that would stand for 24 years, and the A's won 3–1. They took Game 2 with a score of 9–3. When the Series moved to Philadelphia for Game 3, a three-run inning was all the Cubs needed, as Guy Bush held the A's to just one run.

In Game 4, Charlie Grimm's fourth-inning two-run homer brightened the day for the visiting Cubs. They then exploded with five straight singles in the sixth on their way to five more runs. When they tacked on their eighth run in the seventh, the Cubs looked certain to tie the Series at two games each.

Cubs starter Charlie Root had allowed just three hits as the last of the seventh began. So when Simmons led off with a homer, the Cubs weren't frightened, even though the hit landed on the roof atop the left-field stands. Foxx followed with a sharp single. Miller's short fly to center dropped in front of Wilson, who lost the ball in the sun. Then Jimmy Dykes smacked a single to left, and the A's had another run. At this point, Mack offered his men some sage advice: Since Root is losing it, he'll be trying to groove every pitch. Swing at everything.

Joe Boley responded by rapping a single, and the score was 8–3. A pop to short by the next batter didn't slow things down, because Max Bishop swatted in another run with a liner over Root's head. Cubs manager Joe McCarthy had seen enough, and he brought in veteran Art Nehf to face Mule Haas. Wilson lost Haas's fly ball in the sun, but this time it went over his head. By the time he chased it down, Haas had a three-run, inside-the-park homer. The A's were just one run down.

And they weren't through. Cochrane was walked, a new pitcher was called in, and Simmons came to bat again. Al grounded to third, but a weird hop sent the ball over the third baseman's head. Foxx then swatted his second hit of the inning, and Cochrane scored the tying run. McCarthy called in his fourth pitcher of the inning, who promptly hit Miller with a pitch and then gave up a two-run double to Dykes, which was nearly flagged down by a diving Stephenson.

The A's had scored ten runs. Wilson, normally a good fielder, bore the brunt of the criticism for his two bad plays on a terribly sunny day. As for the Series, the A's won it in Game 5 with three runs in the bottom of the ninth.

Great War Withers Great Game

World War I moves manpower from diamond to trenches, and ballplayers are forced to struggle with their place in a war-torn society.

During the four years World War I raged in Europe, the great American game endured several blows in the national consciousness, as people questioned baseball's role in the midst of global conflict. Was it important to keep baseball going as a way to boost civic morale? Or was this a questionable way for healthy young men to be occupied in a time of war?

Filling the Seats

The Federal League had started in 1914, just before the war began, but it disbanded after only two seasons. Some of those players later joined the American and National Leagues, but many wound up back in the minors or faded from the game along with the memory of the last upstart major league. Competition for the leisure dollar and public interest—thanks to the growing taste for boxing, horse racing, college football, and picture shows—was greater than it had ever been. Attendance for the AL and NL actually hit a five-year high in 1916—6.5 million total for the 16 teams—but that came after two years of depressed numbers because of the Federal League. In 1917, though, attendance dropped significantly, to 5.2 million paying customers. It fell 2.1 million more the following year.

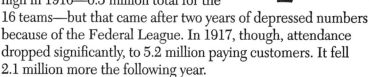

Service and Sacrifice

The United States joined the war effort in 1917, and while American soldiers massed in Europe, baseball players fought the image that they were slackers unwilling to do their duty. The schedule was reduced from 154 to 140 games in 1918 (and again in 1919), and players performed pregame military drills to display their patriotism. But the military wasn't impressed. The May 1918 edict of "work or fight" required all men to be involved in "essential" war industry work by July 1 or risk induction. Baseball got an exemption through Labor Day, leading to the only September World Series in history. In all, nearly 250 major-leaguers joined a war industry or the service in 1918.

Future Hall of Famers Grover Cleveland Alexander and Christy Mathewson were wounded during the war. Alexander recovered, but thereafter suffered from seizures; Mathewson's exposure to poison gas led to his death in 1925. Three former players were killed. The best-known was Harvard grad and Giants third baseman Eddie Grant, a captain who was killed trying to reach the famous "Lost Battalion" in the Argonne Forest on October 5, 1918, five weeks before the end of the war. A plaque was placed in his honor at the Polo Grounds.

Raising the Country's Morale

The war also brought about a notable performance of "The Star-Spangled Banner." Although the song had been played a few times at ball games, it received popular approval during the seventh-inning stretch of Game 1 of the 1918 World Series. Its reception led to the song being played during each game of the Series by the Cubs and Red Sox, though it did not become a regular pregame event until 1942, during America's next great war. In the intervening years, baseball would secure a higher spot in the national perception and be seen as vital to the country's morale.

⚾ ⚾ ⚾

"April 21, 1863. The parade ground has been a busy place for a week or so past, ball-playing having become a mania in camp. Officers and men forget, for a time, the differences in rank and indulge in the invigorating sport with a school-boy's ardor."

—Private Alpheris B. Parker, 10th Massachusetts, Union Army

Major Miscues

What's that they say about life? Oh yeah, that it's not fair. Well, baseball legacies aren't always fair either. Consider Fred Merkle, Mickey Owen, and Bill Buckner, for example. All were above-average players, at times All-Star caliber performers, who were assets to pennant-contending teams. Sadly, this was not to be their legacy in the game. A bonehead play, a passed ball, a missed grounder. Big blunders in baseball are hard to forget.

Merkle's Boner

September 1908. With the pennant on the line in a crucial late-season game against the Chicago Cubs, Al Bridwell of the New York Giants swatted an apparent game-winning two-out RBI single in the bottom of the ninth. Rookie Fred Merkle was the runner at first. When Moose McCormick scooted home from third to score, according to major-league rules all Merkle had to do was advance to second base and touch the bag in order for the run to officially count. When young Merkle failed to do so and instead started to run toward the clubhouse in center field, Cubs second baseman Johnny Evers frantically called for the ball to force him out. The Giants' coach, Joe McGinnity, wrestled the ball away from him, even going so far as to throw it into the stands, but Evers retrieved it and touched second base.

Oddly, this wasn't the first time this had happened. It wasn't even the first time Evers had been involved in such a play. Just two weeks prior, umpire Hank O'Day had turned down a similar appeal by Evers, in part because O'Day had already left the field and hadn't seen the second baseman touch the bag. Furthermore, umpires of the day rarely enforced the rule that stipulates each runner must advance to the next base on a game-winning play with two outs. This time, O'Day came up with a different decision, though he did not announce it right away. Well after thousands of fans had poured onto the field and most of the players had made their way back to the clubhouse, he called Merkle out, negating the run. Either on the field or later that night—it's not clear which—O'Day declared the game a tie. Amid a sea of confusion, and with countless fans scattered over the field, O'Day and his umpiring partner left the field. Enraged by O'Day's decision, the Giants filed a protest but were turned down by National League president Harry Pulliam.

This tie game meant all the difference to the two teams, who finished the regular season in a flat-footed deadlock. It came down to a tie-breaking game on October 8 to decide the pennant. The Giants lost 4–2, and even though Merkle didn't even play in that deciding game, his name became forever linked with the infamous "Merkle's Boner"—no matter that he went on to become an excellent defensive first baseman and a respectable hitter.

Owen's Passed Ball

October 1941. Thirty-three years after Merkle's Boner, a normally sure-handed catcher let down the Brooklyn Dodgers at the worst possible moment. With Brooklyn trailing the Yankees two games to one in the World Series and clinging to a 4–3 lead in the ninth inning of Game 4, All-Star catcher Mickey Owen failed to catch what should have been a game-ending third strike to Tommy Henrich, who swung and missed. As the ball glanced off Owen's glove and squirted away toward the Brooklyn dugout, Henrich raced to first, igniting a four-run rally for the Yankees that earned them a miraculous 7–4 victory. Now up three games to one and with momentum on their side, the Yankees beat Owen's Dodgers the next day to wrap up the World Series.

"It was all my fault," said Owen in a report filed the next day in *The New York Times.* "It wasn't a strike. It was a great breaking curve that I should have had. But I guess the ball hit the side of my glove."

Ironically, earlier in the season Owen had set the NL record for catchers with 476 consecutive errorless chances accepted, also setting a Dodger record with a season-high .995 fielding percentage. Despite these achievements, and his election to the All-Star team in each of the next three years, he would never live down his blunder of 1941. That single play, rather than Owen's defensive excellence over time, would remain firmly embedded in the memories of Brooklyn fans and in the annals of baseball.

Between Buckner's Legs

October 1986. Call it "The Curse of the Bambino," if you will. With the Red Sox leading Game 6 of the World Series by two runs, the New York Mets found themselves with no one on base and two out in the bottom of the tenth, on the verge of elimination. As Red Sox fans jubilantly began to prepare for postgame parties, the Mets suddenly strung together three consecutive singles, bringing them within a run and putting the tying run on third base.

Mookie Wilson stepped up to the plate, and Sox reliever Bob Stanley threw a wild pitch that eluded catcher Rich Gedman, allowing Kevin Mitchell to score and Ray Knight to advance to second. With the game tied, Wilson then chopped a bouncer down the first base line. As Boston fans watched helplessly, and Mets fans looked on with mounting joy, the ball skipped between Bill Buckner's legs and slid down the right-field line. It's debatable whether Buckner would have had a play on the speedy Wilson, but the error made no doubt about the outcome, allowing the winning run to score from second base and handing the Red Sox yet another defeat in their quest for a world title.

After the game, Red Sox manager John McNamara faced a barrage of questions regarding his decision not to replace the aging and hobbled Buckner with utilityman Dave Stapleton as a defensive caddy. It was a maneuver McNamara had used throughout the season, but one he decided to forgo because he wanted Buckner on the field to celebrate the world championship. Alas, it was Buckner's error that ensured there would be no Red Sox celebration. The Mets took Game 7 as well, overcoming a three-run deficit to win the game and the Series. And Buckner, who otherwise would have been recalled as a gritty and skilled .289 lifetime hitter, would forever be linked in infamy with a World Series collapse.

Chatter

"Baseball is only a game, but they keep a book on you. When it's all over for you, the game has got you measured."

—Joe Garagiola, *Baseball Is a Funny Game*

"A big enough boy to enjoy the national game—and a man big enough to guide our country through its greatest crisis."

—Words accompanying a picture of President Woodrow Wilson throwing out the first ball of the season, cover of 1917 World Series program

"I was not a consignment of goods. I was a man, the rightful proprietor of my own person and my own talents."

—Curt Flood on refusing his trade from St. Louis to Philadelphia, *The Way It Is*

"Maybe a pitcher's first strikeout is like your first kiss—they say you never forget it."

—Bob Feller, *Now Pitching, Bob Feller*

"Just give me a happy ballclub, and we'll be hard to beat."

—Billy Southworth, *Baseball's Greatest Managers*

"I don't care if half the league strikes. This is the United States of America and one citizen has as much right to play as another."

—Commissioner Ford Frick to Cardinals players, who had been planning to strike when the Dodgers and Jackie Robinson came to St. Louis in 1947, *The Summer Game*

"...you could look up into the upper deck and recognize your mother, the stands were so close to the field."

—Pee Wee Reese on Ebbets Field

Double Duty

*Baseball is the national pastime, but it's not the only sport around.
Here are several athletes who "played the field."*

Danny Ainge
Baseball:
2 HRs, 37 RBI, .220 BA in 3 seasons
Basketball:
11.5 points per game, 1,002 3-pointers, 2 NBA championships in
14 seasons
Verdict:
Swish.
Danny Ainge was an infielder by summer and a shooting guard by
winter who ultimately was better served shooting the three than
turning two. But it wasn't an easy transition. Ainge was drafted by
the Blue Jays out of high school in 1977 and toiled for five years in
baseball while attending Brigham Young University on a basketball
scholarship. He was midway through a three-year baseball contract
when the Celtics drafted him in 1981, sparking an intersport legal
battle that was ultimately resolved when Toronto released Ainge
from his contract in exchange for a reported half-million-dollar
payment from Boston. It was money well spent: Ainge made his
NBA debut in December 1981, 79 days after playing his last MLB
game, and went on to a 14-year career and two NBA championships. He went on to serve as a Celtics executive.

Chuck Connors
Baseball:
2 HRs, 18 RBI, .238 BA in 2 seasons
Basketball:
4.5 points per game in 2 seasons
Verdict:
Action!
Chuck Connors played pro basketball and pro baseball but didn't
become a star until he played "The Rifleman" in the TV show of
the same name. Connors originally served as a reserve forward on

the 1947 and '48 Celtics, but he gave that up to be a first baseman with the Dodgers (1949) and the Cubs (1951). Farmed out to the Cubs' minor-league team in Los Angeles in 1952, Connors caught the eye of a casting director and before long was a television star.

Dave DeBusschere
Baseball:
3–4, 2.90 ERA in parts of 2 seasons
Basketball:
8 All-Star Games and 6 All-Defense mentions in 12 seasons, NBA Hall of Fame
Verdict:
Slam dunk.

A 6'6" right-hander with a lively fastball, Dave DeBusschere played four years of pro baseball, including parts of two seasons with the White Sox, compiling a big-league record of 3–4 with a respectable 2.90 ERA. But he did his best work preventing scoring on the basketball court, becoming one of the NBA's best-ever defenders.

George Halas
Baseball:
.091 BA in 1 season
Football:
Rose Bowl MVP, six-time NFL coach of the year, Hall of Fame
Verdict:
Gridiron.

The year before Babe Ruth joined the New York Yankees, George Halas had been a young outfielder for the team. Halas eventually became a legend in his own right, becoming a pioneering player, coach, and owner in the National Football League. For the man known as "Papa Bear," baseball was only a passing fancy. His 12-game stint with the Yankees was preceded by a stellar college football career at the University of Illinois and followed by a founding ownership of an NFL franchise, the Decatur Staleys, in 1920. That team eventually relocated to Chicago, where Halas chose the nickname Bears as a tribute to the city's North Side baseball residents, the Cubs.

Cal Hubbard
Baseball:
16-year umpiring career, Hall of Fame
Football:
Star offensive lineman, 4 NFL championships in 9 seasons
Verdict:
Football—in a close call.
The only man enshrined in both the Pro Football Hall of Fame and Baseball Hall of Fame, Cal Hubbard was a legendary Packers offensive lineman of the 1920s and '30s who spent his off-seasons as a baseball umpire. He reached the majors as an American League umpire in 1936, his final year as a football player, and dispensed baseball justice for the next 15 years, working four World Series and three All-Star Games. His experience running football plays helped him design various patterns of positioning for umpires that are still used today.

Bo Jackson
Baseball:
141 HRs, 415 RBI, 1 All-Star Game in 8 seasons
Football:
Heisman Trophy winner, 1 Pro Bowl invitation, 2,782 yards rushing, 18 TDs (16 rushing, 2 receiving) in 4 seasons
Verdict:
Let's play two!
Simultaneous and frequently spectacular success on the diamond and gridiron made Bo Jackson a cultural phenomenon of the 1980s. A slugging outfielder for the Royals, White Sox, and Angels and a bruising running back with the Oakland Raiders, Jackson is the only man to be named a starting All-Star in both sports. He claimed football was his "hobby" and didn't return to that game

following a hip injury suffered in 1990. Aftereffects of the injury eventually ended his baseball career by age 31.

Brian Jordan
Baseball:
184 HRs, 821 RBI, .282 BA in 15 seasons
Football:
1 Pro Bowl in 3 seasons
Verdict:
Can o' corn.
Drafted as an outfielder by the Cardinals (1st round) and a defensive back by the Buffalo Bills (7th round), Brian Jordan spent minor-league off-seasons playing safety for the Atlanta Falcons, where he was named a Pro Bowl alternate in 1992. Though Jordan would say football was his first love, he gave up the game to sign a baseball-only contract with the Cardinals and started a 15-year career that included an All-Star campaign in 1999 and five trips to the postseason.

Michael Jordan
Baseball:
.202 in 1 season in Class AA
Basketball:
14-time All-Star; all-time NBA career points-per-game leader
Verdict:
Are you kidding?
Michael Jordan was already considered among the greatest basketball players of all time when, on October 6, 1993, he shocked the world by announcing his intention to retire from basketball and give pro baseball a try. He signed a contract with the White Sox, where he managed to hit just .202 in one season as a Class AA

outfielder. Humbled, Jordan was back in a Chicago Bulls uniform a year later.

Ron Reed
Baseball:
146–140, 3.46 ERA, 103 saves in 19 seasons
Basketball:
8 points per game in 2 seasons
Verdict:
Out of the park.
A star basketball player at Notre Dame, the 6'6" Reed was drafted by the Detroit Pistons and played two seasons as a reserve forward in the NBA while toiling in the minor leagues for the Milwaukee Braves' system. But Reed gave up hoops for good after emerging as an All-Star pitcher in his rookie baseball season of 1968. A control artist, Reed was an anchor of the 1969 Braves' rotation and later had a long run as a set-up man with the Phillies in the 1970s, pitching into his 40s.

Deion Sanders
Baseball:
.263 BA, 186 SBs in 9 seasons
Football:
8 Pro Bowls in 14 seasons; excelled as a defensive back, kick returner, and wide receiver
Verdict:
Touchdown!
On October 11, 1992, Deion Sanders played an afternoon football game for the Falcons in Miami, then flew to Pittsburgh in time for the Braves' NLCS game against the Pirates. Though Sanders didn't get into the latter game, he would end his dual-sport career as the only man to appear in both a Super Bowl and a World Series. Though far more accomplished as a rare two-way player in football, Sanders was a fine basestealer and outfielder in baseball, and, had he chosen neither sport, he might even have made a go as a track star.

Jim Thorpe
Baseball:
7 HRs, 82 RBI, .252 BA in 6 seasons
Football:
52 NFL games in 6 seasons, 6 TDs, Hall of Fame
Olympics:
Gold medals in the decathlon and pentathlon, 1912 Olympics
Verdict:
What season is it?

Considered among the greatest American athletes of all time, Jim Thorpe achieved world prominence by blowing away the field in the pentathlon and decathlon events at the 1912 Games in Stockholm, Sweden. When it was revealed Thorpe had played semipro baseball for pay prior to the Olympics, his medals were stripped. But the scandal called attention to Thorpe's baseball skills, and he was subsequently signed to a contract by the New York Giants. Thorpe played outfield for three teams over six seasons, ending in 1919. At the same time, Thorpe was a magnificent fullback for pre-NFL teams and the first president—and superstar—of what would become the NFL, playing for six different teams until 1928.

⚾ ⚾ ⚾

The top ten states to produce the most major-leaguers in the 20th century were: California with 1,828 players; Pennsylvania with 1,324; New York with 1,107; Illinois with 985; Ohio with 956; Massachusetts with 635; Missouri with 552; Michigan with 405; New Jersey with 377; and North Carolina with 368.

⚾ ⚾ ⚾

"Baseball is pitching, fundamentals, and three-run homers."
>   —Earl Weaver, *How Life Imitates the World Series*

Magical Moments

The catch that made 111 wins irrelevant.

The Setting: Polo Grounds, New York; September 29, 1954
The Magic: Willie Mays hauls down Vic Wertz's drive and changes the World Series.

The 1954 World Series was unusual primarily because of the absence of the Yankees, who had appeared in the championship the previous five years (and won every time). The Giants and Indians faced each other that year and had a lot in common: Both had led their leagues in home runs and runs scored, and each had that year's batting champion (Willie Mays for the Giants and Bobby Avila for the Indians). Mays was in the top five in on-base percentage, slugging average, and the combination of the two, as was the Tribe's Al Rosen. Both team's pitching staffs led their leagues in fewest hits, earned run average, and lowest opponent batting average. But those who set the odds made Cleveland the favorite, for two reasons: The Indians had set an American League record with 111 wins, and the AL was considered the stronger league by far. (The Yankees alone won 103 games that year.) But the oddsmakers hadn't counted on Willie.

It was the first game of the Series, tied at two in the eighth inning, when two Indians reached with nobody out. Indian first baseman Vic Wertz slugged a ball into the deep canyon of the Polo Grounds' right center. But Mays zoomed out there, made the catch with his back to the plate, then spun and fired an immense strike to second to force the runner on first to return. The catch was sensational; the throw otherworldly. The Giants won in ten innings, and the Indians never got back in it. New York swept them, and it was a dose of Mays Magic that made the difference.

◐ ◐ ◐

"What a blessing is conveyed by these two words, base ball."

—*Philadelphia City Item*, 1866

Fast Facts

- *Tris Speaker played center field like no one else. He played so shallow and with such incredible speed that he was like a fifth infielder, even turning double plays by himself on six occasions.*

- *Three former major-leaguers have been both fathers and grand-fathers to major-leaguers. Ray Boone fathered Bob, who is the father of Aaron and Bret. Gus Bell was Buddy Bell's dad, and Buddy's kids include David and Mike. Sammy Hairston's son Jerry is father to Jerry and Scott.*

- *In 1957, Warren Spahn became the first left-handed pitcher to win a Cy Young Award.*

- *Pitcher Lefty Grove won the ERA title nine times—more than any other player. Some others who have won the title multiple times are Roger Clemens with seven wins, and Walter Johnson, Sandy Koufax, Christy Mathewson, Grover Cleveland Alexander, and Pedro Martinez with five each.*

- *In 1881, if spectators "hissed or hooted" at or insulted the umpire, they could be ejected from the grounds.*

- *In the 1870s, batters were not required to swing at a delivery they didn't think they could hit, because there was no such thing as a called strike. In fact, the batter could indicate to the pitcher whether he wanted a high ball or a low ball, and the pitchers were supposed to comply.*

- *Long before Frank Thomas, Yankee pitcher Stan Williams was known as "The Big Hurt." He got the nickname during his first road trip with the team—when he accidentally spiked the bare-foot Mickey Mantle in an adjacent toilet stall.*

The House of David

*They were barnstorming religious proselytizers—
and snazzy ballplayers, too.*

In Benton Harbor, Michigan, around the turn of the 20th century, a religious community called the Israelite House of David was looking for ways to earn money. As a fundraiser in 1907, the House of David folks opened an ice cream parlor, which was so successful it rapidly expanded into a full-scale amusement park with a zoo, miniature car races, bowling alleys, miniature train rides, and a dance hall. Another feature of the amusement park was a ball field, complete with a two-tiered grandstand.

By 1913, ball games were part of the regular weekend activities. Thanks to some genuine baseball talent, the House of David was soon playing games around the region against local nines, and by 1920 they were a full-time barnstorming team, traveling throughout the Midwest with great success. One reason they stood out was because of the way they looked: They became famous for their long hair and beards, which were highly unusual in the United States at the beginning of the 20th century. Another reason was their skill: These players were good at what they did. And in the fifth inning of every game, they really turned on the charm, pausing to do a little Globetrotter-style performance—the legendary "pepper game," in which three members of the team did impressively energetic, nearly magical, tricks with the ball as they tossed it around. The original pepper stars, Jesse "Doc" Tally, John Tucker, and George Anderson, would throw the ball back and forth, gradually increasing the speed and using sleight-of-hand tricks that made the ball seem to disappear, delighting the crowds.

The team held its own in barnstorming games against major-leaguers and often traveled with the Negro League Kansas City Monarchs. And when the prime club was on the road, various "house" teams were established—including a girls' team and a junior boys' team.

Over the first ten years or so of their existence, the House of David teams won about 75 percent of their games. "Membership" requirements were loosened to attract star players to the traveling team. Grover Cleveland Alexander played with the team for a time. So did Babe Didrikson and Jackie Mitchell. In 1934, the team won the prestigious *Denver Post* semipro championship, with the great Satchel Paige and his personal catcher, Cy Perkins, joining up for a time to give them a little boost. And yep, these visitors were made to don false beards to fit in with the rest of the team. (Except for the ladies.)

At one time there were as many as three teams with legitimate claims to the House of David name, but there were also totally bogus "H of D" teams. These groups, who had no connection to the official religious group, understood the promotional value of the name and even wore fake beards for the purpose. At one time there was even a team of African-Americans calling themselves the "Black House of David."

The House of David was easily the most recognizable of the white barnstorming teams during their 40 years of existence. As members of the community aged, the league died out, but teams with the "H of D" moniker and facial hair played in weekend semipro leagues and barnstormed as late as 1955, and the religious organization exists to this day.

◖ ◖ ◖

"Whiskers! Whiskers! Whiskers!
Strangest of all baseball attractions
Weird and Eccentric!"

—1930 poster promoting a game between the House of David baseball team and the Buffalo Bisons of the International League

◖ ◖ ◖

The House of David team played in the first professional night baseball game, in Independence, Kansas, in 1930.

The Origins of the Game

The Abner Doubleday Fan Club isn't going to like this.

It was long believed that Abner Doubleday invented baseball in 1839. While we now know this is not true, we still don't know exactly how baseball came about. Games involving sticks and balls go back thousands of years. They've been traced to the Mayans in the Western Hemisphere and to Egypt at the time of the Pharaohs. There are historical references to Greeks, Chinese, and Vikings "playing ball." And a woodcut from 14th-century France shows what seem to be a batter, pitcher, and fielders.

Starting with Stoolball

By the 18th century, references to "baseball" were appearing in British publications. In an 1801 book entitled *The Sports and Pastimes of the People of England,* Joseph Strutt claimed that baseball-like games could be traced back to the 14th century and that baseball was a descendant of a British game called "stoolball." The earliest known reference to stoolball is in a 1330 poem by William Pagula, who recommended to priests that the game be forbidden within churchyards.

In stoolball (which is still played in England, mostly by women), a batter stands before a target, perhaps an upturned stool, while another player pitches a ball to the batter. If the batter hits the ball (with a bat or his/her hand) and it is caught by a fielder, the batter is out. Ditto if the pitched ball hits a stool leg.

The Game Evolves

It seems that stoolball eventually split into two different styles. One became English "base-ball," which turned into "rounders" in England but evolved into "town ball" when it reached the United States. The other side of stoolball turned into cricket. From town ball came the two styles that dominated baseball's development: the Massachusetts Game and the New York Game. The former had no foul or fair territory; runners were put out by being hit with a thrown ball when off the base ("soaking"), and as soon as one out was made, the offense and defense switched sides. The latter established the concept of foul lines, and each team was given three "outs" to an inning. Perhaps more significantly, soaking was eliminated in favor of the more gentlemanly tag. The two versions coexisted in the first three decades of the 19th century, but when the Manhattanites codified their rules in 1845, it became easier for more and more groups to play the New York style.

A book printed in France in 1810 laid out the rules for a bat/base/running game called "poison ball," in which there were two teams of eight to ten players, four bases (one called "home"), a pitcher, a batter, and flyball outs. Different variations of the game went by different names: "Tip-cat" and "trap ball" were notable for how important the bat had become. It was no longer used merely to avoid hurting one's hand; it had become a real cudgel, to swat the ball a long way.

The Knickerbocker Club
In the early 1840s, Alexander Cartwright, a New York City engineer, was one of a group who met regularly to play baseball, and he may have been the mastermind behind organizing, formalizing, and writing down the rules of the game. The group called themselves The Knickerbocker Club, and their constitution, enacted on September 23, 1845, led the way for the game we know today.

The Myth Begins
Even though the origins of baseball are murky, there's one thing we know for sure: Abner Doubleday had nothing to do with it. The Mills Commission was organized in 1905 by Albert Spalding to search for a definitive American source for baseball. They "found" it in an ambiguous letter spun by a Cooperstown resident (who turned out to be crazy). But Doubleday wasn't even in Cooperstown when the author of the letter said he had invented the game. Also, "The Boy's Own Book" presented the rules for a baseball-like game ten years before Doubleday's alleged "invention." (See pages 206–207 for more information about the Doubleday myth.) Chances are, we'll never know for sure how baseball came to be the game it is today.

All-Time Great

Honus Wagner

The only player from his era who is still arguably the all-time greatest at his position.

Born: February 24, 1874; Chartiers (now Carnegie), PA
MLB Career: Louisville Colonels, 1897–99; Pittsburgh Pirates, 1900–17
Hall of Fame Resume: Led NL in batting eight times * Led NL in doubles seven times * Led NL in RBI and steals five times each * Eighth on the all-time hits list
Inside Pitch: His first name is not pronounced "Hoe-nus" but "Hah-nus." He was the first player to have his name inscribed on a Louisville Slugger bat.

Often mentioned alongside Ty Cobb as the greatest dead-ball-era players produced by each league, Johannes Peter Wagner could not have been more different from his AL contemporary. The Pride of the Pirates was a genuine Mr. Nice Guy, as modest and even-tempered as Terrible Ty was vicious and bull-headed. Most famous these days as the guy whose 1910 baseball card could pay for a new house and college education, "The Flying Dutchman" also happened to be a .327 lifetime hitter with a National League–record eight batting titles and 722 stolen bases—as well as the greatest fielding shortstop this side of Ozzie Smith.

Supposedly discovered by Ed Barrow tossing coal chunks at a boxcar near his tiny Pennsylvania hometown, Honus demolished minor-league hurling for parts of three years before joining Louisville of the NL as an outfielder in 1897. Squat (5′11″, 200 pounds) and bowlegged with a long, beaked nose, Wagner didn't look like a ballplayer—until he got on a field. Once there, the right-handed, barrel-chested slugger with deceptive speed hit .299 and .336 his first two full seasons, with more than 100 RBI per year.

The Louisville franchise shifted to his hometown of Pittsburgh in 1900, and Wagner celebrated by collecting his first National League batting title with a career-high .381 mark. He led the NL in doubles (45), triples (22), and slugging (.573), despite hitting just four homers. League leader in RBI (126 and 91) and stolen bases (49 and 42) each of the next two seasons, he hit .353 and .330 as the Pirates won back-to-back NL flags.

After playing as many as five positions in a season without one to call his own, Wagner thrived after being made Pittsburgh's starting shortstop in 1903. Becoming the game's best fielder at the spot, he developed a rifle arm and used his huge hands to scoop up everything hit near him. He also hit .350 with seven batting titles over the next nine seasons, earning the first in '03 when he hit .355 with 101 RBI, 46 steals, and a league-high 19 triples to power the Pirates to their third straight league championship.

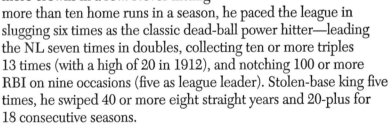

Repeating as batting champ in 1904 at .349, Wagner was second at .363 the next year before winning four more crowns in a row. Never hitting more than ten home runs in a season, he paced the league in slugging six times as the classic dead-ball power hitter—leading the NL seven times in doubles, collecting ten or more triples 13 times (with a high of 20 in 1912), and notching 100 or more RBI on nine occasions (five as league leader). Stolen-base king five times, he swiped 40 or more eight straight years and 20-plus for 18 consecutive seasons.

Retiring at age 43 in 1917 as NL leader in hits (3,415), runs (1,736), doubles (640), and triples (252), the charter Hall of Famer still ranks high on each list. The Flying Dutchman came back at age 59 to coach for the Pirates and stayed on for 18 years, keeping himself young and spinning many a yarn about the good ol' days.

Red Sox vs. Yankees: Rivalry Redux

Ruth and Frazee. Williams and DiMaggio. Fisk and Munson. Torrez and Dent. Roger and Pedro. Wakefield and Boone. Jeter and Nomar. Rivera and Ortiz.

Run-of-the-mill Red Sox and Yankees rooters may know the story behind some of these pairings; true aficionados will get them all. When it comes to these two teams, it's hard to think of one without the other. Sox fans have been known to reserve as much passion for hating the Yanks as they do for cheering their own team, and vice versa. And although the bad blood between these rivals dates back to 1904—when the Boston Americans snatched the pennant from the New York Highlanders on the season's final day—it has reached epic proportions in recent years as the franchises with baseball's two highest payrolls have pushed each other to the limit.

The Yankees' Long Reign

Unfortunately for Red Sox partisans, the Yankees have usually emerged victorious in these summer-long scuffles. New York finished first and Boston second in the American League East each regular season from 1998 through 2005, the longest such stretch of repetitive rankings in big-league history. The Yanks won five pennants and three World Series during this period, twice topping the Sox in the playoffs. New York fans quickly added these feats to a mental checklist of Sox slayings that had given their club a 26–0 edge in world championships over their nemesis from the time Boston owner Harry Frazee sold slugger Babe Ruth to the Yanks in 1920 through the 2003 campaign.

The drought, titled by many as "The Curse of the Bambino," made Red Sox fans easy pickings for their brash counterparts. Bostonians tried to hold their heads high, but for decades they carried a chip on their shoulders bigger than Reggie Jackson's ego. New York had the swagger, personified throughout the years in guys like Ruth, Lou Gehrig, Joe DiMaggio, Whitey Ford, Mickey

Mantle, Jackson, and—most recently—shortstop Derek Jeter and ace reliever Mariano Rivera, superstar talents who came through when it counted. The Sox had their own share of great players through the years, including Ted Williams, Carl Yastrzemski, Jim Rice, Roger Clemens, and Pedro Martinez, but they always seemed to lack the pitching depth and bench strength to overcome their adversaries.

For more than half a century, in fact, this was more like a chase than a rivalry. First sparked to the top by a series of one-sided trades that sent Ruth and other future Hall of Famers from Boston to New York, the Yankees dominated the American League for nearly 50 years—winning or contending for the pennant almost every season from 1920 through 1964. The machinelike efficiency of the "Bronx Bombers" came to symbolize the nation as a whole, and as the United States rose to superpower status after World War II, so did the expression that "rooting for the Yankees is like rooting for U.S. Steel." Satisfaction was guaranteed and, in most cases, delivered.

An Exercise in Futility?

Red Sox loyalists had a much different experience. Other than the period from 1939 to '50, when strong Boston teams led by Williams routinely battled DiMaggio's clubs for American League supremacy—a fight that left Ted's crew with a lone pennant and no World Series titles to show for their efforts—cheering for the Sox was most often an exercise in futility. Even when vaunted Yankee manager Joe McCarthy traded pinstripes for crimson hose, he couldn't win in October. After a while the only excitement at Boston's Fenway Park seemed to be when Williams came to bat or the Yankees came to town. Once Ted retired, attendance at Fenway plummeted, while Mantle, Yogi Berra, and company continued to roll in the Bronx.

Not until the 1970s, once the Red Sox had undergone a revival behind Yastrzemski and the Yankees a decade of rebuilding, were both teams again contenders. At the center of this renewed rivalry were the starting catchers: square-jawed, no-nonsense New Hampshire native Carlton Fisk of the Sox and scruffy, surly Thurman Munson of the Yanks. Tremendous leaders on and off the field, their allegedly acrimonious relationship—spurred on by the tabloids and one infamous fistfight at home plate—helped raise the heat.

Fisk's club gained an edge by copping the 1975 American League pennant, but the Yanks won the next three AL titles (and two World Series) behind Munson and Jackson. In 1978, although

the Red Sox blew a 14-game lead over New York, these were arguably the two best teams in baseball, and they finished tied atop the AL East with 99 wins apiece. A one-game playoff was held at Fenway, where a three-run homer by New York's weak-hitting shortstop Bucky Dent off former Yankees star Mike Torrez proved the biggest blow in New York's epic 5–4 win.

The Struggle Continues

Big games between the clubs were rare over the next 15 years, during which Boston actually enjoyed more regular-season success but struck out in the playoffs. In the late 1990s, however, things picked up again when ex–Red Sox pitching ace Roger Clemens joined the Yankees. New York was in the midst of a five-year stretch in which Jeter, Rivera, and manager Joe Torre carried the team to four world championships, and the Sox—now led by Clemens's successor, Martinez, and their own super shortstop, Nomar Garciaparra—were consistently on their heels.

The new "wild card" playoff format offered a postseason berth to each league's winningest runners-up, and in 1999 Boston made the cut. That fall's best-of-seven American League Championship Series marked the first time the Red Sox and Yanks had ever met in the postseason, and New York won in five games. (For an idea of just how much this meant to some people, consider that four tickets for the Game 3 battle at Fenway pitting Martinez against Clemens went for $12,100 in an online auction.) Red Sox fans once again left empty-handed.

The Tables Are Turned

After Boston missed the playoffs the next three years, a new ownership group committed emotionally and financially in 2002 to toppling the Bombers and their free-spending owner, George Steinbrenner. Sox team president and CEO Larry Lucchino dubbed Steinbrenner's franchise "The Evil Empire"—thus giving "Yankees Suck" T-shirt hawkers outside Fenway new material to work with—and the two teams dueled again in the 2003 ALCS. This series went a full seven games but ended in familiar fashion: Boston took a 5–2 lead late in the finale at Yankee Stadium, but New York came back to tie and then win when Aaron Boone led off the bottom of the 11th with a homer off Tim Wakefield.

The teams had yet another matchup in the 2004 ALCS, and it looked like more of the same when New York captured the first three contests—including a 19–8 drubbing in Game 3. The next night the Yanks were just three outs from a series sweep with Rivera on the mound, but unbelievably the Sox rallied to victory on a 12th-inning homer by clutch-hitting slugger David Ortiz. Thus began the most incredible comeback in the history of American team sports, as the Sox captured the next three games as well (the last two at New York) to claim the pennant. For the first time, Yankees fans were the ones feeling the ache of coming so close, only to finish empty-handed.

A four-game sweep of the Cardinals in the World Series followed for the Sox, meaning Boston had conquered both its greatest nemesis and its 86-year championship jinx with eight wins in eight games. The Yanks still held a 26–1 edge in world titles since the Ruth trade, but the biggest "choke" in sports history had somehow made things equal in the minds of Boston fans.

◎ ◎ ◎

"Joe, it's been a while. Do the batters still get three strikes?"

—Red Sox catcher Moe Berg to manager Joe Cronin
upon making a rare appearance in a game,
The Picture History of the Boston Red Sox

A Catcher Like No Other

*Roy Campanella's tragic car accident halted his ability to catch—
but not to inspire.*

Roy Campanella's brilliant catching career ended on a slick road on January 28, 1958, when his car slid into a telephone pole. Paralyzed below the shoulders, Campanella could no longer be a ballplayer, but he could still be an inspiration. He'd already inspired many during his baseball journey: starting in the Negro Leagues at age 16, taking a steep pay cut to sign with the Dodgers in 1946, integrating the American Association, helping Brooklyn win its only world championship, catching in five World Series, and becoming the only catcher to win three NL Most Valuable Player Awards. He hit 41 home runs in 1953, a record for catchers that lasted until 1996, and had an NL-high 142 RBI that same year. He ended his career with a .276 batting average, 242 home runs, and 856 RBI.

On May 7, 1959, a major-league-record crowd of 93,103 came to the Los Angeles Coliseum for Roy Campanella Night, even though Campy had never played in that city. The Yankees traveled across the country for the benefit game against the Dodgers. The lights were turned down, and everyone in the crowd lit a match in tribute to Campanella. "This is something I will never forget," he said. "I thank God I'm here living to be able to see it. It's a wonderful thing."

The evening raised an estimated $75,000 for Campy, who faced mounting debt in the days before lucrative autograph sessions and big-league pensions. The Dodgers hired Campanella to work in the community relations department, and the always upbeat Hall of Famer—he was elected to Cooperstown in 1969—served as a spring training instructor and a mentor to young catchers. Campy died in 1993 at the age of 71, years beyond the life expectancy of most quadriplegics. But then, Roy Campanella wasn't most men.

How to Be a Better Fielder

Effective fielders make it look easy because they're smart and prepared. Here's how they get that way.

Preparation: Break in your glove enough so the fingers lay flat on the ground.

Readiness: Stand square to home plate. Give yourself a balanced foundation by distributing your weight evenly on the balls of your feet, with your knees bent and your legs a comfortable width apart.

Alertness: Check playing field conditions, and continuously keep tabs on wind and sun conditions. Anticipate that every ball is going to be hit to you. Think, "What am I going to do?" *(From Cal Ripken)*

Grounders: Keep your feet wide, your butt down, and your hands out in front.

Fly balls: Take a direct route to where you think the ball is going to land. Run on the balls of your feet—if you run on your heels, your eyes will bounce. Keep your glove above your eyes.

Throwing: Generate momentum toward your target, and follow the throw. Make a straight overhand throw with backspin.

On pop flies: Holler, "I've got it!" if you do or "Take it!" if you don't.

Stance: Position yourself as far back as you feel comfortable, but take into consideration how fast the batter runs to first. *(From Robin Ventura)*

And most important: Don't take your eyes off the ball.

The Owner Fills Out the Lineup Card

Some managers have gotten so exasperated with second-guessing from their owners that they've been tempted to shout, "If you're so smart, why don't you manage the team?" Well, that's exactly what some owners have done over the course of baseball history.

Charles Ebbets (Brooklyn Bridegrooms/Dodgers): Ebbets began his Brooklyn career as a bookkeeper for the team, then rose through the ranks, becoming a partial owner. He managed most of the 1898 season, not because he thought he was smarter than any manager, but as a cost-cutting measure. Ebbets should have spent the money. In ninth place at the time Ebbets took over, the Bridegrooms went 38–68 under the owner's managerial watch and sunk to tenth place in the National League by season's end. Despite his failure as a manager, Ebbets became an effective and innovative owner. He devised baseball's rain-check system for postponements, instituted regularly scheduled batting and fielding practice prior to each game, and pushed to have ballplayers wear numbers on their uniforms. Popular among New Yorkers, Ebbets lent his name to the beloved ballpark constructed for his team.

Judge Emil Fuchs (Boston Braves): After the 1928 season, Judge Fuchs decided to trade his player-manager, Rogers Hornsby, who had guided the team to a record of 39–83 after taking over mid-season. Fuchs installed himself as manager, though he was smart enough to allow former star infielder Johnny Evers to actually run the team. Under the Fuchs-Evers regime, the Braves showed some improvement over the Hornsby reign. With Fuchs taking credit for the wins and losses, the Braves went 56–98 and finished dead last in the National League. Fuchs did take a few games off during the season so that he could work a courtroom case, but not as a judge. Contrary to his nickname of "Judge," Fuchs actually worked as an attorney. Manager Bill McKechnie took over in 1930.

Connie Mack (Philadelphia Athletics): Dignified, suit-wearing Mack handled the dual duties of ownership and managing with such long-term success that he earned a place in baseball's Hall of Fame. During Mack's half-century helming the A's, the team won nine pennants and five World Series. Mack built two dynasties (1910–14 and 1929–31), which are considered to be among the best teams of all time. But he broke up both of them for financial reasons—baseball being primarily a business concern to him. Mack holds the major-league record for lifetime wins (3,731), losses (3,948), and games managed (7,755).

Ted Turner (Atlanta Braves): With his Braves mired in a 16-game losing streak in May 1977, Turner decided it was time to put on a uniform and step into the dugout himself. He sent manager Dave Bristol on a ten-day scouting trip and took over the team for its May 11 game against the Pittsburgh Pirates—though in reality, it was coach Vern Benson who called the shots. The change in managers didn't alter the team's fortune, as the Braves lost their 17th consecutive game. National League President Chub Feeney then stepped in, citing a league rule that prohibited anyone who owned a financial interest in a team from acting as its manager. Turner handed the managing reins to Benson for the May 12 game (which they won) and returned to the owner's box, where he could concentrate on other efforts, such as captaining his yacht, *Courageous,* to the America's Cup. Bristol cut his trip short and rushed back to retake control of his team. He was fired later that year.

◐ ◐ ◐

"Gimme good pitching and long hitting, and let the rest of them managers get just as smart as they want!"

—Manager Wilbert Robinson

Magical Moments

You wouldn't blame Haddix if he cried himself to sleep that night.

The Setting: Milwaukee County Stadium; May 26, 1959
The Magic: Harvey Haddix pitches a game that will go down in history—but not in the record books.

On a cool, damp night in Milwaukee, Pittsburgh Pirate lefty Harvey Haddix, while battling a Braves lineup featuring two future Hall of Famers, pitched what is probably the greatest game in history, retiring 36 batters in a row before one reached base. Yet he lost the game. And then years later Major League Baseball said he hadn't pitched a no-hitter at all. You had to wonder what Harvey had done in a previous life to merit this kind of treatment.

The Braves had won back-to-back NL pennants and even toppled the legendary Yankees in the World Series two years before. The pitching star of that Series was Lew Burdette, the rangy right-hander who may or may not have thrown a spitball but made sure everyone thought he did. Harvey was up against Lew again on May 26, 1959. That night Harvey was perfect, while Lew defined the notion of "good enough." The Pirates managed 12 singles and two walks, but the Braves turned three double plays and erased a baserunner at third on an overaggressive move.

Harvey's perfect game continued into extra innings, but the Pirates kept failing to score. Then, in the last of the 13th, Braves leadoff hitter Felix Mantilla reached on an error. There was a sacrifice bunt and an intentional walk before Joe Adcock hit the ball to deep right center. In the dismal conditions it was hard to tell if it cleared the fence—but it did. Amid the confusion, the runner on first, Hank Aaron, was passed by Adcock, turning the home run into a double. But it didn't matter. The run had scored, and Haddix's near-perfect masterpiece had ended.

In 1991, after a few questionable "no-hit" efforts began to clog the record books, MLB ruled that a pitcher had to finish the game, win, and not allow a hit in order to be credited with a no-hitter. Harvey was out of the record books despite what many consider the finest pitching performance in the history of the game.

Fast Facts

- In the first five games of the 1931 World Series against the Philadelphia A's, St. Louis Cardinals center fielder Pepper Martin batted in or scored ten of his team's 14 runs.

- Ten men have won the American League Pitching Triple Crown (leading the league in wins, ERA, and strikeouts) a total of 15 times, including Walter Johnson three times, and Lefty Grove, Lefty Gomez, and Roger Clemens two times each. (The other winners were Cy Young, Rube Waddell, Bob Feller, Hal Newhouser, Pedro Martinez, and Johan Santana.)

- Babe Ruth would often wear a cabbage leaf under his hat. He said it kept him cooler on hot days.

- In 1921, Walter Johnson struck out his 2,804th batter, which moved him past Cy Young as the all-time leader in strikeouts. His record lasted until 1982, when Nolan Ryan surpassed him. Currently, Johnson ranks ninth.

- The record for the most games played without appearing in a World Series is held by Rafael Palmeiro, who played in 2,831 games from 1986 to 2005.

- In 1931, Chick Hafey of the St. Louis Cardinals became the first batting champion to wear glasses.

- Actor William Bendix, who played the title role in The Babe Ruth Story, was once Ruth's batboy.

- Ebbets Field organist Gladys Gooding earned her spurs the second day on the job (May 9, 1942). As umpires Bill Stewart, Ziggy Sears, and Tom Dunn walked onto the field, Gooding burst into song with "Three Blind Mice."

Willing to Pay the Price

Prices have risen at ballparks over the years, but so has the diversity of food and merchandise.

Teddy Roosevelt once commented, "When money comes in at the gate, sport flies out the window." Money's been coming in the gate for baseball since manager William Cammeyer fenced off a field in Brooklyn in 1862 and started charging admission to the games. Since the teams were amateurs, he kept every penny of the ten-cent admission at Union Grounds. Players soon realized they were missing out. With a cut for the clubs figured in, the price rose to 25 cents in 1866. Big games generally cost more, and scalpers could already be found outside the stadium trying to entice the paying public to purchase tickets from them.

The National League charged 50 cents in its formative years (the late 1870s), except in Philadelphia, where a price cut was the only thing that brought people out to see a poor club. By 1886 this lower-price policy extended to other weak sisters in the NL, especially those in competition with the rival American Association.

Beer Here!
Concessions have always been an important revenue source at the ballpark. Especially beer. The Cincinnati Reds felt so strongly about it, they were willing to get bounced out of the National League in 1880 for continuing to peddle brew (even on Sundays) when NL rules strictly forbade it. They joined the American Association, known as the Beer and Whiskey League, which charged only 25 cents (rather than 50 cents) to get in. That left more money to spend on beer and whiskey.

Keeping Score and Hawking Dogs
In 1885, Ohio entrepreneur Harry M. Stevens invented scorecards as a way to keep track of the players and the action (and to sell some advertising space). He sold them at various ballparks for five cents each. By the turn of the century he was also selling ice cream and sodas to baseball fans. When no one was buying those items

on cold early season days at New York's Polo Grounds, he sent out some of his salesmen to buy "dachshund" sausages and buns, then had them yell to the crowd to "get them while they're red hot!" Thus the term "hot dog" was popularized. Even today, when everything from nachos to sushi can be purchased at a ball game, people still line up for the staples that have been sold for more than a century, including bags of peanuts and soda drunk through a straw (both of which were also Stevens's ideas).

Fan Cost Index
Prices for everything at the ballpark have increased by leaps and bounds through the years. This has become especially true in the last two decades as the corporate culture has provided a base of customers willing to pay more for better seats and fancier eats. The Fan Cost Index, which measures the amount a family of four spends at a game—factoring in tickets (two for adults and two for children), two programs, two adult baseball caps, four hot dogs, two beers, four small soft drinks, and parking—was $180 for the average major-league team in 2006. The cost was almost $100 more for fans at Fenway Park, the most expensive place to see a game. (Kansas City's Kauffman Stadium is the least expensive.) A day at the ballpark isn't the cheapest activity around, but for many fans it's still worth it, no matter what the cost.

Some selected ballpark prices from selected seasons (not adjusted for inflation):

	1920	1942	1962	1980	2006
Program/Scorecard	$.10	$.10	$.25	$.50	$4.00
Hot Dog	$.10	$.15	$.35	$1.00	$4.50
Soda	$.05	$.10	$.25	$.55	$4.75
Beer	Prohibition	$.25	$.45	$1.00	$6.50
Box Ticket	$1.00	$2.20	$3.50	$6.00	$41.00

Greatest Games of All Time

1924 World Series, Game 7

Senators 4, Giants 3

The Setting: Griffith Stadium, Washington, D.C.

The Drama: Lightning strikes twice in the same place as fate rewards Walter Johnson's usually hapless Senators and punishes John McGraw's arrogant Giants.

Walter Johnson was one of the greatest pitchers in baseball history. Unfortunately, he played for a terrible team. The Washington Senators of Johnson's era were routinely second-division fodder. Walter could win, but few others could. It had gotten so bad by 1924 that the 36-year-old Johnson, winner of 354 big-league games (only Cy Young and Christy Mathewson had won more), announced he would retire after the season.

His team rallied behind him, knocking over the Yankees (three-time consecutive AL champs) by two games to give Washington its first pennant ever in 38 seasons of professional D.C. baseball. Led by their spunky second baseman/manager, Bucky Harris, the Senators faced off in the Series against NL powerhouse New York. John McGraw's Giants, four-straight NL winners and twice world champions, were the opposite of the new-kid winners in Washington.

Senators mania had gripped Washington, but the team got off to a poor start. In Game 1, Johnson was rapped around for 14 hits and four runs as he took the loss in a 12-inning thriller. The two teams took turns winning in Games 2, 3, and 4, but in Game 5 Johnson allowed 13 hits and six runs for another Senators defeat. The Nats took Game 6, though, setting up the amazing events of Game 7.

In an attempt to get red-hot lefty hitter Bill Terry out of the Giants lineup, Harris started seldom-used right-hander Curly Ogden, then switched to lefty George Mogridge after just one out in the first inning. McGraw didn't take the bait; Terry started and stayed in the game. For a while.

Giants starter Virgil Barnes held the first ten Nats hitless, but then Harris got his team rolling with a solo homer. In the sixth, his pitching ploy worked. With two on and none out, McGraw sent in a pinch-hitter for Terry. And Harris promptly inserted relief specialist Firpo Marberry. Terry's left-handed power was gone from the game, but it didn't hurt—yet. A fly ball, a single, and two consecutive infield errors pushed three Giants across. The score stayed 3–1 until the bottom of the eighth. The exceptionally durable Muddy Ruel, who had caught all but seven of the Nats' games that year and every inning of the World Series, picked the perfect time for his first Series hit, as he advanced a runner to third. Then, with the bases loaded and two men out, Harris grounded sharply to third, where 18-year-old Freddy Lindstrom (the youngest player ever in a World Series) could only watch in dismay as the ball hit a pebble and bounced over his head into short left field. Two runners scored. The game was tied. And coming in to pitch for the Senators was none other than Walter Johnson. His chance to be on a winning World Series team was now in his hands.

He faced some tough situations, including a one-out triple by Frank Frisch in the ninth and two men on in the 11th. All in all, six batters reached against him. But Johnson kept the Giants off the scoreboard, fanning five of them in four innings. When it came to the last of the 12th, the score was still knotted at 3.

With one out, Ruel came to bat and lifted a foul pop-up around home plate. Giants catcher Hank Gowdy tossed his mask aside and waited for the ball to drop. But as Hank circled under it, he stepped into his mask. Trying to shake the mask off his foot and simultaneously chase the pop, Hank failed at both. The ball fell for an error, and Ruel responded by rapping a double past third.

Next up, Johnson, who was also an excellent hitter. He slapped a grounder to short, where Travis Jackson fumbled the ball. Johnson safe at first, Ruel holds at second.

Then lightning struck twice. Earl McNeely grounded to third, but the ball bounced over Lindstrom's head—again! Ruel romped home as the Senators became world champs in highly improbable fashion. As for Johnson, he decided not to retire. He stuck around and took the Nats to the Series again in 1925.

Pitch It Like the President

The Oval Office is okay, but there's no place like the ballpark.

On April 14, 1910, President William Howard Taft decided on a whim to attend the Senators' Opening Day game against the Philadelphia A's, showing up unannounced at National Park. Umpire Billy Evans noticed President Taft sitting in the stands and asked him if he would throw out the first ball, something that was usually done by a local politician. Taft's toss began a tradition of first pitches that has been carried out by every American president since then, with the exception of Jimmy Carter.

Presidential first pitches have featured dramatic and comedic highlights—and lowlights. Following are some of the more memorable first pitch moments.

William H. Taft: When making his trendsetting first pitch in 1910, Taft had a Hall of Fame partner. Washington Senators ace Walter Johnson, normally on the pitching end of the baseball battery, received Taft's historic throw. President Taft gave Johnson the ball the next day with the following inscription: "To Walter Johnson with hope that he may continue to be as formidable as in yesterday's game. William H. Taft."

Two years later, Taft missed the opener in Washington while tending to the aftermath of the *Titanic* disaster. Vice President James Sherman filled in for Taft, throwing out the first pitch on April 19 before a scant crowd of just over 10,000 fans.

Woodrow Wilson: He ventured out of the nation's capital to become the first president to attend a World Series game. On October 9, 1915, Wilson threw out the first pitch at Philadelphia's Baker Bowl, moments before Game 2 of the Series matchup between the Boston Red Sox and the Philadelphia Phillies.

Franklin Delano Roosevelt: A true fan of the game, FDR holds the record for most Opening Day first pitches (eight) and overall first pitches (11). In FDR's case, practice didn't make perfect: At the 1940 opener in Washington, Roosevelt made an errant toss, breaking the camera of a *Washington Post* photographer.

Harry Truman: Due to World War II, Roosevelt refrained from visiting major-league ballparks in 1942, '43, and '44. Truman ended the presidential drought when he threw out the first pitch before a game on September 8, 1945, between the Senators and the St. Louis Browns. Truman's return to the ballpark signaled that baseball, depleted because of players' involvement in military service, was now back to full strength.

John F. Kennedy: An avid fan of the Boston Red Sox, JFK stayed to watch every inning of the four games he attended while in office. As president, he threw out the first pitch at the newly built D.C. Stadium in 1962. The stadium was later renamed in honor of Kennedy's brother Robert.

Lyndon Johnson: In 1965, Johnson was supposed to throw out the first pitch at the exhibition game that marked the opening of the Houston Astrodome, but he arrived late and missed the opportunity. Three years later, Johnson missed the Opening Day game in Washington, which had been delayed because of the assassination of civil rights leader Martin Luther King, Jr. Vice President Hubert H. Humphrey attended the rescheduled Washington opener in Johnson's absence.

Richard Nixon: Arguably the most knowledgeable baseball fan of all American presidents, Nixon took part in a unique first pitch ceremony on April 6, 1973. A POW named Major Luna and Nixon, participating in his first ceremonial toss away from the city of Washington, both threw out first pitches before the game at Anaheim Stadium in California. According to Dick Young of the *New York Daily News,* Nixon was not just "a guy that shows up at season openers to take bows and get his picture in the paper and has to have his secretary of state tell him where first base is. This man knows baseball."

Gerald Ford: At the 1976 All-Star Game, the athletic president thrilled fans by doing double duty: throwing out one pitch right-handed to Johnny Bench of the Cincinnati Reds and a second pitch left-handed to Carlton Fisk of the Boston Red Sox.

Jimmy Carter: Carter once told Commissioner Bowie Kuhn that he preferred playing sports to watching them, which explains why he attended only one major-league game while in office—the seventh game of the 1979 World Series between the Orioles and the Pirates. Carter chose not to throw out the first pitch on that occasion, and he remains the only president since Taft who has not thrown one.

Ronald Reagan: A die-hard fan of baseball and a former radio broadcaster, Reagan attended a World Series game between the Baltimore Orioles and Philadelphia Phillies on October 11, 1983, but declined an opportunity to throw out the first pitch due to security reasons. Five years later, Reagan threw out two first pitches at Wrigley Field and then joined the legendary Harry Caray in the broadcast booth to announce the game for an inning and a half. "You know, in a few months, I'm going to be out of work," joked the outgoing president, who had once re-created games on radio, "and I thought I might as well audition."

George H. W. Bush: The elder Bush became the first sitting president to attend a major-league game north of the border. On April 10, 1990, Bush traveled to Toronto to throw out the first pitch before a matchup between the Blue Jays and his beloved Texas Rangers. Two years later, Bush joined Hall of Fame slugger Ted Williams in throwing out dual first pitches at the All-Star Game in San Diego.

George W. Bush: The younger Bush continued the old tradition into the new millennium, throwing out the first pitch at the first game ever played at Milwaukee's Miller Park on April 6, 2001. Later that year, he became the first president to throw out the first pitch before a World Series game being played at Yankee Stadium.

His visit to New York occurred on October 30, less than two months after the terrorist attacks of September 11 and was part of an effort to restore normalcy to the nation.

President	No. of "First Pitches"	Year(s)
William H. Taft	1	1910
Woodrow Wilson	4	1913–1916
Warren Harding	3	1921–1923
Calvin Coolidge	6	1924–1928
Herbert Hoover	4	1929–1932
Franklin Delano Roosevelt	11	1933–1941
Harry Truman	8	1945–1952
Dwight Eisenhower	7	1953–1960
John F. Kennedy	3	1961–1963
Lyndon Johnson	3	1964–1967
Richard Nixon	3	1969–1973
Gerald Ford	2	1976
Ronald Reagan	3	1984–1988
George H. W. Bush	8	1989–1992
Bill Clinton	3	1993–1996
George W. Bush	5	2001–2006

◐ ◐ ◐

"Nolan says throw it high because amateurs get out there, no matter how good they are, and throw it in the dirt. You get more of an 'ooooh' [from the crowd] if you heave it over the [catcher's] head instead of going with the fast-breaking deuce into the dirt."

—George H. W. Bush on advice Nolan Ryan gave him on throwing out the first pitch while president

Baseball Lingo

Sprechen sie baseball?

Airmail: A throw, often from the outfield, that overshoots its intended target. **Origin:** Descriptive.

Banjo hitter: A hitter with little power. **Origin:** Refers to the banjo's twangy sound and/or describes the fragile musical instrument as if it were a bat.

Barber: A talkative player. **Origin:** Descriptive of the stereotypical chatty barber.

Battery: The pitcher and catcher, together. **Origin:** Telegraphy, referring to the transmitter (pitcher) and receiver (catcher).

Bees in the hands: The "stinging" sensation that occurs after swinging the bat, particularly when not wearing protective gloves and/or in cold weather. **Origin:** Descriptive of stings.

Bullpen: Where relievers warm up. **Origin:** "Bull Durham" tobacco advertisements often appeared on outfield walls near the area. May also refer to an area of the park where relief pitchers gather and "shoot the bull" for long stretches of the game.

Catbird seat: A favorable ball-strike situation for a pitcher or a hitter. **Origin:** Refers to the perch of the catbird. Popularized by broadcaster Red Barber.

Cleanup hitter: The fourth batter in the lineup. **Origin:** He clears, or cleans, the bases occupied by the first three hitters.

Deuce: Curveball. **Origin:** Usually signaled for with two fingers.

Fireman: A relief pitcher, usually the ace. **Origin:** Descriptive.

Get the thumb: To be ejected from the game. **Origin:** Descriptive of an umpire's hand signal.

The good face: A positive but unscientific assessment of a player's fitness, attitude, and "makeup." **Origin:** Scouting. A player possessing such qualities is said to have "the good face."

Hospital throw: A throw to a base that forces the fielder to take his eye off an approaching runner. **Origin:** Descriptive of the potential for injury.

Jack: A home run, or to hit a home run. **Origin:** Descriptive of jack, meaning "to lift."

Keystone: Second base, or the second baseman. **Origin:** Like the keystone of an arch, second base is considered a key supporting element (for scoring runs) and a key defensive position.

Matador: A timid fielder. **Origin:** Bullfighting. Refers to a player who fields a ball to his side, like the movement of a bullfighter, rather than get in front of it.

O-fer or Ohfer: Going hitless over a game or other period. **Origin:** Puns. O-fer is "zero-for," and "ohfer" includes the exclamation "oh" as in "oh-for-5."

Ribbies: Runs batted in. **Origin:** Phonetic, plural pronunciation of the acronym "RBI."

Southpaw: A left-handed pitcher. **Origin:** In most ballparks, home plate faces east so as to keep the sun from a batter's eyes, meaning south would be on the pitcher's left side.

Tablesetter: The first and second hitters in a lineup, or a player who reaches base early in an inning. **Origin:** Descriptive of preparation for the cleanup hitter.

Spitballers and Greasers

Toss me that Vaseline, and keep your eye on the ball.

Pitchers began seeking an advantage over hitters almost as soon as Jim Creighton developed the wrist snap in the 1850s. The rules were much simpler then, leaving more room for creative interpretation. So in 1868, when 16-year-old Bobby Matthews of the Lord Baltimores spat on the ball and fired it with the underhand stiff wrist the rules then required, the ball danced, and the batters went crazy.

Doctoring the Ball

The spitball has had dozens of names, from "country sinker" to the "aqueous toss" and "humidity dispenser" or, more directly, "the wet one." But the spitball belongs in a larger class of pitches in which the ball is altered in one way or another to break or twist when it heads toward the batter. These pitches haven't always been fair, but they've usually done the trick.

In the 1890s, Clark Griffith, who amassed more than 200 wins in his pitching career, would bang the ball against his spikes, cutting it and leaving it subject to off-balance aerodynamic forces—thereby baffling hitters. In later years, pitchers would alter their gloves to leave a hole through which they could scrape the ball on a doctored ring. Or they would have a friendly teammate wear a belt with a sharp buckle and tear it against the ball as they warmed up before an inning.

How the Spitball Got Its Name

In the early 1900s, Ed Walsh of the Chicago White Sox learned how to moisten a ball just right on the tips of his fingers so it would slide off and be harder to hit. Before long, the spitter was the pitch of choice for dozens of hurlers. Historians John Thorn and John Holway have said, "The dead-ball era could be called the doctored ball era."

Walsh's spitball was especially devastating because he could make it break four different ways: down and in, straight down,

down and out, and up (which he threw underhand). So that the batters wouldn't know what to expect, Walsh put his hand to his face on every pitch, but he threw the spitter only about half the time. He and fellow spitball artist Jack Chesbro became the only two pitchers to win 40 games in one season in the 20th century.

Cleaning Up and Playing Dirty

After years of wild pitches (culminating in the death of Ray Chapman, who was hit in the temple by a pitched ball), baseball decided to clean up its act. Since the 1890s, it had been "illegal" for pitchers to damage a ball to alter pitches, but that rule was rarely enforced. The spitter was officially banned before the 1920 season (with stricter punishments for rule-breakers), although 17 pitchers were grand-fathered in and allowed to throw it until their careers ended. The new rule outlawed spit, sandpaper, resin, talcum powder, and other "foreign substances" that pro-duced trick pitches. So hurlers had to find better ways to cheat.

Some did and later admitted it; some have denied all wrongdoing. Hall of Famer Whitey Ford of the Yankees has been accused of using every trick he could muster, from gouging the ball with a ring, to covering one side of the ball with mud, to creating a special invisible gunk that he slathered on his fingers between innings.

Lew Burdette of the Braves in the 1950s always said that having the hitters *think* he had a spitter was just as good as actually throwing one. He'd wipe his hands on his pants and in his hair and then spit between his teeth.

But the all-time artist of loading the ball was Gaylord Perry, who used his wiles (and a lot of Vaseline) to win Cy Young Awards in both leagues. Perry's gyrations between each pitch were phenomenal. He'd grab here, scratch there, flick here, wipe there. No one could possibly know what was coming. In all his years of cheating, Perry was caught just once.

Bill Klem: The Greatest Umpire of All Time

There have been other fine umpires—Al Barlick, Doug Harvey, Billy Evans. But there was only one Bill Klem.

Try to start a discussion that begins, "Who was the greatest [blank] of all time?" and you'll be in for some argument—unless the blank is "umpire." In that case, the answer is unquestionably Bill Klem. He was so good, and it was so obvious that he was so good, that for 16 of his record-setting 37-year National League career he only umpired behind the plate. That wasn't a reward for years of quality service—it started the first day he umped in the major leagues. He was uniquely skilled at calling balls and strikes.

Klem wasn't large, but he commanded respect because of his hard work and integrity. He took grief from some of the game's legendary grief-givers, but when the heat got to be too much, Klem would draw a line in the dirt with his toe, announce, "Don't cross the Rio Grande," and turn his back. Anyone who crossed that line was headed for the showers. He was often called "The Old Arbitrator," and that nickname (which Klem loved) is on his Hall of Fame plaque. But if you called him "Catfish" (because of his looks), you were tossed immediately.

Klem pioneered the inside chest protector, which allowed for a better view of the pitch than the protectors that were previously worn outside the shirt. And he was one of the first to use hand signals for strikes and fouls. He umpired 104 World Series games in 18 Series—almost twice as many Series as any other ump—and he worked at the first All-Star Game in 1933. When he retired in 1941 at age 67, he was the oldest ump in baseball history.

Klem did one very important thing that many umpires never do, although they should: *wait.* He would hesitate and let the facts clarify themselves in his mind before making a call. Once when Klem paused before signaling safe or out, the frustrated catcher shouted, "Well, what is he?" Klem answered, "He ain't nothing till I call it."

Fast Facts

- Joe and Dom DiMaggio are the only brothers with hitting streaks of 30-plus games.

- On July 14, 1946, Lou Boudreau set a major-league mark as the first player with five extra-base hits in a single game.

- In 1880, the number of base on balls, also known as walks, was reduced to eight "called balls" from nine.

- The only person to win the batting title in his first two major-league seasons was Tony Oliva of the Twins. In the 1964 season, he hit .324; in 1965, he hit .321.

- In 2000, Diamondback Luis Gonzalez became the first player to hit home runs into two bodies of water. In April he cracked a long ball into the pool at Bank One Ballpark in Phoenix, and in September he knocked one into McCovey Cove in San Francisco.

- When normal rail routes were disrupted by a New England hurricane in 1938, the New York Giants used an overnight steamboat to get to Boston for a series with the Braves.

- In 1985, Dwight Gooden of the New York Mets became the youngest player to win a Cy Young Award, at age 20.

- In 1979, Bob Watson became the first player to hit for the cycle in both the National League and the American League. John Olerud duplicated the feat in 2001.

- Two of the worst seasons for pitchers in the 20th century were 1954, when Baltimore's Don Larsen went 3–21 for a .125 winning percentage, and 1962, when New York Met Roger Craig went 10–24 for .294.

All-Time Great

Lou Gehrig

Despite playing in Babe Ruth's shadow, and doomed to an early death, he was a powerful batter who dominated slugging for years.

Born: June 19, 1903; New York, NY
MLB Career: New York Yankees, 1923–39
Hall of Fame Resume: Led league in games seven times * Led in RBI five times * Led in home runs three times * Led in runs four times * 184 RBI in 1931 is still American League record * Had more than 400 total bases per season five times
Inside Pitch: Gehrig was banned from intercollegiate sports his first year at Columbia University because he had played professionally (under a phony name) the summer before. The person who recommended he do that was New York Giants manager John McGraw.

Now that his incredible streak of 2,130 consecutive games played has been topped by Cal Ripken, Jr., there is a new opportunity to examine the career of Lou Gehrig. The record once thought unbreakable no longer stands, but what Gehrig accomplished in the seasons comprising his string remains a remarkable achievement—and only his own Yankee teammate Babe Ruth can claim a more prodigious level of sustained offensive excellence.

It seems fitting that a player of Ripken's disposition toppled Gehrig's mark; Gehrig was himself a wise and modest man who drew far more solace from family than from nightclubs. A native New Yorker and left-handed slugger at Columbia University, the sturdy six-footer joined the Yanks at age 20 in 1923 and saw limited duty behind star first baseman Wally Pipp for two seasons. Gehrig's first game of his streak came as a pinch-hitter on May 31, 1925, and when he started the next day after Pipp complained of a headache, nobody thought much of it. In the end, Pipp was out of a job as Gehrig played the final 126 games of the season, finishing at .295 with 20 homers.

The cleanup hitter for the Yankee pennant-winners of 1926, Lou paced the American League with 20 triples while adding 47 doubles, 16 homers, and 112 RBI. He also hit .348 in a World Series loss to St. Louis, but Ruth (who preceded him in the New York batting order) remained the main man with 47 homers and four more in the Series. "The Iron Horse" lessened the gap in '27, running neck-and-neck with Babe much of the season before finishing with 47 dingers. Ruth set the world afire by smashing a record 60 for the world champs, but Gehrig was AL MVP with astounding totals of 218 hits, a .373 average, a league-best 175 RBI, and 52 doubles, 18 triples, and a .765 slugging percentage never topped by anyone not named Babe or Barry.

Lou upped his average to .374 in 1928, leading the league with 47 doubles and 142 RBI. Similar stats followed each of the next nine years. Over 11 full seasons from 1927 to '37, Lou averaged .350 with 39 homers and 153 RBI (including an AL-record 184 in '31) while playing on five world champions. His numbers fell off to .295–29–114 when the Yanks took their third straight Series in '38, and some said the streak was getting to him. In fact, the problem was actually a rare and incurable disease called amyotrophic lateral sclerosis—now known as Lou Gehrig's disease—that was eating away at his body.

On May 2, 1939, with a .143 average, the suddenly sluggish and feeble-footed star took himself out of the lineup. Shortly there-after, his doctors informed him he would never play again. A July 4 "day" at Yankee Stadium honored a classy man who told the hushed crowd, "I have an awful lot to live for," but Gehrig died less than two years later at age 37.

"I didn't have nothin'... I had no license to beat anybody. But they coulda cut off my arm in that clubhouse if I'd won that one."

—Dizzy Dean on his 6–3 loss to the Yankees in Game 2 of the 1938 World Series

Best Single-Game Performances

When the stars align for one day of glory.

Some of these men had long and glorious careers; others were journeymen. But what they have in common is that for one day (or night) they put together a game for the ages. Some single-game sensations are detailed elsewhere (like Harvey Haddix's 12-inning no-hitter—see page 152—and Don Larsen's perfect World Series game—see page 204). Here are other highlights.

Jim Abbott
September 4, 1993. Jim Abbott was born without a right hand, but the combination of his athleticism and dogged determination brought him to the bigs. The highlight of his baseball career happened when, as a member of the New York Yankees, he stiffed the Cleveland Indians by throwing a no-hitter. Jim walked five Tribe men, but there was never an inning with more than one man on base. And the Indian lineup that day featured Albert Belle, Manny Ramirez, and Jim Thome.

Joe Adcock
July 31, 1954. It was a hot, humid day in Brooklyn, so the Braves' Adcock wasn't wasting time taking pitches from Dodger hurlers. He came out swinging and rapped four homers and a double off four different pitchers, needing only seven pitches to do it. The record he set for total bases in a game (18) wouldn't be broken for 48 years.

Jim Bunning
June 21, 1964. Bunning had seven children, which may be why he pitched his best game on Father's Day. The Phillie hurler faced just 27 Mets that day

and struck out ten of them. He also doubled in a pair of runs to add to his 6–0 perfecto win. Manager Gene Mauch said, "We knew when he was warming up that this was something special."

Ty Cobb
May 5, 1925. Thirty-eight-year-old Cobb, tired of hearing how super Babe Ruth was, announced he was going for the home run that day. And did he ever! He swatted three out of the park, tacked on two singles and a double, and set a still-standing AL record for total bases in a game (16). Only two other American Leaguers had ever homered three times in one game. (Ruth wouldn't do it for five more years.)

Ed Delahanty
July 13, 1896. Some historians will tell you that Delahanty was the greatest right-handed hitter ever. They could point to this day as proof. Only one person (Bobby Lowe) had ever homered four times in one game before, and this day at Chicago, Delahanty singled his first time up and crushed four inside-the-park homers. After the last one, the opposing pitcher was there at home to shake his hand.

Shawn Green
May 23, 2002. It took six Milwaukee Brewer pitchers to get through this Thursday afternoon game at Miller Park. Dodger Shawn Green was having a lot of fun leading the attack. He not only went 6-for-6, but among his six hits were four homers, a double, and a single, and he knocked home seven runs as the L.A. men romped the Brewers 16–3.

Catfish Hunter
May 8, 1968. The 1960s were definitely the decade of the pitcher. Hunter's perfect game against Minnesota on this date was the third perfecto in the decade. He fanned 11 Twins in the game. Hunter's A's won 4–0, and Catfish joined in the batting fun, too, driving in three of the runs himself and hitting a homer.

Addie Joss

October 2, 1908. Both the National and American League pennant races were exceptionally tight in '08. Cleveland, Detroit, and Chicago were within percentage points of each other when Cleveland's immensely likable Joss faced off against rugged 40-game White Sox winner Ed Walsh. Walsh was excellent, pitching a four-hitter, fanning 15. But Joss was perfect. He faced 27 batters and not one reached first.

Rick Wise

June 23, 1971. The story is told that in 1971, Wise was complaining about the lack of offense in his teammate Phillies' bats and said, "To win around here, you have to pitch a shutout and hit a homer." He did even better than that on this day: He pitched a no-hitter against the Reds (only one batter reached base, on a walk) and slugged two homers. One was a two-run dinger.

Four-Homer Hitters

Including Adcock, Delahanty, and Green mentioned above, only 15 players have hit four homers in one game. It is a rarer feat than pitching a perfect game. Six men have done it on consecutive at-bats: Bobby Lowe for Boston, May 30, 1894; Yankee Lou Gehrig on June 3, 1932; Rocky Colavito for Cleveland, June 10, 1959; Mike Schmidt for the Phils, April 17, 1976; Mike Cameron for Seattle, May 2, 2002; and Carlos Delgado for Toronto, September 25, 2003. Schmidt drove in eight runs that day in a windy, 18–16, 10-inning win over the Cubs. Chuck Klein hit four for the Phillies on July 10, 1936, while Pat Seerey of the White Sox did it in 11 innings on July 18, 1948. Dodger Gil Hodges accomplished the feat on August 31, 1950; Giant Willie Mays slugged a quartet on April 30, 1961; and Brave Bob Horner bopped four on July 6, 1986. Mark Whiten slugged four out of the park on September 7, 1993, for the Cardinals and tied the major-league record for single-game RBI, with 12.

Marathon Men

A 1985 Mets–Braves game lasted nearly seven hours and featured 29 runs and 46 hits over 19 innings.

It was getting late on July 4, 1985, at Atlanta's Fulton County Stadium. Rick Aguilera was scheduled to start for the New York Mets the following night against the Braves, so the pitcher returned to his hotel room for some rest. When he woke up at 3:00 A.M. and saw Braves–Mets baseball on his TV, Aguilera assumed it was highlights from the game and went back to sleep. Never in his wildest dreams would he have imagined his teammates were still playing. But they were.

It was the game that wouldn't end, which was a shame for those among the 44,947 in attendance who were there mainly for the Independence Day fireworks after the game. First, there were two rain delays. Then when the Mets took a 10–8 lead in the 13th and it appeared the end was at hand, the Braves scored twice in the bottom of the inning. New York took another lead in the 18th, but a home run by Braves reliever Rick Camp extended what had already become the longest game in major-league history.

Camp, however, gave up five runs in the top of the 19th. Atlanta scored twice in the bottom of the frame, but the time had come to surrender. The Mets won 16–13, recording the final out at 3:53 A.M. after six hours and ten minutes of play.

New York's Keith Hernandez hit for the cycle. The Mets pounded out a club-record 28 hits. Only one position player, third-string Mets catcher Ronn Reynolds, did not get in the game. New York's Darryl Strawberry and manager Davey Johnson were ejected in the 17th inning for arguing balls and strikes. They were outlasted by about 8,000 fans.

As a reward to those who stuck it out, the Braves decided to go ahead with the fireworks—to the dismay of those who lived near the ballpark. Several Atlanta residents awoke to what they thought were gunshots at just past 4:00 A.M.

"It probably wasn't the best game I ever played in," said Braves third baseman Ken Oberkfell, "but it certainly was the oddest."

The Catcher Was a Spy

When it comes to character assessments, you gotta listen to Casey Stengel. And the Ol' Perfessor claimed Moe Berg was "the strangest man ever to put on a baseball uniform." But Berg wasn't just strange in a baseball uniform, he was strange and mysterious in many ways—some of them deliberate.

Moe Berg lived a life shrouded in mystery and marked by contradictions. He played alongside Babe Ruth, Lefty Grove, Jimmie Foxx, and Ted Williams; he moved in the company of Norman Rockefeller, Albert Einstein, and international diplomats; and yet he was often described as a loner. He was well-liked by teammates but preferred to travel by himself. He never married, and he made few close friends.

"The Brainiest Guy in Baseball"

Moe was a bright kid from the beginning, with a special fondness for baseball. As the starting shortstop for Princeton University, where he majored in modern languages, Moe was a star. He was fond of communicating with his second baseman in Latin, leaving opposing baserunners scratching their heads.

He broke into the majors in 1923 as a shortstop with the Brooklyn Robins (later the Dodgers). He converted to catcher and spent time with the White Sox, Senators, Indians, and Red Sox throughout his career. A slow runner and a poor fielder, Berg nevertheless eked out a 15-season big-league career. Pitchers loved him behind the plate: They praised his intelligence and loved his strong, accurate arm. And while he once went 117 games without an error, he rarely nudged his batting average much past .250. His weak bat often kept him on the bench and led sportswriters to note, "Moe Berg can speak 12 languages flawlessly and can hit in none." He was, however, a favorite of sportswriters, many of whom considered him "the brainiest guy in baseball."

He earned his law degree from Columbia University, attending classes in the off-seasons and even during spring training and partial seasons with the White Sox. When Berg was signed by the

Washington Senators in 1932, his life took a sudden change. In Washington, Berg became a society darling, delighting the glitterati with his knowledge and wit. Certainly it was during his Washington years that he made the contacts that would serve him in his espionage career.

Time in Tokyo and on TV

Berg first raised eyebrows in the intelligence community at the start of World War II when he shared home movies of Tokyo's shipyards, factories, and military sites, which he had secretly filmed while on a baseball trip in 1934. While barnstorming through Japan along with Ruth, Lou Gehrig, and Foxx, Berg delighted Japanese audiences with his fluency in their language and familiarity with their culture. He even addressed the Japanese parliament. But one day he skipped the team's scheduled game and went to visit a Tokyo hospital, the highest building in the city. He sneaked up to the roof and took motion picture films of the Tokyo harbor. Some say those photos were used by the U.S. military as they planned their attack on Tokyo eight years later. Berg maintained that he had not been sent to Tokyo on a formal assignment, that he had acted on his own initiative to take the film and offer it to the U.S. government upon his return. Whether or not that was the case, Berg's undercover career had begun.

On February 21, 1939, Berg made the first of several appearances on the radio quiz show *Information, Please!* He was an immense hit, correctly answering nearly every question he was asked. Commissioner Kenesaw Mountain Landis was so proud of how intelligent and well-read the second-string catcher was that he told him, "Berg, in just 30 minutes you did more for baseball than I've done the entire time I've been commissioner." But Berg's baseball time was winding down; 1939 was his last season.

Secret Agent Man

Berg's intellect and elusive lifestyle were ideal for a post-baseball career as a spy. He was recruited by the Office of Strategic Services (predecessor to the CIA) in 1943 and served in several capacities. He toured 20 countries in Latin America early in WWII, allegedly on a propaganda mission to bolster the morale of soldiers there. But what he was really doing was trying to determine how much the Latin countries could help the U.S. war effort.

His most important mission for the OSS was to gather information on Germany's progress in developing an atomic bomb. He worked undercover in Italy and Switzerland and reported information to the States throughout 1944. One of his more daring assignments was a visit to Zurich, Switzerland, in December 1944, where he attended a lecture by German nuclear physicist Werner Heisenberg. If Heisenberg indicated the Germans were close to developing nukes, Berg had been directed to assassinate the scientist. Luckily for Heisenberg, Berg determined that German nuclear capability was not yet within the danger range.

Life After the War

On October 10, 1945, Berg was awarded the Medal of Freedom (now the Presidential Medal of Freedom) but turned it down without explanation. (After his death, his sister accepted it on his behalf.)

After the war he was recruited by the CIA. It is said that his is the only baseball card to be found in CIA headquarters. After his CIA career ended, Berg never worked again. He was often approached to write his memoirs. When he agreed, in 1960 or so, the publisher hired a writer to provide assistance. Berg quit the project in fury when the writer indicated he thought Berg was Moe Howard, founder of the Three Stooges. But his unusual career turns were later immortalized in the Nicholas Dawidoff book *The Catcher Was a Spy*. At age 70, Berg fell, injuring himself. He died in the hospital. His last words were to ask a nurse, "What did the Mets do today?"

◐ ◐ ◐

"There are two things I teach the boys that are all American. One's the good old flag and one's baseball."

—Sportswriter Tim Murnane, 1908

Can of Corn

"The only mistake I made in my whole baseball career was hitting .361 that one year, because ever since then people have expected me to keep doing it."

> —Tigers slugger Norm Cash, who, after batting .361 in 1961, never hit above .283 in 13 more seasons, *Behind the Mask*

"When they start the game, they don't yell 'Work Ball!' They say 'Play Ball!'"

> —Willie Stargell

"The umpiring of the game by Mr. Chandler was fair and impartial, notwithstanding the growling which was to be expected from a New York club."

> —*Boston Herald* sportswriter, getting in a barb at his team's opposition, May 13, 1872

"We cheer for the Senators, we pray for the Senators, and we hope that the Supreme Court does not declare that unconstitutional."

> —Lyndon Johnson, July 10, 1962

"Many baseball fans look at an umpire as a sort of necessary evil to the luxury of baseball, like the odor that follows an automobile."

> —Christy Mathewson

"It depends on the length of the game."

> —King Kelly's response to a reporter asking if he ever drank while playing, late 19th century

"If you have to begin fining them, it's time to get rid of them."

> —Hughie Jennings's managerial theory

The Baseball, Then & Now

The evolution of one of the game's most important components.

Throughout the history of the game, the folks who make the decisions have not been above tinkering with the game's rules or equipment. This tinkering is done to please the public, the players, and management. Even the baseball, the central object of the game, has changed quite a bit since the advent of the sport. The ball has evolved to make the game better and more exciting as well as to please those honchos wielding the funds.

The Dead-Ball Era

Some historically minded fans revere the dead-ball era at the start of the 20th century. Back then it was a slow, slogging game. Players concentrated more on baserunning, hit-and-run plays, and similar strategies instead of home runs. The balls were poorly manufactured with a solid rubber center and not wound as tightly as the baseballs of today. The cost-conscious early baseball leagues also insisted that each ball be used for the entire game if possible. As they were batted and thrown around, the balls became softer. The pitchers also had their way with the sphere, shining them up, wetting them, scraping them, and doing anything they could to make the balls harder to see and hit.

Cork at the Center

In the 1910 World Series, the first ground ball hit to Cubs shortstop Joe Tinker had him shaking his head; he could tell something was wrong. He had just met the new cork-center ball. It was much livelier all right: in five games, the teams combined for 50 runs.

When the cork-center ball became the standard in 1911, things really got interesting. AL runs per game jumped by a full run. Thirty-five American Leaguers batted over .300, and two batted over .400. NL teams experienced a similar leap.

In 1920, Babe Ruth's glamorization of the long ball—hitting the ball hard and up to give it the trajectory to go out of the park—made people believe it had been "livened up." However, there was no change in the horsehide. The only change was that doctored balls, such as spitballs and shiners, became illegal. Umpires were instructed to replace old, battered, dirty balls with hard, clean, white ones. This rule was introduced after Ray Chapman's fatal beaning, which most believe happened because the ball was too dirty for him to see.

The leaps in offense, particularly homers, led to much concern. A typical headline read, "Lively Ball Pushes Cubs to Win." While fans liked the offense, by 1929 things seemed to be getting out of control. The next year was also the highest scoring in National League history, with teams averaging five or six runs per game, totals not seen since the pitcher's plate was pushed back five feet.

More Changes

What came next is proof that the National League owners were embarrassed by the explosion in offense. For the 1931 season, they raised the stitches on the ball and introduced a thicker horsehide cover. Scoring dropped an alarming 21 percent, and it fell by another 14 percent two seasons later. Per game, National League home runs had increased 24 percent in two years, but then they plummeted 30 percent in the following three. On the other hand, while the NL was pulling in its haunches, the AL was doing the opposite. From 1929 to 1939, American League teams averaged more than five runs per game every season, and in 1939, they averaged 4.97, or about two runs less per week.

In 1931, the cushioned cork center was introduced, consisting of cork wrapped in layers of rubber. Although the quality of material and means of manufacturing have changed slightly, the baseball and its specifications have remained predominantly the same ever since.

Even so, whenever there seems to be an offensive spurt, whether it lasts a week or a decade, someone starts hollering, "Juiced ball!" The major leagues refuse to divulge whether or not they have instituted changes in the sphere. Tests have been inconclusive, and the offensive jumps of the late 1990s seem to have come from forces other than the actual baseball. Thus, it looks like we'll never really know.

Relief Is Just
Two Pitches Away

Make way for the men from the 'pen.

The idea of a "relief pitcher" being someone to help *win* the game was unheard of for the first 50 years of baseball. Usually called a "change pitcher," this person was brought in to take the beating when the main pitcher was getting wracked.

Frequently during the first several decades of the 20th century, a team's primary starter would be given a chance to protect a lead late in the game. The first "relievers" were players like Mordecai "Three Finger" Brown, Ed Walsh, and Christy Mathewson. The term "relief pitcher" was first mentioned in *Harper's Weekly* in 1914.

Using starters in the clutch remained the rule into the 1930s. Firpo Marberry of Washington was the first to specialize in relief pitching in the 1920s, and he became the first reliever to register 100 saves. However, this was only done retroactively, because saves didn't become an official stat until decades later.

In 1969, longtime Chicago sportswriter Jerome Holtzman encouraged baseball to adopt the "save" as a formal statistic. This came about because, for the first time in history, a single stat changed the way the game was played on the field. The save gave management a way to measure the performance of their best reliever. Around 1978, closers came to be used for only one full inning and only when their team was ahead by three runs or less— in other words, when they were in a "save situation." This choice forced managers to create a new job in their bullpen: the "setup man." That's the person who pitches the inning or two leading up to the ninth. The era of the man who could pitch almost every day had essentially disappeared.

The importance of relief pitchers has increased considerably in the last decade. Today, a reliever is not brought in simply to close the game. There are many types of relief pitchers, such as a long reliever, who comes in any time between the first inning and the fourth inning to get the game under control for the offense.

There's even a left-handed specialist, a pitcher whose job is to retire left-handed batters.

If anyone doubts that relief pitchers have drastically changed the game, just look at how much (or how little) starting pitchers are being asked to pitch today. In 2004, the National League had 71 complete games. The total was almost twice that five years earlier, and five times that just 25 years before. In 2005, the American League had 85 complete games, and in 1980, that number was 549. No pitcher has had ten complete games in a season in either league since 1999.

There are signs that the use of the closer is changing. Although 50 saves is no longer unusual, Bobby Thigpen's 57 for the White Sox in 1990 has since held as the most saves in one season.

The first reliever to earn 200 saves was Hoyt Wilhelm. The first with 300 was Rollie Fingers in 1982. Lee Smith landed his 400th save in 1993 and retired as the leader with 478, until Trevor Hoffman passed him in 2006.

⚾ ⚾ ⚾

"Scold him, find fault with him and he could not pitch at all. Praise him and he was unbeatable."

—Former Chicago manager Cap Anson on Hall of Fame pitcher "Sensitive John" Clarkson, *The Sporting News*, April 6, 1963

⚾ ⚾ ⚾

"Nothing makes a pitcher feel more secure than the sight of his teammates circling the bases during a ballgame."

—Reliever Jim Brosnan, *Pennant Race*

⚾ ⚾ ⚾

"How do I pitch him? I wish I could throw the ball under the plate."

—Don Newcombe on Hank Aaron, *Young Baseball Champions*

Magical Moments

And you thought walking on water was impossible.

The Setting: The National League, 1969
The Magic: The Mets went from lovable losers to world champs—and did it in heroic fashion.

The New York Mets, one of the first two National League expansion clubs, set an all-time record for losses their first season (120 in 1962). They improved some, but not a lot, garnering at least 100 defeats in five of their first six years. Some wags said, "A man will walk on the moon before the Mets win a pennant." In 1968, they lost "only" 89 games. But this was a talented group at the core, led by superstar pitchers Tom Seaver and Jerry Koosman and such able batters as Cleon Jones and Tommie Agee.

In 1969, the National League expanded again and split into two six-team divisions. The Mets were picked to finish near the bottom. But they stayed surprisingly competitive and were second behind the Cubs on June 15 when they pulled off a miraculous deal, obtaining 33-year-old first baseman Donn Clendenon from the Montreal Expos. At least it turned out to be miraculous: In his first 16 games as a Met, Clendenon knocked home either the lead run or the winning run four times. But the Cubs hung tough, and they led the Mets by five games on July 19. That day two Americans walked on the moon. But some might say an even bigger miracle happened as the Mets fell 9½ games back in August but then went on to win 22 of their last 27 games. The Cubs collapsed under their martinet manager, Leo Durocher. But the magic continued for the Mets as they swept the Braves in the League Championship Series and toppled the powerful Baltimore Orioles in five games to win the world title. The Miracle Mets had pulled off one of the biggest upsets in baseball history.

Fast Facts

- *The first indoor World Series game was played on October 17, 1987, in Minnesota's Hubert H. Humphrey Metrodome. The Twins beat the Cardinals 10–1.*

- *Bill Mazeroski, Pittsburgh Pirates second baseman from 1956 to 1972, broke the record for double plays by a second baseman in a single season, with 161 in 1966, and the most career double plays by a second baseman, with 1,706.*

- *At age 20, Al Kaline of the Detroit Tigers became the youngest player ever to win a batting title by hitting .340 in 1955.*

- *The Brooklyn Dodgers were the first team to purchase their own airplane, in January 1957.*

- *Greg Maddux and Randy Johnson are the only two pitchers to win four consecutive Cy Young Awards.*

- *Since 1876, there have been only two years when not a single triple play occurred in the major leagues: 1961 and 1974.*

- *The first regular season interleague game was played on June 12, 1997, when the AL Texas Rangers hosted the NL San Francisco Giants. The Giants won 4–3.*

- *Since 1900, only 34 American Leaguers and 26 National Leaguers have had six hits in a single nine-inning game. No player comes into a game expecting even three or four hits, so six hits in one game is nothing short of remarkable. Even more impressive, Rennie Stennett of the Pirates had seven hits in a single game in 1975.*

- *The youngest player to reach 3,000 hits was Ty Cobb at age 32.*

Best Baseball Books

The shelf of great books written about the game is a long one, but some stand out even there.

Baseball has stories, baseball has history, and baseball has stats. All three play important roles for every fan's enjoyment of the game. (Although how much of each you prefer determines what kind of fan you are.) These books do the best job of connecting us to the game we love in one way or another. And we didn't have room to mention the absolutely critical statistical works, such as encyclopedias, that belong on every fan's bookshelf.

Book: *Babe*
Author: Robert Creamer
What's the story?: It's only fair that the greatest player should get one of the greatest biographies.
Why we like it: Ruth comes across as a talented, but largely undisciplined, lovable lug. Which is how we want to think of him.

Book: *Baseball: The Early Years; Baseball: The Golden Age; Baseball: The People's Game*
Author: Harold Seymour
What's the story?: Academic research comes to baseball, and the results are serious yet pleasurable.
Why we like it: The first two volumes, which track professional baseball from its beginnings through the late 1920s, are indispensable. The third, a history of nonprofessional baseball, is truly breathtaking.

Book: *Baseball Before We Knew It*
Author: David Block
What's the story?: Finally, an in-depth study of the question "Where did baseball come from?"
Why we like it: It goes everywhere in search of the answer, and what it delivers is very satisfying.

Book: *The New Bill James Historical Baseball Abstract*
Author: Bill James
What's the story?: Using Sabermetrics to discover the historically best players.
Why we like it: James knows his stuff, and his style is always engaging and appropriately light. He takes his place in the first rank of baseball historians.

Book: *The Boys of Summer*
Author: Roger Kahn
What's the story?: A bittersweet look at what happened to the adored Dodgers of the late 1940s and early '50s when they left baseball and glory to face the often harsh realities of the world.
Why we like it: They were our heroes, but we love and respect them even more when we see them as mere mortals.

Book: *The Glory of Their Times*
Author: Lawrence Ritter
What's the story?: The men who played for and against John McGraw, and with and against Honus Wagner and Christy Mathewson, relate the tale of baseball life in the first decades of the 20th century.
Why we like it: Their voices leap off the page and draw us in.

Book: *The Hot Stove League*
Author: Lee Allen
What's the story?: Stories from baseball's golden age.
Why we like it: Lee Allen was one of the game's first true historians, and he's a writer with a fine, strong, yet mellow style.

Book: *The Long Season*
Author: Jim Brosnan
What's the story?: It's hard to understand today what a clamor this book set off in the early 1960s. It looked behind the puffery of the sports pages into the actual lives of the players.
Why we like it: It isn't always pretty, but it is fascinatingly honest.

Book: *The New Dickson Baseball Dictionary*
Author: Paul Dickson
What's the story?: The first edition, in 1990, had 5,000 citations; the second, in 1999, had 7,000. A third, underway, should have 10,000.
Why we like it: Baseball's language is as rich as its history, and the two are wedded beautifully under Dickson's talented hand. The definition of "Chinese home run" alone is worth the price of this book.

Book: *Nice Guys Finish Last*
Author: Leo Durocher and Ed Linn
What's the story?: For 50 years, whenever there was a battle going on in baseball, Durocher wasn't far from the middle of it. This is his autobiography—nasty, bristling, and full of the giants of the game, from Branch Rickey, Babe Ruth, and Rabbit Maranville to Jackie Robinson, Willie Mays, and Bobby Thomson.
Why we like it: It's a rare sports book that puts so much lively storytelling between two covers.

⚾ ⚾ ⚾

An official major-league baseball must weigh no less than 5 ounces and no more than 5.25 ounces. It must measure no less than 9 inches and no more than 9.5 inches in circumference.

⚾ ⚾ ⚾

"Like dysentery through the Army camps, [baseball swept] down the South Atlantic coast, and out into the Midwest . . . by the time the nation's wounds were bandaged . . . [it had become] the most popular game in the land."

—Tristram Potter Coffin

The Sad Decline of Denny McLain

In baseball, it doesn't take long to fall from the attic and land in the cellar.

The last major-league pitcher to win 30 games in a single season, Denny McLain dominated the American League so thoroughly during the final two years of the 1960s that he seemed destined for the Hall of Fame. In 1968 and '69, he won a combined 55 games, captured an MVP Award, and earned two Cy Young Awards as the league's most outstanding pitcher. McLain then experienced one of the most abrupt declines in major-league history, in large part because of his own reckless behavior.

Finding His Stride—and His Slide

Originally signed by the Chicago White Sox as a bonus baby, McLain never pitched a game for the Windy City franchise. The White Sox failed to promote the highly touted prospect to their major-league roster in 1963, making McLain eligible to be selected by another team. The Detroit Tigers gladly swooped in, selecting the hard-throwing right-hander off waivers. Within three years, McLain became a 20-game winner for Detroit.

Still, McLain had not reached his peak. He relied too much on his fastball, while struggling to command his breaking pitches. That changed in 1967 when Tigers pitching coach Johnny Sain taught McLain a sidearm slider. Now equipped with two devastating pitches, McLain soon raised himself to an All-Star level. In 1968, he became the ace of the American League's best team, helping the Tigers clinch the pennant in a runaway. He won 31 games during the regular season, marking the first time a major-league pitcher had reached the 30-win plateau since 1934. To top off the season, McLain earned a World Series ring as the Tigers beat the St. Louis Cardinals in seven games.

Living Large and Loving It

McLain also excelled off the field, showing skill in music and aviation. He became an accomplished piano player and a licensed pilot. McLain also became a favorite of the media. Highly quotable, he gave writers plenty of material with brash, almost boastful responses to questions. One year he showed up for spring training with a mop of red hair, yet he denied dyeing it. "I did not dye my hair, no matter what anyone says," he explained to reporters. "It was Mother Nature."

On top of the pitching world in 1968 and '69, McLain enjoyed his success—perhaps a little too much. During the 1968 season alone, McLain appeared on *The Ed Sullivan Show, The Smothers Brothers Comedy Hour,* and the *Today* show. He made his television appearances in between starts, which ultimately affected his daily routine and his preparation for his next outing. And then there were his bad habits. Wrapped up in a fast-paced lifestyle that was popular in the late 1960s, McLain spent a significant amount of time enjoying the nightlife. He also didn't worry about conditioning himself, instead drinking a case of Pepsi a day.

Big Trouble

McLain's career began to fully unravel in 1970. When a story in *Sports Illustrated* linked him to illegal bookmakers, the Commissioner's Office investigated and found enough evidence to suspend McLain for half the season. Even after he returned in midsummer, McLain continued to cause trouble. In one instance, he dumped a bucket of ice water on a Detroit sportswriter. Furious over his behavior, the Tigers suspended McLain again. He then received a third suspension—this one again coming from the commissioner—for carrying a gun.

After the 1970 season, the Tigers traded McLain to the lowly Washington Senators, where he constantly feuded with manager Ted Williams, who didn't approve of the trade to begin with and grew to dislike McLain intensely. Struggling with increasing weight and a decreasing fastball, McLain won only ten games while losing a league-leading 22 decisions in 1971. During the spring of 1972, McLain was traded to the Oakland A's for two minor-league pitching prospects.

In five starts with the A's, McLain pitched poorly and with extremely low velocity, causing Oakland to part ways with him just a few days after he made his fifth start. Instead of releasing him and paying off his guaranteed contract in full, the A's demoted McLain all the way down to Double-A Birmingham. He never returned to Oakland. On June 29, A's owner and general manager Charlie Finley traded McLain to the Atlanta Braves in a deal that brought Orlando Cepeda to the team.

Post-Career Problems

McLain finished out the season in Atlanta but drew his release the following year, ending his career just three days shy of his 29th birthday. McLain's problems continued after he left the game. After allowing his weight to balloon to 300 pounds, he looked unrecognizable to those who remembered him as a player. He declared bankruptcy twice and lost his house in a 1979 fire. During the mid-1980s, McLain served 29 months in prison on drug, extortion, and racketeering convictions. Unfortunately, he seemed to learn few lessons from his punishments. In 1997, McLain returned to federal prison after a jury convicted him of stealing millions of dollars from a union pension fund. In 2003, McLain was granted an early work release under the provision that he would have to work as a clerk in a Michigan 7-Eleven.

Few players have endured such a sad fate as Denny McLain. If only the young major-leaguer had taken better care of himself, he might have pitched longer, perhaps enough to merit serious consideration for election to Cooperstown.

◖◖ ◖◖ ◖◖

"Don't look back. Something might be gaining on you."

—Satchel Paige

Greatest Teams of All Time

1906–08 Chicago Cubs

Record: 116–36 (1906)
Manager: (and first baseman) Frank Chance
Hall of Famers: Chance, Mordecai "Three Finger" Brown, Johnny Evers, Joe Tinker
The Season: Brown's 1.04 ERA in 1906 is still the lowest for a season in NL history.
The Legacy: No team would match their number of wins in a season (116 in 1906) for 95 years (and Seattle had eight more games in which to do it).

No team has ever dominated a league the way the 1906–08 Cubs did. For those three years, they won an average of 107 games a season. In 1906, they won 116 games and took the pennant by 20 games. In 1907, they won by 17. Yet such was the intense competition with the other two splendid teams of the time, the Pirates and Giants, that when the Cubs took their third straight title, they did it by winning a game that had to be replayed because of one New Yorker's baserunning gaffe. The "gift" victory gave the Cubs a one-game edge over the tied Bucs and Giants.

These Cubs were the team built by brainy manager Frank Selee, called by some the best pilot ever. Under Selee, the Cubs moved from sixth in 1901 to fifth, then to third, then to second. Tuberculosis forced Selee to retire in mid-1905, and the reins of management were handed to first baseman Frank Chance. The husky 27-year-old soon earned the moniker "The Peerless Leader."

Between 1905 and '06, the Cubs obtained outfielder Jimmy Sheckard and third sacker Harry Steinfeldt, and their starting eight was set for the next three glorious seasons. Chance held down first, Johnny Evers played second, and Joe Tinker was at short. The outfield was patrolled by Wildfire Schulte, Jimmy Slagle, and Sheckard, none a great hitter but all excellent fielders.

The Chicago club was built on speed, defense, slashing if not powerful hitting, a sturdy pitching staff ably handled by catcher Johnny Kling, and brains. The Steinfeldt-Tinker-Evers-Chance infield was not just solid, it was smart.

The pitching staff was superb. With the deep and reliable starting unit of Brown, Jack Pfiester, Ed Reulbach, Carl Lundgren, and Orvie Overall, no Cub hurler had to risk blowing out his arm. The Cubs didn't need a 30-game winner (although Brown won 29 in '08); they just had two 20-game winners each year, plus a few other guys sprinkled in the teens.

The 1906 World Series featured both Chicago teams: the indomitable Cubbies and the "Hitless Wonder" White Sox, whose team batting average was nearly 50 points below the league leader. The North Siders took the South Siders too lightly. Even though Reulbach pitched a one-hitter in Game 2, the Sox spanked Brown and Pfiester with two losses each. Ed Walsh won two for the Sox, and the mighty Cubs were defeated in six games.

The 1908 NL pennant race has gone down in baseball legend and lore. The Cubs, Pirates, and Giants maintained a furious pace. By late September, the three contenders were bunched at the top, ten games above the next team. On September 22, the Cubs won both games of a doubleheader against the Giants at the Polo Grounds, and the race tightened further. The next day, the Giants thought they had won the game 2–1 in the last of the ninth when Al Bridwell singled home Moose McCormick with two out and Fred Merkle on first. But 1) Merkle failed to touch second before he left the field, 2) eagle-eyed Evers spotted the fact, and 3) after a scuffle for the ball, Evers showed the umpire he had the ball on second. Merkle was forced out, and the game was declared a tie, to be replayed the day after the last scheduled game. At season's end, the Giants and Cubs were tied for first. In the make-up game, the Cubs beat Christy Mathewson 4–2 to win the title.

In the World Series contests of 1907 and '08, the Cubs dominated the Ty Cobb–led Tigers, winning eight of the ten games played. One ended in a tie. With only one change in the starting eight, but the addition of a few new pitchers, the Cubs won 104 games in 1910 to take the pennant once more.

Chatter

"...the exponent of American Courage, Confidence, Combatism; American Dash, Discipline, Determinism; American Energy, Eagerness, Enthusiasm; American Pluck, Persistency, Performance; American Spirit, Sagacity, Success; American Vim, Vigor, Virility..."

—A portion of Albert Spalding's 1911 analysis declaring baseball as "America's Game"

"There is always some kid who may be seeing me for the first or last time. I owe him my best."

—Joe DiMaggio

"Branca throws... There's a long drive! It's going to be... I do believe! The Giants win the pennant! The Giants win the pennant! The Giants win the pennant!"

—Radio broadcaster Russ Hodges, October 3, 1951

"I'd walk through hell in a gasoline suit to play baseball."

—Pete Rose

"...A kind of baseball that none of us had ever seen before—throwing and running and hitting at something close to the level of absolute perfection, playing to win but also playing the game almost as if it were a form of punishment for everyone else on the field."

—Writer Roger Angell, describing the performance of Roberto Clemente in the 1971 World Series, *Five Seasons*

"You can learn little from victory. You can learn everything from defeat."

—Christy Mathewson

Noodle Bats

These guys believed Ted Williams when he said that hitting was the hardest thing to do in professional sports.

Great hitters receive the fans' adulation and respect. It's not an easy thing to hit a baseball—and do it with power and precision. In fact, there are plenty of men who make a career of professional baseball but never quite master what seems such a basic skill of the game.

Bill Bergen, Catcher
947 games   3,028 ABs   2 HRs   193 RBI   .170 BA   .194 OBP

Most notoriously weak hitters don't maintain careers for as many as 900 games. Bergen, who played for Cincinnati and Brooklyn, was one of the exceptions. Bergen set a record for the lowest season batting average by a player with enough plate appearances to qualify for the batting title. He achieved that piece of immortality in 1909, when he hit .139 in 346 at-bats. But what he lacked in hitting skills, he made up for behind the plate. Considered an exceptional catcher and handler of pitchers, Bergen caught a majority of his teams' games for more than half his career.

John Vukovich, Third Base
277 games   559 ABs   6 HRs   44 RBI   .161 BA   .203 OBP

Over the span of a ten-year career with the Philadelphia Phillies, Milwaukee Brewers, and Cincinnati Reds, Vukovich came to bat 559 times—roughly equivalent to one season's worth of at-bats. He batted .161 with six home runs, 44 RBI, and 29 walks, while striking out 109 times. In spite of those numbers, Vukovich managed to last a decade in the majors because of his slick fielding at third base, a willingness to play anywhere on the infield, and a professional work ethic that helped him become a highly respected coach. He passed away during spring training in 2007 at the age of 59.

Doug Flynn, Second Base
1,308 games   3,853 ABs   7 HRs   284 RBI   .238 BA   .266 OBP

Flynn's best remembered for being one of the players the New

York Mets acquired in 1977 as part of the Tom Seaver trade with the Cincinnati Reds. Well, Flynn didn't make anyone forget "Tom Terrific." Although an adept fielder, which kept him in the starting lineup for some weak Mets teams, Flynn finished his career with a batting average, on-base percentage, and slugging percentage all below .300. In a total of 1,308 games, Flynn hit a mere seven home runs, with four of those coming during the 1979 season.

Mario Mendoza, Shortstop
686 games   1,337 ABs   4 HRs   101 RBI   .215 BA   .245 OBP

Mendoza was a brilliant defensive shortstop who would have been better off bringing his glove to the plate. His hitting futility in the 1970s gave birth to a brand-new baseball term: the "Mendoza Line." Since Mendoza rarely hit above .215 (his career average) for the Pittsburgh Pirates, Seattle Mariners, and Texas Rangers, anyone who hit below that figure was said to be hitting "below the Mendoza Line." Some baseball observers adjusted the line to the .200 mark, making the Mendoza club even more exclusive (though not one people were anxious to join).

Darrell Chaney, Shortstop
915 games   2,113 ABs   14 HRs   190 RBI   .217 BA   .296 OBP

Chaney was a switch-hitter, but that didn't help him much. He struggled to hit against both left-handers and right-handers. Managing to last 11 seasons with the Cincinnati Reds and Atlanta Braves because of his versatility and slick glove, Chaney swatted a grand total of 14 home runs, with a lifetime slugging percentage of .288. Chaney never hit higher than .252 in any one season (1976 was his best year), but he did hit .201 or worse six times in his career (with a low of .125 in 1971).

Bob Gilks, Outfield
339 games   1,385 ABs   1 HR   142 RBI   .231 BA   .265 OBP

A 19th-century outfielder who played with Cleveland in the American Association before joining the National League, Gilks was a smart player who used to cleverly trap balls in the outfield and then start double plays against unsuspecting baserunners.

Unfortunately, smarts didn't help Gilks at the plate. Playing with the Cleveland Spiders and Baltimore Orioles of the National League, Gilks had no power (one home run in five seasons) and wasn't good at getting on base (a lifetime on-base percentage of .265). He also never managed to hit higher than .238 in a full major-league season.

Jack McGeachy, Outfield
608 games   2,464 ABs   9 HRs   276 RBI   .245 BA   .265 OBP

Another 19th-century player who unskillfully swung a bat, McGeachy compiled a lifetime batting average of .245 with only nine home runs over six seasons. A veteran of the National League, the Players League, and the American Association, McGeachy didn't draw any walks, either, reaching base just 27 percent of the time.

Ted Beard, Outfield
194 games   474 ABs   6 HRs   35 RBI   .198 BA   .315 OBP

Formally known by his birth name of Cramer Theodore Beard, this former Pittsburgh Pirate and Chicago White Sox fly-chaser of the 1940s and '50s might have been the worst hitting outfielder of all time. Gifted with the glove, Beard managed to last seven seasons, but his lack of hitting limited his playing time. He had little power, compiling a slugging percentage of .285 while batting .198 lifetime. A look at these statistics explains why he never came to bat more than 177 times in a single season.

Ron Herbel, Pitcher
332 games   206 ABs   0 HRs   3 RBI   .029 BA   .065 OBP

This right-hander for the San Francisco Giants, San Diego Padres, New York Mets, and Atlanta Braves was a moderately successful reliever, but he faced a monumental struggle each time he strode to the plate with a bat in his hand. In 206 major-league at-bats, Herbel collected a total of six hits. Of those, none were home runs. His lifetime average? A miniscule .029—the lowest batting average ever for a player with at least 100 at-bats. If ever a pitcher needed a designated hitter, it was Herbel, but he had already retired by the time the American League adopted the DH rule in 1973.

All-Time Great

Rogers Hornsby

He was a nasty, rude person but possibly the greatest right-handed batter of all time. And he had power, too.

Born: April 27, 1896; Winters, TX

MLB Career: St. Louis Cardinals, 1915–26; New York Giants, 1927; Boston Braves, 1928; Chicago Cubs, 1929–32; St. Louis Cardinals, 1933; St. Louis Browns, 1933–37

Hall of Fame Resume: Won seven batting titles, six consecutively * Led the league in hits four times; had more than 200 hits three other times * His .424 batting average in 1924 was the highest in the 20th century * Led the league in homers and triples twice, in doubles four times

Inside Pitch: Hornsby refused to read or go to the movies for fear of damaging his eyesight.

It's been almost 70 years since Ted Williams last cracked it, but there was once an era when a .400 batting average was not an unheard-of feat. Six men achieved the magic mark a total of 11 times from 1910 to 1930, but Rogers Hornsby's performance from 1921 to '25 should still be considered the greatest hitting stretch in major-league history. Through 696 games, 2,679 at-bats, and countless doubleheaders in the St. Louis sun, the Cardinals second baseman averaged a .402 batting mark.

Hornsby's achievement becomes even more remarkable upon viewing his early career. A 140-pound shortstop with a .232 average in the low minors during 1914, the righty-hitting Texan eventually put on 20 pounds and hit .313 as a Cards rookie in 1916 before upping the mark to .327 (second in the National League) a year later. Not much of a power threat in those dead-ball days (36 home runs his first five full seasons), Hornsby was moved to second base in 1920 and paced the NL in batting (.370), slugging (.559), RBI (94), hits (218), and doubles (44) despite just nine homers. It was the best offensive season by an NL second baseman in the 20th century, but it was only the beginning.

In 1921, the man called "Rajah" for his regal, hazel-eyed appearance upped his average to .397 with 44 doubles, 18 triples, 126 RBI, 131 runs, and 21 homers—leading the league in each department except the last while maintaining a hold on the NL batting, slugging (.639), and on-base-percentage (.458) leads that would last four more years. His first .400 season (.401) followed, with Hornsby completing his full maturation as a slugger by belting 42 homers (then a record for second basemen), good for 152 RBI and the 1922 Triple Crown.

An aloof free-thinker nearly as despised as the only man to compile a higher lifetime average—Ty Cobb—Hornsby outdid even the Georgia Peach during his infamous 1921–25 run. Limited by injury to 107 games in '23, he still averaged 216 hits, 123 runs, 41 doubles, 13 triples, 29 homers, and 120 RBI over the span—highlighted by the highest NL average of the 20th century (.424) in '24 and his second Triple Crown in 1925 (.403–39–143). Named player/manager of the underachieving Cards that same year, he led St. Louis to its first pennant and a stunning seven-game World Series upset of the Yankees in 1926 while batting .317.

As with Cobb, however, success couldn't calm Hornsby's bitter disposition. He routinely clashed with Cardinals owner Sam Breadon over money matters and, before the

1927 season, was traded to the Giants for Frankie Frisch and Jimmy Ring. After more quarrels with New York ownership during his lone season there (.361), he passed through Boston (a seventh and final batting title at .387 with the '28 Braves) and Chicago (.380–39–149 totals a year later) before his production slipped. He eventually ended up back in St. Louis for part-time duty with the Cardinals and Browns, and his final .358 average, 301 homers, 1,584 RBI, and .577 slugging percentage earned him a Hall of Fame plaque—even if his attitude was anything but golden.

Fighting Mad

Baseball players might not rival hockey players as fighters, but there have been some memorable scraps on the diamond.

A lack of boxing or wrestling skills has not prevented several epic, dugout-clearing brawls in the majors. As former player and skipper Bill Rigney once said, "Baseball players are the worst fighters I've seen in my entire life."

Senators vs. Yankees (July 4, 1932)

This historic scrap did not take long to settle after Senators outfielder Carl Reynolds collided hard with Yankees catcher Bill Dickey on a play at the plate. As Dickey would later describe: "It was hot, the games had been close, and I had been banged around for days. When Reynolds came at me, I just had to hit somebody." So Dickey slugged Reynolds, breaking his jaw with one punch. The star catcher was fined $1,000 and suspended for 30 days.

Dodgers vs. Giants (August 22, 1965)

As these archrivals battled it out for the NL pennant, tensions ran high. Giants ace Juan Marichal had been backing the Dodgers off the plate all day, and Dodgers catcher John Roseboro had had enough. Putting a new twist on brushback pitches, he tried to fire the ball as close to Giants hitters as possible on his throws back to pitcher Sandy Koufax. Finally, after a Roseboro throw whizzed past his head a little too close for comfort, Marichal turned and bashed the Dodgers catcher on the head with his bat, opening a gash that required 14 stitches to close. It also triggered a 14-minute brawl and resulted in an eight-game suspension and $1,750 fine for Marichal.

Reds vs. Mets (October 8, 1973)

Pete Rose was never shy about playing physically, and in this NLCS game, with the Reds trailing 9–2, he tried to break up a fifth-inning double play by taking out Bud Harrelson at second base. Rose's hard slide started a scrap between the two players, clearing the benches for a brawl that lasted ten minutes and saw Reds reliever Pedro Borbon tearing up a Mets cap with his teeth.

Shea Stadium fans showered Rose with trash when he took his place in left field in the top of the sixth inning, and Reds manager Sparky Anderson pulled his team from the field when one bottle nearly hit Rose. The umps finally succeeded in settling everyone down, and the game was eventually completed. The 9–2 score held up as the final, and the Mets took the series in five games.

Braves vs. Padres (August 12, 1984)
Some contend this game set baseball back 50 years. After Braves starter Pascual Perez beaned Padre Alan Wiggins with the first pitch of the game, there was more brawling than baseball. The Padres retaliated by throwing at Perez every time he came to bat. When Perez waved his bat at San Diego pitcher Ed Whitson after a fastball whizzed behind his helmet in the second inning, the fight-fest began. It started with a bench-clearing melee—the first of two in that inning. More brawling broke out in the fifth, eighth, and ninth frames. In the later innings, even the fans jumped onto the field to participate in the fray.

Eventually, five of those fans, one of whom had poured a beer over Kurt Bevacqua's head, and 14 participants were ejected, managers Joe Torre and Dick Williams among them. After the game, Torre called Williams an idiot and compared his actions to those of Hitler. While Torre took some criticism for that comment, it was Williams who absorbed the worst of the punishment—a $10,000 fine and ten-day suspension for his role in the altercation.

Blue Jays vs. Red Sox (June 23, 1985)
Toronto's George Bell set the standard by which all "mound charges" can be compared—if the goal is comedy, that is. Boston starter Bruce Kison beaned Bell and, instead of throwing a punch or trying to wrestle Kison, Bell charged the mound and tried a ridiculous karate kick. Kison easily avoided it, then dropped Bell with a nifty left hook. The laughs kept coming as the benches cleared. Blue Jays reliever Bill Caudill got into the action wearing an undershirt and unbuttoned pants.

Orioles vs. Yankees (May 19, 1998)

After Orioles closer Armando Benitez gave up an eighth-inning, go-ahead home run to Yankee Bernie Williams, he put a fastball between the shoulder blades of the next batter, Tino Martinez. Rather than waiting to get revenge when the Orioles came to bat, reliever Graeme Lloyd came charging from the bullpen to take a swing at Benitez. Next, Yankee Darryl Strawberry took a swing at Benitez with what many called a sucker punch. It caused Strawberry to spill into the Baltimore dugout, where he was roundly pummeled by Alan Mills.

White Sox vs. Tigers (April 22, 2000)

Even hockey players were entertained by this one. "It was a pretty vicious fight for a baseball game," Chris Osgood of the Detroit Red Wings noted. It started when Tigers pitcher Jeff Weaver plunked Carlos Lee in the sixth inning. Chicago's Jim Parque retaliated against Dean Palmer in the seventh, prompting Palmer to throw his helmet at him. What followed was some of the best "real" fighting to ever take place on a baseball diamond. Keith Foulke of the White Sox suffered a cut that required stitches. When Major League Baseball reviewed tapes of the bench-clearing incidents in the seventh and the ninth, they suspended 16 players—five more than the number ejected from the game.

Red Sox vs. Yankees (July 24, 2004)

The Red Sox and Yankees have scrapped no less than six times since 1938. This incident was the most notable. After being hit by a pitch in the third inning at Fenway Park, Yank Alex Rodriguez had words for Boston starter Bronson Arroyo as he made his way to first base. Red Sox catcher Jason Varitek stepped between the two, giving A-Rod a faceful of catcher's mitt before Rodriguez put him in a headlock. The benches cleared, and Yankees pitcher Tanyon Sturtze had his face bloodied in the fracas. Four players were ejected. The Red Sox had the last laugh, however: They heated up down the stretch and won their first World Series title since 1918.

Fast Facts

- Bert Blyleven set the record for most home runs allowed by a pitcher in 1986 when he gave up 50. The following year he held the opposition to 46. Second behind Blyleven is Jose Lima, who allowed 48 home runs in 2000.

- The only two brothers to ever win the Cy Young Award are Jim Perry in 1970 and Gaylord Perry in 1972 and '78.

- Barry Bonds had 232 walks in 2004, the most ever recorded by a batter in a single season. He's also in second place with 198 in 2002, and third with 177 in 2001.

- The last National League player to steal second base, third base, and home in the same inning is Eric Young of the Colorado Rockies, who did it on June 30, 1996.

- On October 9, 1951, Gil McDougald became the first rookie to hit a grand slam in a World Series game.

- The National League began play in 1876 with eight teams: the Philadelphia Athletics, the Boston Red Caps, the Chicago White Stockings, the Cincinnati Red Stockings, the Hartford Dark Blues, the Louisville Grays, the New York Mutuals, and the St. Louis Brown Stockings.

- Norm Cash had the biggest drop in batting average from one season to the next. In 1961, his average was .361; the next year it dropped to .243.

- Tony Cloninger is the only pitcher to hit two grand slams in the same game. He did it for the Atlanta Braves on July 3, 1966.

Nuttiest Fans

Love is strange... and noisy, too.

Some fans skim through the daily game reports and nod at the stats. Some pore over articles and numbers from across the country. And then there are the ultimate devotees—the ones whose lives would scarcely seem to exist without their team.

Hilda Chester—Brooklyn Dodgers

Famous for ringing her cowbell from the center-field bleachers in Ebbets Field, Chester was the epitome of the raucous Dodger fan. She carried not just one cowbell but two, to ring out in celebration or in mourning. (One of the bells is now in Cooperstown.) She also carried a large sign that let everyone know "Hilda Is Here."

Wild Bill Hagy—Baltimore Orioles

In Section 34 of Baltimore's Memorial Stadium in the late 1970s rose up a large, long-haired, full-bearded, well-beered cab driver who spelled out O-R-I-O-L-E-S with his body, and the crowd went bonkers. One writer said Hagy had "a voice that sounds like a cement mixer in action." When told he was "amazing," Wild Bill responded, "There ain't nothing amazing about it. They could do the same thing if they drank a case of beer every night."

Lolly Hopkins—Boston Red Sox

Unlike other famous fans, Lolly was a Boston fan of the pre–World War II era who would never think of hollering. She used a megaphone. And, in polite New England style, she was perfectly willing to cheer for good play on the part of either team.

Bruce "Screech Owl" McAllister—Pittsburgh Pirates

It wasn't a pleasant sound, but it was memorable. When Bruce McAllister let go one of his patented screams back in the 1930s, no one sitting in Forbes Field could miss it. Of course, with KDKA beaming Pirate games all over the East and Midwest, Bruce would often be heard in Missouri and Connecticut, too.

Mike "Nuf Ced" McGreevy—Boston Red Sox

The man's moniker came about because he was the ultimate authority on any sports question you threw at him. Bartender McGreevy headed the Royal Rooters, a raucous group of Boston fans who drove the Pirates wacky in the 1903 World Series with their pronounced singing of "Tessie" (words altered to hassle the Pirates players). In 1912, when a front-office blunder shut the Rooters out of Game 6 of the World Series, they just broke down the gates and marched around the field.

Mary Ott—St. Louis Cardinals

One writer called Ott's voice "a neigh known to cause stampedes in Kansas City stockyards." That's particularly impressive when you realize Mary lived in St. Louis! Ott's voice carried, but she testified to her love of what she called "scientific rooting," the art of getting the other team's goat with her scornful laugh. The "Horse Lady of St. Louis" first came to national attention when revered umpire Bill Klem threatened to throw her out of a game in 1926.

Patsy O'Toole—Detroit Tigers

In Detroit in the 1930s, the fan who made the most noise was Patsy, who rightfully earned his nickname as the "All-American earache." Opposing players got the full brunt of a Patsy attack, and he was especially tough on the hated Yankees.

Jack Pierce—Brooklyn Dodgers

Pierce's fandom bordered on obsession. He was sure that Dodger infielder Cookie Lavagetto was the greatest player ever. So to honor his idol, Pierce showed up at Ebbets Field every day, bought ten seats, and—using the containers of gas he brought along—blew up dozens of balloons with "Cookie" on them and released them throughout the game. He even continued this ritual in 1942, when Cookie was in the Army, not in Brooklyn.

Magical Moments

Don Larsen summoned greatness once,
when it mattered the most.

The Setting: Yankee Stadium; October 8, 1956
The Magic: Don Larsen's perfect World Series game is one for the ages.

In 1954, Don Larsen, then a member of the Baltimore Orioles, had a record of three wins and 21 defeats. He was one of seven Orioles swapped for ten Yankees that off-season, and he obviously took to his new surroundings, sporting a 9–2 record in a partial '55 season and an 11–5 record as a swingman in '56. That year he started 20 games and relieved in 18 others.

But on one October afternoon, the solid but until then unremarkable Larsen gave one of the greatest pitching performances of all time, retiring all 27 Brooklyn Dodgers he faced. There were three turning points in his perfecto (the first perfect game in the majors in 34 years). One was a heads-up piece of defensive work on a second-inning Jackie Robinson grounder, which Andy Carey deflected to shortstop Gil McDougald, who threw to first in time to nail Robinson by an eyelash. Second was Mickey Mantle's fourth-inning home run (the first hit allowed by Sal Maglie that day), and third was a nifty running grab of a Gil Hodges line drive by Mantle the next inning. Beyond that, Larsen was utterly dominant: He used only 97 pitches, and only one batter ever saw a three-ball count. Larsen lasted ten more years in the bigs, mostly as a reliever and without much success, but his one perfect day of World Series glory is an achievement that remains unmatched.

◎ ◎ ◎

"You ain't gonna get nothin' but fastballs, so don't look for anything else, and be ready."

—Cardinals ace Dizzy Dean, yelling to Braves batters as they approached the plate; Dean won 13–0

Spread the Glove

A future glove manufacturer started the trend, while the need for protection and some ingenuity resulted in the baseball glove we know today.

Albert Spalding was not the first pro baseball player to sport a glove, but he was probably the first star of the game to wear one. He saw his first baseball glove in Boston on the hands (one on each) of first baseman Charles C. Waite in 1875. Spalding started wearing one when he moved to first base in 1877, and soon everyone was asking about them. Conveniently, Spalding and his brother owned a sporting goods store in Chicago, a company that would go on to produce innumerable gloves over the next 130 years and counting.

In 1883, a hard ball broke two of shortstop Arthur Irwin's fingers. Since he wanted to continue to play, Irwin purchased a large buckskin glove, added padding, and sewed the third and fourth fingers together. Within a few years most players were using the "Irwin glove." The baseball glove was improved upon again in 1919 thanks to St. Louis spitball pitcher Bill Doak. He suggested to the Rawlings Sporting Goods Company that a webbed thumb and forefinger be added to create a pocket. The result was the revolutionary "Doak model," the standard baseball glove used to this day.

One player whose glove couldn't be found on the field was Bid McPhee. The son of a saddlemaker, McPhee eschewed the leather on his hand long after almost everyone else had relented. Instead he soaked his hands in brine every spring to toughen them. It worked. His 529 putouts at second base for the 1886 Cincinnati Reds of the American Association has never been surpassed, glove or no glove. Yet with his fielding slipping and his finger sore to start the 1896 season, McPhee finally donned a glove in his 15th season. The future Hall of Famer led second basemen in fielding, and his .978 fielding percentage stood as a record for 23 years.

The Doubleday Myth

It's a great story that's been passed from one generation to the next. It's also a work of fiction.

"The first scheme for playing Baseball, according to the best evidence available to date, was devised by Abner Doubleday at Cooperstown, N.Y. in 1839."

That finding, announced after a three-year study by the Mills Commission in 1907, is the main reason the tiny central New York hamlet was chosen to be the home of the National Baseball Hall of Fame and Museum. This "creation myth" has since been debunked from so many angles it seems positively ridiculous now, but it was accepted as truth back then.

Had Abner Doubleday truly invented baseball in 1839 in Cooperstown, New York, as so many generations of children have been told over the years, pundits could answer the question "Why Cooperstown?" in far fewer words. As it stands, the response requires a little more explanation.

So why Cooperstown? "The answer involves a commission, a tattered baseball, a philanthropist, and a centennial celebration," describes the Hall of Fame in its official statement. The commission was the brainchild of sporting goods magnate Albert G. Spalding in 1905, in response to a story that baseball had evolved from the British game of rounders. The baseball in question was an old, tattered, homemade ball discovered in a dusty attic trunk in a farmhouse near Cooperstown in 1934. It became known as the "Doubleday Ball," and it served to support the commission's 1907 findings. Singer sewing machine magnate Stephen C. Clark purchased the "Doubleday ball" for $5 in 1935 and pushed for the formation of the Hall of Fame. The museum's opening was planned to coincide with a "century of baseball" celebration set to take place in Cooperstown in 1939. Thanks largely to Clark and his family, the Hall of Fame opened its doors in June of that year.

Even before the Hall of Fame opened, many people questioned the findings of the Mills Commission, which said that Doubleday, a West Point cadet and Union general in the Civil War, had set down rules for a game of "town ball" for a group of Cooperstown boys to take on those from a neighboring town. The tale was based largely on the testimony of Abner Graves, a retired mining engineer who claimed to have witnessed the event. But historians later learned that Graves's testimony was questionable at best and that baseball's presumed "founding father" was likely not in or even near Cooperstown in 1839.

Abner Doubleday's credibility as the inventor of baseball wasn't helped by the dozens of diaries he wrote after retiring from the U.S. Army in 1873. Neither the diaries nor the Doubleday obituary that appeared in *The New York Times* 20 years later include any mention of baseball.

In fact, the Hall of Fame plaque of Alexander Cartwright credits *him* as the "Father of Modern Base Ball." Cartwright, a New York bank teller and talented draftsman, organized the first regular team, which he called the New York Knickerbockers. Rather than play "town ball," where scores could top 100, Cartwright devised rules for a game that would feature bases 90 feet apart on a diamond-shape infield, nine players per side, a three-strikes-and-you're-out policy, and "force outs" at first base if the ball got to the infielder before the runner—all rules that have stood the test of time. The first game under Cartwright's rules was played at the Elysian Fields in Hoboken, New Jersey, on June 19, 1846.

⚾ ⚾ ⚾

"I like to see Quentin practicing baseball. It gives me hope that one of my boys will not take after his father in this respect, and will prove able to play the national game."

—President Theodore Roosevelt

⚾ ⚾ ⚾

"Baseball is more than a game to me; it's a religion."

—Umpire Bill Klem

Greatest Teams of All Time

1927 New York Yankees

Record: 110–44
Manager: Miller Huggins
Hall of Famers: Huggins, Babe Ruth, Lou Gehrig, Tony Lazzeri, Earle Combs, Waite Hoyt, Herb Pennock
The Season: In Gehrig's third year, this powerhouse team scored 975 runs, 130 more than the runner-up. Ruth himself out-homered every other team in the league.
The Legacy: Still often referred to as the best team of all time.

They came to call it "Five O'Clock Lightning." The Yankees of the 1920s and '30s were such a powerful group of hitters that almost no opposing pitcher could hold them back for a full game. After the pitcher had faced the Yank lineup once or twice and tired a bit (about five in the afternoon, since most games started at three), the slugging men from the Bronx had seen all they needed, and they were almost certain to break the game open.

Every list of the greatest teams of all time begins with the 1927 Yankees. Yankee manager Miller Huggins, in his tenth year as their skipper, was known for being irascible and moody, but all he had to do in 1927 was sit back and watch his men work.

As an offensive powerhouse, the Yanks were simply awesome. It should be remembered that the "big bomber" mentality had not yet taken over the game. As the 1927 season began, only three men in major-league history had swatted 40 or more homers in a season. That year, Babe Ruth belted 60 and Lou Gehrig 47. Ruth's record and the Ruth-Gehrig combo total stood until 1961, when Roger Maris and Mickey Mantle topped them in an expansion year. The 1927 Yankees weren't riding the wave of a livelier ball or other offensive fluke season; the league batting average was actually lower than it had been two of the previous three years.

The '27 Yankees had the top three run scorers in the American League; the top two in hits, RBI, and triples; the top three in home runs and total bases; and the top two in walks. As a team, they led the AL in hits, triples, homers (102 more than the runner-up), batting average, on-base percentage, and slugging average. Not surprisingly, they scored 130 more runs than the next highest-scoring team. Their 110 victories stand as the second best by any American League team in a 154-game season.

The Yankee starting eight was mostly blossoming young talent, with only third baseman Joe Dugan, outfielder Bob Meusel, and Ruth qualifying as veterans. Gehrig, in his third full year, set a record for slugging percentage by anyone not named Babe Ruth. In addition to his 47 circuit clouts, he led the AL in doubles with 52 and tied for second in triples with 18. His 175 RBI were the most in baseball history at that time and are still fourth best. Second baseman Tony Lazzeri, just a rookie the season before, finished third in the league (and on the Yanks) with 18 homers and knocked in 102 runs. Switch-hitting shortstop Mark Koenig, in his second full season, swatted 11 triples and scored 99 times. Earle Combs, the speedy center fielder in his third full season, had the best totals he would ever have in hits, triples, and batting average.

And then there was the Babe. His 60 home runs were 18 more than anyone else had ever hit. His 158 runs scored tied himself for second (he was also first) for runs in the 20th century, and he drove in 164 runs, too.

Naturally, the Yankee pitching staff enjoyed having such a crop of sluggers around. They were a group of seasoned veterans. Staff ace Waite Hoyt led the team in wins with 22. Herb Pennock (age 33), Urban Shocker (36), and Dutch Ruether (33) each started more than 25 games. Pennock chalked up 19 wins, Shocker 18, and Ruether 13. Ace swingman Wilcy Moore (30) started a dozen games and relieved in 38 others. He was around when Five O'Clock Lightning hit often enough to earn 19 wins, and he's credited (retroactively) with 13 saves. He also led the league with a 2.28 ERA, with Hoyt and Shocker right behind him.

With the exception of one inning, the 1927 Yankee power didn't show up for that year's World Series. But it didn't matter. Aided by Pirate errors and two final-game, ninth-inning wild pitches by Pirate hurler John Miljus, the Yanks easily swept the Bucs in four games.

The Men Behind the Microphone

Besides being excellent announcers, each of these men became the living, breathing connection between a team and its town.

Mel Allen

New York Giants and Yankees, 1939–43
New York Yankees, 1946–64

After being fired by the Yankees (after 24 years!), Allen returned to the air a decade later on the national TV show *This Week in Baseball.* His voice was warm and mellifluous, and his signature phrase was "How 'bout that?" He nicknamed Joe DiMaggio "The Yankee Clipper" and Phil Rizzuto "Scooter," and his home run call was the simply perfect "Going, going, gone!"

Red Barber

Cincinnati Reds, 1934–38
Brooklyn Dodgers, 1939–53
New York Yankees, 1954–66

Red was first and foremost a reporter, yet his easy Southern tone and rural phrases were a big hit in Brooklyn. Among them: "rhubarb" (a real battle) and "catbird seat" (sitting pretty). When his Dodgers rallied, Barber said, "The boys are tearin' up the pea patch." He also trained two other broadcasting greats: Ernie Harwell and Vin Scully.

Jack Buck

St. Louis Cardinals, 1954–2001

Buck was so vital to the St. Louis baseball scene that Busch Stadium sports a statue of him behind a microphone. His trademark tag line, "That's a winner," was also the title of his autobiography. But his most famous call came when non-slugger Ozzie Smith belted a homer to win Game 5 of the 1985 National League Championship Series. Buck hollered, "Go crazy, folks, go crazy!"

Harry Caray

St. Louis Cardinals, 1945–69
Oakland A's, 1970
Chicago White Sox, 1971–81
Chicago Cubs, 1982–97

He supposedly talked his way into his first interview and was told by the owner of St. Louis's largest station, "Your voice has an exciting timbre." Caray went on to share that excitement with fans for more than four decades, primarily in Wrigley Field. He was known for saying "Holy Cow!" and singing "Take Me Out to the Ball Game" during the seventh-inning stretch. His signature home run call was "It could be, it might be, it is!"

Ernie Harwell

Brooklyn Dodgers, 1948–49
New York Giants, 1950–53
Baltimore Orioles, 1954–59
Detroit Tigers, 1960–91, 1993–2002

His calm, intelligent style came about because he started his baseball career as a writer. For Harwell, who became known as "the voice of the Tigers," each game was a mini-seminar on baseball personalities, tactics, and history. One sports columnist said he had "authenticity."

Russ Hodges

Cincinnati Reds, 1932–33
Chicago Cubs and White Sox, 1935–37
Washington Senators, 1938–45
New York Yankees, 1946–48
New York/San Francisco Giants, 1949–70

He was the Giants announcer in both New York and San Francisco, and his home run call was "Bye bye, baby!" But Hodges's spot in broadcasting history was sealed after his famous call of the "Shot Heard 'Round the World"—Bobby Thomson's three-run homer in the last of the ninth, which pulled out the 1951 pennant for the men from New York. "The Giants win the pennant!" Hodges hollered . . . nine times.

Waite Hoyt

Cincinnati Reds, 1942–65

His style was described as "casual, sincere, matter of fact." Fellow broadcaster Russ Hodges said the result was an authoritative tone: "When Hoyt says it's so, the Cincinnati public goes by what he says." Radio listeners were entertained by the anecdotal stories Hoyt shared during rain delays. Fans loved the stories so much that two record albums of "Hoyt's best" were released.

Bob Prince

Pittsburgh Pirates, 1948–75, 1982–85
Houston Astros, 1976

There was no more outrageous phrase-turner and home-team cheerleader than Pittsburgh's Bob Prince. If they were down by a run he'd announce, "All we need is a bloop and a blast." On a Bucco homer, Prince would roar, "You can kiss it good-bye." After every Pirate victory, he bellowed, "We had 'em all the way!"

Vin Scully

Brooklyn/Los Angeles Dodgers, 1950–present

In 1976, Dodger fans voted Scully the Most Memorable Personality in Dodger history. His tone and style are absolutely one of a kind, always matching the rhythm of his perfectly parsed sentences to the action on the field. Some of his game calls are so notable, they have been transcribed and anthologized in books of baseball literature.

⚾ ⚾ ⚾

"If I have to win one game, I want something to say about it myself, so I've got to be in there."

—Ralph Kiner on why he picked himself as a member of his "Ultimate Lineup," *The Greatest Team of All Time*

Chatter

"Whoever wants to know the heart and mind of America had better learn baseball, the rules and realities of the game."

—Jacques Barzun, philosophy professor

"A base hit meant more to [Cap] Anson than a week's pay."

—Grantland Rice

"To do what he did has got to be the most tremendous thing I've ever seen in sports."

—Pee Wee Reese on the rookie season of Dodger teammate Jackie Robinson, *The Boys of Summer*

"One of the secrets of the Babe's greatness was that he never lost any of his enthusiasm for playing ball, and especially for hitting home runs. To him a homer was a homer, whether he hit it in a regular game, a World Series game, or an exhibition game."

—Sportswriter Frank Graham on Babe Ruth, *The New York Yankees*

"Guessing what the pitcher is going to throw is 80 percent of being a successful hitter. The other 20 percent is just execution."

—Hank Aaron, *Hank Aaron...714 and Beyond*

"Baseball's unique possession, the real source of our strength, is the fan's memory of the times his daddy took him to the game to see the great players of his youth."

—Bill Veeck, *The Hustler's Handbook*

"Don't pull that stuff on me. How can a pipsqueak like you be Babe Ruth's manager?"

—Doorman to Yankees skipper Miller Huggins

No Man's Land

Imagine a ballplayer who reaches base 215 times, attempts 203 stolen bases (caught only twice)—and happens to be a woman.

There was such a ballplayer, and her name was Sophie Kurys. She was a star player in the All-American Girls Baseball League (AAGBL) of the 1940s and '50s. Kurys's 201 steals in 1946, a year the basepaths were actually lengthened, were six times more than Brooklyn Dodger Pete Reiser's major-league high of 34 that year—and Pistol Pete didn't have to slide with bare legs. Sliding was excruciating in the short skirts of the All-American Girls Baseball League, especially in Fort Wayne, where the grounds crew burned the infield with gasoline to dry it on rainy days. But the players all slid, and never headfirst. It was a running league, and the constant sliding caused deep cuts—known to ballplayers as strawberries—that would painfully stick to clothes after games. "I had strawberries on strawberries," Kurys recalled.

Kurys stole 1,114 bases in just eight seasons—most of them as a Racine Belle—and her 140-steal annual average was higher than major-league record holder Rickey Henderson's best season. Kurys's most memorable moment, though, was beating the throw home for the only run of a 14-inning game to win the 1946 league championship. Max Carey, the all-time National League stolen-base leader back then (with 738), and president of the AAGBL, called it "even in the majors, the best game I've ever seen."

The league was started in 1943. Most able-bodied men were serving in the armed services, and the major leagues—not to mention the minors—were forced to use many players who would have been laughed out of the ballpark before World War II started. The AAGBL wasn't just a wartime phenomenon, though. The league lasted until 1954, making several attempts to branch out. A 1949 tour of Central America featured exhibition games in four different countries. There were also junior teams, most notably the Junior Belles in Racine, where teenage girls learned fundamentals, participated in a short-season schedule, and occasionally played before the start of AAGBL contests.

The AAGBL had some outstanding players. Two-time batting leader Dorothy Kamenshek (.292 lifetime) was sought by a men's minor-league team in Fort Lauderdale, but she turned them down. Joanne Weaver, at 14, followed her sister Betty into the league and later became the only .400 hitter in AAGBL history. Bonnie Baker, a Saskatchewan-born catcher and former model, was the only player ever hired as a manager in the league. Pitcher Jean Faut, whose husband would eventually be her manager, had a baby in March 1948, then went out and won 16 games on the season while also playing third base; she later pitched two perfect games and led South Bend to consecutive championships. Rose Gacioch once had 31 outfield assists in a season and converted to pitcher, helping the Rockford Peaches win four titles. Dottie Schroeder was the only woman to play every season—and nearly every game—of the league's existence, winning her only title in 12 seasons by driving in the winning run for the Kalamazoo Lassies in the last game in league history.

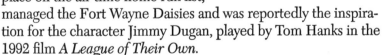

The managers were better known: ex-Cub Woody English, former Pirate Carson Bigbee, Bill Wambsganss (noted for turning an unassisted triple play in the 1920 World Series), and future Hall of Famers Carey, Dave "Beauty" Bancroft, and Jimmie Foxx. Heavy-drinking Foxx, who retired from the majors in 1945 at second place on the all-time home run list, managed the Fort Wayne Daisies and was reportedly the inspiration for the character Jimmy Dugan, played by Tom Hanks in the 1992 film *A League of Their Own*.

Hollywood likes to stretch the truth, but *A League of Their Own* wasn't too far off base. If anything, the movie condensed the 12 seasons the league existed into one year and pieced many real-life stories together to create characters with fictional names. The most memorable aspects of the film are mostly true: the Midwestern locale, the mass tryout in Chicago, the compulsory charm school, the chaperones, the bus trips, the camaraderie, a player's child in uniform on the bench, and the candy magnate who started the whole thing (fictional Walter Harvey, proprietor of Harvey Field, as opposed to Chicago Cubs owner Philip Wrigley). A brief 1993 television series with the same name as the film could have shed more light on other facets of the league, but its six-episode run was shorter than some homestands.

Contrary to what was depicted in the movie, though, the league began with a 12-inch softball thrown underhand from 40 feet away. The ball got smaller, the mound got farther away, and the distance between the bases grew as the league wore on. By 1954, the ball was 9½ inches, or the same size as a regulation major-league ball; the mound was 60 feet from home plate; and the bases were 85 feet apart. But all these changes weren't enough to keep the league from folding.

Mismanagement by independent owners, too much expansion, and dwindling attendance eventually killed off the AAGBL. In the last year, the players drove their own cars to games when teams could no longer afford a bus, and they even played without pay at the end. The ride had been a good one, though. The $45–$75 average weekly salary was far more than most women would have earned in occupations they enjoyed far less. What's more, the 600 women who made the grade earned the right to play baseball professionally. That's something only a handful of women have been able to claim in the half-century since then.

◖◖◖

"When I said the hardest thing for me to leave behind was baseball games, I was eyed as a nut of some kind. I'm not sure that anyone understood, but when you have baseballs for red corpuscles, you don't give up the game without a constriction of the blood vessels."

—Sister Mary Barbara Brown, C.S.C., of San Francisco, who became a nun the same year (1936) that Joe DiMaggio left town to play for the Yankees

How to Be a Better Hitter

Priceless tips from the master batsmen.

Of course there's some innate talent involved, as well as a bit of luck. But for the most part, great hitting comes down to hard work and lots of practice.

Ted Williams: Hit only strikes.

Ty Cobb: Keep your left elbow cocked on a level with your hands or higher. And keep your hands well away from your body.

Willie Keeler: Hit 'em where they ain't.

Cal Ripken: Choose the right bat. Repetitive practice is essential.

Mike Piazza: Try to spread your feet a little wider than shoulder width for balance.

Tony Gwynn: For me the most effective way to practice hitting is to use a batting tee and a bag of Wiffle balls. The sooner you can hit a Wiffle ball cleanly off a tee, the sooner you will become a better hitter.

Manny Mota: The most valuable advice that I can give a young hitter is to think about hitting the ball up the middle. If you think about hitting up the middle, you can adjust to hit the ball wherever it is pitched.

Ted Williams again: Hitting is 50 percent above the shoulders.

And some general advice: Never speak to the catcher. And no matter what the count, always expect fastballs, but be prepared to adjust to other pitches.

Larry Doby:
The Other Pioneer

Recognition for a man who often found himself overshadowed.

Larry Doby must have resigned himself to finishing second. In 1947, he made his debut for the Cleveland Indians, becoming the second African-American to play major-league baseball in the 20th century. Three decades later, Doby became the second black man to manage a major-league team. (Frank Robinson was the first, for the Cleveland Indians in 1975.) Yet, Doby never publicly complained about being a bridesmaid. He handled his role as a secondary baseball pioneer with dignity and grace, advancing the cause for other African-Americans who would succeed him.

Doby starred in the Negro Leagues from 1942 to 1947, though he did lose some of that time to service in World War II. His abilities as a hard-hitting second baseman caught the attention of Cleveland Indians owner Bill Veeck, who was aggressively seeking black talent for his major-league team in 1947. In the early days of July, Veeck arranged to purchase Doby's contract from the Newark Eagles. Veeck paid $15,000 to Eagles owner Effa Manley for Doby, who was hitting .414 at the time.

Jackie Robinson had broken the game's color barrier only 11 weeks earlier, making his Brooklyn Dodgers debut on April 15. Unlike Robinson, Doby did not receive the benefit of playing minor-league ball, which would have allowed him to make a gradual transition to the majors. Instead, Veeck brought Doby directly from the Negro Leagues to the Indians.

Veeck also laid out some ground rules. "He sat me down and told me some of the do's and don'ts," Doby recalled. "Don't even turn around at a bad call at the plate, and no dissertations with opposing players—either of those might start a race riot."

On July 5, Veeck personally escorted Doby to Comiskey Park, where the Indians were playing the Chicago White Sox. Doby didn't start the game but would immediately find himself tested. Pinch-hitting in the seventh inning with two men on base, Doby struck out, swinging and missing badly. It didn't matter. In the larger scheme, Doby had arrived—second overall, but the first black player in American League history.

Over the years, historians have carefully examined the racism that Jackie Robinson faced from teammates, opponents, and fans during his early days in the majors. But the similar obstacles that Doby faced have not received nearly as much scrutiny. Like Robinson, Doby heard insults from opposing players and taunts from fans who didn't want a black man sharing the diamond with his white counterparts. Most of Doby's teammates showed him a cold indifference, but a few were outright nasty and rude. Some even refused to shake Doby's hand before his first game. On one occasion, an opposing player spit on Doby as he slid into second base, but he chose not to retaliate. "I couldn't react to [prejudicial] situations from a physical standpoint," Doby once said. "My reaction was to hit the ball as far as I could."

Doby's debut season did not unfold as dramatically as Robinson's did. While Robinson played well enough to win Rookie of the Year and helped the Dodgers advance to the World Series, Doby played sparingly and flailed at the plate, hitting only .156 in 32 at-bats. But Doby rebounded in 1948. He became the Indians' regular center fielder, hit .301 with 14 home runs, and helped Cleveland clinch the AL pennant.

Although baseball's color barrier had delayed his major-league career, Doby diligently overcame the late start. By the time his career ended, he had qualified for seven All-Star teams, led the American League in home runs twice, and finished second in the MVP voting in 1954. In 1978, he was hired again by Veeck, this time to manage the White Sox.

Doby didn't always end up in second place. He was the first African-American to lead his league in home runs, the first to hit a homer in the World Series, and the first to be on a Series-winning team (the Indians in 1948). Coupled with his performance in the Negro Leagues, Doby's many pioneering accomplishments helped earn him election and induction to the Baseball Hall of Fame in 1998. Always a man of great strength and dignity, Doby passed away in 2003 at the age of 79.

Fast Facts

- Hank Aaron, Willie Mays, and Stan Musial played in the most All-Star Games: 24.

- In 1953, respected and innovative National League umpire Bill Klem was the first ump elected to baseball's Hall of Fame.

- The four players who have won pitching's Triple Crown (leading the league in ERA, wins, and strikeouts) in two consecutive years are Roger Clemens, Sandy Koufax, Lefty Grove, and Grover Cleveland Alexander (who won it three consecutive years: 1915, 1916, and 1917).

- The 1899 Cleveland Spiders won 20 games and lost 134 for a .130 "winning" percentage—the worst ever recorded.

- Only Hughie Jennings was hit by more pitches than Craig Biggio—287 and 282, respectively. However, Biggio is still an active player, so his number could grow.

- From 1885 to 1892, the baseball bat could have one flat side.

- On May 17, 1939, the first televised baseball game took place. It was a college game between Princeton and Columbia broadcast on W2XBS. Princeton won 2–1.

- In 1968, Bob Gibson pitched 13 shutouts (five consecutively). Only two men have ever thrown more shutouts in a single season (George Bradley—a rookie—in 1876 and Grover Cleveland Alexander in 1916 each pitched 16), and no player has thrown more than ten since 1985.

- On April 18, 1956, Ed Rommel was the first umpire to wear glasses in a regular-season game.

Duty Calls,
Ballplayers Respond

*Several baseball players sacrificed for their country
during World War II.*

When World War II broke out, many baseball players stepped up
to the plate to serve. Some were drafted, some volunteered, and
some were called to bring America's pastime to the soldiers to
provide an outlet during the interminable downtime of the military. No matter what their call to duty, all emerged changed men.
Two major-leaguers—Elmer Gedeon and Harry O'Neill—as well
as 40 minor-leaguers were killed. What follows are stories of just
some of the survivors.

Zeke Bonura

Bonura drove in 100 runs four times in seven seasons and was a
.307 career hitter. An Army master sergeant still trying to get back
into the big leagues, he was recalled to the service after Pearl
Harbor. Driven by his passion for baseball, Bonura was an expert
organizer of players, games, ball fields, and equipment from
Mississippi to Algeria. He organized games even as German planes
strafed overhead. Soldiers referred to him as the "Judge Landis of
North Africa." General Dwight D. Eisenhower presented Bonura
with a Legion of Merit for his contribution to military athletics.
Subsequent orders brought him (and baseball) to Italy and France.
There Bonura continued his mission while editing a military sports
periodical, offering personal instruction, and keeping an eye out
for talent as a scout for the minor-league Minneapolis Millers.

Bob Feller

Although many of the game's top stars avoided combat, Bullet Bob
was an exception. Despite being his mother's sole supporter with
no chance of being drafted, Feller enlisted in the Navy the day
after Pearl Harbor. He became an antiaircraft gunner on the USS
Alabama in 1942 and served in the treacherous North Atlantic,

avoiding German U-boats before heading to the South Pacific Theater. There he saw plenty of combat duty in Kwajalein and the Marshall Islands as well as in the "Marianas Turkey Shoot" that destroyed much of Japan's remaining air force. Feller, who'd won 25 games in his last season before the war, won 26 in his first full season back with the Indians in 1946.

Hank Greenberg

By age 29, Greenberg had won the American League MVP twice and placed third the year he hit 58 home runs. Yet a high draft number led him to join the Army Air Corps early in the war. Greenberg had actually been honorably discharged on December 5, 1941 (after being drafted in 1940), but he reenlisted immediately after Pearl Harbor and was put in charge of a bomber squadron in China. After serving nearly five years, Greenberg was among the first baseball stars to return to the game. His home run clinched the 1945 pennant for the Tigers, and he hit .304 with Detroit's only two home runs in its World Series triumph.

Ted Lyons

Lyons joined the Marines 20 years after his major-league debut. Though three years past the maximum draft age of 38, Lyons signed up anyway and was assigned mostly athletic duties. He returned to pitch for the White Sox as the game's oldest player at age 45. He then spent three years managing the Chicago team.

Bert Shepard

Shepard was a minor-leaguer whose plane was shot down during a bombing mission in 1944. A German doctor amputated his leg, but he pitched with a prosthesis and received a tryout with the Senators. He threw 5⅓ innings, allowing just one run in his lone major-league outing.

Warren Spahn

Spahn was 21 years old when he debuted for the Boston Braves in 1942. He made just two starts before spending more than three years as a combat engineer. He took part in the Battle of the Bulge and received a rare battlefield commission for helping take the crucial Remagen Bridge in Germany. Spahn received a Bronze Star as well as a Purple Heart after he was hit with shrapnel. He served another six months in the service after the war, then went on to become the winningest left-hander in major-league history.

Cecil Travis

An excellent hitter before the war, Travis suffered severe frostbite in his legs during the Battle of the Bulge. The Senators were thankful to get the three-time All-Star shortstop back, but he wasn't the same. Travis mostly played third base because of his diminished quickness. Before World War II he was a .327 hitter over nine seasons; after the war he hit .241 and didn't last through 1947.

Ted Williams

Teddy Ballgame had already batted .406, won two batting titles, and averaged 32 home runs and 129 RBI over his first four seasons when he became a Marine pilot. Williams served as an instructor and did not see action in World War II, but he later saw extensive combat and was shot down in Korea. He gave almost five full years to the military and was still among the greatest hitters ever to play the game.

⚾ ⚾ ⚾

"To protect and benefit ourselves collectively and individually. To promote a higher standard of professional conduct. To foster and encourage the interests of . . . Base Ball."

—Preamble for The Brotherhood of Professional Base Ball Players, 1885

⚾ ⚾ ⚾

"May the sun never set on American baseball."

—President Harry Truman, marking the 75th anniversary of the major leagues, February 2, 1951

Can You Put a Price on Greatness?

Who earned more: Babe Ruth or Todd Hollandsworth?

These numbers, when dragged from the years of Cobb and Ruth into the present for inflation adjustments, seem remarkable—and absurd. Babe Ruth making less than Todd Hollandsworth? Wagner, Cobb, and Gehrig all earning less than Ryan Vogelsong? What's going on here?

The difference, of course, is the amount of money baseball takes in nowadays as opposed to the days of old. Back then there was no television revenue, very little radio, and almost no merchandising. Teams had to make do with ticket sales, the profit on the hot dogs and sodas they sold, and what they could make selling players. Today we add stadium naming rights and plush rich kids' boxes, parking revenues, and shares of merchandise earnings. George Steinbrenner bought the Yankees in 1973 for $10 million; today some estimates put the team's value at $1 billion.

Year	Player	Annual pay	Inflation-adjusted value today
1900	NL salary limit	$2,400	$53,170
1910	Nap Lajoie	$12,000	$246,000
1910	Honus Wagner	$18,000	$369,500
1915	Ty Cobb	$20,000	$364,800
1930	Babe Ruth	$80,000	$864,376
1934	Dizzy Dean	$3,000	$42,800
1936	Lou Gehrig	$36,000	$484,800
1939	Joe DiMaggio	$26,500	$656,000
1946	Major-league minimum	$5,000	$51,343
1957	Don Newcombe	$30,000	$206,940

1958	Major-league minimum	$7,000	$45,900
1959	Ted Williams	$125,000	$798,431
1968	Major-league minimum	$10,000	$55,300
1969	Willie Mays	$145,000	$770,000
1970	Major-league minimum	$12,000	$60,454
1980	Nolan Ryan	$1,000,000	$2,540,000
1981	Dave Winfield	$2,000,000	$4,475,000
1988	SL Cardinals median	$240,000	$389,400
1989	Major-league average	$512,000	$798,000
1990	Mark Davis	$2,125,000	$4,759,000
1992	Major-league average	$1,084,000	$1,354,000
1994	Cal Ripken, Jr.	$5,500,000	$6,893,000
1996	SL Cardinals median	$625,000	$758,000
2001	Todd Hollandsworth	$1,450,000	$1,642,000
2001	Major-league average	$2,264,000	$2,451,000
2005	Alex Rodriguez	$26,000,000	$26,000,000
2006	Major-league minimum	$327,000	$327,000
2006	Ryan Vogelsong	$555,000	$555,000
2006	SL Cardinals median	$1,000,000	$1,000,000
2006	Kris Benson	$8,333,000	$8,333,000

All-Time Great

Cy Young

No other pitcher has been so consistently good for so long.

Born: March 29, 1867; Gilmore, OH
MLB Career: Cleveland Spiders, 1890–98; St. Louis Cardinals, 1899–1900; Boston Pilgrims, 1901–08, 1911; Cleveland Naps, 1909–11; Boston Braves, 1911
Hall of Fame Resume: Most wins by a pitcher (511) * Most complete games (749) * Five 30-win seasons * Ten other 20-win seasons * Led league in shutouts seven times * Started 40 games a season 11 times * Six seasons with an ERA below 2.00
Inside Pitch: The last seven batters Young faced in his career hit a triple, three singles, and three doubles.

At one point, Babe Ruth's 714 homers were the career baseball record most people predicted would never be broken. Once Henry Aaron topped it, Lou Gehrig's streak of 2,130 consecutive games became the popular choice. Now that Cal Ripken, Jr., has put that thought to rest, the question arises anew: 511 wins? Twenty-five a year for more than 20 years? Don't worry, Mr. Young, your mark appears safe.

Walter Johnson, Lefty Grove, and others have each been lauded as the greatest pitcher of all time, but Denton True Young's 511 victories remain the benchmark for all hurlers—and far ahead of runner-up Johnson's 417. Pitching in an era when arms often burned out after a handful of 350-inning seasons, Young exceeded that total 11 times over a 14-year span and was a 20-game winner on a record 15 occasions. His 7,354 innings are more than 1,300 ahead of runner-up Pud Galvin, and even his record 316 losses looks secure for the moment.

Growing up just after the Civil War in Gilmore, Ohio, Young picked up his nickname (shortened from "Cyclone") from a minor-league catcher impressed by his speed. The hardy 6'2" farm boy reached the majors with the National League Cleveland Spiders in 1890, and after a 9–7 debut, won 20 or more games each of the next nine seasons. Those early years were spent hurling from a pitcher's "box" some 50 feet from home plate, and when the distance was increased to 60′6″ with a mound added in 1893, the right-hander didn't seem to miss a beat.

The hard-throwing Young led the NL only twice in wins, and he routinely gave up more hits than innings pitched (although that was the norm in the 1890s). Far from dominating in many of his first 11 seasons, his records grew instead through consistency and durability. His best NL years came in 1892 (36–12 with a league-leading nine shutouts and 1.93 ERA) and 1895 (35–10), but it was after joining the Boston Pilgrims of the new American League in 1901 that Young had his most dominating campaigns. Leading the AL in victories his first three years with Boston (going 33–10, 32–11, and 28–9), he had a 1.95 ERA and walked just 127 in 1,098 innings over the span—topping it off in 1903 with two wins as Boston beat Pittsburgh in the first modern World Series.

Author of three no-hitters (including a 1904 perfect game), Young went 21–11 with a 1.26 ERA at age 41. After his career ended in 1911, he lived well over 40 more years, attending old-timer's functions and tossing out the first ball at the 1953 World Series. Others may have been flashier, but when the two major leagues honor their best pitchers each season, they do so with a plaque named for the game's winningest hurler—Cy Young.

⚾ ⚾ ⚾

"I pitched 874 major-league games in 22 years, and I never had a sore arm until the day I quit. My arm went bad in 1912 when I was in spring training, and I guess it was about time."

—Cy Young, *Baseball Digest*, October 1943

⚾ ⚾ ⚾

"Son, I won more games than you'll ever see."

—Cy Young, responding to a youthful reporter

Baseball Lingo

Sprechen sie baseball?

Ace: Top pitcher on a staff. **Origin:** In playing cards, ace is high.

Around the horn: The path of a baseball being thrown around the infield, either following a strikeout, as part of a warmup, or in a double or triple play. **Origin:** Nautical term referring to sailing ships that would pass Cape Horn in southern Chile.

Band box: A small ballpark. **Origin:** From small bandstands frequently found in parks and town squares.

Barnstorming: A tour, often of exhibition games. **Origin:** An old vaudeville term that implied the performers were so eager to strut their stuff they'd even play in a barn during a storm.

Bermuda Triangle: Any area between three or more fielders where a ball drops safely for a hit. **Origin:** Refers to the triangular area in the Atlantic Ocean where, legend has it, numerous boats have mysteriously disappeared.

Billyball: An aggressive style of play. **Origin:** The style favored by former manager Billy Martin.

Bleeder: A safe hit that just eludes the grasp of a fielder. **Origin:** Like blood, it often trickles.

Climbing the ladder: When a pitcher tries to retire a batter by using a series of ascending pitches. **Origin:** Descriptive.

Five o'clock hitter: A player who does his best work in batting practice. **Origin:** Refers to the hour at which batting practice usually takes place.

Gamer: A player who is enthusiastic and aggressive at game time. **Origin:** Descriptive.

Goat: A player held responsible for a loss or poor play. **Origin:** Variation of scapegoat, meaning the one held responsible for a loss, but not necessarily the culprit.

Hot corner: Third base. **Origin:** Scene of hard, pulled hits by right-handed batters.

In his wheelhouse: A pitch precisely where the batter likes to hit it. **Origin:** Nautical term referring to the room where the boat is controlled.

Jake: To beg out of the lineup with a dubious injury, or to fake an injury. **Origin:** Probably refers to Garland "Jake" Stahl, the early 20th-century ballplayer and manager who reportedly begged out of a game citing a sore foot.

Murphy money: Per-diem stipend provided to players for meals and spring-training expenses. **Origin:** Named for Robert Murphy, an attorney who led an unsuccessful attempt to unionize the Pirates in 1946. He did succeed in getting owners to provide the stipend as a preventative measure against future uprisings.

Rubber arm: A pitcher who is, or can be, used frequently. **Origin:** Descriptive of the flexibility and durability of rubber.

Station-to-station: An offense that tends to move baserunners one base at a time, either due to a relative lack of speed or a need to play conservatively. **Origin:** Descriptive of commuter trains.

Walk-off hit: A hit that ends a game, often a home run. **Origin:** Recent term, descriptive of the losing team walking off the field dejectedly. Similar to a sayonara home run.

The Halls of Fame

Baseball history doesn't live just in Cooperstown.

Babe Ruth Birthplace and Museum

Three blocks west of Camden Station (follow the 60 painted baseballs along the sidewalk), Baltimore, Maryland

Here you can see the very room where the Babe drew his first breath, plus a display dedicated to the members of the 500 Home Run Club, a special exhibit tracing the "Curse of the Bambino" through history, and a section called "Babe and Lou" that illustrates Ruth's bumpy relationship with Lou Gehrig.

Braves Museum & Hall of Fame

Turner Field, Atlanta, Georgia

The Ivan Allen, Jr. Braves Museum & Hall of Fame at Turner Field holds more than 600 Braves artifacts and photographs that trace the team's history from its beginning, including exhibits on the 1914 and 1948 World Series, and Babe Ruth as a Brave.

Canadian Baseball Hall of Fame

St. Marys, Ontario, Canada

This shrine pays homage to 78 inductees who have made their mark on Canadian baseball—both historic players such as Fergie Jenkins as well as current Canadian-born big-leaguers.

Cincinnati Reds Hall of Fame and Museum

West side of Great American Ballpark, Cincinnati, Ohio

Professional baseball began here in 1869, and this impressive museum includes memorabilia from that year up until now. One of the most interesting displays is a huge scale model of the "Palace of the Fans," one of the greatest early ballparks (from the 1880s).

Another treat is the "treasures" room, full of the stuff your parents wanted you to throw out years ago (advertising signs, cups, baseball cards, pennants), all plastered with the Reds logo and information.

Louisville Slugger Museum
Louisville, Kentucky

Here's where they turn out bats for everyone from Little Leaguers to the game's greatest stars. And they've been doing it since 1884. Honus Wagner signed on to have them exclusively make his bats in 1905. (He was the first player to have his autograph on the bat.) You can get a bat with your own name on it at the gift shop.

Negro Leagues Baseball Museum
Kansas City, Missouri

Located in the historic 18th and Vine Jazz District of Kansas City, Missouri, the Negro Leagues Baseball Museum houses multimedia computer stations, several film exhibits, hundreds of photographs, and a growing number of baseball artifacts that illustrate the rich history of African-American baseball from the late 1800s through the 1960s.

New England Sports Museum
TD Banknorth Garden, Boston, Massachusetts

Housing one of the most comprehensive collections of film, video, photographs, and research material in North America, this eclectic museum features exhibits from all professional sports played in New England.

Peter J. McGovern Little League Museum
Next to Lamade Stadium, South Williamsport, Pennsylvania

Paying homage to Little League baseball and softball, this museum, located in the birthplace of Little League, houses both exhibits and hands-on sections, such as batting and pitching areas. It even provides the opportunity to do your own play-by-play commentary on a past Little League World Series game.

Sports Legends Museum at Camden Yards
In historic Camden Station at the gateway to Oriole Park, Baltimore, Maryland

Two and a half blocks from the Babe Ruth Birthplace and Museum, this museum highlights the many professional sports teams that have played in Maryland, including the Baltimore Orioles, the Baltimore Ravens, and the Baltimore Colts.

St. Louis Cardinals Hall of Fame Museum
St. Louis, Missouri

Located inside the International Bowling Museum, the St. Louis Cardinals Hall of Fame is the official resting place for St. Louis professional baseball history. Artifacts and information about the team's ten world championships and 16 National League pennants are on display.

Ted Williams Museum and Hitters Hall of Fame
Tropicana Field, St. Petersburg, Florida

The first museum ever dedicated at the time of its opening to a living athlete, the Ted Williams Museum provides an illustrative showcase for some of the most significant triumphs in hitting, with video footage, photographs, and memorabilia.

Ty Cobb Museum
Royston, Georgia

Rare art and memorabilia here includes the medal Cobb was awarded when he won his first of a record 12 batting titles.

Western Pennsylvania Sports Museum
Pittsburgh, Pennsylvania

Its 20,000 square feet of exhibits cover the history of all sports in the area, which means a lot of baseball, including the Negro Leagues. Don't blink or you'll miss movie footage of Ty Cobb and Honus Wagner bantering before a game during the 1909 World Series.

Yogi Berra Museum
Montclair State University, Little Falls, New Jersey

Naturally, one of the greatest Yankees should have one of the best museums. Here you'll find countless relics of the game, including the mitt Berra wore when he caught Don Larsen's perfect game in the 1956 World Series and all the championship rings he won. A must for Yankee fans.

Fast Facts

- An embarrassing situation occurred when Ebbets Field opened on April 5, 1913, in Brooklyn. No one could locate the keys to the gates, leaving thousands of fans roaming outside the ballpark waiting to be seated.

- Jackie Robinson played his first game in the International League on April 18, 1946, for the Montreal Royals.

- The meddling Yankees owner George Steinbrenner paid a known gambler $40,000 for dirt on Dave Winfield—one of his own players, with whom he'd had a falling out. He was suspended and banned from running the day-to-day operations. The gambler went to prison.

- The New York Yankees have won 26 World Series titles. The St. Louis Cardinals are a distant second with ten.

- In 1981, Dodger Fernando Valenzuela was the first player to win the Rookie of the Year and Cy Young Awards in the same season.

- On January 21, 1953, Joe DiMaggio was passed over by the Hall of Fame in his first year of eligibility. In fact, it wasn't until 1955, his third eligible year, that he was voted in.

- Mark Bellhorn and Carlos Baerga are the only two switch-hitters to hit home runs batting from both sides of the plate in the same inning. Baerga did this on April 8, 1993, and Bellhorn on August 29, 2002.

- The Baseball Writers' Association of America's first MVPs were awarded in 1931. The recipients were Frankie Frisch for the National League and Lefty Grove for the American League.

Greatest Games of All Time

1951 NL Playoffs, Game 3

Giants 5, Dodgers 4

The Setting: Polo Grounds, New York

The Drama: The Dodgers had held a 13½-game lead in the National League, but now they found themselves in a playoff series with the crosstown Giants—in the third and final game.

No rivalry in any professional sport has ever surpassed the intensity and wackiness of the one between the New York Giants and Brooklyn Dodgers. And no game typified this brash, brilliant rivalry more than the third game of the 1951 playoffs. It was the culmination of a sensational pennant race featuring the greatest come-from-behind charge to the top ever, which ended the season in a flat-footed tie. Yet the winner would not be crowned until another comeback in the final half of the final inning of the final playoff game, with the outcome ultimately sealed by the most dramatic home run in baseball history—the "Shot Heard 'Round the World."

The Dodgers, who had won the pennant in 1947 and '49 and narrowly missed in '50, were expected to win the National League once again. By the middle of May, they had established themselves in first; the Giants were in second.

But then two important things happened. First, the Giants brought up Willie Mays from Minneapolis, where he was batting .477. Mays had a poor start for the Giants, but manager Leo Durocher made it clear to Willie that the kid would be in center field "as long as I'm the manager." Second, with Mays in center, a place had to be found for Bobby Thomson. He obligingly took over the third base spot, and the team began to click.

By early July, the Giants had moved into second place, but the Dodgers were still comfortably in front. On August 11, in fact, Brooklyn had a 13½-game lead, and Dodger manager Charlie Dressen offered this opinion to a writer: "The Giants is dead."

Durocher's boys didn't take kindly to that. They went on an incredible tear, winning 39 of 47 games, including the last seven of the regular season. It took a 14th-inning home run by Jackie Robinson on the final day of the season to keep the Dodgers from winding up in second. The two teams finished with identical 96–58 records, and the National League prepared for its second-ever playoff, a best-of-three confrontation.

Monte Irvin and Thomson homered off Ralph Branca to give the Giants a 3–1 victory in Game 1 in Brooklyn, but Clem Labine shut them out 10–0 in the Polo Grounds in Game 2. The amazing season was down to one game again.

For Game 3, the teams started their aces: Don Newcombe for Brooklyn, Sal Maglie (nicknamed "The Barber" for his willingness to throw close to batters) for New York. Maglie stumbled in the first, allowing two walks and a single to give the Dodgers a run. After that, he was untouchable for six innings. Newcombe was unscored on until the seventh, when the Giants tallied on a double, bunt, and sacrifice fly.

In the eighth, the Dodgers punched out four singles around a wild pitch and intentional walk for three runs and a lead that looked insurmountable. From his station in the third base coaching box, Durocher had been trying to rattle Newcombe, calling him every name he could think of. But Newk wasn't being affected. He put the Giants down in order in the last of the eighth.

But in the bottom of the ninth, Newcombe tired. Al Dark singled. Don Mueller pushed a single to right past Gil Hodges's outreaching glove. One out later, lefty hitter Whitey Lockman went with a Newcombe outside pitch and comfortably slapped it into the left-field corner. One run scored to make it 4–2, and runners were on second and third.

Dressen called for a new pitcher, and Branca headed in. The second pitch was a high inside fastball, which Thomson muscled down the left-field line. It cleared the fence 315 feet away. The fans went bonkers. Giants broadcaster Russ Hodges screamed, "The Giants win the pennant!" into his mike nine times. The Giants had come back again. No one had ever seen anything like it.

All-Star Quiz

1) Which two future Hall of Fame second basemen were traded for each other in 1926?

A: Rogers Hornsby and Frankie Frisch

2) Which Hall of Famers are the only three pitchers inducted with a losing record in the major leagues?

A: Satchel Paige, Rollie Fingers, and Bruce Sutter

3) Who in the Hall is also a member of the Mexican and Cuban halls of fame?

A: Martín Dihigo

4) Who once pitched two nine-inning complete games on the same day three times in the same month?

A: "Iron" Joe McGinnity (winning all six)

5) Who in the Hall of Fame stole second, third, and home in the same inning four times?

A: Ty Cobb

6) Which Hall of Famer is the only player to play every inning of every game in a season, straight through the World Series?

A: Cal Ripken, Jr. (of course!) in 1983

7) Whose 81-year-old, NL-record 44-game hitting streak did Pete Rose tie in 1978?

A: Willie Keeler

8) Who holds the major-league record with 24 consecutive pitching wins?

A: Carl Hubbell

9) Who is the Hall's only pitcher never to have started a game?

A: Bruce Sutter

A Recipe for Success: Pickled Eels, Dirty Shirts, and Lucky-Sounding Wood

No one is more superstitious than a player on a winning streak.

What makes a baseball team successful? Is it a player who can slug dingers over the fence, a fielder who snags the ball with ease, a pitcher who blazes a flame over the plate? Or is there something more? Many players are firm believers in luck, and they aren't satisfied to let it come to them. Instead they participate in elaborate rituals designed to keep their luck running.

On-Field Rituals

Many well-known baseball superstitions are practiced by everyone from Little League players to Hall of Famers. Step on one of the bases as you leave the field between innings, or spit on your hand before picking up your bat for good luck. Comment on a pitcher's performance when it looks like he might throw a no-hitter, and you're guaranteed to jinx it. These traditions are as much a part of baseball as chewing tobacco, batboys, and the seventh-inning stretch. Said Ralph Kiner, who never stepped on the foul lines, "It didn't help or hurt me. I just didn't want to take any chances."

But other players don't court luck as casually as Kiner. Instead they perform individualized rituals. Some may have evolved from those well-known superstitions, but others are, well, out of left field. For instance, Hall of Famer Clark Griffith thought shutouts were unlucky and went through his first 127 starts without one (in the dead-ball era). He once ordered rookie Frank Chance to drop a pop-up to allow a score and break up his own shutout in a one-sided game. He finally completed one

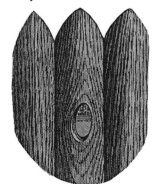

in 1897, then went on to tie Cy Young for the most shutouts in two different leagues in 1900 and 1901. Not so unlucky after all.

Eat, Drink, and Be Lucky

Food can be the key to ensuring a good game. Baltimore Orioles pitcher Jim Palmer had to eat pancakes before every start, while Wade Boggs stuck to chicken. After Lou Gehrig's mom sent a jar of pickled eels to the clubhouse, the Yankees went on a hitting streak—and an eel streak. To ensure the streak continued, each team member, including Babe Ruth, would have at least a few bites of eel before every game. Pitcher Turk Wendell would chew licorice (and brush his teeth) between innings.

For Denny McLain of the Tigers, Pepsi-Cola was his magic elixir. McLain would sometimes drink more than 20 bottles a day, even taking a bottle to bed so he could sip it when he woke up during the night. Despite drinking himself through 31 victories in the 1968 season, McLain was never appointed official spokesperson for Pepsi.

Magical Equipment

Bats receive royal treatment because of the luck they hold. Every baseball fan knows you never lend your bat to another player, and if you need an extra shot of luck, you can always try sleeping with your bat. Some players would make an annual trip to Hillerich & Bradsby Company in Louisville, Kentucky, to ensure that their bat was lucky. Both Ted Williams and Al Simmons would roam the warehouse to pick out the perfect piece of wood for their bat. Williams needed a narrow grain while Simmons swore by the widest. Apparently they were both on to something: Their lifetime batting averages were .344 and .334, respectively.

For Hugh Duffy, whose average was .324, the wood had to sound just right. Duffy would bounce pieces of wood off the concrete, listening for the sound of success only he could discern. Orlando Cepeda wasn't that particular about wood or sound, just as long as his bats were "productive." Cepeda would only use bats that had never made an out. Len Dykstra felt the same way about his batting gloves, throwing them away if he failed to get a hit in a single at-bat.

Since Mark "The Bird" Fidrych was a pitcher, it only seems reasonable that he centered his superstitions around the pitcher's mound. In addition to playing with the dirt, Fidrych would talk to his ball before a pitch.

Don't Go Changing...

Routine is the driving force behind many players' superstitions. If you have good luck, you must do everything exactly the same; if you have bad luck, change, change, change! Many of the routines involve clothing. Rafael Palmeiro wears the same T-shirt under his jersey if he's hitting well. Charlie Kerfeld of the Houston Astros was another member of the T-shirt club. He wore the same George Jetson shirt the entire 1986 season and finished with 11 wins and two losses. Craig Biggio, an Astros second baseman, keeps his luck in his cap. He doesn't wash it all season.

For some, their superstition was their undoing. Blue Jays catcher Rick Cerone wore long johns under his uniform for an April game and promptly began a hitting streak. He refused to abandon the thermals responsible for his good luck even as the season wore on and the temperature climbed. Although he kept his thermals, he didn't keep his luck. His season's batting average was a career-low .239. Cerone could have learned a thing or two from Milwaukee Brewers pitcher Pete Vukovich, who stopped the final game of the 1982 World Series so he could change a shoe. (Mismatched shoes had brought him luck in the past.) Perhaps he should have changed both shoes: The Brewers lost to the St. Louis Cardinals.

Sometimes the rituals work, and sometimes they don't. But that doesn't stop the players from believing in the old ones and creating new ones. After all, you never know....

⚾ ⚾ ⚾

"I never shave on days I'm gonna pitch. I try to look extra mean on those days. It helps me get batters out."

—Cleveland fireballer Sam McDowell, *The Suitors of Spring*

Magical Moments

Reggie, Reggie, Reggie!

The Setting: Yankee Stadium; October 18, 1977
The Magic: Reggie Jackson earns the title "Mr. October" with three homers on consecutive pitches in the Yankees' World Series victory-clinching game.

Reggie Jackson didn't just crave the spotlight—he hogged it. Before he signed with the Yankees, he announced of New York: "If I played there they'd name a candy bar after me." (When he got there, they did.) Upon his arrival in 1977 he told a reporter, "I'm the straw that stirs the drink." And he proved it with one night of amazing power.

The Yankees had returned to the Series in 1976 for the first time in 12 years (a mighty long stretch for the Yanks), only to get stomped in four games. In '77, they led the Series 3–2 over the Dodgers, but the men from L.A. had gone ahead in Game 6 on a solo homer by "the other Reggie," Reggie Smith. With one on and none out in the fourth, Jackson swatted the first pitch he saw from Burt Hooton over the right-field fence, and the Yanks were up 4–3. Jackson came to bat again in the fifth, with a Yank on first and two down. He cracked the first pitch he saw from Elias Sosa even farther back into the right-field stands. Two pitches, two homers for Reggie; Yanks up 7–3. Jackson batted again in the eighth, this time against Charlie Hough. Hough's first offering was his famous knuckleball, and Reggie creamed it. That made three homers on three swings. Jackson became only the second player to knock three dingers in one Series game (Babe Ruth was the other). On that night for sure, Mr. October didn't just stir the drink—he shook it.

Babe Zaharias

Perhaps the greatest female athlete of all time, Babe Didrikson Zaharias left her mark on baseball.

It was the most unusual of baseball showdowns. Two of the 20th century's greatest sports icons stared each other down across a distance of 60 feet, 6 inches. At the plate: Joe DiMaggio, the Yankee legend whose Hall of Fame plaque would one day show three American League MVP Awards, two batting titles, and a record 56-game hitting streak. On the mound: a woman.

But this was no ordinary woman. She was, perhaps, the greatest female athlete of all time. Babe Didrikson Zaharias had been throwing harder, running faster, and playing better than the boys since she was a girl in Port Arthur, Texas. On this day, she was pitching for the barnstorming House of David men's team, a club whose players wore long beards. Zaharias's arm had impressed the team enough that her lack of a beard was easily overlooked.

The details of this legendary face-off between DiMaggio and Zaharias have become cloudy with the passage of time. However, DiMaggio once described it to writer Bert Sugar. "Struck him out on three pitches," Sugar said, the clincher an overhand fastball.

Born Mildred Ella Didrikson, Babe earned her nickname after a Ruthian feat: smashing five home runs during a childhood game. Truth is, baseball was not even her best sport. She set Olympic records at the 1932 Games in Los Angeles, winning the javelin and the 80-meter hurdles and breaking a world record in the latter. She was also a basketball star, a world-class swimmer, and—above all else—a brilliant, big-hitting golfer whose titles included the 1948, 1950, and 1954 United States Women's Opens.

In 1934, Zaharias pitched in two major-league spring training games in Florida. She threw the first inning of a Philadelphia Athletics match against Brooklyn, walking one batter but not allowing a hit. Two days later, she pitched an inning for the Cardinals against the Red Sox, yielding her first runs. She did not bat in either game, but in warm-ups she reportedly chucked a baseball from center field to home plate—a distance of 313 feet.

Sign Language

*Communication between coaches and players is like
a well-choreographed game of charades.*

Anyone who has watched a base coach flash crazy-looking signs to
a hitter knows that baseball has a hidden language. Sometimes,
however, that language isn't really so hidden. Take the case of a
Dodgers player who gave third base coach Preston Gomez a
quizzical look while being given a squeeze-bunt sign and yelled
out, "This pitch?" The squeeze was taken off.

Nonverbal Communication

Coaches convey signs to hitters in a variety of ways—touching a
hand to their ear, to their cap, to their chest. The order of the signs
can mean completely different things from different coaches.
There is no "how-to" book for signaling. Where the coach is standing, how many times he claps his hands, where in a progression of
hand signals a shoulder-touch falls—these can all indicate that a
batter should hit away, take a pitch, or bunt. "It's one of the biggest
parts of baseball," former Mets manager Davey Johnson once said
of this nonverbal communication. "And it always has been."

Baseball historian Paul Dickson estimates that more than
1,000 nonverbal instructions are given in the course of a nine-
inning major-league baseball game. That includes a variety of signs
from catchers to pitchers for every hitter, but it also includes a
number of subtle and not-so-subtle signals from coaches to batters
and baserunners—signals that might be completely lost on the
average fan. A player must watch carefully and be prepared to hit
and run, steal a base, throw to second, or do whatever else the
coach is directing him to do.

Vital Signs

Coaches and managers consider their instructions vital to the
outcome of a game. Former Yankees skipper Billy Martin once
relayed signs via phone from a hospital bed. Legend has it that
Jack McKeon, after being ejected from a game, returned in the

team mascot's uniform and continued calling plays. (McKeon, for the record, denies that story.) After having been ejected from a minor-league game in the Florida State League, Don Zimmer once climbed a light pole and flashed signs from outside the park.

Signs and signals have been around in baseball for more than a century, perhaps for as long as the game has been played. And while the gestures have gone from simple hand waves and numbers-of-fingers to elaborate brushes of the chest, doffs of the cap, and swipes of the sleeve, the most effective signs are still those that are easiest to remember and pick up from the batter's box or the basepaths. Each coach comes up with his own set of signals for the team, so it's his responsibility to make sure the players understand the messages he's sending.

Stealing Signs

Still, signs that are *too* simplistic can lead to easy sign-stealing from the opposing team. The Cleveland Indians of the 1940s were said to have used an elaborate sign-stealing system that included an arm wave from a man in the outfield scoreboard each time a curveball was coming. Other teams have been accused of using everything from old-fashioned telescopes to modern video equipment to swipe opponents' signs, whether from coaches to players or catchers to pitchers.

To combat such tactics, coaches and catchers frequently flash decoy signs that have nothing to do with the called-for pitch or plays. However, these decoys and extra gyrations of the body can fool one's own players, too. And if not executed correctly, they might not even serve their purpose in fooling the opposition.

"If you rush through the decoy signs and go slow when you're giving the real signs, they'll know something is going on," explains Yankees coach and former player Luis Sojo. Players have to pay close attention for an "indicator" sign that lets them know the next sign is not a decoy.

Baseball games can be orchestras of sorts, with managers, coaches, and catchers serving as the conductors. They're trying to create a harmony that only their team can understand. Because in baseball, some of the most compelling strategy is best left unsaid.

Defensive Wizards

The most underrated part of the game has its own set of superstars.

Luis Aparicio
No shortstop in history has played in more games (2,583) than Aparicio. He defined the position for slick glovework until Ozzie Smith came along. He still holds the American League lifetime records for assists (8,016) and putouts (4,548). When he first came to the big leagues, he played very shallow. When he was asked to move back, people were astonished at his arm.

Johnny Bench
Bench put it all together: size, strength, quickness, and a powerful arm. He invented the art of one-handed catching, the perfect style to cut down the newer and faster basestealers of his era (although some old-timers will tell you that the style has ruined every other catcher since). Bench was named an All-Star 14 times, and he won ten consecutive Gold Gloves.

Hal Chase
Some say there was never a better fielder at the initial sack. Smooth and handy, first baseman Chase was often able to charge a bunt, snatch the ball, tag the man heading to first, and then make a strong throw to third to nail the runner. In 1906, he had 22 putouts in a single game, tying a record that still stands. His Achilles' heel was errors, and many were probably intentional. "Prince Hal" was repeatedly accused of throwing games for money or trying to bribe others to do the same.

Roberto Clemente
The Pirate right fielder could get the ball and throw it as well as anyone had ever seen. And no one had ever seen it done with such ferocity, as though each ball hit his way was a personal threat. The list of great Clemente catches and throws is a long one. Particularly memorable was a play early in the 1971 World Series that turned the usually aggressive Orioles into timid baserunners.

Eddie Collins

Collins was the heart of one of baseball's first great infields—the "$100,000 Infield" of Connie Mack's Philadelphia Athletics. He may have been the most complete player of his time, and he played for a long time (1906–30). Nine times he led the American League in fielding average. He's the all-time career leader in assists and chances by a second baseman.

Ray Dandridge

Because African-Americans were banned from playing in the major leagues during his career, most fans never saw the artistry of Dandridge, a man with bowed legs, soft hands, and a superior arm. Roy Campanella once said, "I never saw anyone better as a fielder." In the late '30s, when Dandridge was playing third for the Newark Eagles, someone offered the opinion that the team's infielders would be worth a million dollars if they were white.

George Davis

George Davis was one of the unsung heroes of the 19th century. He started as an outfielder, but his hands and range were such that he was moved to shortstop. He was the star on the "Hitless Wonder" White Sox team that engineered one of the greatest upsets in World Series history—the toppling of the 116-game-winning Cubs in 1906.

Joe DiMaggio

He was grace and elegance personified, and although others (including his brother Dom) put up better defensive stats, Joe DiMaggio patrolled the ominous spaces of Yankee Stadium with remarkable efficiency for a team that hardly ever seemed to lose. DiMaggio was careful to position himself for hitters' tendencies, and his arm was excellent. Joe occasionally neared perfection in his outfield play.

Buck Ewing

Although his name is largely forgotten now, Ewing was considered one of the greatest players (not just catchers) of all time during his

1880–97 stint in the majors. Ewing was said to be the first catcher to throw from a crouch position and the first to back up other bases. He was blessed with a sensational arm. Three times Ewing led his league in assists.

Keith Hernandez
Hernandez put together a string of 11 consecutive Gold Glove titles (1978–88) because he was simply the best of his time. He holds the major-league record for most seasons leading first basemen in double plays (six). Hernandez, like Hal Chase, was known to charge to the third base line on bunts. In the "fielding runs" statistic created recently to compare how many runs are saved by an above-average fielder, Hernandez is the all-time leader among first basemen.

Andruw Jones
While some outfielders are famous for their flashy catches, Jones makes the impossible look like a walk on the beach. As of the 2006 season he had won nine consecutive Gold Glove Awards; no National Leaguer had done that since Ozzie Smith. And Jones has years of baseball left; he broke in when he was just 19.

Jim Kaat
Even though he was a big guy, at 6'4" and 200-plus pounds, pitcher Kaat fielded his position like his idol, the tiny Bobby Shantz. No one was quicker off the mound to snag bunts or cover first. His 16 Gold Gloves tie him with Greg Maddux and Brooks Robinson for the most at any position.

Willie Mays
Perhaps the most complete baseball player ever, Mays stood in center field and dared anyone to hit the ball to him. He could dive, leap, or slide for the tough ones, or use his trademark basket catch on the easy ones. His great catch in the 1954 World Series (one of the first such plays immortalized on film) was just as notable for the unbelievable throw he released after the backward grab.

Bill Mazeroski

The Babe Ruth of defense, Mazeroski holds more defensive records than anyone else who has ever played. He holds major-league records for double plays by a second baseman, with 1,706 (Nellie Fox is a distant second, with 1,568), as well as double plays in a season, with 161 in 1966. Mazeroski led NL second sackers in double plays a record eight times, in chances a league-record eight times, and in assists a record nine times (including five in a row—another record).

Brooks Robinson

Nobody ever did it better at third than Brooks. He holds the highest lifetime fielding percentage among third sackers (.971) and is also the all-time leader in putouts (2,697), assists (6,205), and double plays (618). No wonder he won 16 Gold Gloves and started in the All-Star Game 15 years in a row. His defensive work in the 1970 Series is an absolute classic.

Ivan Rodriguez

"Pudge" Rodriguez redefined the idea of a catcher's arm. He had several seasons where he threw out half of those who tried to steal against him (when around 40 percent is considered good for other catchers). His ability to remove the opposition's running game greatly helped his pitchers. He won ten Gold Gloves in a row, missed two seasons, then won another two.

Ozzie Smith

"The Wizard" was one of the flashiest, most exciting shortstops ever. And he didn't miss the easy ones, either. He leads all shortstops in career assists. No other shortstop has led his league in assists (eight times) or chances (eight) more often. Smith's 1980 record of 621 assists smashed by 20 what was thought to be an untouchable record.

Tris Speaker

A lifetime .345 hitter, "Spoke" played the best outfield anyone had ever seen. Playing a shallow center, he turned an unassisted double play from the outfield a record six times (plus another in the 1912 World Series) in his career. No major-league outfielder ever threw out more runners or took part in more double plays. Only Willie Mays caught more fly balls.

Omar Vizquel

When the last batter in Chris Bosio's 1993 no-hitter attempt grounded to Vizquel, Omar grabbed the ball barehanded and threw him out. Vizquel, who won nine consecutive Gold Gloves, and 11 overall, has been delivering exceptional defense with a flair stylish enough to remind folks of Ozzie Smith, and he's been doing it since 1989.

Honus Wagner

Wagner was so good every place he played that he didn't become a full-time shortstop until he was almost 30 years old. But he still ranks as the best overall shortstop of all time. Built more like a barrel than an infielder, he was incredibly fast, and he had a powerful arm that could throw runners out from anywhere. He won eight batting titles in his career and fielded as well as he hit.

⚾ ⚾ ⚾

"I don't want to embarrass any other catcher by comparing them to Johnny Bench."

—Sparky Anderson, *50th Anniversary Hall of Fame Yearbook*

⚾ ⚾ ⚾

"He took great delight in fielding a base hit in right field with a man on first base and pausing. He'd just stand there, sometimes in deep right, and hold the ball saying, 'Go ahead to third.' Runners wouldn't dare go because Clemente nailed them every time."

—Maury Wills on Roberto Clemente, *On the Run*

Fast Facts

- Jason Bay, the 2004 National League Rookie of the Year, was the first Canadian-born player to win that award. He was also the first member of the Pittsburgh Pirates to earn the honor.

- Nolan Ryan is the only pitcher to have his number retired on three different teams: the California Angels, the Houston Astros, and the Texas Rangers.

- Rod Carew is the only American League player ever to win a batting title without hitting a single home run. He accomplished this in 1972 with a .318 average.

- On September 25, 2001, Jeromy Burnitz and Richie Sexson of the Milwaukee Brewers became the only players in major-league history to both hit three home runs in the same game for the same team.

- In 1934, the Los Angeles Angels of the Pacific Coast League won an all-time organized baseball record of 137 games.

- Active managers Tony La Russa and Bobby Cox are now among the top five managers in lifetime wins, with more than 2,000 victories each. However, they have combined for a total of just three World Series championships. The other managers in the top five are Connie Mack, John McGraw, and Sparky Anderson.

- The first American League pitcher to throw a perfect game was Cy Young on May 5, 1904.

- Vince Coleman of the St. Louis Cardinals missed the 1985 World Series because of a freak leg injury. During the NLCS, the grounds crew started the electronic tarp machine because of rain, not realizing Coleman was on the tarp. The machine rolled over his leg and trapped him, chipping a bone in his knee.

Greatest Teams of All Time

1929–31 Philadelphia A's

Record: 104–46 (1929)
Manager: Connie Mack
Hall of Famers: Mack, Jimmie Foxx, Al Simmons, Mickey Cochrane, Lefty Grove
The Season: The A's finished just 2½ games behind the Yankees in 1928, with a team that included Ty Cobb, Eddie Collins, and Tris Speaker. But the old-timers were pushed aside in '29, and a dynasty was born.
The Legacy: Their 104 wins in '29 were followed by 102 in 1930 and 107 in '31.

Of all the teams that merit ranking in baseball's all-time top ten, the Athletics of 1929–31 were the most complete. They had sluggers who hit both for power and for average, their defense was first-rate, and their pitching was superior. Three of their starting eight those years are now in the Hall of Fame. Their ace pitcher, another Cooperstown resident, might be the greatest lefty of all time. They dominated their NL opponents in two of the three World Series they played. And perhaps most impressive, they had to beat out Babe Ruth and Lou Gehrig's Yankees every year just to get there.

The A's were managed and owned by Connie Mack, the angular patrician who wore a business suit in the dugout—not a baseball uniform. Mr. Mack managed 20 years longer than anyone else ever did, which is why he won nearly a thousand games more than the next most successful manager.

After having caught and played third and first in previous years, Jimmie Foxx was given the first-base job for the 1929 season. He hit .354 with 33 homers and 118 RBI. And he scored 123 times, too. Outfielder Al Simmons swatted 34 circuit clouts himself, led the league with 157 RBI, and batted .365.

But the Athletics' run-scoring was no two-man tag team. Leadoff hitter and second baseman Max Bishop hit just .232, but he walked

128 times, the most in the majors, which drove his on-base percentage up to nearly .400. He crossed the plate 102 times. Along with Simmons in the outfield were Bing Miller and Mule Haas. Miller belted the ball at a .335 clip and drove in 93. Haas hit .313 and knocked home 82. Catcher Mickey Cochrane, such a potent batsman that Mack batted him third in the order (catchers had always been eighth-place hitters), hit for a .331 average and drove in 95.

On the mound, George Earnshaw won 24 games to lead the league, losing just eight. But Lefty Grove had a better winning percentage, topping all other AL hurlers with a 20–6, .769 mark. Thirty-two-year-old Rube Walberg tossed in 18 more victories. Even 45-year-old Jack Quinn won 11. The staff ERA of 3.44 was the best in baseball by a half-run.

The A's toppled the Cubs in the 1929 World Series with dispatch. In Game 4, with the Cubs up 8–0 in the seventh inning of a game that would have tied the Series, they were struck by Philadelphia lightning. The A's ran around the bases to score ten times that inning. Two days later, the Cubs blew a 2–0 lead in the last of the ninth on a Bishop single, a Haas homer, and Simmons and Miller doubles, and the Series was over in five games.

The 1930 season was an instant replay. Foxx batted .335 with 37 homers and 156 RBI. Simmons swatted the ball at a .381 clip to win his first of two consecutive batting titles; he hit one less homer than Foxx and drove in 165. Cochrane's .357 average included 42 doubles. Even defensive specialist Jimmy Dykes joined Miller to top the .300 mark. Grove went 28–5, 2.54 to lead the league in wins and ERA. Earnshaw won 22 and Quinn, now 46, was 9–7. In the World Series, the Cardinals found Earnshaw and Grove nearly unhittable as each won two games. Series to Philadelphia in six.

Then to prove it was no fluke, they did it again. Grove had the greatest season of his great career, winning 31 (16 in a row) and losing just four. His .886 winning percentage was the major-league record for 47 years. He had 27 complete games in 30 starts, and his league-leading ERA was 2.06. Earnshaw won 21 times; Walberg 20. Even the surprising World Series loss to the red-hot Pepper Martin and the Cardinals could not diminish the remarkable achievements of the 1929–31 A's.

For Cubs and Their Fans, There's Always Next Year

We know all about their postseason travails, but for Cubs fans, suffering happens throughout the year.

In failing to win a World Series since 1908 or even make it to the fall classic since just after World War II, the Chicago Cubs have suffered enough late-season collapses to leave their loyal fans feeling as lost as a ball in the ivy-covered walls of Wrigley Field. Then again, dramatic losses are not just a September/October habit for the lovable Cubbies—they've perfected the art in April and May as well.

On April 17, 1976, Chicago held a 13–2 lead over Philadelphia after just four innings at Wrigley, but the Phillies stormed back to go ahead 15–13 on three home runs by third baseman Mike Schmidt. The Cubs evened things up at 15-all in the ninth, but Schmidt untied it with his record-tying fourth homer in the tenth—giving Philadelphia an 18–16 victory.

The Phillies were the visitors once again on May 17, 1979, when Chicago went down 7–0 in the top of the first, answered with six runs in the bottom of the inning, then fell behind 17–6 in the fourth before eventually knotting the game 22–22 through eight innings. Such a comeback deserved a win, but, being the Cubs, they lost 23–22 in the tenth on a homer by—who else?—Mike Schmidt.

A bit less energy but no less frustration was issued on April 21, 1991, when Chicago traveled to Pittsburgh and led a fairly routine game,

3–2, through seven. The Cubs went up 7–2 with four runs in the eighth, but the Pirates countered with four in the bottom of the frame and then scored once more in the ninth to send things to extra innings. After an Andre Dawson grand slam and five runs in the 11th, the Cubs seemingly had the game locked up, but the Pirates scored six of their own in a steady drizzle to win 13–12.

The new century has brought no relief. In 2006, the 99th season since the Cubs' last World Series title, the club showed a prime example of why it would be yet another case of "Wait until next year" at Wrigley Field. Up 4–1 after one inning against the Braves on May 28, they fell behind 11–5 in the sixth before eventually rallying to tie the game with four ninth-inning runs. In the 11th, however, a pop-up by Atlanta's Ryan Langerhans hit third baseman Aramis Ramirez in the head for a two-base error, and Marcus Giles stroked a two-out single for a 13–12 Braves victory. "You think you've seen everything and wonder what else can happen, and something else happens," Chicago manager Dusty Baker said after the game.

Cubs fans everywhere know just what he was talking about.

◎ ◎ ◎

"If you're in professional sports, buddy, and you don't care whether you win or lose, you are going to finish last. Because that's where those guys finish, they finish last."

—Leo Durocher, *Nice Guys Finish Last*

◎ ◎ ◎

"Professional clubs, to keep in existence, must have gate money; to receive gate money, they must play games; and to enable them to play games, their opponents must have faith that such games will prove remunerative."

—Excerpt of letter from Boston manager Harry Wright of the American Association to business executive William Hulbert, backing his plan to form a new "National League," 1875

Temper, Temper, Ty

*Ty Cobb had to be the best at whatever he did, whether it was
hitting a baseball or hitting someone who got in his way.
The Georgia Peach did plenty of both.*

At a function in the late 1950s, a catcher confessed to Ty Cobb
that some 40 years earlier he had used a trick—tagging a runner at
home with two outs and then tossing off his mitt to indicate the
third out, even when the runner was safe—that led to Cobb being
called out at home when he was really safe. It probably happened
seven or eight times, the old catcher chuckled. Cobb reached out
and started strangling the old-timer. "You cost me eight runs!"
Cobb seethed as his hands grew tighter on the man's neck. The
game was never over for Ty Cobb.

He had a burning desire to win, no matter who got hurt or
what it might cost him personally. Cobb was like this at age 18, and
he was that way until a combination of alcoholism, diabetes, and
cancer ended his life in 1961 at age 74. He made millions through
shrewd investments, endowed a hospital and an educational fund
in his hometown in Georgia, and yet lived a miser's life. Cobb
never mellowed, never relented.

Tyrus Raymond Cobb was raised by a disciplinarian father in
Royston, Georgia, among relatives who had served as Confederate
officers in the Civil War. His mother shot and killed his father
accidentally, mistaking him for a prowler. Cobb, 18, was playing
minor-league ball at the time, and the tragedy made the focused
young ballplayer bitter and angry at the world. He debuted with
the Tigers just three weeks after his father was killed. Sam Crawford was there when Cobb arrived in Detroit in 1905.

"Every rookie gets a little hazing," Crawford recalled, "but
most of them just take it and laugh. Cobb took it the wrong way.
He came up with an antagonistic attitude, which in his mind
turned anything into a life-or-death struggle. He always figured
everyone was ganging up against him."

God help anyone who was. In 1912, a heckler in New York
loudly questioned the bigoted Cobb's racial ancestry, and the Tiger

tore into the man. Cobb was suspended from the team indefinitely. His teammates stood up for their meal ticket, refusing to play the next game. Detroit fielded a team of collegians against the A's and lost 24–2, and Cobb told his mates to return. In 1921, Cobb pulverized Hall of Fame umpire Billy Evans under the stands following a game where two calls went against him.

Off the field, accolades were hard to come by. Cobb carried a revolver and was as mean to people on the street as he was to the players in the other dugout. He attacked elevator operators, butchers, and groundskeepers over perceived slights. Three men who tried to steal his Chalmers automobile, the one he'd won in an epic batting race with Cleveland's Nap Lajoie in 1910, were beaten senseless by their would-be victim.

Davy Jones, who played alongside Cobb and Crawford in Detroit's outfield, admitted that he was Cobb's only friend on the team. "He was one of the greatest players who ever lived, but he had very few friends. I always felt sorry for him."

Jones, like Crawford, disclosed his teammate's shortcomings to Lawrence S. Ritter in *The Glory of Their Times,* which was published a few years after Cobb's death. Few dared go on the record maligning or pitying Cobb while he was still alive and kicking.

⚾ ⚾ ⚾

"I recall when [Ty] Cobb played a series with each leg a mass of raw flesh. He had a temperature of 103 and the doctors ordered him to bed for several days, but he got three hits, stole three bases, and won the game. Afterward he collapsed on the bench."

—Grantland Rice, *Cooperstown: Where The Legends Live Forever*

⚾ ⚾ ⚾

"Every great batter works on the theory that the pitcher is more afraid of him than he is of the pitcher."

—Ty Cobb, *The Tiger Wore Spikes*

Eight Hours, 25 Minutes, and 33 Innings to History

A look at the longest professional game of all time.

The longest game in professional baseball history took 33 innings and parts of three days to complete, and while many of the players who suited up for the Class AAA epic between the Pawtucket Red Sox and Rochester Red Wings on April 18, 1981, later saw action in the majors, this is one minor-league contest they would never forget. Both starting third basemen are in the Hall of Fame, as is the scorecard.

The "PawSox"—Boston's top farm club, led by star third baseman Wade Boggs—played host for the game, which began on a cold and windy Rhode Island night before 1,740 fans at McCoy Stadium. They watched the visitors (affiliates of the Baltimore Orioles) take a 1–0 lead in the seventh, but Pawtucket knotted the score in the ninth. And there the seemingly endless string of zeroes on the scoreboard began, altered only with matching "1s" when both teams scored in the 21st.

Conditions grew so frigid after midnight that pitchers broke up benches and lit fires in the bullpen. Umpires could not find a rule about International League curfews, so action continued until league president Harold Cooper was reached by phone and suspended play after 32 innings at 4:07 A.M. on Easter Sunday. At that time only 19 fans remained, and Red Wings third baseman Cal Ripken (like Boggs, destined for Cooperstown) later remembered that it was the only time in his distinguished career that his post-game meal consisted of breakfast.

The 2–2 contest made national headlines, both in the days that followed and when it resumed on June 23. By then Major League Baseball players were on strike, so reporters descended 140 strong on Pawtucket. They were joined by a sellout crowd of 5,746, who waited just 18 minutes before Dave Koza singled in Marty Barrett to give Pawtucket a 3–2 victory in the bottom of the 33rd. All told, 41 players saw action over 8 hours, 25 minutes of play, but only one stat mattered to Pawtucket center fielder Dallas Williams: 0-for-13, the worst one-game batting line ever.

Can of Corn

"When I broke in, they didn't keep track of things the way they do now. These days they have a stat for how many times a guy goes for a cup of coffee."

—Mark McGwire on the habit of sportswriters charting the distance of his home runs, *Sports Illustrated,* August 26, 1996

"Shall I get you a net, or do you want a basket?"

—Red Sox shortstop Heinie Wagner needling Giants shortstop Art Fletcher during the second game of the 1912 World Series; Fletcher had made three errors in the contest

"I know, but I had a better year than Hoover."

—Babe Ruth's response when a reporter pointed out that his 1930 salary demand of $80,000 topped the President's $75,000 salary

"Show me a good loser, and I'll show you an idiot."

—Leo Durocher

"All I could think about was, 'We beat the Yankees! We beat the Yankees!' I was in a kind of daze."

—Pirate Bill Mazeroski on his thoughts as he rounded the bases following his World Series–winning home run in 1960, *Clout! The Top Home Runs in Baseball History*

"You spend a good piece of your life gripping a baseball and in the end it turns out that it was the other way around all the time."

—Jim Bouton, *Ball Four*

All-Time Great

Mickey Mantle

The slugger, speedster, and party animal overcame injury and charmed the fans.

Born: October 20, 1931; Spavinaw, OK
MLB Career: New York Yankees, 1951–68
Hall of Fame Resume: 536 home runs * 1,509 RBI * Named to 16 All-Star teams * Played in 12 World Series * Three MVP Awards * Led league in runs six times
Inside Pitch: Mickey was named after Hall of Famer Mickey Cochrane.

To those who saw him play, Mickey Charles Mantle was something special: a combination of power, speed, and presence possessing so much natural talent that some viewed him as an underachiever despite his titanic accomplishments. A switch-hitter from the time his father pitched to him in the family's Commerce, Oklahoma, backyard, he overcame the bone disease osteomyelitis in his left leg to make the Yankees as a 19-year-old outfielder in the spring of 1951.

Mantle was touted as the next Joe DiMaggio (who, for one year before retiring, played alongside Mantle in the outfield). He recovered from a tough start to have a fine rookie year dimmed only by an injury to his good leg in the Yanks' World Series win over the New York Giants. It was just the beginning of the health hazards that would plague Mantle's career, but as the starting center fielder on the most dominating team in baseball history, Mantle's star rose quickly. He batted .311 his second season, and he had already hit 121 homers by age 23 when he led the AL with 37 in 1955.

Superb defense, blistering power (the term "tape-measure home run" was coined after his 565-foot shot in Washington), and annual totals of 100-plus runs and 90 to 100 RBI were not enough for some fans awaiting the next DiMaggio. Only after putting together an MVP/Triple Crown season in '56 (pacing the league with a .353 average, 52 homers, 130 RBI, 132 runs, and a .705 slugging percentage) did Mantle win everyone over. He hit a career-high .365 with 34 home runs to cop a second straight MVP trophy in '57, and in 1961 he waged a season-long assault against Babe Ruth's record of 60 homers. He wound up six short when he was sidelined in September by a hip infection, and teammate Roger Maris broke the record with his 61st blast.

Mick had become the fan favorite, and when he recovered to win a third MVP prize in 1962 (.321–30–89), it was still thought he might challenge Ruth's all-time record of 714 homers. But injuries (including surgery on one shoulder and both legs) and years of hard drinking had worn down Mantle's body. After a strong year in '64 capped by three World Series home runs (his 18 homers in 12 Series broke Ruth's record), he and the Yankees began a rapid decline. Mantle was in constant leg pain and relegated to first-base duties when he quit in 1968 at age 37.

Mantle's 536 homers, 1,509 RBI, and leadership on seven World Series champions guaranteed him a Hall of Fame plaque, but his perseverance alone became legendary. When he died in 1995, baseball fans who came of age in the 1950s and '60s found themselves questioning their own mortality. If the great Mickey Mantle was vulnerable, they wondered, how safe are any of us?

⚾ ⚾ ⚾

"Nobody is half as good as Mickey Mantle."

—Al Kaline, responding to a young boy who told him he wasn't half as good as Mickey Mantle

⚾ ⚾ ⚾

"You say Mickey Mantle, I'll say Willie Mays; if you say Henry Aaron, I'll say Roberto Clemente. When you're competing at that level of ability, the margins of difference aren't that great."

—Tom Seaver, *The Greatest Team of All Time*

All-Star Classics

From the moment Babe Ruth swatted the first All-Star Game home run to MLB's recent decision to award the winning league home-field advantage in the World Series, baseball's All-Star Game has held an appeal unmatched in other sports.

In 1933, *Chicago Tribune* sports editor Arch Ward set the Mid-summer Classic in motion when, with much prodding, he convinced owners to stage an exhibition between the best of the American and National Leagues. Commissioner Kenesaw Mountain Landis wasn't too keen on the idea until Ward suggested all proceeds be used to augment the pension fund for needy ex-players. The first game, planned to coincide with the Chicago World's Fair, was held on July 6, 1933, in Chicago's Comiskey Park.

Via a newspaper poll, fans from all over the country selected the players to represent the two leagues. The top vote-getter was the A's Al Simmons, followed by Chuck Klein of the Phils. (Philadelphia fans did a lot of voting!) Babe Ruth finished sixth overall. But the Babe didn't let that bother him. In the third inning, with the American League leading 1–0 and Charlie Gehringer on base, Ruth lined a homer to right that opened up the game for good. Baseball's first All-Star Game had been decided by its greatest player.

The game caught on instantly. Over the years, fans have played a large part in choosing the participants, and managers have racked their brains trying to concoct ways to get all their big bats and strong arms into the lineup.

Between 1965 and '85, the National League won 19 All-Star Games while losing just twice. Entering 2007, however, the American League was unbeaten over a stretch of ten years, narrowing the Senior Circuit's overall lead to 41–34–2. The All-Star Game has provided more than its share of drama along the way.

1933: The Babe Gets It Started

It could not have been scripted better. Babe Ruth, 38 years old and in his next-to-last season with the Yankees, socked the first home run in All-Star Game history, a two-run liner in the third inning that powered the American League to a 4–2 lead in Chicago. But the Babe was not finished.

Though not known for his fielding—and certainly not at this stage of his career—Ruth made a fabulous leaping catch in right field to rob Chick Hafey of a hit in the eighth inning. The defensive gem helped preserve the first All-Star Game pitching victory for Ruth's teammate, Lefty Grove.

1934: K-K-K-K-K

"I can recall walking out to the hill in the Polo Grounds that day," the National League's starter, Carl Hubbell, recalled, "and looking around the stands and thinking to myself, 'Hub, they want to see what you've got.'"

One by one, future Hall of Famers stepped to the plate for the American League: Babe Ruth. Lou Gehrig. Jimmie Foxx. Al Simmons. Joe Cronin. And one by one, National League starter Hubbell struck them out in the single greatest performance in All-Star Game history.

Hubbell's five consecutive Ks did not keep the American League from rallying for a 9–7 win. It did, however, leave some of the greatest hitters in the history of the game scratching their heads as they failed to make contact with Hubbell's devastating screwball.

1946: A Splintered Eephus

Back home from the war, which had prompted cancellation of the 1945 All-Star Game, Ted Williams treated his Fenway Park faithful to a classic performance. His 4-for-4, two-homer game remains one of the greatest, and most unusual, in All-Star history.

By the time the Splendid Splinter strode to the plate in the eighth inning, he was 3-for-3 with a home run and an RBI single for the American League, which held a 9–0 cushion. National League pitcher Rip Sewell was on the mound. Williams had warned him not to throw his zany "eephus" pitch—a ball that was lobbed some 25 feet in the air before it fell on a sharp downward plane, often through the strike zone—in a showcase as grand as the All-Star Game itself. But Sewell, smiling, warned Williams that it was coming. And when the eephus crossed the plate, Williams attacked it, stepping up in the box and hammering it over the right-field fence. "He hit it right out of there," Sewell described. "And I mean he hit it."

1949: No More Barriers
The 1949 All-Star Game was not about the score, but the circumstance. Two years earlier, Jackie Robinson had broken baseball's color barrier. Now, for the first time, black players would stand in their rightful place in the game's showcase of its best players.

Robinson, Roy Campanella, and Don Newcombe took the field for the National League, and Larry Doby suited up for the Americans. Robinson, the first African-American to start an All-Star Game, crossed the plate three times, but it was not enough to keep Joe DiMaggio from leading the AL to an 11–7 win.

"The 1949 All-Star Game was a huge step because it proved to baseball and all the naysayers that we were in fact here to stay," said Newcombe 50 years after the milestone day. "By us being chosen to play in that game, it affirmed that African-American players were stars and would continue to be stars and there was nothing anybody could do to stop it."

1955: Stan the Comeback Man
It was the greatest comeback in All-Star Game history. By the time the National League erased a 5–0 deficit to win 6–5, however, it wasn't so much the comeback that people were talking about, but the dramatic blow that ended the game.

Before Stan Musial stepped to the plate to lead off the bottom of the 12th inning in Milwaukee, National League coach Harry Walker pulled the Cardinals star aside and said, "Let's end this now. I'm hungry." Musial made sure it was dinnertime when Boston's Frank Sullivan threw him a mouthwatering fastball, and Stan the Man launched it into the right-field seats to end the game in dramatic fashion.

1970: Playing to Win

In 1970, Ray Fosse was one of baseball's best young catchers, and Pete Rose was on his way to becoming the majors' career hits king. When their paths collided, literally, in one of the most debated moments in the history of the All-Star Game, fate was knocked on its heels.

In the bottom of the 12th inning, Rose came charging home as third-base coach Leo Durocher waved him on. When Amos Otis's throw from center went a few feet up the third base line, Fosse moved up to field it. As he did, Rose, rather than leaping into one of his patented head-first dives, dropped his shoulder and sent Fosse flying, separating the catcher from his glove while Rose tumbled across the plate with the winning run in a 5–4 decision.

Many people chalked it up to Charlie Hustle's aggressive style of play. Others were appalled by the violent contact, particularly in an exhibition game. Fosse sustained a fractured and separated left shoulder that was not diagnosed until the following year, and his career was never the same.

1971: Power Play

Six future Hall of Famers—Hank Aaron, Johnny Bench, Roberto Clemente, Reggie Jackson, Harmon Killebrew, and Frank Robinson—homered to account for every run in the 1971 All-Star Game, a 6–4 American League victory.

Although the AL snapped an eight-year losing streak with the power-fueled triumph, one home run stood out above all else. With one runner on in the third inning, Reggie Jackson laced a Dock Ellis offering high into the Detroit sky for a home run off the Tiger Stadium roof's light tower some 520 feet from home plate. "To this day, I can still see Reggie hit that ball," said National League manager Sparky Anderson of Cincinnati. "It was incredible. I don't know where the ball would have went if the light tower had not been there."

1983: Slammin' Freddy

The 50th anniversary of the All-Star Game was celebrated where it all began—Comiskey Park. And just as the very first edition featured a memorable home run by Babe Ruth, the golden anniversary marked a milestone blast. Hard to believe, but there had never been a grand slam hit in All-Star Game play until the California Angels' Fred Lynn cleared the bases in the third inning.

Lynn's blast off Atlee Hammaker followed an intentional walk to Robin Yount. "I take it personally," Lynn said. It also helped the American League snap an 11-game losing streak with a 13–3 romp.

1984: King Carl Would Be Proud

If the All-Star Game's 50th birthday was a bash, the golden anniversary of Carl Hubbell's memorable five-strikeout run may have been even more remarkable. Fifty years after Hubbell fanned five straight hitting legends, National League aces Fernando Valenzuela and Dwight Gooden did one better, combining to set down six in a row on strikes.

The Dodgers' Valenzuela started the streak in the fourth inning, whiffing future Hall of Famers Dave Winfield, Reggie Jackson, and George Brett consecutively. Gooden, at age 19 the youngest player in All-Star history, relieved Valenzuela in the fifth and used his heat to handcuff the next three hitters: Lance Parrish, Chet Lemon, and Alvin Davis. Their performances led the NL to a 3–1 win in San Francisco.

1999: For Starters, None Better than Pedro

Great pitching performances are nothing new to the All-Star Game. In hitter-friendly Fenway Park, however, Pedro Martinez's efforts in the 1999 edition were a cut above. The Red Sox ace, who entered the game with 15 wins on the season, was surrounded by history on this night. Ted Williams teared up as he threw out the ceremonial first pitch, and baseball's All-Century Team pregame celebration brought out the likes of Bob Feller, Warren Spahn, Stan Musial, Hank Aaron, and Willie Mays.

And then there was Pedro. He struck out the first three NL batters—Barry Larkin, Larry Walker, and Sammy Sosa—and then fanned Mark McGwire to lead off the second inning. The four consecutive strikeouts to start a game set an All-Star Game record, garnering Martinez MVP honors in the 4–1 AL win.

2001: Farewell, Cal

Cal Ripken, Jr., will be remembered for what he did over the long haul—playing in a major-league–record 2,632 consecutive games and providing Baltimore with All-Star shortstop play for the better part of two decades. But this Iron Man will also be remembered for a tremendous one-night performance in the last of his 18 All-Star Games.

The 40-year-old received a long standing ovation when he came to bat for the first time in the bottom of the third inning and another when he sent Chan Ho Park's first offering over the left-field fence, becoming the oldest player in All-Star Game history to hit a home run. His efforts led the AL to a 4–1 win, earned game MVP honors for Ripken, and prompted one of the most emotional curtain calls ever for a man who had taken many of them in his career. "I tried to acknowledge [the fans] very quickly because I didn't want the game to be delayed for that," Ripken said.

2002: The Tie Goes to the . . . Well, Who Wants It?

It was an amazing game with an anticlimactic outcome. In fact, calling the outcome anticlimactic is an understatement. After 11 innings and some terrific baseball, with both teams out of players on their 30-man rosters and the bullpens depleted, commissioner Bud Selig and managers Bob Brenly and Joe Torre decided to call the game. With that, the 2002 All-Star Game was declared a 7–7 draw, prompting chants of "Let them play!" from the capacity crowd at Milwaukee's Miller Park.

The decision was the subject of fan debate and disappointment in the coming days. It also put a damper on an otherwise spectacular showcase that featured 25 hits, home runs by Barry Bonds and Alfonso Soriano, and one memorable deep fly to center by Bonds that was headed over the wall until Twins star Torii Hunter leaped up and pulled it back for an out.

"The fans got to see the stars, they got to see good pitching, good hitting, great plays," said Hunter's teammate, reliever Eddie Guardado. "The only thing they didn't get to see was a winner."

Steve Dalkowski: The Best That Never Was

The most incredible pitcher no one's ever heard of.

Statistics don't always tell the whole story about a baseball player, but in the case of Steve Dalkowski—widely acknowledged as the fastest, wildest pitcher in history—they do a pretty good job.

Take 1960, for instance, when the left-hander was with the Stockton Ports, Class C affiliate of the Baltimore Orioles. In just 170 innings, he struck out 262 batters, *walked* another 262, and hit countless backsides and backstops throughout the California League. Or how about the 1957 game when he had 24 strikeouts and 18 walks? He had 39 wild pitches in 62 innings that year.

The picture is clear, even if the numbers are almost unfathomable. Dalkowski is the most incredible pitcher few people have ever heard of, simply because he never made the major leagues. His lifetime stats of 995 innings, 1,396 strikeouts, 1,354 walks, and a 46–80 record from 1957 to 1965 were compiled predominantly in the low minors, as the Orioles kept hoping he would harness his incredible gift.

Just 5′11″ and about 170 pounds, with thick glasses and an easygoing manner, the New Britain, Connecticut, native couldn't fully explain how he threw a fastball an estimated 105–110 miles per hour—5 to 10 mph faster than anybody else. Dalkowski was never accurately timed in the pre–radar gun era; once, throwing at a makeshift device with a laser beam, he took about 40 minutes to hit the beam and clocked in at an exhausted 93.5.

Steve admitted his fondness for booze didn't help him any. He also suffered from over-tinkering, and with this in mind, minor-league manager Earl Weaver used a patient, simpler approach with Dalkowski during the 1962 season at Class A Elmira. Weaver sent him to major-league spring training in '63, and "White Lightning" was dominating big-league batters when he felt a pop in his elbow during an exhibition game. The Orioles uniform he had been fitted for that same day would not be needed—then, or ever.

Fast Facts

- Hall of Fame player Frank Robinson was the first black manager in the majors, but the Blue Jays' Cito Gaston was the first black manager whose team won the World Series.

- Roger Maris didn't hit the first home run of his record-breaking 1961 season until April 26, two weeks in, though before September 1 he had hit 51. He was the only player to reach 50 home runs before September 1 until Sammy Sosa and Mark McGwire did so in 1998.

- The only pitcher to save three All-Star Games was Dennis Eckersley, in 1988, 1990, and 1991.

- Abner Doubleday, credited (erroneously) with the invention of baseball, is also credited with firing the first shot of the Civil War.

- Babe Ruth hit his first career home run at the Polo Grounds against the New York Yankees on May 6, 1915.

- On August 6, 1930, Gene Rye of Waco in the Texas League launched three home runs in one inning.

- There have been 12 unassisted triple plays in major-league history. Most were accomplished by shortstops or second basemen catching a liner, touching second base, and then tagging the runner coming from first. Only two were turned by first basemen.

- Philadelphia is the only city to produce two Triple Crown winners in the same season. Chuck Klein for the Phillies and Jimmie Foxx for the Athletics both won in their respective leagues in 1933.

- In 1928, the Hollywood Stars of the Pacific League became the first team to travel by air.

Stars of the Negro Leagues

*Real or exaggerated, the great Negro League performances
are surrounded by a legendary aura.*

Most of the numbers can't be found in record books. The documentation simply doesn't exist. Many of the tales cannot be read in newspaper or magazine clippings. Negro League baseball games were not covered with the same media blanket as their major-league counterparts, leaving many of the best stories to be passed from one generation to the next by word of mouth.

This is both the curse and the blessing of the Negro Leagues. While it's a shame the records and statistics, in many cases, don't hold up to encyclopedic accuracy, there's a certain charm and reverence in the way these heroes have had their remarkable stories told and retold.

The Black Babe Ruth

Josh Gibson, without a doubt, would have challenged major-league home run records had he been given the chance to swing his mighty bat against white contemporaries. The "Black Babe Ruth" is said to have hit as many as 962 home runs in his career, though some came against semipro competition.

In Negro League games, the number is agreed to be in the vicinity of 800—nearly 50 more than Hank Aaron's major-league record of 755. In 1936, one year before he traded his Pittsburgh Crawfords jersey for the Homestead Grays, Gibson is said to have hit 84 round-trippers, 11 more than Barry Bonds's big-league record.

It was not only the frequency of Gibson's home runs that stood out. Some say he once hit a ball right out of Yankee Stadium, making him the only man in history to do so. A taller tale has him hitting a ball so far in Pittsburgh that it dropped into an outfielder's glove in Philadelphia the next day, prompting an umpire to declare, "You're out! Yesterday in Pittsburgh."

Said Hall of Famer Monte Irvin, "I played with Willie **Mays** and against Hank Aaron. They were tremendous players, but they were no Josh Gibson."

Speaking of Home Runs...

Dale Long, Don Mattingly, and Ken Griffey, Jr., share the major-league record of belting home runs in eight consecutive games. Had any of them extended their streaks by three more games, they would merit mention with John Miles's feat of 1948. Stated Negro League historian Dean Lollis, "You can take the greatest home-run hitters in baseball history—Babe Ruth, Hank Aaron, Willie Mays, Mark McGwire, Sammy Sosa, Barry Bonds—and even in their greatest years, they never came close to that streak."

Miles, a tall man with long arms and big, strong wrists, could not recall the locations of those 11 consecutive games. His team, the Chicago American Giants, played almost all of their games in major-league parks, such as Comiskey Park, the Polo Grounds, and Yankee Stadium, so the legitimacy of the accomplishment is seldom questioned.

Speed Kills

By his own count, James "Cool Papa" Bell once stole 175 bases in a 200-game season. The dazzling leadoff man, baserunner, and center fielder hit .400 or better several times. He once forfeited a Negro League batting title to Monte Irvin to increase Irvin's chances of being allowed to play in the majors.

Two tall tales were Bell's most lasting legacies. Fellow Negro Leaguers liked to say that this Mississippi native was so fast he could turn out the light and be tucked in bed before the room got dark. They also said that he once hit a ball up the middle and was called out because it hit him as he was sliding into second base.

Tales from the Mound

Of course, Satchel Paige is widely considered the greatest pitcher of the Negro League era. He dominated major-league hitters in exhibition games, fared well against them when he finally got his big-league chance at age 42, and made a career out of entertaining fans, not only with his deep repertoire of first-rate "stuff" and crazy trick pitches, but also as a showman.

Bell once said Paige "made his living by throwing the ball to a spot over the plate the size of a matchbook." Satch, as he was called, threw so many no-hitters in his 1,500 (or more)-game career that somewhere along the line the count was lost. He is said to have tossed more than 300 shutouts, but that, too, is a number that will never be verified.

Paige was hardly the only pitcher with an amazing tale. "Smokey" Joe Williams, pitching for the Homestead Grays at age 44 in 1930, once struck out 27 Kansas City Monarchs in a 12-inning, 1–0 victory. He is said to have pitched dozens of no-hitters himself. "If you have ever witnessed the speed of a pebble in a storm," Leland Giants owner Frank Leland once said of Williams, "you have not seen the equal of the speed possessed by this wonderful Texan."

The Unsung Iron Man

One of the Negro Leagues' most robust accomplishments came from a man who stood only 5′8″ and weighed 160 pounds. Larry Brown arrived from Pratt City, Alabama, as a 17-year-old catcher for the Birmingham Black Barons and gained acclaim as one of the greatest defensive backstops of all time.

If Lou Gehrig was the "Iron Horse" and Cal Ripken, Jr., was baseball's record-setting "Iron Man," Brown deserves a metallic nickname as well. In 1930, he reportedly caught 234 games in one season. No one knows how many consecutive games he played in during a career that spanned more than four decades and ten teams, but it would likely compare with the well-documented streaks of Gehrig (2,130) and Ripken (2,632).

And, like his durable white counterparts, it was not only the number of games played by Brown that was impressive, but also the quality of his performance. He led his clubs to three championships and played in six East-West All-Star Classics while calling games for the likes of Paige, Willie Foster, and Ted "Double Duty" Radcliffe. "He was strong as an ox and could throw bullets to catch stealing baserunners," Radcliffe said of Brown.

Although we'll never know the exact numbers racked up by these legends of the Negro Leagues, their talent and feats can never be disputed.

Chatter

"I honestly feel that it would be best for the country to keep baseball going... if 300 teams use 5,000 or 6,000 players, these players are a definite asset to at least 20,000,000 of their fellow citizens—and that in my judgement is thoroughly worthwhile."

—President Franklin Delano Roosevelt's "green light" letter to Judge Kenesaw Mountain Landis, January 15, 1942

"I don't want to take anything away from Dr. [Martin Luther] King [Jr.]. But through baseball, Jackie did more to segregation, hotels, and sports arenas than any other man."

—Don Newcombe, *Baseball Quotations*

"Only in baseball can a team player be a pure individualist first and a team player second, within the rules and the spirit of the game."

—Branch Rickey, *The American Diamond*

"Look at it. 'World Series. Saturday. 8 P.M.' Nice. That is nice."

—Yankee manager Joe Torre, observing the marquee outside Yankee Stadium, *Sports Illustrated*, October 28, 1996. Torre had waited 36 years as a player and manager to reach his first fall classic.

"Nobody taught me about hitting. I learned."

—Ted Williams, *Voices From Cooperstown*

"Baseball is the very symbol, the outward and visible expression of the drive and push and rush and struggle of the raging, tearing, booming nineteenth century."

—Mark Twain, 1889

"Against that guy, we should all get four strikes."

—Anonymous batter on facing Sandy Koufax

Greatest Games of All Time

1960 World Series, Game 7

Pirates 10, Yankees 9

The Setting: Forbes Field, Pittsburgh, PA

The Drama: Five lead changes, three clutch home runs, bizarre fielding along with baserunning genius—this has to be the greatest seventh game of all time.

Out of 102 World Series, only 35 have gone to the limit. Most of those final games were not terrifically close, nor very exciting. Only 13 were decided by one run. Of those 13 one-run seventh games, one stands out for having the least likely script of all: Game 7 of the 1960 Series between the New York Yankees and Pittsburgh Pirates.

When Rocky Nelson homered for the Pirates with Bob Skinner on first in the bottom of the first inning, Pirates fans may have seemed relieved, but they couldn't get too cocky. They knew this Yankee club could score. (In their three Series matchups, the Yanks had pulverized the Pirates 16–3, 10–0, and 12–0.) The Bucs tacked on two more in the second for a 4–0 lead, but the hair-raising roller-coaster ride was just getting started.

Through the first four innings, Pirates starter and Cy Young winner Vern Law allowed only two singles. A fifth-inning homer by Bill Skowron put the Yanks on the board. Yankee power exploded in the sixth. After a single and a walk, Law was replaced by Roy Face. After one out, Mickey Mantle singled, and Yogi Berra crushed a three-run homer. The Yankees had taken the lead, 5–4.

Face disposed of the first two Yankees in the top of the eighth, then walked Berra. Two singles and a double later, the New Yorkers had quickly extended their lead to 7–4. The Pirates were three runs down with just six outs to go. A leadoff single by pinch-hitter Gino Cimoli got the eighth off and rolling for Pittsburgh. The next batter, Bill Virdon, chopped down on a pitch and grounded it toward short, a likely double-play ball. But Yank shortstop Tony Kubek, uncertain how to play the wicked hops of the notorious Forbes Field infield, hesitated, moved back, then in, and the ball hit him in the throat. Both runners were safe with nobody out.

Dick Groat, National League bat champ and MVP, rapped a single to left, scoring Cimoli. Yanks hurler Bobby Shantz was replaced by Jim Coates. A sacrifice bunt moved runners to second and third, and then Nelson hit a short fly-out. The Bucs' last chance was Roberto Clemente, hitless in this game. Clemente chopped one to first, where Skowron gloved it and waited to toss to Coates for the third out. But Clemente was in full flight, and he outhustled the pitcher to the bag. Another run in, 7–6 Yanks.

Hal Smith, a former Yankee farmhand, got around on a pitch from Coates and powered it over the left-field wall. Three Pirates scored, and the Bucs had turned the tide once again. Now they took a 9–7 lead into the top of the ninth.

But the Yankees weren't done, either. To try and end the Series, Bucs manager Danny Murtaugh brought in Bob Friend, the burly right-hander who had won 18 games in the regular season but who had been no puzzle for Yank batters; they had swatted him around for 11 hits and eight runs in just six innings of work. Bobby Richardson and former Pirates slugger Dale Long quickly rapped singles, and Harvey Haddix entered the game in relief.

With one out, Mantle singled in Richardson, and the score was 9–8 Bucs. Then Mantle provided one of the most electrifying moments in World Series history. Berra lined a one-hopper down the first base line that Nelson speared. He stepped on first and then raised his arm to throw to second for the tag on Mantle that would end the Series.

But Mantle had not gone to second. His remarkable instincts sent him back to first, where his diving dance-step kept him away from Nelson's attempted tag. This allowed the runner on third to score, and the Yanks had impossibly tied the score at nine runs each.

Then second baseman Bill Mazeroski, a great fielder, opened the last of the ninth with a home run over the left-field fence. The Pirates had won a World Series in highly improbable fashion. Shortly afterward, New York fired manager Casey Stengel.

Fanning the Flames

Sometimes players and fans cross the line that separates
participants from spectators—and end up with ugly results.

Don't Mess with Babe
Senators at Yankees, 1922

Mired in a slump, Babe Ruth tried to stretch a single into a double at the Polo Grounds, was called out at second base, and threw dirt in the face of umpire George Hildebrand. The Babe was ejected and booed by the home fans. One called the Yankees slugger a bum and, according to Ruth, "other names that got me mad." Ruth went after the heckler in the stands. Once the man ran out of reach, Babe returned to the top of the dugout and screamed, "Anyone who wants to fight, come down on the field! Ah, you're all alike, you're all yellow!"

Rocky, Outside the Ring
Tigers at Yankees, 1961

Although many Rockys have graced the boxing ring over the years, it was baseball's Rocky Colavito who did some of the most notable battling in 1961. The former Indians slugger, who'd been very popular with Cleveland fans, wasn't as well received as a Tiger, and the pressure apparently got to him. He once went after an official scorer who charged him with a controversial error. Then, at Yankee Stadium, a drunken fan crossed him, heckling Colavito about his wife and father. The outfielder climbed into the stands behind third base to attack the man, earning an ejection.

Getting His Kicks
Indians at Yankees, 1961

A few weeks after Jimmy Piersall kicked a fan who approached him at Yankee Stadium (Piersall said he thought the man could have been wielding a knife), two teenage fans charged the Indians outfielder in the first game of a doubleheader at the same site. He dropped the first one with a punch, then chased the other but was too far out of reach to land another swift kick. No matter. Piersall's teammates and the police helped out. Asked if he wanted to press charges against the fans, Piersall refused, saying, "I've had 117 fights, and that's the first time I've ever won."

Jekyll or Hyde? Hard to Tell
Dodgers at Giants, 1981

Reggie Smith, a fine player and normally quiet man, could only take so much harassment. Michael Dooley, a 6'4", 218-pound Giants fan, had been taunting the Dodgers outfielder from behind the Giants dugout. "You stink! You have no class!" Smith recalled the heckler saying. Smith could tolerate the verbal barbs, even tossing a few back. However, when the fan threw a souvenir batting helmet at him in the sixth inning, Smith climbed into the stands and landed a solid punch on Dooley that tipped off a five-minute fracas between Dodger players and Giant fans. Eight fans were taken into custody, and Dooley was treated for injuries at Stanford University Hospital.

Belle's Bull's-Eye
Angels at Indians, 1991

From his seat in the left-field stands, a fan taunted Cleveland outfielder Albert Belle, inviting him to a keg party after Belle had completed a ten-week stay in an alcohol rehabilitation program. In response, the Indians slugger picked up a foul ball in the seventh inning, turned, and unleashed a laser into the fan's chest from 15 feet away. Belle had his one-week suspension reduced to six games on appeal and was ordered to pay $3,846—one week's salary—to a charity of his choice.

"Nasty Boy" Scores Takedown
Astros at Cubs, 1995

When he pitched for Cincinnati, reliever Randy Myers was one of the "Nasty Boys" trio (along with Rob Dibble and Norm Charlton). After giving up a two-run, eighth-inning home run to Houston's James Mouton in a 1995 game at Wrigley Field, Myers used his martial arts background to deliver a nasty blow to a fan who charged the mound. "He reached for his pocket, and I thought it could be for a knife or a gun, so I dropped him with a forearm," Myers said. He expertly kept Murray pinned to the ground, holding his hands in place, until teammates rushed to help.

Unhappy Homecoming
Astros at Brewers, 1999

Bill Spiers used to play for the Brewers, but he was back in Milwaukee as an Astros outfielder when a fan ran onto the field and jumped him. Said Spiers, "I looked down and saw blue jeans wrapped around my neck. I couldn't move, so I fell down backwards trying to get him off me." Mike Hampton and other teammates came to the rescue. Hampton delivered some hard kicks to the instigator, who was arrested and held on $250,000 bail. Spiers tried to stay in the game despite scrapes, bruises, and whiplash but was removed in the next inning.

Hats Off, But Dodgers Object
Dodgers at Cubs, 2000

In the ninth inning of a game at Wrigley Field, a Cubs fan swiped rival catcher Chad Kreuter's cap and may have hit him as well, while others doused the Dodgers bullpen with beer. Kreuter went after the main offender, and some of his teammates followed. Chaos ensued for several minutes. Nine days after the Dodgers 6–5 win, Major League Baseball suspended 16 players and three coaches for their involvement, though some of the suspensions were reduced on appeal. The moral of the story? "If you wanted a hat that bad, be polite and ask for one," said Dodger Todd Hundley.

Not One of His Best Pitches
Rangers at Athletics, 2004

Oakland fans had been taunting the Rangers bullpen, so pitcher Frank Francisco made the ill-fated decision to take matters into his own hands. More specifically, he took a plastic folding chair and threw it toward the hecklers. The chair hit a man in the head, then a woman in the face, breaking her nose. Francisco, facing a misdemeanor assault charge, pleaded no contest and was sentenced to a work program and anger management classes.

"I Can Pitch Forever"

When the Providence Grays lost one of their two pitchers to a rival franchise in 1884, Charley "Old Hoss" Radbourn literally took matters into his own hands.

Charley "Old Hoss" Radbourn had a rubber arm and an iron will. When his team, the Providence Grays, found themselves without one of their pitchers in 1884, the gritty right-hander made a deal with team owners: He would pitch the rest of the season, he said, but if the Grays won the National League pennant, he'd get a bonus and the right to free agency.

So began one of baseball's most remarkable tales of endurance: When it was all over, the Grays were pennant winners, and Radbourn had logged 73 starts—including a stretch of 19 consecutive starts and wins—and 678⅔ innings, just four outs short of Will White's all-time record of 680 innings, set in 1879. Radbourn's 59 victories that year are an all-time record and six more than his closest challenger. Radbourn then pitched three straight victories over American Association champion New York, sweeping the Mets in what some consider the first World Series. He collected a $2,000 bonus (more than $40,000 by today's standards) and then re-signed with Providence in 1885.

Radbourn's stamina was outstanding even in his day, an era when teams carried two pitchers, 30-win seasons weren't uncommon, and the concept of relief pitching was barely developed. Radbourn tried to conserve his achy arm using a variety of deliveries, but the strenuous workload took its toll nonetheless; the dependable Old Hoss reportedly had difficulty combing his hair before and after games.

The record feats of rubber-armed 19th-century hurlers such as Radbourn and White get safer every year. Bill Hutchison, who threw 622 innings in 1892, was the last pitcher to surpass 600—and 500—innings in a season. Ed Walsh in 1908 was the last 400-inning pitcher. And it's been more than a quarter-century since Steve Carlton in 1980 was the last player to throw more than 300 innings in one year.

The Black Sox

*Baseball's Golden Age was preceded by its darkest hour: the
1919 World Series–fixing scandal in which Shoeless Joe Jackson
emerged as a shameful symbol. Though acquitted by a jury,
Jackson and his co-conspirators were convicted in the court of
public opinion and banned from baseball for life.*

The *Chicago Herald and Examiner* described him as "a little
urchin," the young lad who emerged from the crowd outside a
Chicago courthouse on that September day in 1920 and was said
to have grabbed Joe Jackson by the coat sleeve. The newspaper's
report of the exchange went on:

"It ain't true, is it?" the lad said.

"Yes, kid, I'm afraid it is," Jackson replied.

"Well, I'd never have thought it," the boy exclaimed.

Nowhere did the newspaper report that the boy demanded,
"Say it ain't so, Joe," although this version of the story became the
standard that was passed down through the years among generations of baseball fans. Almost three decades later, a few years
before his 1951 death, Jackson told *Sport Magazine* that the entire
story was a fictional account, made up by a sportswriter. He said
the only words exchanged on the way out of the courthouse that
day were between him and a law enforcement officer. Had there
been such a boy, Jackson added, he would have told him, "It ain't
so, all right, just like I'm saying it now."

What is so is this: Members of the 1919 Chicago White Sox
committed baseball's cardinal sin, deliberately losing the World
Series to the Cincinnati Reds for pay. Eight members of that team,
including the great and graceful "Shoeless" Joe Jackson, were
banned from baseball for life for their part in the scandal.

Two years after their 1917 world championship, the White Sox
fielded a powerful team that took the American League pennant.
The White Sox were favored to defeat Cincinnati in the World
Series—heavily favored, in some gambling circles.

By all accounts, Sox infielder Chick Gandil was the ringleader
among the "Black Sox"—the man who made contact with known

gamblers and indicated that the Series could be thrown. He immediately involved 29-game-winner Eddie Cicotte, and others followed: Jackson, pitcher Claude Williams, infielders Buck Weaver and Swede Risberg, outfielder Oscar "Happy" Felsch, and utility man Fred McMullin. Some of the players would play lead parts in the fixing of games. Others, notably Weaver and some say Jackson, had knowledge of the plan but were not active participants.

When the Series began, the players were promised a total of $100,000 to throw the games. But by the time the Reds won the Series in eight games, the payout was considerably less, and whispers about what had taken place began swelling to a roar. Sportswriters speculated in print about a possible fix even before Cincinnati wrapped up the Series, but nobody wanted to believe it could be true. No official action was taken, however, until the following September.

The 1920 season began with rumors about gambling in other big-league dugouts. Something had to be done, and in September a grand jury convened to examine allegations of other instances of gambling in the game—and soon looked at the 1919 World Series as well. Eight White Sox players were called to testify, and several, including Jackson, admitted knowledge of the fix. All eight were indicted for conspiracy to defraud the public and injure "the business of Charles Comiskey and the American League." Although the group was acquitted due to lack of evidence when Jackson and Cicotte's testimony "disappeared," the damage had already been done in the form of huge black headlines across the country. Baseball, America's game, was facing its darkest hour.

The Black Sox were not as fortunate on the scales of baseball justice as they had been in the court of law. Kenesaw Mountain Landis, baseball's newly appointed commissioner, suspended all eight players for life in an effort to restore credibility to the game. It was a crushing blow for Chicago, and for Weaver and Jackson in particular. While Gandil had received $35,000 and Cicotte $10,000 for the fix, Weaver received nothing. Actually, it was proven that he had turned down an invitation to participate in the scam. And Jackson, considered one of the greatest outfielders and hitters—and certainly one of the most sympathetic figures—in the history of the game, hit .375 with six RBI in the 1919 Series while playing errorless defense.

Many still clamor for Shoeless Joe to be enshrined in the Hall of Fame, arguing that his numbers support the claim that he did nothing to contribute to the fixing of the 1919 World Series. The $5,000 he accepted from the gamblers, however, nearly matched his $6,000 salary during that campaign and sealed his fate as a tragic figure in baseball's most infamous 20th-century scandal.

Say it ain't so, Joe.

It is.

"The idea staggered me . . . it never occurred to me that one man could start to play with the faith of fifty million people—with the single-mindedness of a burglar blowing a safe."

—Character Nick Carraway describing the 1919 Black Sox scandal
in *The Great Gatsby*

". . . Worthless, dissipated gladiator; not much above the professional pugilist in morality and respectability. To employ professional players to perspire in public for the benefit of gamblers . . . furnishes to dyseptic moralists a strong argument against any form of muscular Christianity."

—*The New York Times* editorial condemning baseball and its
players as all things evil, March 8, 1872

". . . the toughest of the toughs and an abomination of the diamond . . . a rough, unruly man . . . he uses every low and contemptible method that his erratic brain can conceive to win a play by a dirty trick."

—Umpire John Heydler on player-manager John McGraw, 1890s

Fast Facts

- The World Series champion with the poorest regular season record was the 2006 St. Louis Cardinals, who finished just 83–78.

- Several times in 1959, Elroy Face gave up the tying or lead run; his impressive single-season winning percentage of .947 (18–1) only came about because his team (the Pittsburgh Pirates) came back to score with winning runs for him.

- On June 6, 1892, Benjamin Harrison became the first sitting U.S. president to attend a major-league game. The game went into extra innings, and Cincinnati beat the Washington Senators 7–4.

- The 1970 Pittsburgh pitching staff might have been mistaken for a butcher shop. It included players named Moose, Lamb, and Veale.

- During a doubleheader on May 2, 1954, Stan Musial became the first player to hit five home runs on the same day.

- Richie Ashburn hit the same fan twice with foul balls in the same at-bat on August 17, 1957.

- Willie Mays is the only member of the 500 home run club to hit his first homer off a future Hall of Fame pitcher (Warren Spahn). Sammy Sosa, another member of the club, hit his first homer off Roger Clemens, who will certainly be a Hall of Fame pitcher, too.

- In 1979, Garry Templeton of the St. Louis Cardinals became the first player to get 100 hits batting from each side of the plate.

- Prior to 1931, balls that bounced over or through the fence were considered home runs.

All-Time Great

Joe DiMaggio

His record of hitting safely in 56 consecutive games is a perfect metaphor for his style of play—quiet, consistent excellence.

Born: November 25, 1914; Martinez, CA
MLB Career: New York Yankees, 1936–42, 1946–51
Hall of Fame Resume: Batted .340 or better five times * Hit 13 or more triples four times * Hit 30 homers or more seven times * Led league in homers and RBI twice; triples and runs once each
Inside Pitch: Joe could have been a Yankee a year earlier, but the cash-poor San Francisco Seals, who owned his contract, figured they could get more for the sale if he played an extra year for them.

He was the most regal of performers during his career with the New York Yankees, and the quiet, somewhat mysterious way he carried himself outside the game only added to the sense of elegance surrounding Joe DiMaggio. Upon first coming to the Yankees in 1936, DiMaggio was no early candidate for nobility. This poor son of an Italian fisherman had what reporters called "squirrel teeth" and the naïveté to believe a "quote" was some kind of soft drink. Asked for plenty of "drinks" after hitting .323 with 44 doubles, 15 triples, 29 home runs, and 125 RBI his rookie season, he outdid even the great Lou Gehrig his second year, leading the league with 46 homers (15 in July alone), 151 runs, and a .673 slugging average while batting .346.

One of three DiMaggio brothers (along with Vince and Dom) to play in the majors, Joe appeared to have no weaknesses as a ballplayer. A right-handed batter who almost always made contact—never striking out more than 39 times in a season—he was hurt by the 457-foot "Death Valley" in left-center field of Yankee Stadium but still managed to hit .315 there over his career. As a center fielder, he was fast and graceful but never flashy, making great plays look easy and always delivering strong throws to the right man. He was seldom called upon to steal bases (he stole 30 in 39 career attempts), but nobody doubted he was one of the fastest players of his generation. Though quiet, he was a leader in the Yankee clubhouse.

After winning batting titles in 1939 (when his .381 mark earned him the MVP Award) and '40 (.352), DiMaggio captured the attention of the entire country in 1941. Beginning with a single off Chicago's Edgar Smith on May 15 and ending with two great stops by Cleveland's Ken Keltner on July 17, Joe compiled a major-league-record 56-game hitting streak—during which he hit .408 with 15 homers. He was the subject of songs, prompted contests and endless media coverage, and beat out Ted Williams (a .406 batter on the season) for his second MVP trophy.

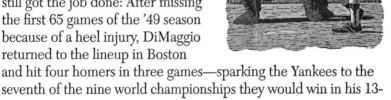

World War II intervened in 1943, and 31-year-old Joe came back three years later slightly below his previous form. His average and power numbers were down (he won a third MVP Award with subpar .315–20–97 totals in 1947), but he still got the job done: After missing the first 65 games of the '49 season because of a heel injury, DiMaggio returned to the lineup in Boston and hit four homers in three games—sparking the Yankees to the seventh of the nine world championships they would win in his 13-year career.

Age and mounting injuries hampered Joe's effectiveness, and he retired after a final World Series win in 1951 to go about marrying Marilyn Monroe, peddling Mr. Coffee, and simply being Joe DiMaggio. His final statistics (361 homers, .325 average, and 1,537 RBI) do not approach the all-time greats, but when injuries and military service are factored in, Joe's average season translates into 34 homers, 143 RBI, and a .579 slugging percentage—numbers worthy of his 1969 selection by Major League Baseball as its "greatest living player."

A Woman on the Mound

Pioneers who brought new meaning to "ERA."

The year was 1931, and the New York Yankees were making their trip north from spring training, stopping to play exhibition games along the way. Facing the Chattanooga Lookouts, they must have been surprised when they saw their mound opponent was a 17-year-old girl named Jackie Mitchell. Was she serious? She certainly thought she was, and she bent off several wicked curveballs, striking out Babe Ruth and Lou Gehrig consecutively on only seven pitches. A few days later, Commissioner Kenesaw Mountain Landis voided her contract, insisting that baseball was "too strenuous" for a woman. Disappointed and defeated, Mitchell began barnstorming with the House of David team. She eventually grew tired of the sideshow antics and retired to work at her father's optometry office. Although she continued to play with local teams from time to time, Mitchell did not play professional baseball again.

It would be 66 years until another woman played in a professional game. Her name was Ila Borders, and she got her chance with the St. Paul Saints of the independent Northern League. Borders, who also had the distinction of being the first woman to pitch and win a game at the collegiate level, was signed by son-of-a-legend Mike Veeck. He claimed it wasn't a publicity stunt, and his team was sold out for the season anyway. Unfortunately, Borders didn't pitch well for the Saints and was traded to the Duluth-Superior Dukes. In her third appearance of the 1998 season, she earned a 3–1 win with six scoreless innings, becoming the first woman to win a men's pro game. She also developed quite a fan club.

Borders was praised for her nearly perfect mechanics, "a curve with a variety of breaks, a changeup that worked like a screwball," her control, and her "pitching smarts." However, her fastball just wasn't strong enough for her to compete consistently. Although *Sports Illustrated* named her one of the top 100 female athletes of all time while she was still active, and she had a 1.67 ERA in 15 appearances in 1999 for the Madison Black Wolf, she retired after the 2000 season.

Magical Moments

Move over, Babe—here comes Henry!

The Setting: Atlanta Fulton County Stadium; April 8, 1974
The Magic: Hammerin' Hank passes the Babe.

In spring training 1969, Hank Aaron felt old. He was seriously considering retirement. But Lee Allen, one of the first great baseball historians, took him aside and explained how close he was to setting some serious lifetime records. He was just one homer behind Mel Ott and two behind Ernie Banks for second place in NL history. The 3,000 hits milestone wasn't far away, and Aaron even had a chance to get the most at-bats of all time.

Aaron listened, and he heard the deeper truth behind Allen's comments. If he could set those records, people would have to take notice, and Aaron could use his increased visibility to see that changes were made within the game—against discriminatory hiring practices and segregation in spring training. Aaron accepted the challenge and went on to finish his career second lifetime in at-bats, third in games and hits, and tenth in doubles.

But the big record was broken in Atlanta on a chilly April night, and not everyone was happy about it. Although many fans were cheering him on, Aaron also received racist hate mail and death threats; the Atlanta police even provided him with a bodyguard. But Aaron maintained his cool, as he always had. And, just as he had done 714 times before, he stepped up to the plate and hit a round-tripper, this time off an Al Downing pitch that he deposited into the Atlanta bullpen. Babe Ruth's home run record had been surpassed. But this moment wasn't just about Aaron's place in baseball history; it resonated throughout the country on many different levels.

⚾ ⚾ ⚾

"Say this much for baseball—it is beyond question the greatest conversation piece ever invented in America."

—Bruce Catton, *Fascinating Baseball Facts*

Best Hitting Pitchers

Easy outs? Think again!

Nowadays a "good hitting pitcher" is one who knows how to bunt. But the game has nearly always had one or two folks who made their money on the mound but were stalwarts with the stick as well. Many of them often served as pinch-hitters for their team.

Jack Bentley
They were calling Bentley "the next Babe Ruth" in 1922, when he hit .349 in 153 games, finishing second in the International League for the Baltimore Orioles (Ruth's first team, too). In 1923, he won 13 games for the pennant-winning Giants and hit .427 in 52 games. He also had two pinch hits in that year's World Series. In Game 5 of the 1924 Series, he slugged a two-run homer off Walter Johnson. His lifetime batting average was .291.

Doc Crandall
Crandall was one of the game's first true relief pitchers. His ability with the stick made him a valuable pinch-hitter as well. He swatted the ball at a .285 clip for his career. He had a sensational season in 1910, when he won 17 games for the New York Giants, lost just four, and slugged his way to a .342 average.

Wes Ferrell
Ferrell's 38 homers outdistance the career mark of any other pitcher, and his nine in 1931 are best for a single season. In 1935, he won back-to-back games with homers, one pinch-hitting and one for himself. Ferrell's hitting ability was a matter of hard work. He said, "A lot of guys could do it if they tried." At the age of 40, he managed and played in the minors and won the batting title with a .425 average.

Mike Hampton

Mike Hampton didn't hit his first double until his third season in the majors, but before long he was topping the leader board for batting by pitchers. In fact, he won the pitching spot on the Silver Slugger team five years in a row. One year he had three doubles and three triples and knocked home ten runs. When he became a free agent, he moved to the hitter's paradise of Colorado, where in 2001 he slugged seven homers and drove in 16 runs.

Don Newcombe

In 1955, Newcombe had quite a year. Not only was he 20–5 for the pennant-winning Dodgers, but he hit .359 and set a National League record for homers by a pitcher in a season, with seven. Twice that season he hit two homers in one game. He even stole home once. His .271 lifetime average ranks among the best for pitchers in major-league history.

Al Orth

This turn-of-the-20th-century pitcher banged out 389 career hits as a hurler, and 78 times he was used to pinch-hit. His lifetime average of .273 is one of the best marks ever for a pitcher, and he hit .290 or better seven times. Oh, and he also won 204 games.

Schoolboy Rowe

Rowe was more than just a pitcher who occasionally pinch-hit; he was counted on off the bench. In 1943, playing for Philly, he led the NL in pinch-hit appearances and pinch hits, going 15-for-49. He is one of just five pitchers to slug a pinch-hit grand slam. He hit another grand slam to aid his own pitching cause.

George Uhle

In 1923, slider pitcher Uhle tore the American League apart. He won 26 games, threw 29 complete games, and pitched 357 innings; all led the league. He also batted .361, one of the highest marks ever for a pitcher. He hit a grand slam off Dutch Leonard in 1921, and he holds the highest batting average (.289) of 20th-century pitchers (minimum 1,000 at-bats).

Baseball Lingo

Sprechen sie baseball?

Annie Oakley: A walk. **Origin:** Named for the riflewoman who could shoot holes in a playing card, making the card resemble a punched ticket, or free pass.

Bases drunk: Bases "loaded." **Origin:** Euphemism.

Bean: A player's head. A "beanball" is a pitch aimed at it. **Origin:** Descriptive.

Bonehead, Boner: A mistake-prone player or a botched play. **Origin:** Descriptive of a head that contains no brain, just a bone. Popularized by journalists writing of Fred Merkle's costly base-running blunder in 1908.

Cakewalk: An easy win or easy opponent. **Origin:** Dance contests that offered a cake as the prize.

Chin music: Inside brushback pitch close to the jaw. Also "a close shave." **Origin:** Descriptive. "Music" is the whooshing of the ball.

Clubhouse lawyer: A player who frequently talks about and/or undermines a manager or teammate. **Origin:** Descriptive of verbose prosecutors or defense attorneys. Probably began with sportswriters alarmed at "Bolshevik" views among early attempts at unionization.

Collar: Going hitless in a game. **Origin:** Descriptive. The shape of a collar resembles the number zero.

Cup of coffee: A brief stay in the majors or with one team. **Origin:** Hyperbole, suggesting a player was there only long enough to have a cup of coffee.

Gas: An especially quick fastball. **Origin:** The automobile. Stepping on the gas to accelerate.

Gopher ball: A pitch hit well, often for a long home run. **Origin:** A pun on "go for," as in a hit that will "go for extra bases," or a pitch a batter will "go for."

Handcuff: An inside pitch at the hands, or a batted ball directly at a fielder that is difficult to field. Also: *shackle.* **Origin:** Descriptive.

Hot Stove League: The baseball off-season. **Origin:** Descriptive of winter gatherings around a stove.

Mendoza Line: A batting average of .200, marking the threshold between a below-average hitter and an extremely poor one. **Origin:** A remark by George Brett (some accounts say Bruce Botche or Tom Paciorek) referring to his batting average relative to that of Mario Mendoza, the light-hitting infielder and career .215 hitter of the 1970s and '80s.

Muffin: An unskilled player. **Origin:** Common in the 19th century, probably descriptive of something new like a freshly baked muffin. A muffin is prone to "muff," or make a foolish mistake.

Paint the black: A pitch on the inside or outside corners of the strike zone. **Origin:** Descriptive of the black outline of home plate.

Pickle: A rundown play. **Origin:** Dates back to Shakespeare, as a description for a compromising position.

The Show: The major leagues, often from the perspective of a minor-leaguer. **Origin:** Descriptive of larger crowds, parks, and more media and amenities relative to the minors.

Squeezed: When an umpire calls a tight strike zone. **Origin:** Descriptive.

Stretching the Story

The history (and lore) behind a seventh-inning tradition.

The seventh-inning stretch, a ritual practiced today at ballparks throughout the major and minor leagues and beyond, was long rumored to have originated at a 1910 Washington Senators game attended by President William Howard Taft. Seeking relief from his confining seat at American League Park, the 300-pound chief executive rose in the seventh. Fans, thinking he was leaving, did likewise as a sign of respect, and when he wound up sitting back down they did the same.

Thus a rite of fandom was born—or so it was thought.

Turns out this tale of President Taft might just have stretched the truth a bit. Researchers found evidence of a seventh-inning stretch all the way back in 1882. During an exhibition game between Manhattan College and the semipro Metropolitans, Manhattan's coach, a prefect named Brother Jasper of Mary, noticed the student fans growing fidgety. Calling time, he asked them to stand and unwind, and when the break proved to have restorative powers, he called for it to occur at the same time—the seventh inning—in all subsequent games. When the New York Giants squared off with Manhattan and saw Brother Jasper's practice, they took it back to the majors and started its spread.

Even this may not be the earliest incidence of the trend, however. A letter written in 1869 by player-manager and future Hall of Famer Harry Wright of the Cincinnati Red Stockings—baseball's first acknowledged professional club—makes mention that at games of that era, "The spectators all arise between halves of the seventh inning, extend their arms and legs, and sometimes walk about. In so doing they enjoy the relief afforded by relaxation from a long posture on hard benches."

Harry sounds like he's on the level, but wouldn't it be great if we really *could* give President Taft the credit?

All-Star Quiz

1) Who holds the record for most Opening Day pitching starts?

A: *Tom Seaver (16)*

2) Who are the only three players to hit safely in seven consecutive All-Star Games?

A: *Mickey Mantle, Joe Morgan, and Dave Winfield*

3) Which Hall of Famer hit major-league home runs off two former NBA players?

A: *Harmon Killebrew, off Dave DeBusschere and Gene Conley*

4) Who was the only shortstop to lead the majors in home runs in the 20th century?

A: *Ernie Banks, in 1958 and 1960*

5) Which two Hall of Famers were teammates at Locke High School in Los Angeles?

A: *Eddie Murray and Ozzie Smith*

6) Who is the only player ever to get five hits in his first nine-inning major-league game?

A: *Fred Clarke, on June 30, 1894*

7) Who was the first manager to win a World Series in each league?

A: *Sparky Anderson*

8) Which two Hall of Famers reached the 300-win milestone and the 3,000-hit mark on the same day?

A: *Rod Carew and Tom Seaver, on August 4, 1985*

9) What is Ozzie Smith's real first name?

A: *Osborne*

Bending, but Not Breaking, the Color Barrier

Integration? Not if baseball's big boys could help it.

In the history of baseball, nothing is more shameful than what Jackie Robinson had to endure as the major leagues' first African-American player. He was brought to the majors over vigorous protest, but once he reached the spotlight at Brooklyn's Ebbets Field in 1947, his emotions courageously in check, he was there to stay. As he continued to be snubbed and demeaned, newspapers, magazines, radio, and newsreels followed his every move. As Jackie succeeded, and then excelled, more African-Americans followed. And the rest, as they say, is history.

In the previous century, though, progress for players of color on the diamond had been stopped dead in its tracks.

African-Americans were barred from the newly formed National League in 1876 when owners came to a backroom "gentleman's agreement" that was not challenged outright until Robinson's debut 71 years later. The minor leagues, however, were a different story. Anywhere from 25 to 50 African-Americans found spots on individual teams in the 1870s and 1880s. Bud Fowler and Frank Grant were probably the best of this group, but neither man crossed the line into the major leagues, despite competing against white players deemed to be of big-league caliber.

Moses Fleetwood Walker broke that line. He and his brother Welday had helped launch the Oberlin College baseball team in 1881, and both later played at the University of Michigan. In 1883, "Fleet" joined the Toledo Blue Stockings of the Northwestern League. When Toledo joined the American Association, a major league that was competing with the National League, the club brought along all its top players.

On May 1, 1884, the Toledo Blue Stockings debuted in the major leagues, with Walker a proud member. A barehanded catcher, Fleet teamed with Tony Mullane to form an intimidating battery. He wasn't exactly welcomed into the league with open arms: He was hit with six pitches in one game alone. Fleet batted .263 in 42 games before a broken rib off a foul tip essentially ended his season. His brother Welday, who had joined him in Toledo in July, appeared in five games as an outfielder and batted .222. At the end of the season Toledo exited the AA, and the Walker brothers' major-league careers came to an end.

Recent research has shown that the Walkers may not have been the first African-Americans to play in the majors, however. William Edward White, who played one game for the Providence Grays in 1879 while he was a student at Brown University, may have been a light-skinned African-American.

Six of ten International League teams fielded African-American players in 1887, with Fleet Walker and George Stovey forming a formidable "colored battery" for the Newark Little Giants. But Cap Anson, player-manager of the NL Chicago White Stockings, refused to take the field for an exhibition against the integrated team. Anson had tried to do the same in 1883 against Walker in Toledo, but when the Blue Stockings threatened not to pay Anson, he relented, unhappily. This time, Anson got his way, and leagues voted to ban new contracts with African-Americans. In 1889, Fleet Walker became the last African-American in the International League until Jackie Robinson debuted with the Montreal Royals in 1946.

Even the new American League, at war with the established National League, fell in with the same unwritten agreement. In 1901, the AL's first year, Baltimore Orioles manager John McGraw tried to pass off Negro Leaguer Charlie Grant as a Native American named Chief Tokohama, but Chicago White Sox owner Charlie Comiskey foiled the plan when he recognized Grant as the catcher from the Columbia Giants. The AL would not integrate until Larry Doby joined the Cleveland Indians in 1947.

𝄞 𝄞 𝄞

"If Judy Johnson were white, he could name his price."

—Connie Mack on the top third baseman of the Negro League during the 1920s and '30s

Magical Moments

It's a Brave new world thanks to Cabrera's dramatic hit.

The Setting: Atlanta Fulton County Stadium; October 14, 1992
The Magic: The Braves rally in the last of the ninth to pull out the League Championship Series against the Pirates in dramatic form.

There was little doubt that these were the two best teams in the National League: Both were young and talented, and both had easily taken their divisions. The Pirates had won their third consecutive Eastern Division crown; the Braves their second consecutive West title. The Pirates were primarily an offensive threat; the Braves focused more on pitching. Barry Bonds, Andy Van Slyke, Jay Bell, Doug Drabek, and Jose Lind were Pirate stars. The Braves featured John Smoltz, Tom Glavine, Steve Avery, Terry Pendleton, Sid Bream, and David Justice. The two teams had played each other close in their dozen matches that year, with Atlanta holding a 7–5 lead in victories. In the previous two years, four of the top ten MVP vote-getters were from these two teams. In Cy Young voting, two of the top five were Braves or Pirates; the year before, two of the top three.

A 13–4 Buc win in Game 6 of the LCS led to a finale face-off between Drabek and Smoltz. Single runs in the first and sixth gave the Pirates a 2–0 lead as the Braves came to bat in the last of the ninth. Drabek seemed in charge; he had retired eight of the last ten batters he'd faced. But 1991 National League MVP Terry Pendleton led off with a double. A mishandled ground ball by the usually sure fielder Jose Lind put runners on the corners. After a walk and a pitching change, a sac fly got one run home, and another walk loaded the bases. A pop-out moved the Pirates to within one out of the World Series, but in a flash it was all over: A line single by pinch-hitter Francisco Cabrera and a shabby throw by Barry Bonds got two runs home. (The final score was 4–3.) The Braves went on to win a record 14 straight division titles, while the Pirates have barely sniffed the first division since.

Fast Facts

- *The only player to appear in three consecutive World Series with three different teams was Don Baylor, with the Boston Red Sox in 1986, the Minnesota Twins in 1987, and the Oakland A's in 1988.*

- *Jose Canseco was the first player to hit 40 home runs and steal 40 bases in the same season.*

- *Hall of Famer Robin Roberts gave up 505 home runs in his 19 years of pitching, the most home runs given up in a career.*

- *On August 23, 1953, Phil Paine became the first ex-major-leaguer to play in Japan.*

- *In the early days of the game, the pitcher was required to deliver the ball by tossing it underhand.*

- *The only full brothers in the Baseball Hall of Fame are Paul and Lloyd Waner.*

- *The two pitchers to give up the most hits to Pete Rose in his record-breaking career were Phil Niekro, with 64, and Don Sutton, with 60.*

- *The Giants have turned the most triple plays in history. The Braves have hit into the most.*

- *Dan Bankhead of the Brooklyn Dodgers became the first African-American pitcher in the major leagues on August 26, 1947. Although he did not have much success and only played for three seasons in the bigs, he was the first black player to hit a home run in his first major-league at-bat.*

Baseball's Bad Boys

Some major-leaguers have become infamous not for their play but for their antics on and off the diamond.

Baseball has its share of good guys, to be sure. And their deeds look extra special when compared to those of their not-always-such-good-guy counterparts.

Roberto Alomar: Splish Splash

It was one reactionary smudge on Roberto Alomar's otherwise clean resume, and it was a wet one. After being called out on strikes by John Hirschbeck in a 1996 game in Toronto, an enraged Alomar argued the call, then spit in the umpire's face. The act, caught by TV cameras and replayed over and over, earned the Orioles infielder a five-game suspension and the ire of fans. Years later, Alomar and Hirschbeck became friends, the player helping the ump raise money to support research of a rare brain disease that took the life of Hirschbeck's eight-year-old son in 1993.

Albert Belle: His Tricks Were No Treat

Albert Belle's drinking and run-ins with fans and media were well-documented, making him one of baseball's least loved players. This deal was sealed in October 1995. On Halloween night (one week after shouting obscenities at NBC reporter Hannah Storm before a World Series game), Belle got in his truck and chased a group of teenagers who had thrown eggs at his home. He was fined $50,000 for the Storm incident and $100 for turning a trick-or-treat stunt into a potentially dangerous pursuit.

Hal Chase: Dollars, Not Sense

Hal Chase was one of the best defensive first basemen of all time. It makes perfect sense, as he was generally on the defensive. He was accused as early as 1910 of throwing games after betting against his own team. Chase beat such charges until 1918, when Reds skipper Christy Mathewson grew suspicious and suspended him for "indifferent play." Chase was indicted in 1920 on bribery charges relating to the Black Sox scandal and was eventually banned for life by Commissioner Kenesaw Mountain Landis.

Vince Coleman: An Explosive Personality

After a loss at Dodger Stadium in 1993, Mets outfielder Vince Coleman threw a powerful firecracker out a car window toward a group of fans in the parking lot. The explosion injured two children and a woman. Coleman, who later said he was not aware that throwing firecrackers at people could result in injury, avoided felony charges by pleading guilty to possession of an explosive device, a misdemeanor. He received three years' probation, 200 community service hours, and a $1,000 fine.

Dave Kingman: That Dirty Rat

Slugger Dave Kingman never got along particularly well with the media. No matter how badgering reporters can be, though, none deserve the fate that befell the *Sacramento Bee*'s Susan Fornoff in 1986. Kingman, playing for Oakland late in his career, sent a present to Fornoff in the press box one night with a tag that read, "My name is Sue." Inside the package was a live rat. The incident earned Kingman a $3,500 fine and a reputation as a troublemaker that many feel led to the resistance he met when trying to sign as a free agent. When asked if he planned to apologize to Fornoff, Kingman said, "I've pulled practical jokes on other people, and I didn't apologize to them."

John Rocker: Mr. Offensive

John Rocker saved 38 games for the Atlanta Braves in 1999. The biggest news he made, however, was not with his arm, but with his mouth. A December 1999 *Sports Illustrated* article quoted the Macon, Georgia, native as saying he would never play for a New York team because he might find himself on the train next to "some queer with AIDS" or "some 20-year-old mom with four kids." He added that he was "not a very big fan of foreigners" and mocked Asian women. Needless to say, Rocker was not greeted warmly when the Braves played in New York—or anywhere else, for that matter.

One-Year Wonders

The music world has one-hit wonders. Baseball has something similar: players who have one season of greatness.

Every baseball player would love to have the legacy of a sustained career of Hall of Fame–level excellence. Though few achieve that, there are some ballmen who have one brilliant season in which they rise above their mediocrity and truly shine. In some cases, their outstanding season was sparked by a change in ballpark or team; in other cases, a hotshot rookie simply caught the league by surprise. Then there were those players who benefited from a league-wide shift, a change in the equipment, or an adjustment to their conditioning and approach. If only these players could have bottled their single seasons of glory and carried them through the rest of their careers, they would all be residing in Cooperstown today. But, as we've come to realize in baseball, it's just not that easy.

Earl Webb

Webb entered the majors at age 27, playing sporadically for the New York Giants and Chicago Cubs. He showed flashes of hitting potential but had little extra-base power. He was a below-average outfielder and couldn't run very fast. It seemed as though Webb would be a quick blip in the baseball annals, but things changed when Webb joined the Boston Red Sox in 1930. Playing half of his games at Fenway Park, Webb batted .323 (up from .250 in 1928), clubbed 16 home runs, and even improved his defensive play.

In 1931, Webb raised his level of play even higher. He had a career-high .333 batting average, 14 home runs, and 103 RBI. But his most amazing feat was banging out 67 doubles—more than doubling his career-best output for one year while setting a single-season major-league record that stands to this day.

While Webb's continued improvement at the plate was certainly a factor in his record-breaking season, there's one other theory behind it, too. According to some sportswriters, Webb had a habit of intentionally stopping at second base, when he could have advanced to third and received credit for a triple. It was not exactly a team-first concept, which might partially explain why Webb's major-league career came to an end two years later.

Walt "Moose" Dropo

With some one-year wonders, the first impression is the best. That was certainly the case with the 6′5″, 220-pound Dropo, who had one of the best rookie seasons in major-league history. In 1950, Dropo hit .322, pounded out 34 home runs, and tied for the league lead with 144 RBI while playing first base for the Boston Red Sox. Dropo's performance earned him American League Rookie of the Year honors, a nice topping to a season in which he won a spot as the starting first baseman in the All-Star Game.

But Dropo's sophomore effort was a letdown for Red Sox fans who thought they had found the perfect right-handed complement to Ted Williams. Dropo batted a disappointing .239 in his second season, as opposing pitchers found some holes in his swing. One year later, the Red Sox sent him packing as part of a nine-player trade with the Detroit Tigers. Dropo hit well for the Tigers over the balance of the 1952 season, but he would never come close to approaching his first-year numbers. Over the final nine seasons of his career, Dropo hit no more than 19 home runs in a single season and had a batting average that never topped .281. All in all, he had a decent career, but it wasn't the stuff of legends, which some had come to expect after his incredible rookie season.

Jim Hickman

A right-handed hitter with power and patience, Hickman experienced some moments of brilliance during a respectable major-league career. He became the first player in the history of the New York Mets to hit three home runs in a single game. He also became the first Met to hit for the cycle. Yet the Mets felt that Hickman could do more. They fretted over his lack of aggressiveness at the plate and grew frustrated with his batting choices. All in all, Hickman provided the Mets with some needed power but didn't become the star they were hoping for. After the 1966 season, the Mets traded Hickman to the Los Angeles Dodgers, who passed him on to the Chicago Cubs.

Things finally clicked in 1970. Hickman hit 32 home runs for the Cubs, eclipsing his previous high of 21. He also reached career highs in doubles (33) and RBI (115). Hickman's breakthrough season earned him a trip to the All-Star Game, where he drove in the game-winning run for the National League.

So what happened to make Hickman a star in 1970? Well, there may have been something going around the National League that summer. Hickman, like a number of other NL players—including Bob Bailey, Donn Clendenon, Dick Dietz, Clarence Gaston, Billy Grabarkewitz, and Wes Parker—all enjoyed breakout seasons. While impossible to prove, it's conceivable that something may have been done to juice up the baseball in the NL that season. If that's the case, no one benefited more than Hickman, who experienced the biggest breakthrough of any player—and who would never put up such impressive numbers again.

Brady Anderson

For much of his career, Anderson was a fine defensive center fielder who stole bases with regularity and hit 15 to 20 home runs a season. In 1992, his first-half performance with the Baltimore Orioles earned him a place on the American League All-Star team.

Yet it all paled in comparison to his accomplishments in 1996. That year, Anderson muscled up and exceeded his best single-season home run total by June, hitting 27 home runs during the first three months of the season. By season's end, he had hit a stunning 50 home runs, more than doubling his career best. Anderson also set a record (since broken) by hitting 12 home runs to lead off games. He was aided by a serious commitment to weight lifting and a batting approach that emphasized swinging harder. Not even an attack of appendicitis could prevent Anderson from putting up one of the best offensive seasons ever enjoyed by a major-league center fielder.

Unfortunately, Anderson was never able to duplicate those numbers—for the rest of his career, he didn't hit more than 24 dingers in a season. After the 2001 season, he was released by the Orioles and signed by the Cleveland Indians. He left baseball altogether in 2003.

How to Be a Better Pitcher

Effective pitching involves a lot more than just throwing the ball.

Most coaches advise young pitchers to use an overhand delivery, which puts less strain on the arm. Below are other pitching tips.

In the off-season: Learn mechanics. Practice without the ball. Watch yourself in a mirror. Run. Learn to throw strikes. Learn to change speeds. Move the ball around.

Herb Pennock: Develop your faculty of observation. Work ever-lastingly for control. Keep studying the hitters for their weak and strong points. Keep talking with your catchers.

Cy Young: Pitchers, like poets, are born, not made. Until you can put the ball over the pan whenever you choose, you have not acquired the command necessary to make a first-class pitcher. Therefore, start to acquire command.

The Windup (from *The Complete Pitcher, Inc.*)
  Stay tall.
  Small steps: Take a small step back, and make a small turn to place your pivot foot parallel with the rubber.
  Lift leg into balance position, toe pointing down.
  Hands remain still; head remains still.
  Glide through the catcher. Toes to the target.
  The quicker the break of the hands, the faster one throws.
  When the batter swings, if his rear shoulder drops, pitch him high. When the batter strides, if he steps in the hole, pitch him outside. When the batter strides, if he steps forward a long way, pitch him high. When the batter takes his stance, if he holds his bat high, pitch him low.
  Never give up a hit on a no-ball, two-strike count.
  Make sure your pivot foot makes a full pivot parallel with the rubber.
  Keep your eyes on the target.

Greatest Games of All Time

October 1, 1950

Phillies 4, Dodgers 1

The Setting: Ebbets Field, Brooklyn
The Drama: The last day of the season saw the mighty Dodgers facing Philly's "Whiz Kids" for the NL flag.

The Brooklyn Dodgers of the late 1940s and early '50s were a true powerhouse. In fact, if they hadn't lost two games (this one and Game 3 of the '51 playoffs), they would have been National League pennant-winners five times in a row, and seven out of eight. The Dodgers were sluggers: Gil Hodges, Duke Snider, and Roy Campanella all hit more than 30 home runs in 1950; Jackie Robinson, Carl Furillo, and Snider all topped the .300 mark. They led all National League teams in runs, hits, homers, stolen bases, batting, and slugging. The Dodgers had two 19-game winners on their staff: Don Newcombe and Preacher Roe.

The Phillies were the opposite of a dynasty. They hadn't won a pennant since 1915. But the 1950 squad had some talented young players, as well as a fierce desire to win. Only one Phillie regular in 1950 was 30 years old. Even their starting pitching was young, with 23-year-old Robin Roberts and 21-year-old Curt Simmons the mainstays. Quickly dubbed the "Whiz Kids," they moved into first in late July. By September 18, they had a 7½ game lead over Boston, with Brooklyn nine back.

But before long, it looked like their luck had run out. Two of their starting pitchers got hurt and were out for the season. Simmons, sporting a 17–8 record, was called into the military in mid-September. Ace hurler Roberts slumped, failing at six chances to win his 20th game. And the Dodgers were coming on. The Phillies lost eight of 11 games; Brooklyn won 12 of 15. The Phils were two in front, with the season's final two games scheduled in Brooklyn. The Dodgers took the first game 7–3 to close the gap to one.

Not surprisingly, the final game was attended by the largest crowd of the season at Ebbets Field—35,073. Some reports said 30,000 other fans were turned away. Newcombe, looking for his 20th win, was to square off against Roberts, still stuck on 19. Roberts was pitching for the third time in five days; manager Eddie Sawyer saw little use in saving his star for the future.

Roberts had the Dodgers eating out of his hand, allowing just one hit through the first four innings. The Phils were hitting singles against Newcombe, but they could get no further, managing just one run through six innings.

The Dodgers evened the score in the bottom half of the sixth, in a most Dodger-like way. Shortstop Pee Wee Reese hit a fly ball that got stuck between the screen and the right-center-field wall. When no one could reach it, the umps ruled it a home run. The Dodger faithful could see their prayers coming true.

The Phils put men on base in the seventh, eighth, and ninth, but Newcombe held firm. In the last of the ninth, Dodgers outfielder Cal Abrams led off with a walk. Reese singled him to second. Snider could have bunted the runners over, but instead he lined a single to center. Phils center fielder Richie Ashburn charged the ball, snatched it on one hop, and threw a perfect strike home to catcher Stan Lopata. Abrams, unwisely sent in by the third base coach, was a dead duck. The Dodgers hadn't won—yet. But now they had men on second and third, still with one out.

Robinson was walked intentionally. Furillo then popped out foul on the first pitch from Roberts. Dodger slugger Hodges knocked a long fly to right-center, but Del Ennis snagged it. The Phils and Dodgers headed into extra innings.

Roberts led off for the Phils, smashing a single off Newcombe. A single by Eddie Waitkus followed, but Newcombe pounced on an Ashburn bunt and courageously threw out Roberts at third. Next up was Dick Sisler, 29 years old but playing in only his fourth full season. On a 1–2 pitch, Sisler popped a fly to left that just barely cleared the fence, 348 feet away. A three-run homer.

A fly ball, strikeout, and pop-up were all the three Dodger batters could muster. Roberts finally had his 20th victory, and the upstart Phils had won the pennant against the potent Dodgers.

Best Baseball Movies

Sometimes filmmakers just don't "get" baseball. But when they do, the results can be as intriguing and varied as a long weekend series against a crosstown rival.

Title: *Bang the Drum Slowly*
Particulars: Based on the Mark Harris novel (with a screenplay by Harris) and released in 1973, this film features two rising stars: Michael Moriarty and Robert DeNiro. (It was first presented on television with Paul Newman in the DeNiro role.)
Plot: Moriarty is a star pitcher, and DeNiro's a third-string catcher, but they bond as friends through the ups and downs of one sad, final season.
Why We Like It: It's a touching and honest portrayal of a friendship with imminent death lurking in the background. This one also gets high marks for the game action.

Title: *Baseball: A Film by Ken Burns*
Particulars: A 1994 made-for-TV attempt to tell the full story of the game in nine documentary segments. A highly ambitious project, so of course it has faults, but most of them are detail bobbles rather than factual errors.
Why We Like It: Because it *is* ambitious, and some of the "talking heads" Burns recruited move from historians to stars. Buck O'Neil's generous spirit as he discusses life in the Negro Leagues is inspirational. In fact, the whole "Shadowball" section is excellent. It won an Emmy for "Outstanding Informational Series."

Title: *The Bingo Long Traveling All-Stars and Motor Kings*
Particulars: Made in 1976, this movie stars James Earl Jones (playing a character based on Josh Gibson), Billy Dee Williams (ditto Satchel Paige), Richard Pryor, and "Daddy Wags" himself, Leon Wagner, a 12-season veteran of the California Angels and four other teams.
Plot: Star pitcher Williams doesn't like the way he's being treated by his Negro National League owner, so he secedes and takes a

gang of razzle-dazzle teammates with him to barnstorm their way to success.

Why We Like It: We've heard plenty about how tough the life of a black ballplayer in the 1930s could be, but this film emphasizes the highlights, high jinks, and high times. These guys were darned good players, but they also knew how to give the audience what they wanted in terms of entertainment.

Title: *Bull Durham*
Particulars: Author/director Ron Shelton spent several years in the Baltimore Orioles minor-league system. Released in 1988, this film stars Kevin Costner, Susan Sarandon, and Tim Robbins.
Plot: Well-read (and very attractive) groupie Annie Savoy (Sarandon) "worships at the altar of baseball." Every year she selects one promising member of the Durham Bulls to teach him maturity— among other things. Her choice this year is "Nuke" LaLoosh (Robbins), but longtime journeyman catcher Crash Davis (Costner), who is trying to teach Nuke to pitch, confuses things for Miss Savoy.
Why We Like It: Baseball has never been this sexy, and the depiction of life in the minors rings absolutely true.

Title: *Eight Men Out*
Particulars: John Sayles's 1988 telling of the 1919 Black Sox scandal is based on Eliot Asinof's famous book. It has a powerful ensemble cast, including John Cusack, David Straithairn, D. B. Sweeney, and Charlie Sheen.
Plot: With the help of some gamblers, eight members of the White Sox conspire to let the Cincinnati Reds win the World Series. But things don't turn out as they'd planned. When their grand jury testimony is somehow "lost," they are acquitted. But brand-new Commissioner Kenesaw Mountain Landis has them all banned from baseball for life.
Why We Like It: The story is familiar to every serious fan, but Sayles (who also plays writer Ring Lardner) does a fine job of putting a human face on characters such as Joe Jackson, Charlie Comiskey, and Ed Cicotte.

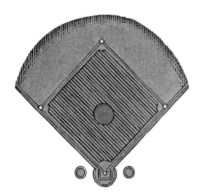

Title: *Field of Dreams*
Particulars: From 1989, this film features Kevin Costner, James Earl Jones, Burt Lancaster, and Ray Liotta (as Shoeless Joe Jackson). It was adapted from the book *Shoeless Joe* by William P. Kinsella, in which baseball is used as a metaphor for life.
Plot: Iowa farmer Ray Kinsella (Costner) begins hearing voices that he believes are telling him to turn his cornfield into a ballfield, which for some reason will invoke the spirits of the Black Sox and help with their redemption. He enlists the help of a reclusive author (Jones) to figure it all out. And of course the ultimate answer is bigger than he expected.
Why We Like It: Although the final payoff is extremely sentimental, the quest for finding the deep answers by looking to the past rings true for those who appreciate the game.

Title: *A League of Their Own*
Particulars: Directed by Penny Marshall and starring Tom Hanks, Geena Davis, Rosie O'Donnell, and Madonna. Released in 1992.
Plot: A fictionalized account of the first season of the first all-female professional baseball league, including both on- and off-field drama and comedy.
Why We Like It: The cast is terrific, especially Hanks as a boozy former major-league star (some say his role was based on Jimmie Foxx). And the baseball action is well done.

Title: *The Natural*
Particulars: Directed by Barry Levinson in 1984, based on Bernard Malamud's novel, and starring Robert Redford, Glenn Close, and Kim Basinger.
Plot: Young superstar Redford is shot by a woman and then disappears for 30 years, only to return to baseball glory.

Why We Like It: Vintage Malamud, which is to say everything is fair game for inclusion, from Arthurian legend to Babe Ruth and Eddie Waitkus. It's a joyously cinematic thrill ride, whether it makes any sense or not.

Title: *Pride of the Yankees*
Particulars: From 1942, starring Gary Cooper and Teresa Wright, both of whom were nominated for Academy Awards. The film itself was nominated for Best Picture. The screenplay was written by Jo Swerling (who worked on *It's a Wonderful Life*) and Herman Mankiewicz (who cowrote *Citizen Kane*), based on a story by Paul Gallico. It also features some wonderful cameos by real Yankees: Bill Dickey, Bob Meusel, Mark Koenig, and that old camera hog himself, Babe Ruth.
Plot: Gehrig's life story, with emphasis on his years as a Yank.
Why We Like It: The best baseball bio ever put on film. The casting is perfect, with many touching moments, including the heart-wrenching "luckiest man" speech.

Title: *The Sandlot*
Particulars: Released in 1993, this film has a cast of unknowns except for small roles played by James Earl Jones and Denis Leary.
Plot: The advertising tagline for the film says it all: "The adventure of a lifetime, the summer of their dreams . . . the dog of their nightmares." The dog is an especially nasty critter they've dubbed "The Beast," who makes off with any baseballs that leave their sandlot field. But like all good villains, he has a secret he's not letting on.
Why We Like It: It brings back all those deep and funny feelings about growing up, acknowledging the huge role baseball can play in those years.

The Minor Leagues: Just a Step or Two from "The Bigs"

It's where they pay you to dream—and work harder than you've ever worked before.

When professional baseball organized itself into a major league in 1876, there were already plenty of other teams around—teams that lacked the playing talent or financial capital to compete with the big boys. They became what we now call the minor leagues. The history of the minor leagues is the story of small towns and mini-entrepreneurs trying desperately to survive while huge economic, social, and technological forces bounced them around. Sometimes they all but disappeared from the face of the earth, but then a new crest pushed through, allowing many others to jump on the bandwagon.

The first successful minor league was the 1883 Northwestern League, which entered into the "Tripartite Agreement" with the two major leagues—National League and American Association—to protect each other's interests, most particularly keeping the rein on players who would "jump" contracts in a second, given the chance. By keeping players from jumping from team to team, both the upper and lower leagues would see greater stability and less financial fluctuation.

The Interstate Association joined the group shortly thereafter. Within five years there were 17 minor leagues; in two more years organized baseball was to be found from coast to coast. Baseball had become America's game, with the minors spreading the gospel outside of the major (mostly East Coast) cities. What they lacked in talent and cash they made up for in flexibility and energy.

It was still rough going for the minors, though. In the 19th century more than 40 percent of the leagues that started a season didn't finish it. When Ban Johnson turned his minor Western League into the American Major League, the Tripartite Agreement fell apart. By boldly moving from minor-league to major-league status on his own initiative, Johnson killed the agreement

In response, in 1901, nine minor-league groups banded together to form the National Association of Professional Baseball Leagues. By the following spring, 15 leagues were in the fold. In 1910, 52 leagues began the season and 44 finished—not a bad percentage. However, the next decade proved a negative one for the minors' health, with everything from new technology, such as movies and the automobile, to the war in Europe shrinking the ranks. Ten leagues began the 1918 season; only one finished it.

Meanwhile Branch Rickey, general manager of the Cardinals, was breathing new life into an old idea: the farm system. As a cost-saving concept, major-league teams had turned away from the idea of owning several minor teams. But under Rickey's arrangement, the Cards would own or be affiliated with a flock of teams at various levels. "Quality from quantity" was Mr. Rickey's motto. Many other teams copied Rickey's mode, and within eight years major-league operations controlled 27 minor leagues. The truly independent minor-league operations were all but gone. By the time the Cards played the Yankees in the 1926 World Series, 14 of their members had come up through their system. By 1936, the Cardinals controlled 28 teams (there were only 26 minor leagues), and they peaked with 33 teams a few years later. The 1942 world-champion Cardinal team featured only two players not produced by the system.

Even though the Depression knocked the pins out from many minor leagues, the postwar economic boom was good to them. By 1949, there were 59 leagues in operation, and the minors set their all-time attendance record.

But the bottom was about to fall out again—this time because of television. By 1963 there were only 18 minor leagues operating. Then, in the late 1970s, the pendulum swung back. Several minor-league clubs recorded attendance figures topping a million a year (while some big-league clubs were getting nowhere near that many fans). In 1983, Louisville crossed the million mark. In 1993, Buffalo rang up its sixth consecutive million-plus season. Meanwhile, fans were flocking to buy minor-league merchandise, too.

While the minors were subject to destabilizing or destructive forces in the past, today they are at their most successful and stable point in history. For one thing, their big-league parents supply them with nearly everything they need. In addition, minor-league games provide an intimate, attractive, inexpensive alternative to the bloated egos, salaries, and sandwich prices of the major leagues. At the minors, a family outing doesn't have to break the bank. New ballparks built in classic style are warm and friendly. Savvy investors have seen the financial opportunities, and new leagues—both independent and affiliated—are being developed all the time. Today, the uniquely small-town American baseball experience minor leagues offer is being enjoyed by more people than ever before.

Best Minor-League Teams of All Time

As part of its 100th anniversary in 2001, Minor League Baseball commissioned two baseball historians to select the best minor-league teams of all time. Their choices:

1. 1934 Los Angeles Angels; 137–50

With their remarkable .733 winning percentage against some serious opposition, this team stands atop the list of all-time minor-league squads. One of their stars was right fielder Frank Demaree. Sent down by the Cubs for more seasoning, Frank tore up the league, hitting .383 with 45 homers and 173 RBI. He led the Pacific Coast League in runs, hits, doubles, total bases, and slugging percentage and was the league MVP. The next year he was back with the Cubs, and he batted .325, .350, and .324 the following three seasons.

2. 1921 Baltimore Orioles; 119–47

Three Orioles teams from this decade made the top ten, but this one was a shade better than the rest. Led by owner/manager Jack Dunn (the man who signed 19-year-old George Ruth to his first professional contract), this group won 27 straight games at one point during the season and scored an amazing 1,140 runs. Star second baseman Max Bishop moved up to the bigs in 1924 and became the table-setter for sluggers Jimmie Foxx and Al Simmons on the potent Philadelphia A's of the '20s and '30s.

3. 1937 Newark Bears; 109–43

Many experts rank this Yankee farm club as the best minor-league team of all time, saying it could have competed against many big-league nines. Their lineup featured future major-league stars such as Charlie "King Kong" Keller (who was named minor-league Player of the Year that season), Babe Dahlgren, Joe Gordon, and George McQuinn.

4. 1924 Fort Worth Panthers; 109–41

This team was one of six consecutive Fort Worth champions, led by aging superstar Clarence "Big Boy" Kraft. The 37-year-old first baseman, who had sampled the majors for only three at-bats in his lifetime, bowed out with a season for the ages. Not only did he hit .349 and knock home 196 runs, but along with his 36 doubles and five triples were 55 homers. Only one man in history at that point had scaled such heights, and his name was Babe Ruth.

5. 1924 Baltimore Orioles; 117–48

By 1924, fans were starting to get tired of seeing the Orioles dominate the International League (they had won five championships in a row). But with another imposing squad, Baltimore once again proved too tough a team to overcome, taking home their sixth consecutive flag thanks in large part to their stalwart left-handed hurler, Lefty Grove. With a record of 26–6 and 231 strikeouts, future Hall of Famer Grove was the International League leader in wins, winning percentage (.813), and strikeouts.

6. 1920 St. Paul Saints; 115–49

What a combination of pitching, defense, and offense this team demonstrated. Not only did they outscore the next-best team by an amazing 201 runs, but at one point their pitching staff threw 45 consecutive shutout innings. For the season they allowed 95 fewer runs than the runner-up.

7. 1903 Jersey City Skeeters; 92–33

In addition to having a terrific nickname, the Skeeters were a dominant team in a tough Eastern League. Their star was outfielder Harry "Moose" McCormick, whose ungulate handle came not from his size but from his long running stride. The 22-year-old led the league with a .362 average that year, then went on to play five seasons in the big leagues. He went down in history as the man who "scored the winning run" on the infamous Fred Merkle play in 1908.

8. 1937 Salisbury Indians; 80–16
Probably the greatest class D team ever, this Maryland collection of players had to overcome a huge obstacle to take their flag. They were 21–5 when an opposition manager claimed Salisbury was using ineligible players. The president took away all 21 of their wins. Bloodied but unbowed, they won 49 of their next 59 games, outscoring the opposition 425–163.

9. 1920 Baltimore Orioles; 110–43
After winning the 1919 pennant, Baltimore was off to a slow start at the beginning of the 1920 season. They battled Toronto and Buffalo for the top position most of the season, then kicked it into high gear and racked up an .812 winning percentage from July 17 through October. And from August 29 through the last day of the season they were perfect, winning all 25 of their games, tying the then-league record for most consecutive wins by a minor-league team, and eking out a narrow victory over Toronto to capture the pennant.

10. 1925 San Francisco Seals; 128–71
In the 1920s, San Francisco won four Pacific Coast League titles. This was the best of those winning teams. Their star was a 22-year-old from Oklahoma named Paul Waner. Playing in his third year with the Seals, the fellow who would be named "Big Poison" a few years later was already strutting his stuff with a bat. He batted .401 to lead the league, also topped other PCLers with 75 doubles, and drove in 130 runs. The next year he'd be in Pittsburgh, on his way to three batting titles and the Hall of Fame.

Chatter

"I was starting my major-league career with one thing in my favor, anyways. I wasn't afraid of anybody I'd see in that batting box. I'd been around too long for that."

—Satchel Paige on his feelings upon joining the Cleveland Indians in 1948, *Maybe I'll Pitch Forever*

"For Lou, the game was almost holy, a religion."

—Sportswriter Stanley Frank on Lou Gehrig

"We Who Are About to Cry Salute You."

—Sign hanging from the left-field stands at Shea Stadium the night Willie Mays said good-bye to baseball and his fans, September 1973

"I believe the joy of getting paid as a man to play a boy's game kept me going longer than many other players."

—Stan Musial

"Baseball is our national game."

—President Calvin Coolidge

"I never ran from signs; I ran on my own. Any good baserunner has to be on his own."

—George Case, who led the American League in steals five straight years, *Baseball Between the Lines*

"To Johnny Bench, a Hall of Famer for sure."

—Inscription on ball signed by Ted Williams for Cincinnati's 20-year-old rookie catcher, spring training 1968

All-Time Great

Hank Aaron

Simply put, one of the greatest hitters ever to pick up a bat.

Born: February 5, 1934; Mobile, AL
MLB Career: Milwaukee/Atlanta Braves, 1954–74; Milwaukee Brewers, 1975–76
Hall of Fame Resume: 755 home runs (first) * 2,297 RBI (first) * 2,174 runs (third) * 3,771 hits (third) * 21 All-Star selections
Inside Pitch: Unlike many superstars who shriveled and faltered in the postseason, Aaron batted .362 and slugged .710 in 17 postseason games.

He never hit 60 home runs in a season—or even 50. Henry Aaron became the all-time Homer King and accumulated his considerable cache of records not by pumping out statistics that jumped off the paper, but rather with a career of steady, consistent play. Each time a current player hits 30 homers a few years in a row, comparisons to great sluggers of lore come up, but consider this: From 1955 through '74, Hank Aaron averaged 36 home runs a year for 20 full seasons.

How could production like this go unnoticed? The former Negro Leaguer had a fine rookie season with the Milwaukee Braves in 1954 (.280 with 13 homers), yet even as he blossomed into one of the National League's top hitters, the slim, shy Alabaman with the quick and powerful wrists was overshadowed by sluggers the likes of Willie Mays, Mickey Mantle, and Duke Snider playing in New York.

A batting title in '56 (.328) and a World Series win and MVP season the following year (.322–44–132) garnered Aaron some notoriety, but when talk turned to someone breaking Babe Ruth's season homer mark (60) or career home run mark (714), Hank's name was rarely mentioned. The heir to Babe's throne would have to be a muscle-bound masher like Mays or Mantle, not a skinny line-drive hitter whose drives happened to find the outfield fence with regularity. Over the next several years, Aaron garnered a second batting title (.355 in 1959) and three Gold Gloves for his outfield play, but he remained in the shadow of teammates Warren Spahn and Eddie Mathews.

Then in the mid-1960s, Willie and Mickey began slowing down, and after the Braves moved their franchise to the homer-friendly climate of Atlanta, Aaron began heating up. He led the NL with 44 and 39 home runs his first two Southern summers and clubbed his 500th homer in 1968. Then he slugged 44 more in 1969, became the ninth major-leaguer to reach 3,000 hits in 1970, and slammed home run No. 600 off Gaylord Perry of the Giants in '71 en route to a career-high 47-homer year at age 37.

When "Hammerin' Hank" passed Mays with his 649th clout in June 1972, the race to catch Ruth began—a race against age, time, and bigotry. Aaron received 930,000 pieces of mail in 1973, including racial slurs, death threats, and plots to kidnap his children. He survived that pressure and rallied to hit 40 homers in just 392 at-bats, finishing the '73 season one home run short of Ruth.

Aaron tied the Babe on Opening Day the following year, then passed him with a shot into the Braves' bullpen off Al Downing of the Dodgers on April 8, 1974, in Atlanta. Hank finished up two years later with 755 homers, 2,297 RBI, 3,771 hits, and 2,174 runs (the same number of runs accumulated by Babe Ruth). Although Barry Bonds will soon surpass Aaron's home run record, that won't diminish the legacy of a man whose consistent years of play made him one of the greatest hitters of all time.

◐ ◐ ◐

"George Thomas Seaver against Henry Louis Aaron—that was a game within a game for me even if he didn't know it. It was the stuff my dreams were made of ever since I began throwing the ball against the chimney, trying to get the ball in on an imaginary Henry Aaron's fists."

—Rookie pitcher Tom Seaver on facing his idol for the first time, *Baseball Is My Life*

Greatest Turnarounds

Every so often, a team manages to turn their fortunes around,
digging themselves out from a huge deficit.

When all is said and done, baseball is a game of streaks. Even the worst hitter seems to get hot for a game or two; even the best puts together a 2-for-30 at some point. What separates the champion from the others is that the former has more "up" streaks than "down" and keeps them going longer.

Here are the tales of three teams that traveled a long way during the course of one season to finish first, plus one that fought back from the verge of elimination to become world champs.

The Team: 1914 Boston Braves
The Deficit: 15 games behind first-place Giants on July 4
The Comeback: 68–19 after July 4

The Braves had lost 100 games or more four years in a row when George Stallings was hired as manager for the 1913 season. Their fifth-place finish that year was a welcome delight, but the team started 1914 back in the cellar and was languishing there as late as the Fourth of July.

Traveling home after a road trip, the Braves stopped for an exhibition game against the minor-league Buffalo team. They got trounced 10–2, which was a serious wake-up call for the Stallings crew. They made their move, thanks in part to near-perfect pitching by 27-year-old Dick Rudolph (18–1 the last half of the season) and 22-year-old Bill James (17–1) and great infield defense from new kid Rabbit Maranville at short and old hand Johnny Evers at second. Manager Stallings relied on platooning to maximize his offensive strength, and his team roared from last place to first in just 37 days.

In early September, Stallings conjured up another marvel by starting a green hurler (only 21 big-league appearances through 1914) named George Davis against the Phils. The spitballer twirled a no-hitter. And once the Braves moved past the Giants, there was no stopping them. They finished the season 10½ games ahead of John McGraw's men. Then they jumped into the World Series and swept Connie Mack's Philadelphia A's in four games. No wonder they became known as "The Miracle Braves."

The Team: 1951 New York Giants
The Deficit: 13½ games back on August 11
The Comeback: 37–7 in the final 44 regular-season games

By 1951, the Giants and the Dodgers had been adversaries for years. So when the Dodgers swept a three-game series at Ebbets Field from their rivals on August 9 to take a huge 12½-game lead, they were in a celebratory mood. Knowing they could be heard in the visiting clubhouse, they began to sing, "Roll out the barrel! We've got the Giants on the run!" Jackie Robinson used a bat to bang out the beat on the door between the clubhouses.

Then Leo Durocher's Giants kicked it up a notch. The Dodgers didn't play badly, but the Giants played amazingly. At one point, they won 16 games in a row. The Dodgers still had a seven-game lead on September 1, but the relentless Giants squeezed into first place on the next-to-last day of the season, and the Dodgers had to win a 14-inning nail-biter against the Phillies to set up the three-game playoff.

In the first game, Giants third baseman Bobby Thomson hit a home run off Dodger pitcher Ralph Branca to give his team a 2–1 lead and eventual 3–1 win. Game 2 was a 10–0 Dodger cakewalk. In Game 3, Branca returned to the mound to face Thomson again, trying to hold a 4–2 Dodger lead with two men on. Thomson attacked a Branca fastball and lined it into the lower deck of the Polo Grounds' left-field seats. The sensational Giants' two-month upswing was capped by an incredible comeback in the final game. Thomson and Branca are forever linked in myth and memory, and Thomson's homer became known as "The Shot Heard 'Round the World." (See pages 234–235 for more about this game.)

The Team: 1978 New York Yankees
The Deficit: 14 games back on July 18
The Comeback: The Boston Red Sox win their last eight games to force a playoff

The 1978 Red Sox were a powerhouse juggernaut. Led by slugger Jim Rice, who would finish the season leading the league in hits, triples, homers, total bases, and RBI, they pounded the ball. By mid-July they were more than 30 games over .500, leading Milwaukee by nine games and the Yankees by 14.

Yankee owner George Steinbrenner couldn't abide scurrilous comments by manager Billy Martin, who resigned and was replaced by the mellow Bob Lemon. The effect on the team was immediate. By mid-August the Yanks had taken ten out of 12. Then they won 12 out of 14. The Sox fell prey to an assortment of injuries, and the Yankees kept up the pressure, capped off by a four-game September sweep in Fenway Park in which the Yanks outscored the Sox 42–9. Naturally the Boston press dubbed it "The Boston Massacre."

In about seven weeks the Yankees had chewed up the 14-game difference and moved into a 3½-game lead. The Sox fought back, winning their final eight regular-season games to force a one-game playoff. In the finale, Yankee shortstop Bucky Dent, who belted a total of five home runs all year, slugged a three-run shot over the Green Monster in Fenway's left field, and the Yankees' huge comeback was complete. To this day Boston fans consider "Bucky Dent" a vile epithet.

The Team: 2004 Boston Red Sox
The Deficit: Down three games to none in the American League Championship Series
The Comeback: Four straight wins, including two in extra innings

The Red Sox seemed to be a team trapped by history. Many a rabid Bostonian believed in "The Curse of the Bambino," which claimed that the Sox were doomed never to win the World Series because they'd had the financial gall to sell the greatest player of all time, Babe Ruth. So when the team began the 2004 American

League Championship Series by dropping three in a row to their rivals, the New York Yankees, few expected them to overturn history's applecart.

To get an idea of the scale of the mountain they had to climb, consider that in 36 League Championship Series and 95 World Series, no team had ever come back from a 3–0 deficit to win a best-of-seven series. In fact, in those series, one team took a 3–0 lead 20 times, and only three times did the opponents win Game 4.

But these Red Sox called themselves "the idiots," because their all-out style of play didn't leave time for fretting over historical matters. The Sox were competitive in Games 1 and 2, but got clobbered 19–8 in Game 3. Three outs away from being swept in the Series, they rallied against longtime nemesis Yank reliever Mariano Rivera to tie Game 4 in the ninth inning and win on a David Ortiz homer in the 12th. The next night it took 14 innings for the Bostonians to eke out another win, this time also on an Ortiz RBI. He fouled off six pitches in a ten-pitch at-bat before he got the one he could knock. In Game 6, Curt Schilling rose to the occasion on a surgically patchworked right ankle (his tendon was temporarily sewn into place) and delivered seven heroic innings as the Sox tied the Series at three in what is now known as the "Blood on the Sock" game. Then they blew the Yanks over and rewrote history with a 10–3 victory in Game 7. They kept it rolling, sweeping the World Series in four games over the St. Louis Cardinals.

⚾ ⚾ ⚾

"Please don't interrupt, because you haven't heard this one before… honest. At precisely 4:45 P.M. today, in Yankee Stadium, off came the 52-year slur on the ability of the Dodgers to win a World Series, for at that moment the last straining Yankee was out at first base, and the day, the game, and the 1955 Series belonged to Brooklyn."

—Lead to Shirley Povich's story in *The Washington Post*,
October 4, 1955

Tragedy at the Polo Grounds

The pitch that haunted Carl Mays all his life was the one that cut Ray Chapman's life short.

"Nobody remembers anything about me except one thing—that I threw a pitch that caused a man to die," wrote Carl Mays in an article in *TSN* in 1963.

Forty-three years after the Yankees sidearmer let loose a fastball that fatally struck the Indians' Ray Chapman, the incident still haunted Mays. He went to his grave in 1971 at the age of 79, professing that the beaning was an accident and that the memory of it denied him enshrinement in the Hall of Fame.

On August 16, 1920, in a showdown between pennant contenders at the Polo Grounds in New York, Mays's first pitch of the fifth inning struck Chapman squarely in the side of the head. Chapman attempted to walk to the clubhouse, but he collapsed and was rushed to a nearby hospital, where he was diagnosed with a massive skull fracture. Doctors performed emergency surgery, but the Cleveland shortstop wouldn't live through the night. It was the first and only fatal accident involving a play on a major-league diamond.

Although Mays had a magnificent record, he had a reputation as an ornery loner and defended his right to pitch inside, suggesting a worn-out ball was to blame. Others pointed to Mays's otherwise extraordinary control and his long history of hit batsmen and doctored pitches, casting him as a villain.

The tragedy prompted officials to rigorously discard used or scuffed balls and added urgency to a recent ban on spitballs, shine balls, and other doctored pitches. These changes hastened an end to the "dead-ball era" and ushered in a new age of offense. One innovation that might have saved Chapman's life, the batting helmet, wouldn't come into popular use until the 1950s.

Heartbroken, but inspired by the memory of their popular teammate, the Indians would hold off the Yankees and the White Sox to win the 1920 American League pennant and defeat the Brooklyn Dodgers in the World Series.

Can of Corn

"You can't hit what you can't see."

—John Daley after pinch-hitting against Walter Johnson in 1912

"What's the matter, son? Did you lose your mother?"
"No, sir, I lost my fastball."

—Exchange between a priest and ex–All-Star Gene Conley
after Conley had been shelled by minor-leaguers
in a comeback attempt, *The Pitcher*

"If I'd known I was gonna pitch a no-hitter today, I would have gotten a haircut."

—Bo Belinsky, *The Suitors of Spring*

"I don't know that it's so important to have Tug McGraw's autograph. It's not like he's Donald Duck or something."

—Elementary schoolgirl on meeting Tug McGraw at his children's
school, *Sports Illustrated,* November 20, 1978

"Last year, more Americans went to symphonies than went to baseball games. This may be viewed as an alarming statistic, but I think that both baseball and the country will endure."

—President John F. Kennedy

"I believe the sale of Babe Ruth will ultimately strengthen the team."

—Red Sox owner Harry Frazee, who in January 1920 sold the
greatest player in baseball history to the Yankees

"Having Willie Stargell on your team is like having a diamond ring on your finger."

—Pittsburgh manager Chuck Tanner, *Time,* October 29, 1979

Greatest Teams of All Time

1936–39 New York Yankees

Record: 106–45 (1939)
Manager: Joe McCarthy
Hall of Famers: McCarthy, Lou Gehrig, Joe DiMaggio, Lefty Gomez, Bill Dickey, Red Ruffing
The Season: In 1939, Gehrig's illness became obvious, and he removed himself from the lineup after 2,130 consecutive games. This powerhouse team was able to keep on winning.
The Legacy: For four years in a row, the Yanks won the pennant; won at least 99 games; and led the league in runs scored, home runs, and ERA.

Were the Yankees of 1936–39 the greatest team of all time? It's not an outrageous claim to make. During that span, they averaged 102 wins a season. They won the pennant each year by an average of nearly 15 games. In each of those seasons, they scored more runs than any team in baseball, averaging 80 more runs per year than the second-best AL team. They beat the other guys by seven or more runs one game out of every four. At least ten times each year, their margin of victory was ten runs or more.

In each of those seasons, the Yankee pitching staff won the ERA title. And after dominating the AL each summer, they did the same to the NL in the World Series, with a 16–3 record in Series games and two four-game sweeps.

The left side of their infield was the same for the four-year span. Red Rolfe held down third, hitting over .300 three times and leading the league in doubles one year and triples another. Not a great hitter, slick-fielding shortstop (and later Yankee coach) Frankie Crosetti had some power and led the AL in stolen bases one year. The 1936 and '37 campaigns were second sacker Tony Lazzeri's final two as a Yank, and when he fell to a .244 average and just 14 homers, he was replaced by Joe Gordon, who banged 25 and

28 homers in 1938 and '39, respectively. First base belonged to Lou Gehrig, of course, until his illness forced him out of the lineup forever after just eight games in '39. From 1936 through '38, Gehrig averaged .334 with 38 homers, 142 RBI, and 140 runs scored.

Bill Dickey was the catcher. In addition to being a superb defensive player and handler of pitchers, his lowest batting average during that span was .302; his highest, .362. The outfield is where brainy Joe McCarthy did most of his tinkering. In June 1936, Ben Chapman was hitting just .266, so McCarthy swapped him to the Senators for Jake Powell, who batted .306 as a Yank that year. Tommy Henrich joined the team in 1937, Charlie Keller in '39. George Selkirk and Joe DiMaggio remained the other outfielders for all four years.

The 1936 campaign was DiMaggio's rookie season, and he showed why he was on his way to Cooperstown, batting .323 with 44 doubles, 15 triples (leading the league), and 29 homers. He also drove in 125 runs and scored 132. In 1937, he led the league with 46 home runs and 151 runs scored, and he drove in 167. In 1939, he won his first batting title with a .381 average.

McCarthy relied on two ace pitchers during the four years: Red Ruffing and Lefty Gomez. Ruffing won 20, 20, 21, and 21 in remarkably consistent style. Gomez won 21 in 1937 and 18 in '38. Surrounding them was a supporting cast that McCarthy utilized perfectly. Johnny Murphy was 13–4 and 8–2 in 1937 and '38 as the top reliever. Others who contributed a dozen wins or more in at least one of those seasons included Monte Pearson, Bump Hadley, Pat Malone, Johnny Broaca, Spud Chandler, and Atley Donald.

This Yankee team was capable of fireworks only dreamed of by previous squads. On May 23, 1936, in Philadelphia's Shibe Park, the Yanks made mincemeat of the Athletics' hurlers, winning a doubleheader 12–6 and 15–1. The Yanks belted seven homers that day and cracked 30 hits. The A's starter in Game 1 was rapped out of the box in the second inning. Connie Mack brought him back in Game 2, and he gave up six more runs. The next day, the Yankees really went to town, hammering the A's 25–2. Lazzeri hit two grand slams that day (the first player ever to accomplish the feat) and added a third homer and a triple. DiMaggio homered, and Crosetti slugged a pair out of the park.

Who Am I?

There are some things about the game's star players that even the most seasoned baseball expert doesn't know. See if you can guess each of the players being described here.

1) He began his career playing for a semipro team called the Amarillo Colts.

2) He once received a grand total of $20 for playing a night game in Lincoln, Nebraska.

3) When he was a child, his father would pay him a nickel in order to get him to play catch.

4) He operated a car dealership while playing in the major leagues.

5) An anonymous phone caller once made a death threat against him during spring training.

6) He never played in a World Series.

A: Ernie Banks

1) He flied out in his first major-league at-bat and made an error in his first game.

2) He suffered from osteomyelitis, an unrelenting bone disease, and doctors took two inches of bone from his left foot when he was eight years old.

3) He seemed to have little fear of injury, a possible reason for his many broken bones, which included a broken collarbone and a broken hand—an injury that caused him to miss a month out of the 1967 season and possibly cost his team the pennant.

4) In 1973, he hit a career-low .255 while playing only 91 games.

5) He finished his career playing primarily as a designated hitter.

A: Al Kaline

1) As a teenager, he temporarily suffered from a heart murmur.

2) He allowed a home run to the first major-league batter who faced him.

3) He was partly responsible for the major league's decision to lower the pitcher's mound by five inches.

4) During one of his team's pennant-winning seasons, he missed two months with a broken leg.

5) He once lost the seventh game of the World Series.

6) He delayed his start in the major leagues to play for the Harlem Globetrotters.

A: Bob Gibson

1) He was first signed by a scout for $1 and an autographed ball.

2) He missed three full seasons and part of a fourth in the middle of his career while serving in World War II.

3) He once lost a World Series game in which he pitched a two-hitter.

4) His manager chose not to pitch him in his final World Series.

5) His mother was hit in the face by a line drive off one of his pitches, leaving her in the hospital for two weeks with cuts, bruises, and two black eyes.

6) He openly feuded with Pete Rose and has been vocal in his opposition to Rose being considered for induction into the Hall of Fame.

A: Bob Feller

1) He began his career playing for Sandersville of the Georgia State League.

2) He went 4-for-4 against Hall of Fame pitcher Robin Roberts in his first major-league game.

3) He was platooned for several seasons at the beginning of his career.

4) His line drive, the final out in the World Series his team lost, became an ongoing element in the *Peanuts* comic strip.

5) In 1977, he was forced to attend spring training as a non-roster player.

A: *Willie McCovey*

1) After struggling in Class D at Williamson, West Virginia, an official with his parent major-league team recommended that he be released.

2) On the verge of being released, he was switched from pitching to playing the outfield due to a shoulder injury.

3) He batted only .222 in his first World Series and also batted .222 in his last World Series.

4) He memorized the speed of the fastball, curve, and slider of every pitcher in the league. He said that he knew how the ball would move by the time it crossed the plate, because he could pick up its speed within its first 30 feet of flight.

5) He missed the entire 1945 season because of military service during World War II.

6) He is an accomplished harmonica player.

A: *Stan Musial*

1) He missed two years because of military service during the Vietnam War.

2) In 1969, he made 11 errors in his first 31 games.

3) Although known for his power, he hit only ten home runs in 1974.

4) After retiring from the major leagues, he won three Emmy Awards for live sports coverage as a broadcaster.

5) He went 0-for-3 in his only World Series.

6) He retired without winning a world championship.

A: Bobby Murcer

1) He was put up for adoption immediately after he was born. Two days later, he was adopted.

2) He played his first professional season for a team in South Dakota in the Northern League.

3) He missed all of the 1968 season with a sore arm.

4) Late in his major-league career, he was an underwear model and donated all the proceeds from the sale of the advertising poster to the Cystic Fibrosis Foundation.

5) After pitching a no-hitter despite allowing six walks, he called it the "ugliest no-hitter ever."

6) He made an unsuccessful comeback seven years after his retirement.

A: Jim Palmer

1) As a minor-league player, he was threatened by a shotgun-toting fan who vowed to kill him if he picked up a hit that night.

2) As a rookie in the major leagues, he hit only .243.

3) During his second LCS, he went 0-for-14 at the plate.

4) Once while trying to steal second base, he realized that he would be out easily and tried to call a time-out.

5) While attempting to break up a fight on the field, he suffered a pinched nerve in his elbow, bringing his season to an early end.

6) Known for his monstrous home runs, he hit two of only four long balls ever hit completely out of Dodger Stadium and seven of the 18 ever hit out of Forbes Field.

A: Willie Stargell

Fast Facts

- In 1954, Joe Bauman hit 72 homers for Class C Roswell, New Mexico, a professional record that stood for 47 years until Barry Bonds of the San Francisco Giants broke it in 2001.

- The only two players to play in four different divisions in the same season are slugger Dave Kingman in 1977 and pitcher Dan Miceli in 2003.

- Pitcher Randy Johnson holds the lifetime record for average number of strikeouts per nine innings with 10.8.

- Each major-league baseball has 108 stitches.

- Cecil Fielder played 1,097 games before stealing his first base, the longest any player has ever gone without a stolen base.

- On September 17, 1947, Jackie Robinson became the first player to be named Rookie of the Year.

- The St. Louis Browns moved to Baltimore in 1953 and became the Orioles in 1954.

- Darryl Strawberry is the only player to play for all four teams that originated in New York: the Yankees, Dodgers, Giants, and Mets.

- In 1974, Mike Marshall became the first relief pitcher to win the Cy Young Award.

- Babe Ruth wore No. 3 because he was batting third in the Yankee lineup when the team decided to add numbers to its uniforms in 1929. Lou Gehrig, who batted behind him, drew No. 4.

When You're Hot, You're Hot!

Some hitters get on a roll and just keep connecting, knocking out hits in game after game. Here are the longest hitting streaks in MLB history.

Joe DiMaggio

1941, New York Yankees
56 games

During his streak, which ran from May 15 until July 17, DiMaggio went 91-for-223, hitting .408. He had 16 doubles, four triples, and 15 home runs, along with 55 RBI. After the 41st game, in which DiMaggio tied George Sisler for the AL record, a fan swiped his bat. He had to use Tommy Henrich's in the second game of the doubleheader to move past Sisler. In the middle of the streak, Joe had a hit in the All-Star Game, too.

In front of the largest night game crowd in history—67,468 at Cleveland Municipal Stadium—DiMaggio was stopped, largely due to two sensational plays by Indians superior third baseman Ken Keltner on hot smashes over the bag. Perhaps most impressive, DiMaggio's team had won 41 of the 56 games in his streak. After it ended, DiMaggio hit safely in his next 16 games.

Even the 56-game streak wasn't DiMaggio's longest—in the minors, he'd had a 61-game streak, which shattered the previous record of 49. Joe's brother Dom had an impressive 34-game streak of his own for the Boston Red Sox in 1949.

Willie Keeler

1897, Baltimore Orioles
45 games

It was the greatest start to any season ever: Keeler hit safely in his first 44 games. Technically, since he had hit in the final game of the 1896 season, he really had a 45-game streak. Throughout his career, Keeler also had two 26-game hitting streaks, and he had 200 or more hits per season eight years in a row—a record that's still unmatched.

Pete Rose
1978, Cincinnati Reds
44 games

Pete Rose had banged his 3,000th career hit on May 5, 1978, and most people figured that would be his outstanding accomplishment of the year. But then on June 14, the 37-old Rose started a 44-game streak. (DiMaggio was only 26 when he hit his streak in 1941; Keeler was 25 in 1897.) Rose finished that season at .302, with 51 doubles. The closest he came to having his streak snapped early was in its 32nd game in the July 19th game against Philadelphia. Rose had gone hitless when he came to bat in the ninth, but his bunt single in the 11th kept the streak alive. The Atlanta Braves finally held Rose hitless on August 1, after 70 hits over 44 games. The next day he had four hits.

Bill Dahlen
1894, Chicago Colts
42 games

Dahlen was a talented shortstop who also had a knack with the bat. After having his 42-game streak snapped on August 7, Dahlen proceeded to smack hits in 28 more consecutive games, meaning he hit in 70 out of 71 games.

George Sisler
1922, St. Louis Browns
41 games

Sisler had 23 multiple-hit games during his streak, and he batted .460. He had 14 doubles and seven triples but not a single homer during that time. He finished the season with a .420 average, the fourth highest ever since 1901, and was voted the 1922 American League MVP.

Ty Cobb
1911, Detroit Tigers
40 games

Cobb's bat was on fire during this streak—he batted .476 with 40 runs, 12 doubles, eight triples, and one home run—and so were his feet: He stole home three times. Cobb also had hitting streaks of 35, 25, and 21 games (twice) during his remarkable career.

Paul Molitor
1987, Milwaukee Brewers
39 games

Of all the major-league hitting streaks, Molitor's came to the most bittersweet end. He had gone 0-for-4 against rookie John Farrell and was on deck waiting to bat against Doug Jones when his teammate Rick Manning delivered the game-winning hit in the bottom of the tenth.

Jimmy Rollins
2005–06, Philadelphia Phillies
38 games

Some people take issue with this record since it was accumulated over two seasons. Rollins batted safely in 36 games in 2005 then, seven months later, in two more. But since the official rule for a streak is "consecutive games in which the player appears," Major League Baseball considers it a 38-game streak.

Tommy Holmes
1945, Boston Braves
37 games

This was just the centerpiece of a monster year for Holmes, in which he batted .352 with 117 RBI, 125 runs scored, and 15 stolen bases. He led the league in hits, homers, and doubles. Unfortunately, the rest of his team wasn't as good, and he finished second in the MVP voting to the first-place Cubs' Phil Cavarretta. Holmes went on to have 20-game streaks in 1946 and 1949.

The World's Love Affair with Baseball

America's game is growing in popularity across the globe.

Of the 16,000-plus players ever to compete in the major leagues, nearly 1,000 have come from the Dominican Republic, Puerto Rico, Venezuela, and Japan (combined). Even Canada, not considered a baseball hotbed, has sent more than 200 players, including Hall of Famer Ferguson Jenkins, to the majors. Mexico has produced approximately 100 big-leaguers—among them, national icon Fernando Valenzuela. With these countries sitting so close to the United States, it seems logical that such a high-paying, high-profile job would attract neighbors. But what about countries far from the U.S.? Turns out the game is a hit with many of them, too.

One reason is the Little League World Series. The winner-take-all-the-glory tournament is immensely popular in many nations. While U.S. teams slug it out in Williamsport for a spot in the national bracket, the rest of the world competes in the other bracket. And the competition is fierce.

Also, the World Baseball Classic brought the professional game to a world stage in 2006. Even as Americans groused about the WBC's timing (during spring training) and its effect on pitchers' arms (a handful of participants suffered injuries), the passion for the tournament in other countries made it a success. Teams from the United States, Dominican Republic, Puerto Rico, and Korea—all considered favorites—were elimi-

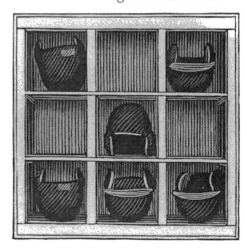

nated in early rounds. The Cubans, winners of three of the first four Olympic gold medals in baseball, reached the finals, where they went up against the Japanese. Using only two players from the American major leagues, Japan won the inaugural title. They could rightfully be called world champions. Other countries, too, hope to have a baseball title of their own someday.

Australia
American gold miners brought baseball to Australia in the 1850s. Joe Quinn, who moved to the United States as a teenager, was the first Australian to reach the major leagues, in 1884. It took another century for the second, Craig Shipley, to make the majors. About 20 Aussies have followed, even as the game has declined in popularity at home. Despite the death of Australia's professional league, the country's silver medal in the 2004 Olympics provided baseball a boost in its constant battle with cricket.

Taiwan
Taiwan won 17 Little League titles between 1969 and 1996. All other non-U.S. countries won just 13 championships combined. Yankee Chien-Ming Wang, Taiwan's first bona-fide major-league star, has caused such a stir that thousands of his countrymen watch his games—broadcast live from New York—in the middle of the night local time on Taiwanese public television. Taiwan's own major league has had to deal with the aftershocks of a gambling scandal. But the renewed interest in baseball, plus Taiwan's history of Little League world dominance, should only nurture a game introduced to the island by the Japanese colonial government in the 1920s.

Korea
Like Taiwan, Korea has become a baseball power in recent decades. Introduced to the game by an American missionary in 1905, Korea started its first professional league in 1982. The Korean Baseball Organization's first alum to reach the major leagues was Chan Ho Park, in 1994. More than a dozen countrymen (and counting) have followed.

China

China may be the last country to host the game on an Olympic stage. Baseball and softball are marked for elimination after the 2008 Games in Beijing. The International Olympic Committee will consider bringing baseball back for the 2016 Games, but with the exception of Italy, few of the influential European IOC countries have ever really taken to baseball. Inroads have, however, been made in the People's Republic of China.

The game was first introduced there in the 1860s by Americans in Shanghai; its slow progress was halted a century later during the Cultural Revolution because the government considered baseball elitist. Yet the government has been instrumental in resuscitating the game in the Middle Kingdom. The Chinese Baseball League has been running since 2002, giving budding ballplayers a chance to hone their skills.

While few Chinese attend the games, despite no admission charge, that didn't stop the New York Yankees from visiting in January 2007. The Yanks met with government officials, promising to send coaches, scouts, and doctors to observe and interact with Chinese players. Their goodwill trip was the first real outreach by the major leagues to China. It may not bear fruit in terms of players for a generation, but out of a country with 1.3 billion people, the Yankees are betting they might find a future superstar.

◖◗ ◖◗ ◖◗

"Baseball is just the great American pastime. I think it's the joy of feeling part of [the game] more than other sports."

—President George H. W. Bush, *The Washington Post,*
March 31, 1989

◖◗ ◖◗ ◖◗

"The game of baseball is a clean, straight game, and it summons to its presence everybody who enjoys clean, straight athletics. It furnishes amusement to the thousands and thousands."

—President William Howard Taft

The Nickname Game

There was a time when ballplayers were apt to receive clever monikers. A man's nickname told you something about him and—occasionally—how he played the game.

Nicknames have been a staple of baseball throughout most of the game's history. Unfortunately, this practice is not quite as exciting now as it once was. Fans who used to revel in colorful names like "The Sultan of Swat" (Babe Ruth) and "Death to Flying Things" (Bob Ferguson) are now subjected to such uncreative monikers as "Jetes" (for Derek Jeter), the effortless shortening of names like "Junior" for Ken Griffey, Jr., and "A-Rod" for Alex Rodriguez, and unintended commercialism, like calling Mark McGwire "Big Mac." Such titles aren't really nicknames at all; most of them are puns or a play on words, which tell us very little about the player. Looking at some of the best from years past might help conjure up a few image-instilling names for today's players.

"Shoeless Joe" Jackson

Sometimes a nickname becomes so synonymous with a player that it becomes attached to the front end of his or her real name. In "Shoeless Joe" Jackson's case, he acquired his handle early in his professional career while playing for Greenville of the Carolina Association. During the 1908 season, Jackson tried to break in a new pair of shoes. The next game, his feet hurt so badly that he switched back to his old pair, but the pain continued. He decided to play the game without wearing any shoes at all, prompting one fan to yell, "Look at Shoeless Joe!"

Jay Hanna "Dizzy" Dean and Paul "Daffy" Dean

In some cases, nicknames fit the player; in other cases, they're contrived to make headlines or accommodate a story line. Jay Hanna "Dizzy" Dean acquired his nickname while pitching in a 1928 exhibition game for the U.S. Army against the Chicago White Sox. When Dean started mowing down opposition batters, White Sox manager Lena Blackburne reportedly yelled to his players,

"Don't let that dizzy rookie fool ya'." In 1930, Dean cemented the nickname when he joined the St. Louis Cardinals and exhibited the unusual behavior and speech patterns that would stamp him as one of the game's most colorful characters. After games, he liked to say to the press, "If you can do it, it ain't braggin'."

Four years later, younger brother Paul Dean made the Cardinals roster. St. Louis sportswriters gave him the nickname "Daffy" because it worked in combination with Dizzy. In reality, Paul was nowhere near as colorful as his brother. Quiet and serious, Daffy was actually called "Harpo" in certain company because he reminded people of the Marx brother who never spoke.

Ted "The Splendid Splinter" Williams

Early in Williams's career, the Boston press dubbed him "The Splendid Splinter." The nickname made sense, given his spindly frame as a younger player. At 6'3", he weighed only 168 pounds, yet he could still crank out the hits. Williams actually preferred two other nicknames: "The Kid," which he began referring to himself as early in his Red Sox career, and "Teddy Ballgame," started rather inadvertently by the young son of a Boston photographer. When asked to name the ballplayer he most wanted to meet, the boy responded by saying, "Teddy... Teddy Ballgame."

Ralph "The Road Runner" Garr

Major-league outfielder Ralph "The Road Runner" Garr became almost as well known for the nickname as the original Looney Tunes cartoon figure created by Chuck Jones. The Atlanta Braves public relations department gave Garr the nickname after he arrived in the big leagues; in fact, the Braves so wanted to market Garr that they wrote to Warner Brothers, Inc., to receive official permission to use the nickname and the catchphrase "Beep! Beep!" in promotional efforts. Warner Brothers came to a history-making agreement with the Braves. "Our contract with the Braves makes Ralph the first licensed nickname to our knowledge anywhere in the world," said Licensing Corporation of America chairman Jay Emmett. The unusual agreement also made it illegal for any other athlete to use the nickname.

Brooks "Vacuum Cleaner" Robinson

Even nice guys are given nicknames. Hall of Fame third baseman Brooks Robinson, a consummate gentleman among the game's greats, acquired two of the best nicknames of the expansion era (1961–1976)—one that is well known and one that is a bit more obscure. Robinson's ability to inhale ground balls with his soft hands earned him the title "Vacuum Cleaner," a nickname that seemed all the more appropriate when artificial turf came into vogue in the late 1960s. And then there was the handle that his Oriole teammates preferred, one that might be considered a little less flattering. Some enjoyed calling Brooksie "The Head," since his receding hairline made his skull appear larger than it actually was.

With all of the above players long since retired, nicknames have become far less commonplace. However, a couple contemporary players have acquired descriptive monikers.

Roger "The Rocket" Clemens

Possessing a high, riding fastball that approached the upper 90s in velocity, Clemens became known as "The Rocket." With his launchpad fastball revving at its peak on April 29, 1986, Clemens struck out 20 Seattle Mariners, setting a nine-inning record and solidifying the nickname. After the new handle took hold, most baseball fans didn't realize that Clemens had earned another nickname during his college days. A star at the University of Texas, he was sometimes referred to as "Big Tex."

Frank "The Big Hurt" Thomas

Some nicknames require a bit of extra creativity. At 6'5" and 275 pounds, Frank Thomas is one of the largest men to ever pick up a major-league bat. His enormous size (which helped him play football as a tight end in college), combined with his ability to hit searing line drives and gargantuan home runs, led Chicago White Sox broadcaster Ken "Hawk" Harrelson to dub Thomas "The Big Hurt." It perfectly captures his immensity in the batter's box and his ability to strike the ball with unusual force.

Oh, My!

Fusing ancient techniques and a singular style, Sadaharu Oh made himself baseball's all-time home run king.

No player in the history of professional baseball hit as many home runs in a career as Sadaharu Oh, the son of a Chinese cook who learned to hit by swinging a bamboo stick in the style of a 15th-century swordsman.

Like Babe Ruth, Oh was a left-handed slugger who began his career as a pitcher. Signed by the Yomiyuri (Tokyo) Giants in 1959, Oh was converted to a first baseman to take advantage of his hitting prowess, but the experiment was nearly a disaster. Possessed of a hitch in his swing that made him vulnerable to inside pitches, Oh batted just .161 in his rookie year, striking out 72 times in just 193 at-bats.

Frustrated, the Giants turned to Hiroshi Arakawa, a former pro baseball player and a martial arts guru who, years earlier, had encountered Oh on a Tokyo sandlot and encouraged the Giants to sign him. Working with Arakawa, Oh would master techniques and discipline drawn from the martial art Aikido, specifically *ki* (concentration) and *ma* (timing). By developing a distinctive swing, lifting his front foot high off the ground in concert with the pitcher, he corrected his hitch. Oh cultivated power—and mental toughness—from practicing *iai-do*, the ancient Japanese art of drawing the sword, which generated strength at the hips and encouraged "life or death" intentions at the plate.

"I craved hitting a baseball in the way a samurai craved following the Way of the Sword," Oh wrote in his autobiography. "It was my life."

The training paid off. By his fourth season, Oh led the Japan Central League in home runs and RBI and was on his way to 19 straight 30–home run seasons and an all-time mark of 868 round-trippers. He won triple crowns in 1973 and 1974, earned five batting titles, and was named Most Valuable Player nine times. Arakawa remained Oh's mentor throughout his 22-year career.

Oh's adherence to traditional methods, and the spectacular results that followed, made him a great favorite of fans throughout Japan. His "flamingo style" batting stance would be imitated by scores of Japanese ballplayers, and pitchers were constantly laboring to disrupt his legendary concentration at the plate. One enterprising opponent, Yutaka Enatsu, was known to intentionally run the count to 3–0 to entice Oh to think of balls and not strikes when at the plate.

By the early 1970s, as Henry Aaron chased Babe Ruth's home run mark in the states, across the world Oh was gaining even faster on both of them. The media were tempted to paint the chase as a rivalry between the two sluggers, but what emerged during meetings of the country's respective home run kings was mutual admiration.

⚾ ⚾ ⚾

"Sixty. Count 'em. Sixty! Let's see some other SOB match that!"

—Babe Ruth in the Yankee locker room after hitting his
60th homer of the season, September 30, 1927,
Clout! The Top Home Runs in Baseball History

⚾ ⚾ ⚾

"I would be the laughingstock of the league if I took the best left-handed pitcher in the league and put him in the outfield."

—Red Sox manager Ed Barrow in 1918 on moving
Babe Ruth from the mound to a full-time position,
The Sporting News, January 16, 1965

Baseball Lingo

Sprechen sie baseball?

Alibi Ike: An excuse-maker. **Origin:** A fictitious nickname often used by famed baseball writer Ring Lardner.

Antkiller: A hard-hit ball on the ground. Also known as a "worm-burner" or "wormkiller." **Origin:** Descriptive.

Baltimore chop: A base hit achieved when the batter chops down on the ball, causing a high bounce and allowing the batter to arrive at first base safely before the ball is fielded. **Origin:** Baltimore refers to the home city of the Orioles, for whom Wee Willie Keeler and his mates of the 1890s perfected the art.

Bird-dog: A scout, particularly a freelancing local who alerts regional scouts of finds. **Origin:** Hunting term.

Breaking his dishes: A hard pitch in on the hands. Also called "getting in his kitchen." **Origin:** Descriptive of shattering the bat, like a dropped dish, or the kitchen, where the dishes are kept.

Clutch: A critical situation, or how a player performs in such. **Origin:** Industry. The clutch is a key part of machinery.

Crank: Fan. **Origin:** Common 19th-century word for "fan."

Ducks on the pond: Runners on the bases. **Origin:** Expression favored by Washington announcer Arch McDonald.

Frozen rope: A hard line drive. **Origin:** Descriptive.

Golden sombrero: To strike out four times in one game. **Origin:** An exaggeration of the common sporting phrase "hat trick," indicating three of something. Originated in cricket, where a batter getting three wickets in one swing was awarded a hat. A sombrero is a large, gaudy Mexican hat. A player who strikes out five times in a game is said to have a "platinum sombrero."

Hot dog: A flashy player, often a show-off. **Origin:** From the word "hot" and the popular ballpark fare. The term "hot dog," a variation of "dachshund sausage," gained popular usage from concessionaire's calls at ballgames. A player "hot dogging it" is trying to attract the same kind of fan attention a hot dog might command over other refreshments at a ballgame.

Iron Mike: A pitching machine with a mechanical arm. **Origin:** Military slang for a man who's tough and durable.

Junior circuit: The American League. **Origin:** The newer of the two leagues, founded in 1901. The National League (1876) is referred to as the "senior circuit."

Knock: A hit. **Origin:** Descriptive of the sound of the bat hitting the ball.

Message pitch: An inside pitch used to back a player away from the plate. **Origin:** Descriptive. Sometimes called a "purpose pitch."

Pull the string: To fool a batter with an off-speed pitch. **Origin:** Descriptive of a ball arriving later than the hitter anticipated, as if pulled back by a string.

Rhubarb: A heated argument or fight on the field, usually between manager and umpire. **Origin:** In acting, extras often repeat the word "rhubarb" to one another to simulate audible but indiscernible background talking. Such incessant chatter is often a feature of manager-umpire confrontations.

Stone hands: A poor fielder. **Origin:** Descriptive.

Magical Moments

Ripken achieves the "unachievable."

The Setting: Oriole Park at Camden Yards; September 6, 1995
The Magic: Cal Ripken, Jr., breaks Lou Gehrig's "unbreakable" consecutive-game streak.

We don't just want our baseball heroes to be good; we want them to be good for a long time. Lou Gehrig's incredible record of 2,130 consecutive games had been a testament to his greatness. It seemed to be a feat that no one else could achieve . . . until Cal Ripken came along, playing inning after inning, game after game, year after year. Ripken's appearance in every game for more than 13 seasons is especially monumental when you realize that during his streak more than 3,700 players spent time on the disabled list.

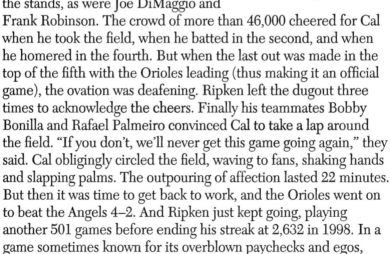

That September night in Baltimore, as Ripken prepared to beat Gehrig's streak, President Bill Clinton and Vice President Al Gore were in the stands, as were Joe DiMaggio and Frank Robinson. The crowd of more than 46,000 cheered for Cal when he took the field, when he batted in the second, and when he homered in the fourth. But when the last out was made in the top of the fifth with the Orioles leading (thus making it an official game), the ovation was deafening. Ripken left the dugout three times to acknowledge the cheers. Finally his teammates Bobby Bonilla and Rafael Palmeiro convinced Cal to take a lap around the field. "If you don't, we'll never get this game going again," they said. Cal obligingly circled the field, waving to fans, shaking hands and slapping palms. The outpouring of affection lasted 22 minutes. But then it was time to get back to work, and the Orioles went on to beat the Angels 4–2. And Ripken just kept going, playing another 501 games before ending his streak at 2,632 in 1998. In a game sometimes known for its overblown paychecks and egos, Ripken proved to be a class act year after year after year.

Fast Facts

- Hank Bauer of the Yankees had hits in 17 consecutive World Series games from 1956 to 1958.

- The only two teams with four 20-game winners are the 1971 Orioles, who lost the World Series to the Pirates, and the 1920 White Sox, who didn't even win the pennant.

- Jim Rice of the Boston Red Sox was a powerful slugger but not speedy afoot. In 1984, he set the record by grounding into 36 double plays.

- Sammy Sosa has the most career home runs without ever being in a World Series.

- On August 9, 1946, for the first time in both leagues, all games were scheduled for play at night, and each game was actually played.

- Barry Bonds's on-base percentage of .609 in 2004 is the highest of all time; second highest is his .582 in 2002.

- On May 27, 1960, Clint Courtney became the first catcher to use the knuckleball "big mitt."

- Dave Stewart of the Oakland A's and Fernando Valenzuela of the Los Angeles Dodgers both threw no-hitters in 1990—on the same day (June 29).

- There have been three World Series in which the home team won every game. One was in 2001, when the Diamondbacks trumped the Yankees. The other two victories were by the Minnesota Twins—over the St. Louis Cardinals in 1987 and the Atlanta Braves in 1991.

Iraq Embraces America's Pastime

Baseball-starved American troops find a way to play during wartime and, in the process, spread the joy of the game.

Bats, balls, and gloves were not high on the U.S. military's list of equipment to bring to Iraq. But that didn't stop the Hawaii-based 25th Infantry Division's 2nd Brigade. With a bit of free time on their hands and an All-American desire to get a pick-up game started, the soldiers improvised as well as any stickball-playing youngsters on a Bronx street ever could. The setting: a soccer field in Altun Kupri, a small and historically safe town north of Baghdad, with Humvees parked at each "outfield pole" and another serving as a center-field wall. The equipment: wadded paper wrapped in duct tape for a ball and an aluminum cot leg for a bat.

As word got back to the sister of Captain Deron Haught in West Virginia, the soldiers became better equipped for games more closely resembling traditional baseball. "She felt bad," Haught noted in 2004. "We were over here serving our country, and we were playing baseball with a tape ball and a cot leg. So she started 'Operation Home Run.'" Soon, balls, bats, and mitts came from the States. And as the equipment arrived, some of the locals began taking interest in a game that differed vastly from the traditional sports of choice in Iraq—soccer and volleyball.

Haught went one step further, convincing the Altun Kupri city council to help interested teenagers form teams for an organized game. The rules were not easy to teach (try explaining baseball to a group of youngsters never exposed to the sport), but the kids caught on quickly to the basics of throwing, hitting, and running. Mainly, what the American soldiers-turned-coaches stressed were traits like teamwork and sportsmanship. "I think baseball is a great example of democracy," Haught said.

Haught served as home plate umpire and public address announcer when Nawruz (Kurdish for New Year's Day) took on Brusik (Team Lightning) in the game that served as the crowning moment of Operation Home Run's efforts. Haught announced: "We'd like to welcome you to the first Iraqi baseball game. This game has been played in America for over a hundred years, and we want to share it with Altun Kupri and with this country."

As the 25th Infantry Division's 2nd Brigade played—and taught—the game, more and more youngsters came out to participate. It was Haught's hope that baseball would continue to spread not only in the Altun Kupri area but also in other parts of the country.

And for the record, Nawruz defeated Brusik 10–7. Said Diller Fakhraddin, the winning pitcher, "I like this game. It's better than soccer."

⚾ ⚾ ⚾

"Well, I don't know anything about base ball, or town ball, now-a-days, but it does me good to see these fellows. They've done something to add to the glory of our city."

—Views of a fan rooting for the Cincinnati Red Stockings,
(Cincinnati) *Commercial,* July 1, 1869

⚾ ⚾ ⚾

Ten Cent Beer Night at Cleveland's Municipal Stadium and Disco Demolition Night at Chicago's Comiskey Park were promotions in the 1970s that both resulted in riots. Ten Cent Beer Night drew more than 25,000 people on June 4, 1974, and the cheap beer caused the crowd to get quite rowdy. Some fans rushed the field, resulting in a spectator hitting an Indians pitcher in the head with a lawn chair. Disco Demolition Night, which drew a crowd of 50,000 people on July 12, 1979, offered a 98-cent admission fee in exchange for an unwanted disco record. When the demolition began between games of a doubleheader, and a mock bomb exploded in the outfield, thousands ran onto the field, starting their own fires and mini-riots. Both promotions resulted in forfeiture of the games for the players' safety.

MVP: Many Voting Peculiarities

Everyone is entitled to his or her opinion, but not every Most Valuable Player candidate or fan is going to like it.

Baseball's Most Valuable Player Award was established in 1911. In the century since, there has been more than a little controversy regarding some of the recipients. In some years, the most valuable player in the league has been an obvious choice. Other years, however, the lines of distinction have blurred. What attributes are *most* valuable? Do stats count more than character? Should a player from a second-division team win? Is a pitcher more or less valuable than a slugger? There are no easy answers.

1925 AL MVP: Roger Peckinpaugh (.294 BA, 4 HR, 64 RBI, 67 R)
Who Could Have Won: Al Simmons (.387 BA, 24 HR, 129 RBI, 122 R)
The Controversy: The value of a winning team.

Veteran shortstop Peckinpaugh won a narrow victory over Simmons, the hard-hitting sophomore center fielder for the A's, primarily because he was credited with leading his Washington Senators to a pennant. Peckinpaugh accepted the award, then had a nightmarish World Series (eight errors, including a critical eighth-inning miscue in Game 7 that allowed Pittsburgh to take the lead and ultimately win the game and the Series). It was no coincidence that, beginning in 1926, all MVP voting results were released after the World Series.

1928 AL MVP: Mickey Cochrane (.293 BA, 10 HR, 57 RBI, 92 R)
Who Could Have Won: Heine Manush (.378 BA, 13 HR, 108 RBI, 104 R)
The Controversy: Value relative to position.

In a magnificent race between two future Hall of Famers in

their prime, Cochrane edged Manush in a vote that rewarded offensive firepower from the catching position ahead of superior numbers from a corner outfielder.

1941 AL MVP: Joe DiMaggio (.357 BA, 30 HR, 125 RBI, 122 R)
Who Could Have Won: Ted Williams (.406 BA, 37 HR, 120 RBI, 135 R, 147 BB)
The Controversy: The value of writing the record books.

Brilliant years from each of the longtime combatants left voters to ponder the more valuable milestone: DiMaggio's record 56-game hitting streak, or Williams eclipsing the .400 mark?

1942 AL MVP: Joe Gordon (.322 BA, 18 HR, 103 RBI, 88 R)
Who Could Have Won: Ted Williams (.356 BA, 36 HR, 137 RBI, 141 R)
The Controversy: The value of relationships.

A frosty relationship with the press couldn't have helped Williams's cause: He led the AL in all Triple Crown categories but saw the hardware go to Gordon, the affable Yankee second baseman.

1952 NL MVP: Hank Sauer (.270 BA, 37 HR, 121 RBI, 89 R)
Who Could Have Won: Robin Roberts (28–7, 2.59 ERA, 148 SO), or any of five Brooklyn Dodgers
The Controversy: Value relative to teammates.

Sauer's surprise win raised questions about whether a top performer on a second-division club was worth more than a solid contributor on a pennant winner. The champion Dodgers were "cursed" with five legitimate candidates in '52, including rookie reliever Joe Black (who finished third in the voting thanks to 15 wins and 15 saves), as well as Jackie Robinson, Pee Wee Reese, Duke Snider, and Roy Campanella, who finished seventh through tenth in the voting, respectively.

1962 NL MVP: Maury Wills (.299 BA, 6 HR, 48 RBI, 130 R, 104 SB)
Who Could Have Won: Willie Mays (.304 BA, 49 HR, 141 RBI, 130 R) or Frank Robinson (.342 BA, 39 HR, 136 RBI, 134 R)

The Controversy: The value of speed.

While Wills's 104 stolen bases more than tripled his next nearest competitor and helped usher in a new emphasis on the running game, there are many who argue the real MVP race that year should have come down to Mays, who finished second, and Robinson, who finished fourth. Robinson actually improved upon his 1961 MVP-winning year and nearly won a Triple Crown. Mays led the league in home runs and led the Giants to the NL pennant, but Wills, true to his talent, stole votes safely.

1988 NL MVP: Kirk Gibson (.290 BA, 25 HR, 76 RBI, 106 R)
Who Could Have Won: Darryl Strawberry (.269 BA, 39 HR, 101 RBI, 101 R)
The Controversy: The value of inspiration.

Occasionally, an inspiring player on an overachieving team steals the hearts of voters at the expense of a candidate with comparable (or better) numbers. It happened in 1979 (Willie Stargell's co-MVP honors with Keith Hernandez), in 1991 (Terry Pendleton over Barry Bonds), and in 1988, when Gibson of the surprising Dodgers edged the mighty Mets' Strawberry in a battle of corner outfielders for respective division winners. Strawberry's cause may also have been hurt by splitting votes with a deserving teammate, Kevin McReynolds, who finished third.

1999 AL MVP: Ivan Rodriguez (.332 BA, 35 HR, 113 RBI, 116 R)
Who Could Have Won: Pedro Martinez (23–4, 2.07 ERA, 313 SO)
The Controversy: The values of the voters.

Results this year spotlighted how sportswriters can affect outcomes based on how they interpret the rules of voting. Martinez's astonishing season, in the midst of an explosive offensive era, garnered him more first-place votes than Rodriguez, but Martinez lost the award when one writer, reportedly George King of the *New York Post,* left Martinez off his ballot completely, arguing that pitchers should not be eligible for the award since they don't play every day.

All-Star Quiz

1) Who is the only major-league player to knock in 1,000 runs with homers and 1,000 more in other ways?

A: Hank Aaron

2) Which Hall of Famer was the first player to start at three different positions in the same World Series?

A: Willie McCovey (1B, RF, LF) in 1962

3) Who in the Hall is the only inductee officially listed as a DH?

A: Paul Molitor

4) Which Hall of Famer played for the so-called "worst team of all time"—the 1962 Mets?

A: Richie Ashburn

5) To what team was Jackie Robinson (who retired instead of reporting) traded in 1956?

A: New York Giants

6) For which team was Joe DiMaggio a coach?

A: The Oakland A's, in 1968 and 1969

7) Which big-leaguer had a statistical title named after him while he was still active?

A: The Lou Brock Award, to the majors' top base thief

8) Who was the first baseball player featured on a postage stamp?

A: Jackie Robinson

9) Who once led his league in home runs without hitting any of them over the fence?

A: Ty Cobb, with nine in 1909

10) Which Hall of Fame inductee received the highest percentage of votes?

A: Tom Seaver, with 98.84 percent in 1992

Greatest Games of All Time

1986 NLCS, Game 6

Mets 7, Astros 6

The Setting: The Astrodome, Houston, TX

The Drama: Three runs by the Astros in the first, three by the Mets in the ninth, one each in the 14th, then five total in the 16th—the longest postseason game in history was also one of the most dramatic.

At least one book has been written calling this the greatest game ever played. That statement may be true considering the game's length (4:42 to play 16 innings) and its importance. Had the Mets lost, they would have been forced to face Astros hurler Mike Scott again. Scott had already held them to one run in two complete-game victories in the Series while striking out 19.

These were the first two NL expansion teams, both starting out in 1962. The Mets had twice before tasted postseason play—in their "Miracle" year of 1969 and again in 1973, winning both LCS. The Astros' only postseason appearance had been in 1980, when they lost an intense five-game series to Philadelphia.

The Mets lost Game 1 of this series to Scott, as Glenn Davis's second-inning homer was the game's only run. Bob Ojeda pitched a complete game in Game 2 to get the Mets even. After the Mets scored four times in the sixth inning of Game 3 to tie things up, the Astros took a one-run lead into the bottom of the ninth. But Wally Backman bunted himself on, and Lenny Dykstra slugged a homer to win it for New York. Game 4 was another Scott victory.

Game 5 went 12 innings, as 39-year-old legend Nolan Ryan faced 21-year-old superstar Dwight Gooden, and the two were knotted at one run each after nine innings. Backman singled in the 12th and scored the winning run on a Gary Carter single.

The Mets hoped to get off to a good start in Game 6 against Bob Knepper, but it was the Astros who jumped ahead. They scored three times off Ojeda—and would have had more if a suicide squeeze attempt hadn't been bungled. Another baserunning blunder cost Houston a scoring chance in the fifth.

But it didn't matter to Knepper, who had no problem holding the Mets to two hits through eight innings. Dykstra led off for the Mets in the ninth, pinch-hitting for Rick Aguilera, and whistled a triple into center field. Mookie Wilson followed with a hard single, and one batter later Keith Hernandez belted a double that brought home Wilson. The Mets were within one run.

Dave Smith was brought in to replace Knepper, but his control was in short supply. Two consecutive walks to Carter and Darryl Strawberry loaded the bases. Ray Knight hit a long fly to right that brought Hernandez in. The Mets had fought their way back to a tie. Neither team could push across any more runs through the 13th inning. Roger McDowell held the Astros in check; Smith and Larry Andersen teamed up to stifle the Mets.

In the top of the 14th, Carter singled, and Strawberry walked. A too-hard bunt by Knight forced Carter at third, but Backman came through again, singling in the lead run. The Mets turned to their relief ace, Jesse Orosco, to close the door. Orosco retired the first hitter in the bottom of the 14th, but then clutch hitter Billy Hatcher knocked an Orosco pitch into the foul-pole screen in left. The Astros had dramatically retied the game.

The Mets came rolling back again, scoring three times in the top of the 16th. Hatcher misplayed a Strawberry pop-fly into a double, then Knight singled Strawberry home. A walk to Backman and two wild pitches by Jeff Calhoun, followed by another Dykstra base hit, sent the Mets into the last of the 16th up by three runs.

But the Astros came back with a roar. With one out, Davey Lopes appeared as a pinch-hitter and reached base on a walk. Both Bill Doran and Hatcher singled to bring one run home. After a force-out at second, Davis—the hero of Game 1—also responded with a single. The score was 7–6, with two out and two men on.

Orosco and Kevin Bass battled it out to a 3–2 count before Bass chased an Orosco slider and missed. The Mets stormed to the mound and mobbed Orosco. New York had prevailed in the longest postseason game ever played.

You Can't Swing a Bat Without Hitting a Celebrity

The ball game is a draw as stars watch stars and fans watch both.

Celebrities have always gone to ball games. While some are in the stands because their agent thinks it's good publicity, others are truly dedicated to their favorite clubs. Ben Affleck attended so many Red Sox games that some people wondered if he was part of the curse. Decades earlier, gangster Al Capone was a fixture at Wrigley Field, just as singer/comedian Danny Kaye was at Dodger Stadium. Comedian Joe E. Brown, a former semipro ballplayer, was such a close friend of Yankees first baseman Lou Gehrig that the Iron Horse gave his mitt to Brown when illness forced him to stop playing.

The Yankees, perhaps more than any other team, continue to draw celebrities—especially in October. Devoted attendees include Jack Nicholson, Tom Cruise, Denzel Washington, and Billy Crystal, who loves the Yankees so much he directed a movie about them (*61**), though he donned a Mets hat to star in another (1991's *City Slickers*). Nicholson, on the other hand, reportedly refused to wear a Red Sox hat for his role in the 2006 blockbuster *The Departed.* Real-estate mogul Donald Trump and former mayor Rudy Giuliani are so well known as Yankees fans that they are booed by Mets fans during their infrequent visits to Shea Stadium. Celebrity is not without its risks, even at the ballpark.

Peter and Bobby Farrelly

The ultimate in sport-meets-celebrity occurred when the Red Sox won the World Series in 2004. When the Sox finally threw off the curse of the Bambino after 86 long years, Hollywood movie cams fortuitously were there to soak in every minute of the excitement and celebration. But directors Peter and Bobby Farrelly, avid Red Sox fans, hadn't expected the baseball gods to throw this at them: They had to rewrite their screenplay for the movie *Fever Pitch* as events unfolded in the Red Sox's favor in October. Stars Jimmy

Fallon and Drew Barrymore were given special permission to be on the field as the Sox cavorted and the cameras rolled.

Tom Hanks

Hanks, who played a fallen slugger-turned-manager of a women's team in *A League of Their Own,* celebrated his 50th birthday by taking a bus tour with Ron Howard and Dennis Miller to several ballparks in 2006. Along the way, Hanks danced to "Thank God I'm a Country Boy" and spelled out O-R-I-O-L-E-S with his body (à la iconic Orioles fan Wild Bill Hagy) at Camden Yards and gave a humorous press conference during a rain delay in Cincinnati.

Glenn Close

During the 1980s, Glenn Close was busy on Broadway (she won a Tony Award for *The Real Thing* and has since won two more) and earned five Oscar nominations in seven years, but she also made it to Shea Stadium whenever she could. The Connecticut native sang the national anthem on numerous occasions and even hosted the Mets highlight video. She remained loyal to the Mets, even as others flocked to the Yankees, and when she sang the anthem during the 2006 postseason, she proudly wore the jersey given to her by the club in 1994 after a 103-loss season.

Charlie Sheen

As a pitcher, Charlie Sheen amassed a 40–15 record at Santa Monica High School. He never made it to the big leagues, but he did play disgraced White Sox center fielder Happy Felsch in *Eight Men Out* and fictitious Cleveland Indian Rick "Wild Thing" Vaughn in two versions of *Major League.* In 1996, Sheen spent $5,000 to purchase all the seats in left field for a game in Anaheim for himself and three friends so he could catch a home run; unfortunately, no one went deep that day, and he went home empty-handed. He once paid $93,500 for the ball that went through Bill Buckner's legs in the 1986 World

Series; Leland's Auction House had expected to get $10,000. Now *that's* a baseball fan.

Kurt Russell

Kurt Russell actually played the game professionally. The son of actor and minor-leaguer Bing Russell, the Disney child star could really hit. (So could Kurt's nephew, Matt Franco, who played eight years in the major leagues.) A shoulder injury curtailed Kurt's baseball career as a second baseman in the California Angels organization. Fortunately, he had a good backup career.

Bill Murray

Chicago native and lifelong Cubs fan Bill Murray is an authority on Cubs angst. Knowing that he would be filming on location in Italy during the team's playoff run in 2003, he had it written into his contract that he'd get a satellite feed to watch the games. As part-owner of the minor-league Charleston River Dogs, Hudson Valley Renegades, Fort Myers Miracle, and the independent St. Paul Saints, Murray has watched games from the owner's box—although he often sits with the fans or appears on the field. But his heart is always with the Cubs. He filled in for a game in the broadcast booth in April 1987 after Harry Caray's stroke and has since sung "Take Me Out to the Ballgame" during the seventh-inning stretch numerous times.

Others who have followed in Caray's shoes singing during the seventh-inning stretch at Wrigley have had some rocky moments. Musician Ozzy Osbourne, along with wife Sharon, mumbled in an unintelligible language; racecar driver Jeff Gordon sang faster than he drove; former Chicago Bear Steve McMichael was ejected for berating the umpire; and actor Jeremy Piven used enough profanity to prompt the team to apologize to the fans.

⚾ ⚾ ⚾

"I don't care or not whether it is childish. Long before I possessed any capacity to examine myself or the reason for the game's appeal to me, I loved it."

—Novelist James T. Farrell on baseball, *Our Game*

Fast Facts

- *The most Gold Gloves any player has won is 16. Brooks Robinson, Jim Kaat, and Greg Maddux have accomplished the feat.*

- *There have been nine combined no-hitters (when multiple pitchers collectively throw a no-hitter during a game). The major-league record for pitchers combining to pitch a no-hitter is six, set by the Houston Astros against the New York Yankees in 2003. The Yankees had gone the longest without a no-hitter thrown against them; their last one had been in 1958.*

- *Sam Crawford is the only player in major-league history to hit more than 300 triples. He hit 309 triples over his 19-year career with the Cincinnati Reds and the Detroit Tigers.*

- *On April 15, 1958, the first West Coast major-league game was won by the San Francisco Giants, who beat the Los Angeles Dodgers 8–0.*

- *Manager Connie Mack's given name was Cornelius Alexander McGillicuddy.*

- *Prior to 1950, the home team had the option of batting first or last.*

- *The oldest player to ever hit a grand slam was Julio Franco, who, on June 27, 2005, accomplished this feat at the age of 46 years and 10 months.*

- *All freak pitches, including the spitball, were outlawed in 1920 with a "grandfather clause," meaning each team was allowed to designate two pitchers as spitball pitchers for the 1920 season. It would take two decades for pitchers to develop new legal pitches to compensate for these restrictions.*

The Most Eccentric Executives

Some baseball owners make a lot of noise and stir up controversy. Some are lovable, some despicable, and most a measure of both.

Chris Von der Ahe was one of the first of the eccentric owners. Proprietor of a St. Louis saloon in the late 1870s, the heavily accented and profit-driven German immigrant took notice of the increase in sales on game days. Before long, he owned the Browns in the American Association and became a sensational (and wealthy) promoter, à la Bill Veeck, and a noisy meddler, à la George Steinbrenner, even though he never really understood the game. In 1895, he modified Sportsman's Park to include nightly horse races and shoot-the-chute rides. Four years later, he had to double its seating capacity. After every game, von der Ahe would roll a wheelbarrow full of that day's gate to the bank, sometimes stopping at the saloon to buy the fans a few rounds. But in 1898, part of the ballpark was destroyed in a fire, and von der Ahe, whose fortunes had dwindled, lost his team.

Born into a prosperous banking family in 1890, **Larry MacPhail** became a lawyer and then used his legal wits to finagle himself into baseball. For the Reds and then the Dodgers, he was an innovator, responsible for the proliferation of night baseball, radio broadcasting of games, airplane travel for teams, and the use of batting helmets. MacPhail's hot-tempered battles with manager Leo Durocher were both legendary and frequent. He fired Leo dozens of times, only to hire him right back. MacPhail left the Reds after the 1937 season and went on to work for the Dodgers and Yankees before hanging up his cap for good in 1947.

Self-made millionaire **Charlie Finley** bought the Kansas City A's in 1960. His slew of wacky promotions—such as using orange baseballs or having a mechanical rabbit hand balls to the umpire behind home plate—didn't help attendance (the team still stunk). So he moved them to Oakland. He hired good scouts because they were cheaper than good players and built a strong team—perhaps made even stronger because of their total unity in their hatred for him. Finley was well known—and infamously disliked—for micro-managing the team and the management. He often demanded that players change their style of play, and he fired any manager who publicly disagreed with him. He paid bonuses to players who would grow mustaches; pitcher Rollie Fingers' handlebar mustache was the most famous result of this. He tried to institute a "designated runner," and he dressed his players in garish green and gold uniforms. But it was his poor business decisions that ultimately did him in, and he stepped away from baseball in 1980.

Marge Schott inherited her husband's Cincinnati business empire when he died in 1968. Under her guidance, the businesses flourished, and she used part of her earnings to become partial owner of the Cincinnati Reds, eventually taking control in 1985. Not only was she a woman in a man's world; her abrasive personality and controversial statements made her even more of an outsider. Fined and suspended for her racial and ethnic slurs, Schott didn't seem upset at all. But she was essentially forced out of the game in 1999, selling her controlling interest in the Reds that year. She died in 2004 at the age of 75.

George Steinbrenner is the only major-league owner to be a character on a hit TV comedy show (though he was portrayed by an actor on *Seinfeld*). His personality is almost a cliché—the boisterous, bullying, infuriating meddler, as capricious as he is strong. His most famous quote came the day he, as leader of a limited partnership buying the Yankees, said, "I won't be active in day-to-day club operations at all." In fact, he has done little else—berating his players, firing his managers (including Billy Martin on five occasions), and "apologizing" to the fans when his team lost the 1981 World Series. After Steinbrenner paid a small-time gambler $40,000 for "dirt" on Yankees outfielder Dave Winfield in 1990, baseball commissioner Fay Vincent banned him from baseball for life. Word of his exile began to spread during a game being played at Yankee Stadium, and the crowd erupted into applause and a standing ovation. Steinbrenner was reinstated three years later and helped lead the Yankees to the American League East championship in 1994 and World Series wins in 1998, '99, and 2000.

Baseball Makes Do in World War II

Shortages, from food to baseballs, didn't deter Americans from playing their favorite game at home or abroad.

Americans learned to do without many things during the Second World War—meat, coffee, gasoline, and loved ones thousands of miles away—but one thing they did not forgo was baseball.

"I honestly feel it would be best for the country to keep baseball going," President Franklin D. Roosevelt wrote in his famous "green light letter" to Commissioner Kenesaw Mountain Landis on January 15, 1942.

Cleveland Indians owner Alva Bradley, perhaps following the lead of the NFL's Cleveland Rams who sat out the 1943 season, advocated shuttering baseball near the war's end. But the War Department identified baseball as the favorite sport of 75 percent of American servicemen; football placed a distant second.

The Changing Face of Baseball

So there would be baseball, but it would be different. More games were played at night to accommodate factory workers, travel and supplies were restricted, and fans were as likely to buy a war bond

as a hot dog. Because many of the game's biggest stars eventually served in the armed forces, teams had to get creative with their lineup cards. Rosters were filled with players deemed unfit for military service, teenagers too young for the draft, or players too old to serve. Scouts began recruiting Latin American players, and fans took great interest in new professional women's teams, which started up in 1943.

Pitcher Joe Nuxhall remains the youngest player in major-league history, appearing at age 15 for the Reds in 1944. Hal Newhouser, who desperately wanted to be sworn into the Army Air Corps on the Briggs Stadium mound but was rejected four times because of a heart problem, won the American League MVP two years in a row for the Tigers.

Have Ball, Won't Travel

The Yankees lost all their starters to the service over a two-year period. With so many strong ballplayers from other teams serving in the war, the St. Louis Browns won their only pennant in 1944. They played—and lost to—the St. Louis Cardinals in the World Series (no travel required). The Browns defended their pennant with Pete Gray (who had only one arm) in the outfield. His 51 hits and 11 strikeouts in 234 at-bats were commendable, but the time it took him to transfer the ball from his glove to his arm allowed opponents to run wild.

Because of travel restrictions, the 1945 All-Star Game was canceled, and the standard home/away/home setup was changed for that year's World Series between the Tigers and Cubs. The first three games were played at Detroit's Briggs Stadium, and the last four were played at Chicago's Wrigley Field. (Detroit won the Series, 4–3.)

Soldiers Stay in the Game

Soldiers serving overseas didn't want to give up their favorite sport. Baseball equipment was supplied to servicemen through the Bat and Ball Fund, established by Washington Senators owner Clark Griffith and National League president Ford Frick. Major-league clubs also passed along used equipment, including foul balls returned by fans. During America's first year in the war, the fund provided close to 100,000 baseballs to the Mediterranean theater alone. Games were played, and morale was boosted.

Friend and foe alike took notice. The Japanese, who had their own infatuation with baseball, shouted at American soldiers: "To hell with Babe Ruth." (He, apparently, returned the sentiment.) The Germans often included baseball diamonds as targets when they bombed the American military in Europe to undermine the morale of servicemen who used the fields as a major source of recreation. Yet the 1945 finals of the Eastern Theater of Operations baseball championship took place at the same Nuremberg stadium where numerous Adolph Hitler rallies had been held.

Baseball also made a big impression in Italy. American servicemen stationed in the town of Nettuno stirred up interest in baseball among the locals. To this day, many young boys there still receive bats and gloves as gifts for their First Communion.

The Pastime Post War

By 1945, the war was over, and fans were flocking to the ballpark in record numbers. The world had changed greatly over the past four years, and baseball had changed, too. Some ballplayers came back as war heroes, while others were forever lost. Women gradually receded from playing pro ball, but their involvement in the workforce at large continued to grow. And through all the changes, during the war and since, Americans have clung to their love for a pastime that still connects us all.

⚾ ⚾ ⚾

"I am glad to hear of their coming, but they will have to wait a few minutes till I get my turn at bat."

—Abraham Lincoln, on being informed of his nomination for president, 1860

⚾ ⚾ ⚾

"By bringing the baseball pennant to Washington, you have made the National Capital more truly the center of worthy and honorable national aspirations."

—President Calvin Coolidge, addressing members of the American League champion Washington Senators

Can of Corn

"You can have it. It wouldn't do me any good."

—Ray Chapman to umpire Billy Evans after taking two strikes from Walter Johnson in 1915; he had already been on his way to the dugout when Evans informed him he still had one strike

"The tradition of professional baseball always has been agreeably free of chivalry. The rule is: Do anything you can get away with."

—Heywood Broun, writing on the game at the turn of the 20th century

"I have always maintained that the best remedy for a batting slump is two wads of cotton. One for each ear."

—Bill Veeck, *The Hustler's Handbook*

"I don't rate 'em, I just catch 'em."

—Willie Mays, when asked if he had a favorite among his defensive gems, *The Baseball Life of Willie Mays*

"I don't room with him; I room with his suitcase."

—Yankee Big Bodie on his mischievous teammate/roommate Babe Ruth, *Babe: The Legend Comes to Life*

"I learned a long time ago you're wasting your time trying to make a player use his head."

—Reds manager Pat Moran

"People found humor in the way the Mets lost or—rarely—won. I suppose it would have been gentler for that team to play in privacy."

—Tom Seaver on the '62 Mets, *Baseball Is My Life*

Game Called on Account of...

Postponements: They're not just about rainouts anymore.

Rain has been the cause of 99 percent of all cancellations and postponements in major-league history. But what about snow? Hurricanes? Bugs? Military invasion? Let's just say you might need more than an umbrella at the ballpark!

Snowed Out

Baseball games have been canceled because of snow many times, but the worst instance came in April 1982. Heavy snow wiped out Opening Day in New York, Detroit, Chicago, Milwaukee, Cleveland, Pittsburgh, and Philadelphia. Fortunately, Minnesota debuted the enclosed Metrodome the day the storm hit.

A Roof Doesn't Matter If the Streets Are Flooded

While the typical rainout is common in outdoor baseball, what about an indoor rainout? The first one in major-league history took place in Houston on June 15, 1976. The Astros and the Pirates both made it to the Astrodome, as did a handful of fans, but the flooded streets made it impossible for the umpires to reach the covered stadium.

That Blows!

When Hurricane Ivan made landfall in September 2004, it wreaked havoc along the Gulf Shore and the islands of the Caribbean. Consequently, it also forced the Marlins to transfer two home games from Miami to Chicago's U.S. Cellular Field.

Well, at Least the Roof Isn't on Fire

The Montreal Expos had no choice but to cancel a game at Olympic Stadium on July 13, 1991, when the luckless facility's retractable roof couldn't keep the rain out. Less than two months later, a 55-ton concrete beam crashed onto a walkway, and the Expos had to play their final 13 home games on the road. The Kingdome in Seattle had a similar problem when four ceiling tiles came down, causing a game against the Orioles to be canceled on July 19, 1994. The strike came along in August to prevent the spectacle of Seattle spending three months on the road.

That was followed by the collapse of a piece of masonry at Yankee Stadium in April 1998, which forced the Yankees to cancel two games against the Angels, reschedule a third game at Shea Stadium, and transfer a weekend series from New York to Detroit.

Buzz Off!

Swarms of bugs have caused many delays, but pesky gnats actually forced the crowd to be sent home from Ebbets Field in the fifth inning on September 15, 1946. With Brooklyn battling for a pennant, the umpires decided that the large number of fans waving scorecards at the bugs made it too difficult for players to see the ball. The Dodgers buzzed off with a 2–0 win over the Cubs.

Riotous Crowds

Even riots have resulted in several forfeits, including the final Washington Senators game in 1971, with two outs in the ninth inning. The Senators, who were up 7–5, were forced to end the game after unruly fans stormed the field. And on August 10, 1995, fans at normally laid-back Dodger Stadium pelted the field with souvenir baseballs, resulting in the first National League forfeit in 41 years.

World Events

On a far more somber note, four events have led to the cancellation of the complete schedule of major-league games for one or more days: the death of President Warren Harding in August 1923; the D-Day invasion on June 6, 1944; President Franklin D. Roosevelt's death in April 1945; and the destruction of New York's World Trade Center on September 11, 2001, after which the schedule was postponed for six days. Games might have been canceled after the assassinations of Martin Luther King, Jr., and Senator Robert F. Kennedy in 1968, but Commissioner William Eckert wavered in his decision, angering players and fans.

Dingers that Went the Distance—Or Did They?

While a few of the numbers are a bit exaggerated, there have been some incredible long-distance shots worth noting.

Big sluggers have had big numbers attached to their names throughout history. Dan Brouthers hit a 500-plus-foot homer on May 4, 1884, in Union Park, Baltimore. And Honus Wagner is said to have tagged one 450 feet in Brooklyn's Washington Park in 1903—then again in the Polo Grounds.

Ruth's Rockets
The story of the breathtaking home run really starts where the home run came to life—with Babe Ruth. Many of his long balls can now be accurately measured because the evidence of where they landed is quite clear. As a rookie, the Babe cracked a Ruthian shot in St. Louis's Sportsman's Park that has been measured at 470 feet. In 1921 alone, he hit at least one 500-foot home run in all eight American League cities.

Killebrew Can-Do
On June 3, 1967, Harmon Killebrew smashed a pitch six rows into the upper deck in Metropolitan Stadium, Minneapolis. What was impressive wasn't just the distance (about 530 feet), but the force. The blast shattered two seats. The next day he hit one almost as far. He (along with Jimmie Foxx, Frank Howard, Cecil Fielder, and Mark McGwire) also cleared the left-field roof at Tiger Stadium.

It's Outta Here—*Really* Outta Here!
Reggie Jackson's 1971 Tiger Stadium All-Star Game blast, which bounced off the light tower, came in an exhibition game but can still draw gasps on the highlight reel. Willie Stargell hit the ball out of Dodger Stadium twice—once in 1969 and again in 1973. But Stargell's greatest slugging feats probably came in his first home

park, Forbes Field. Only ten men ever cleared the right-field roof there. Babe Ruth was the first; Stargell did it seven times.

McGwire Makes His Mark

From 1982 through 1995, there was only one genuine 500-foot-plus home run hit in the major leagues. Cecil Fielder did it in Milwaukee in September 1991, hitting the ball clear out of Milwaukee County Stadium.

During "the era of the homer," from roughly 1996 through 2003, single-season home run records seemed to explode, and the all-time career homer record began to be threatened. The Cardinals' Mark McGwire was at the center of that explosion, with both distance and power. The year he tagged 70 homers to outdo Roger Maris's 61, four of his long balls reached 500 feet. (The longest one, hit 545 feet to center field in Busch Stadium, was commemorated with a bandage on the spot on the wall where it hit.) Fourteen others topped 450 feet.

Even Mickey Wasn't *That* Good

Unfortunately, some long-ball memories are just myth—or, at least, exaggerated truth. The story goes that Mantle once hit a ball 734 feet, which is nearly impossible given the Earth's physics. By his own testimony, the hardest ball Mantle ever hit was on May 22, 1963, at Yankee Stadium. The ball struck the facade on the right-field roof approximately 370 feet from home plate and 115 feet above field level. An optical illusion led observers to believe the ball was still rising when it hit the facade and "would have gone 620 feet."

A claim that Mantle reached 600 feet in 1960 is questionable, as is that of other "legendary" shots, such as Dave Nicholson clearing the Comiskey Park roof on May 6, 1964, and Dave Kingman's homer out of Wrigley Field a dozen years later. *The New York Times* said that one went 630 feet; it probably was more like 530. Josh Gibson's famous homer clear out of Yankee Stadium in 1930 never happened. Gibson's own recollection of his longest home run was measured at "only" 512 feet.

Greatest Teams of All Time

1949–53 New York Yankees

Record: 99–52 (1953)
Manager: Casey Stengel
Hall of Famers: Stengel, Mickey Mantle, Phil Rizzuto, Yogi Berra, Whitey Ford
The Season: The fifth consecutive flag and World Series title for Stengel's men.
The Legacy: The '36–'39 Yanks won four Series in a row. But these Yanks did them one better.

Despite four pennants in the 1940s, by 1949, Yankee management thought it was time for new blood. They called on former big-league clown (but successful minor-league manager) Casey Stengel to take charge. The final days of the legendary 1949 season saw the Yankees win the pennant in dramatic fashion, and the most successful Yankee dynasty was born.

The heavy-hitting Red Sox had swept the Yanks in a three-game Fenway set on the next-to-last weekend of the season to move into first place. When the teams met for the last two games, the Sox were one game in front. Stengel's team topped the Sox twice to take the flag in one of the greatest pennant races in history. The Yankees rolled over the Dodgers again in the Series.

Then Casey began to build his dynasty, starting with a steady starting-pitcher crew of Vic Raschi, Eddie Lopat, and Allie Reynolds and improved by the midseason call-up of 21-year-old Whitey Ford. Joe DiMaggio had a brilliant comeback year after an injury-plagued '49, and Phil Rizzuto hit about 50 points higher than his lifetime average to win the league MVP Award. Yogi Berra, still rough-hewn as a catcher, was a born hitter. He batted .322 and belted 28 homers, driving in 124 runs. New York swept the "Whiz Kid" Phillies in the Series, and Casey's men were world champs for the second year in a row.

The 1951 season marked the appearance of Mickey Mantle and the final year of DiMaggio. Both Boston and a promising young Cleveland team pushed the Yankees to a pennant race that wasn't decided until mid-September. Stengel was in full platoon form now: Bobby Brown/Gil McDougald and Hank Bauer/Gene Woodling were good players who became excellent combos sharing time. Johnny Mize and Joe Collins were spotted against certain pitchers. Peppery infielder Billy Martin, in his second year, quickly became one of Casey's all-time favorite players. In the World Series, Lopat pitched two complete-game wins and Reynolds one as the Yankees offed the "Miracle Giants" in six games.

The 1952 campaign looked to be the year the Yankee string would be broken. DiMaggio had retired, and infielders Brown and Jerry Coleman joined Ford in the military. Stengel's team looked weaker than it had in years. But Martin stepped in to fill the second-base slot with flash, and he and Rizzuto teamed up to form a superb keystone combo. Mantle replaced DiMaggio in center and hit .311 with 23 homers and 87 RBI. Berra's average fell to .273, but he still tagged 30 homers and drove home 98 to lead the team. Thirty-seven-year-old Reynolds remained staff ace, winning 20 and topping the AL with a 2.06 ERA. Raschi added 16 wins.

The 1952 World Series, New York vs. Brooklyn, was the toughest one in decades for the Yanks. Two games were decided by one run, four by a pair. The Yanks were up 4–2 in the bottom of the seventh of Game 7 when Martin saved at least two runs with a spectacular running catch. Two innings later, the Yankees had tied the all-time record for consecutive world championships with four.

The next year, they broke it. There was no pennant chase in 1953, as the Yanks were securely on top by May 1. For the first time in Casey's tenure, the Yankees outscored everyone else in the league. They also led in team ERA. Ford and Lopat were the aces, and Reynolds, in a swing role, won 13 games and saved 13 more.

The 1953 World Series belonged to Martin. He set a record with 12 hits, including two triples and two homers, and tallied eight RBI. And he added the only moment of real drama when he singled in the winning run in the last of the ninth in the final game against the Dodgers.

Magical Moments

Could a Rose by any other name hit as sweet?

The Setting: Riverfront Stadium, Cincinnati; September 11, 1985
The Magic: Pete Rose becomes the new all-time hit leader.

His longtime Reds manager, Sparky Anderson, once said of Pete Rose, "He is Cincinnati. He's the Reds." And even though Rose played for two other teams in his career (and helped one of them to a World Series title), when his career began to wind down there was only one place for him to be—back home in Cincinnati. It was there he chased the seemingly unconquerable record of Ty Cobb's lifetime 4,189 hits.

Rose was both playing for and managing the Reds in 1985 when he faced San Diego pitcher Eric Show at 8:01 P.M. that September night. (Actually, Rose had broken Cobb's record several days earlier, but Major League Baseball had redefined the record as 4,191 hits, so that's the one Pete was after.) The count was two and one when Pete shot a line drive into left field for his 4,192nd hit, and Cincinnati celebrated as though it had just won the World Series, as their favorite son marched (or hustled, if you will) himself atop the leader board for all-time hits. With fireworks blazing above them, the crowd cheered for a full seven minutes.

Rose racked up an amazing lifetime total of 4,256 hits—nearly 500 more than Hank Aaron, 800 more than Carl Yastrzemski, Cap Anson, and Honus Wagner, and 1,000 more than Nap Lajoie, Cal Ripken, and George Brett. Pete's later actions have taken some of the bloom off the Rose, but for that one night, Cincinnati's hustling hometown hero deserved all the adulation he got.

Fast Facts

- In 1973, the American League began allowing the use of a designated hitter (DH). This player bats in place of the pitcher. During an interleague game at an AL ballpark, National League teams may also use a DH. Ron Blomberg of the New York Yankees was the first-ever designated hitter.

- Good day or bad day? On August 6, 2001, Scott Hatteberg of the Red Sox hit into a triple play. However, he also had a grand slam.

- The official mud used to remove the sheen off the baseball is "Lena Blackburne Rubbing Mud," which is obtained from a tributary of the Delaware River in New Jersey.

- On June 30, 1948, Bob Lemon of the Cleveland Indians became the first American League pitcher to throw a no-hitter at night.

- Ricky Bones, middle reliever for the Florida Marlins in 2000, had to be placed on the disabled list after he injured himself changing channels on the clubhouse television.

- Joe DiMaggio is the only person to play on four world championship teams in his first four years in the big leagues, for the 1936–1939 Yankees.

- In 1904, the 154-game schedule was adopted. The season increased to 162 games for the American League in 1961 and the National League in 1962, and that's where it stands to this day.

- Jim "Orator" O'Rourke got the NL's first-ever base hit, for the Boston Red Caps on April 22, 1876. Then in 1904, as a catcher for the New York Giants, he became the oldest player ever to appear in an NL game, at the age of 54.

Baseball with Spice

Una pasión para el béisbol

When Major League Baseball summoned a group of prominent Latino players and ex-players to New York in 2005 to commemorate the history and contributions to the game made by players of Latin-American heritage, it showed them a video of such past superstars as Luis Aparicio, Roberto Clemente, and Orlando Cepeda. Watching it had a visible effect on many of those in attendance.

"Watching that video gave me goose bumps," said Yankees relief pitcher Mariano Rivera, a Panama native. "It was tremendous, watching some of the guys who made the path for us. I'm honored just to be mentioned with them."

A Way of Life

Meriting mention among those greats is indeed a high honor, given the number of All-Star players to hail from Cuba, the Dominican Republic, Venezuela, Puerto Rico, Nicaragua, Mexico, and other Latin American and Caribbean countries.

Though many of these players grew up in some of the poorest nations in the Western Hemisphere, using cut-out milk cartons as gloves and swinging sticks at rolled-up cloth baseballs, they began a parade of talent to the majors that seems to grow richer each year. Latino players will tell you that it's largely because of a collective love for the game that permeates their homelands—not unlike the deep connection Europeans and South Americans generally feel for soccer.

As former Dominican winter-league general manager Winston Llenas once said, "It's more than a game. It's our passion. It's almost our way of life."

Added St. Louis Cardinals manager Tony La Russa, "The Latin-American player understands the game of baseball better than other players. They've been talking about it and playing it their whole lives; they're not confused and distracted by other sports."

Battling Prejudice

Although some Latinos played in the major leagues long before blacks were allowed to do so, others were denied the chance because of their darker skin. Cuban-born Negro League Hall of Famer Martin Dihigo, for instance, never got to show his considerable skills in the big leagues despite being considered one of the greatest, most versatile players of all time.

Like black players, the Latino players of the 1940s, '50s, and '60s endured segregation, ridicule, and hostility. Unlike their African-American counterparts, most of them had a language barrier to overcome as well.

Today, approximately one-quarter of all major-league players are Latino. Every big-league team scouts Latin America for talent. The top Latino prospects earn invitations to academies set up by some of the American clubs. Some people call them "baseball factories" because they produce and train major-league talent at minimum wages.

Desire and Determination

The Dominican Republic has led the way among Latino countries to produce an abundance of major-league talent. Among its heroes: Joaquin Andujar, George Bell, Robinson Cano, Rico Carty, Luis Castillo, Mariano Duncan, Tony Fernandez, Pedro Guerrero, Guillermo Mota, Jose Offerman, Juan Samuel, Alfonso Soriano, Sammy Sosa, and Fernando Tatis.

Of youngsters in the Dominican Republic, sports anthropologist Alan Klein said in the documentary *Stealing Home,* "Every morning you would drive to the Academy, you would see 15, 20 kids out there—not one of them had a uniform; they all had pieces of one uniform or another, poor equipment, they would be right at the gate waiting for the security people to open up the gates, and they would go in for their tryout. If they got signed, they were happy. If they didn't get signed, it didn't even deter them for a minute; they would be on the road hitchhiking to the next location."

That desire has helped boost the number of Latinos playing American professional baseball exponentially over the last few decades.

Fueling the Fire

Beginning in the 1940s, an international amateur baseball tournament named Mundial fueled competitive fires between Latin American nations; interest in the game at all levels soared as a result. Caribbean basin nations won every one of these tournaments from 1940 to '72, with Cuba taking 11 titles in 18 years.

The creation of national agencies to foster amateur baseball development in Cuba and the Dominican Republic, among other countries, contributed to the passion in those nations. And the fact that pro baseball was banned by Cuba's communist regime after the 1961 season certainly helped push some of that island's talented players onto U.S. soil.

Glory and Greatness

The success of players like Aparicio, Cepeda, and Clemente paved the way for others. And those others have followed in huge numbers. While about 27 percent of big-leaguers on 2006 Opening Day rosters were born outside the United States, that percentage was 45 in the minors, according to Major League Baseball. The vast majority of those non-American-born players were Latino.

Venezuelan Johan Santana has been one of the best American League pitchers in recent seasons, and Dominican-born David Ortiz stands near the top of its list of hitters. Ortiz's countryman Albert Pujols has dominated the National League in similar fashion. They are just a few of the big-name Latino stars who now set the standard for greatness.

Commissioner Bud Selig summed it up: "Over the years, major-league baseball has been blessed with a wealth of players of Latin American heritage who have contributed to some of the most memorable moments and accomplished some of the most storied feats in the history of the game."

Latino Legends

In 2005, Major League Baseball had fans vote for the Latino Legends team, choosing 12 players from a ballot of 60. The honored players:

Catcher: Ivan Rodriguez, Puerto Rico
First baseman: Albert Pujols, Dominican Republic
Second baseman: Rod Carew, Panama
Shortstop: Alex Rodriguez, Dominican Republic
Third baseman: Edgar Martinez, Puerto Rico
Outfielders: Roberto Clemente, Puerto Rico; Manny Ramirez, Dominican Republic; Vladimir Guerrero, Dominican Republic
Starting pitchers: Pedro Martinez, Dominican Republic; Juan Marichal, Dominican Republic; Fernando Valenzuela, Mexico
Relief pitcher: Mariano Rivera, Panama

◐ ◐ ◐

The 2006 season opened with 27.4 percent of major-league players having been born outside the United States. The largest numbers came from the Dominican Republic, Venezuela, and Puerto Rico. Following is a breakdown of all the foreign countries in which 2006 Opening Day major-leaguers were born:

Dominican Republic (85)
Venezuela (43)
Puerto Rico (33)
Canada (14)
Mexico (14)
Japan (9)
Cuba (6)
Korea (5)
Panama (4)
Taiwan (3)
Australia (2)
Colombia (2)
Aruba (1)
Curacao (1)

From Diamonds to the Rough

*You might be surprised to learn what interesting twists some
players' lives took when their baseball careers ended.*

Sometimes, the name gives it away. Hi Jasper, an early 20th-
century pitcher for the White Sox, Cardinals, and Indians, had the
perfect first name to greet patrons in his second career as a bartender. Others, like Happy Finneran, might have considered a
name change once their playing days were over. Finneran went
from the pitcher's mound to the funeral home, where he worked
as a funeral director and embalmer.

Joe Quinn: Undertaker

The first Australian to reach the major leagues played second base
sporadically for 17 years, through 1901. He played on five championship teams but was also a player/manager with the 1899 Cleveland Spiders, whose 20–134 record remains the worst in history.

Having been involved with that club must have made Quinn's
"other" job a little easier to bear. This colorful character spent his
off-seasons and part of his post-playing career serving as an under-
taker in St. Louis, where he first took up U.S. residence.

Lu Blue: Chicken Farmer

A switch-hitting first baseman with a terrific eye at the plate, Blue
spent most of his 13-year career with the Detroit Tigers. In 1929,
he finished first in the American League in total times on base and
finished second in the AL in walks four times in his career.

His life after baseball was both decorated and unique. In 1941,
he retired to a career as a chicken farmer in Virginia, dabbled in
chinchilla farming, and later owned a chicken hatchery in Maryland. A World War I veteran, Blue is perhaps the best-known
former big-leaguer buried in Arlington National Cemetery.

Grover Cleveland Alexander: Performer in a Flea Circus

One of the greatest pitchers of all time, Alexander won 373 career
games, led St. Louis to a World Series title with the famous 1926

strikeout of Yankee Tony Lazzeri, and was enshrined in the Hall of Fame in 1938. Alexander ranks third among pitchers in career wins (tied with Christy Mathewson), trailing only Cy Young and Walter Johnson.

Out of uniform, Alexander experienced many struggles in life, such as epilepsy, hearing loss, and double vision. Within a year of his induction to the Hall, Alexander could be found working for Hubert's Museum and Flea Circus on 42nd Street in Manhattan. For $100 a week, Alexander would stand on a small wooden platform and recount tales of his career at 30-minute intervals.

Rocky Colavito: Mushroom Farmer

Rocky Colavito was one of the most popular players—and people—in Cleveland early in his career. He was a skilled fielder and powerhouse hitter, with 41- and 42-homer seasons. In 1959, he hit home runs in four consecutive at-bats in a single game. He was traded to Detroit before the 1960 season for Harvey Kuenn, an act that Tribe fans blamed for putting a curse on their club.

Colavito finished his career with 374 home runs, a .266 batting average, 1,159 RBI, and one season with a perfect 1.000 fielding percentage. Then he slipped away into an unusual post-baseball job. Rocky went from big-slugging outfielder to mushroom farmer, a gig that kept him well out of the limelight that his sometimes tumultuous playing career had attracted.

Mark Fidrych: Pig Farmer

On the mound, he was "The Bird." Fidrych's animated wiggles, gyrations, and head bob made him one of baseball's marquee players. His mastery of opposing hitters helped him win the 1976 AL Rookie of the Year Award and finish second in Cy Young Award voting. He was the definitive one-year wonder, compiling a 19–9 record and 2.34 ERA before winning just ten times over the remainder of his career.

A torn rotator cuff forced Fidrych to retire at the age of 29. He moved to a 107-acre pig farm near his hometown of Northborough, Massachusetts, where he cared for the animals, hauled gravel, and worked as a licensed commercial truck driver.

Special Ks

"For it's one, two, three strikes you're out..."—and sometimes
those strikes come one right after the other, after the other.

A strikeout will put a bully in his place or get a pitcher out of a
jam. It's baseball's ultimate act of defense, often expressing the
dominance of the hurler, the incompetence of his bat-waggling
opponent, or both. The following are some examples of baseball's
foremost—and freakiest—feats of fanning.

19 Ks

In 1884, the birth of the overhand pitching motion resulted in
several dominant one-game pitching performances. Charles
Sweeney of the Providence Grays and Hugh **"O**ne Arm" Daily of
the Chicago Unions each recorded 19-K outings. Dupee Shaw of
the Boston Unions and Henry Porter of the Milwaukee Brewers
each recorded an 18-strikeout game.

Steve Carlton of St. Louis struck out 19 Mets on September 15,
1969, but the celebration was muted: He lost the game 4–3 after
surrendering a pair of two-run homers to Ron Swoboda.

In 1970, Tom Seaver of the Mets also reached the 19-strikeout
mark, and he did it in terrific fashion by consecutively blowing
away the last ten Padres he faced. Seaver's mark is still the all-time
record for consecutive batters struck out.

On June 24, 1997, Randy Johnson struck out 19 Oakland A's—
and coughed up 11 hits that included two home runs, losing 4–1.
The Big Unit, however, won a 19-K game later that year, beating
the White Sox 5–0. Johnson is the only man to strike out at least
19 men twice in the same season. He also holds the single-season
mark for strikeouts per nine innings pitched (13.4 in 2001). As of
the end of 2006, Johnson held the career standard of 10.77 K/9
and is the all-time strikeout leader among left-handers.

Nolan Ryan had four 19-strikeout games (three in extra-inning
affairs) and holds the modern-era single-season strikeout record,
ringing up 383 victims in 1973, one more than Sandy Koufax had in
1965. Ryan tied Koufax by striking out 15 Minnesota Twins in his

final start of the 1973 season and broke the record with an 11th-inning strikeout of Rich Reese. Ryan also owns the career mark for strikeouts, with 5,714, and led his league in strikeouts 11 times.

20 Ks

Roger Clemens is the only pitcher to fan 20 men in a game twice, completing the tricks nearly a decade apart for the Red Sox—in 1986 at Fenway Park against Seattle and in 1996 at Detroit. His record-setting 1986 outing received an unlikely assist from his first baseman, Don Baylor. With Gorman Thomas batting for Seattle in the fourth inning, Baylor dropped a foul pop behind first and was charged an error for prolonging the at-bat. Thomas proceeded to be called out on strikes. Clemens had a chance to retire 21 by strikeout in that game, but Ken Phelps grounded to shortstop for the final out. It should be noted that in neither of Clemens's two 20-strikeout games did he walk a single batter.

When rookie Kerry Wood of the Cubs struck out 20 Houston Astros in only his fifth career start, he tied Clemens's all-time nine-inning game mark and caused a sensation. Not only was the game a one-hitter, but it also marked only the second time in history that a pitcher had matched his age in years with strikeouts in a game. (Rookie Bob Feller whiffed 17 Philadelphia Athletics in 1936.)

21 Ks

Washington Senator Tom Cheney, a journeyman who would fashion a 19–29 career record, whiffed 21 Baltimore Orioles on September 12, 1962. Thirteen of those Ks came in the first nine innings, and he racked up the rest in the final seven innings of the 16-inning, 2–1 victory. Cheney's mark remains the highest total for any single baseball game.

Single-Season Ks

The single-season strikeout king of all time is Matthew Kilroy, who fanned 513 batters (in 583 innings) for the American Association's Baltimore Orioles in 1886. Kilroy, a 20-year-old left-handed rookie, did most of his work at the plate: His 182 walks were the second most in the league that year.

Unusual Ks

Because rules allow for batters to try to advance to first base (if unoccupied) on a wild pitch or passed ball on strike three, there have been 48 occasions since 1900 when a pitcher has struck out four men in an inning. Remarkably, one pitcher, Chuck Finley, accomplished the feat on three separate occasions, including twice in one year (1999). No other pitcher has struck out four men in an inning twice. Finley is also among 15 pitchers to record four strikeouts in one inning in consecutive order. Orval Overall of the Cubs is the only player to whiff four men in an inning of a World Series game. He did it in Chicago's decisive Game 5 victory in 1908.

A dropped third strike led to one of baseball's most unusual plays. On April 25, 1970, Earl Wilson appeared to have ended the Tigers inning by striking out, but the ball was actually trapped by Twins catcher Paul Ratliff, who failed to tag or force Wilson and instead rolled the ball back to the pitcher's mound. The Twins trotted off the field as Wilson raced around the bases, rounding third before the Twins took notice. Left fielder Brant Alyea picked up the ball at the mound and threw to shortstop Leo Cardenas near home plate. Wilson retreated to third, but Alyea hustled there to receive a throw from Cardenas and tag him out.

Mark Whiten is among a handful of players in baseball history to hit four home runs in a game, but the outfielder is in even more select company as a pitcher. Called in by the Indians in 1998 to do mop-duty in a game they were losing by nine runs, Whiten struck out the side, becoming the only position player ever to do this in his only inning of work as a pitcher.

On May 29, 1982, Roy Smalley of the Yankees struck out into a triple play. With Bobby Murcer and Graig Nettles on the move from second and first, respectively, Smalley swung and missed at strike three. Twins catcher Sal Butera fired to third base to catch Murcer, who retreated to second only to find Nettles approaching from the other direction. Nettles then turned back to first base but was tagged out there by Kent Hrbek. In the meantime, Murcer broke once again for third but was nailed at the base when Hrbek fired to pitcher Terry Felton covering. Murcer later remarked, "We need a second base coach."

Chatter

"...the perfect hitter. Joe's swing was purely magical."

—Ty Cobb on Shoeless Joe Jackson, *Baseball Digest,* July 1973

"I told Cronin I didn't want that. If I couldn't hit .400 all the way, I didn't deserve it."

—Ted Williams on his response to Red Sox manager Joe Cronin's offer to sit out the final two games of the 1941 season so his .39955 batting average could be rounded up to .400; Williams went 6-for-8 in a doubleheader to finish at .406, *My Turn At Bat*

"It's more timing than anything else. You don't have to be real big. Time it right, and the ball will go far enough."

—Henry Aaron on hitting homers, *Young Baseball Champions*

"Above anything else, I hate to lose."

—Jackie Robinson, *Giants of Baseball*

"A surge of joy flooded over me that I shall never forget. I felt like shouting out that I had made a ball curve; I wanted to tell everybody; it was too good to keep to myself."

—Candy Cummings, who claimed to have invented the first curveball around 1864, "How I Curved the First Ball"

"If a black boy can make it on Okinawa and Guadalcanal, hell, he can make it in baseball."

—Baseball commissioner Happy Chandler on the breaking of the major-league color line

"Here lies a man who batted .300."

—What Cap Anson wanted put on his tombstone; his lifetime average was .329

All-Time Great

Ted Williams

He wanted to be known as "the greatest hitter who ever lived,"
and most would agree he got his wish.

Born: August 30, 1918; San Diego, CA
MLB Career: Boston Red Sox, 1939–42, 1946–60
Hall of Fame Resume: Last man to bat .400 for a season (1941) *
Hit more than 30 homers eight times * Led league in runs six
times * Led league in walks eight times * Led league in homers
and RBI four times each
Inside Pitch: He was the first person elected to both the Baseball
and Fishing Halls of Fame.

He struck out in his first major-league at-bat, homered in his
last, and during the 21 years in between made the art of hitting his
personal quest. Ted Williams looked at the goal of wood meeting
ball in a scientific way, and if grades were awarded instead of
statistics, his achievements—a .344 lifetime average, 521 homers,
and a slugging average (.634) second only to Babe Ruth—would
rank him at the head of his class.

The lessons started early: swings taken before, after, and sometimes during school as a pencil-thin teen in San Diego. He signed
with the Red Sox in the summer of 1937, and although Williams
didn't make the big club the following spring, his parting shot to
Boston's starting outfielders who had ridiculed him—"I'll be back
and make more money than the three of you combined"—would
prove dead-on. A year later, he returned for good.

The major leagues were packed with sluggers in the years just
prior to World War II, but rookie Ted was able to distinguish
himself in 1939 with a .327 average, 31 homers, and a rookie-
record 145 RBI. In '41, Joe DiMaggio captured the attention of
the nation with a 56-game hitting streak, but Ted out-hit him
.412 to .408 over the course of the streak and finished the season

with 37 homers, 120 RBI, and a .406 batting mark—the last major-leaguer to reach the charmed .400 level. Sportswriters awarded the MVP Award to DiMaggio in what turned out to be the first of many times the outspoken Williams (a two-time MVP winner) would be snubbed due to friction with the press.

Williams was a decent left fielder, but when he said he lived for his next at-bat it was no exaggeration. His goal was perfection at the plate; he sought the same from pitchers, and his careful eye enabled him to lead the American League in walks seven times in his first nine full seasons (each time with more than 125). He was criticized for not swinging enough and not hitting in the clutch—

this despite an incredible .482 on-base percentage (the best in history) and a .359 lifetime batting average in September (his best month).

Winner of Triple Crowns in 1942 and '47 (he missed a third in 1949 by .0002 on his batting average), Ted led the American League nine times in slugging, seven times in batting, six times in runs scored, and four times in homers and RBI. The Player of the Decade for the 1950s hit .388 with 38 homers at age 38 in 1957, won his final batting title (.328) a year later, and slugged 29 long ones in just 310 at-bats in his swan-song season of 1960. Despite missing nearly five full seasons as a Navy and Marine flyer and parts of two more due to injury, Williams retired as third on the all-time homer list—and first in many never-ending debates about the greatest hitter of all time.

Famous Feuds

The Yankees have had some not-so-civil wars.

The Enemies: George Steinbrenner and Billy Martin
The Feud: Their intense competitive fires kept tearing them apart—and then bringing them back together.
The Upshot: After losing Martin for the fifth time, it took Steinbrenner eight years to find a manager he could deal with.

Billy Martin seemed an obvious choice for Yankee manager. A former Yank himself, a battler and bruiser and notorious party pal of Mickey Mantle and Whitey Ford, he had managed weaker teams to divisional titles. And George Steinbrenner loved his fire. But every Martin mistake was amplified by his combative comments afterward, and sometimes he preferred to let his fists do the talking. While Martin dug himself plenty of holes over the years, Steinbrenner's sniping remarks and micromanaging certainly didn't make things easier for the feisty manager.

In July 1978, as the Yankees were chasing the Red Sox, Martin stated disparagingly that his team's superstar, Reggie Jackson, and owner were made for each other. "One's a born liar, and the other's convicted," he said, referring to Steinbrenner's convictions for illegal contributions to Richard Nixon's reelection campaign. The day after making the comment, Martin tendered his resignation. He came back in 1979 but was ousted by Steinbrenner after the season for getting into a fight with a marshmallow salesman. Rehired for 1983, Martin was fired before the 1984 season, then rehired in 1985. He was let go after that season, during which he got into an ugly fight with one of the Yankee pitchers. Steinbrenner tried him once again in 1988, but he lasted only into late June. At the time of his death in 1989, Martin was hopeful of someday managing the Yanks again.

The Enemies: Babe Ruth and Miller Huggins
The Feud: Babe felt his home runs made up for his lack of discipline; Huggins disagreed.
The Upshot: Huggins died while still the Yank manager.

When Babe Ruth joined the Yankees and started slamming home runs all over the American League, he was also leading the league in partying. His diminutive manager, Huggins, tried to get him to settle down, but Babe wouldn't budge. After Huggins berated him during a July 1925 train trip, Babe dangled the little guy over the railing of the train by his ankles. Later that year, when Huggins had finally had enough, he fined the big guy $5,000—a fine ten times larger than any ever levied in major-league baseball. Babe got the message. Huggins's health, never rosy, worsened as the years went on, and he struggled to keep his charges in line. He died in 1929 at age 51, and Babe Ruth cried at his funeral.

The Enemies: Billy Martin and Reggie Jackson
The Feud: Martin thought Jackson was Steinbrenner's man; Reggie said of himself that he was "the straw that stirred the drink."
The Upshot: Reggie was gone before Billy returned for a third go-round.

It was a Saturday afternoon in 1977, and the game was being broadcast on national television. When Reggie apparently "loafed" on a play in right field, manager Billy Martin sent Paul Blair out to replace him—on the spot. Naturally, Reggie was perturbed, and words between the manager and the player boiled over into a near-brawl in the dugout—as the TV cameras caught it all. The bad blood was there for everyone to see, yet the Yankees pushed the distractions aside and won the pennant and the World Series that year. Jackson led the way with three homers in the final game.

By the following July, things were sour again. During a game on the 17th, Jackson tried to bunt after Martin had ordered that he swing away. The result was a five-day suspension for Reggie. A week later, Martin made his "born liar...convicted" statement and then resigned. Yet, despite the turmoil, the Yankees went on to win the World Series again.

Martin's return as manager in 1979 stoked the fire once again, though the feud between the men cooled as each moved further from Steinbrenner. Martin lasted only until the end of the season, and Reggie stopped being a Yankee after two more. Thus ended one of the trickiest triangles in the history of the game.

Monkey See, Monkey Do

If you buy into baseball superstition, the "Rally Monkey" helped swing the 2002 World Series in the Angels' favor.

It all began when the Angels were trailing the Giants in an inter-league game during the 2000 campaign. Video board operators Dean Fraulino and Jason Humes showed a clip of a monkey from the movie *Ace Ventura: Pet Detective* along with the words "Rally Monkey." The Angels then rallied from a two-run deficit in the ninth inning to win the game, and a furry tradition was born.

Following this victory, the team decided to bring in a white-haired capuchin monkey named Katie, whose previous gigs included appearances on the hit television series *Friends.* They filmed Katie dancing to House of Pain's "Jump Around" holding a sign reading "Rally Time!" and edited her into clips from popular films and television shows. The goal in each case was to get the crowd (and the Angels) pumped when the team trailed by three runs or less in the last three innings of a game.

In 2002, the Angels made it to the World Series, where they faced the Giants. Trailing 5–0 in Game 6, the Angels pulled out the Rally Monkey for a needed boost. With their mascot springing across the scoreboard in the seventh inning, the Angels staged one of the greatest comebacks ever by a team facing elimination, winning 6–5 and forcing a seventh and deciding game. The following night the Angels won their first-ever championship.

Some people credit the Rally Monkey with mystical game-changing powers, but others believe she just helped to motivate the crowd—and the team. Angels first baseman Scott Spiezio, whose three-run homer started the six-run rally in that memorable Game 6, enthused about the monkey's motivational abilities, "To have the fans behind you, they never gave up," he said. "If it takes the Rally Monkey to get them going a little bit more, we love it."

The Rally Monkey became the Angels' official mascot. She is never seen live, but her image on video screens around the Angels' stadium is always a welcome sight whenever the team needs a late-inning boost.

Fast Facts

- Even though he was playing for the lowly Pittsburgh Pirates, Ralph Kiner set a record by winning seven consecutive home run titles from 1946 to 1952.

- Orel Hershiser pitched 59 consecutive scoreless innings in 1988.

- When his team topped the Diamondbacks 10–1 on April 30, 2002, Mets pitcher Al Leiter became the first pitcher to beat all 30 major-league teams.

- Reggie Jackson had four consecutive home runs spanning Games 5 and 6 of the 1977 World Series.

- In 1968, Johnny Bench became the first catcher to win the Rookie of the Year Award.

- Earl Weaver, manager of the Baltimore Orioles, holds the record for the most games anyone has been ejected from: 98. In one doubleheader, Weaver was ejected from both games.

- On May 30, 1956, Mickey Mantle almost hit a home run out of Yankee Stadium, missing by only 18 inches.

- As a rookie for the San Diego Padres, Benito Santiago hit safely in 34 straight games. This rookie record still stands.

- While hitting his record 61 homers for the New York Yankees during the 1961 season, Roger Maris never received an intentional walk: Mickey Mantle was batting behind him.

- Rogers Hornsby averaged .402 (over nearly 2,700 at-bats) from 1921 to 1925. He is the only National Leaguer since 1900 to hit above .400 more than once. (He did it three times.)

Magical Moments

Gibson limps to plate, swats walk-off blast.

The Setting: Dodger Stadium; October 15, 1988
The Magic: An injured Kirk Gibson leaves the bench to pinch-hit a game-turning homer that gets the Dodgers rolling in the Series.

When Kirk Gibson, All-American football star at Michigan State, signed with his hometown Tigers, many people compared him to Mickey Mantle. No one with this combination of speed and power had come along since the great Mick. By his second full season (1984), Gibson helped power the Tigers to a World Series victory. He clubbed two upper-deck homers in the decisive Game 5 to seal Detroit's triumph over the San Diego Padres.

As a Dodger in 1988, Gibson was such a critical part of the team's success that he won the League MVP Award despite stats that looked less than sensational. And he was superb in the League Championship Series. But when the World Series started, he wasn't even in the lineup. A bad left hamstring and a swollen left knee had him in street clothes when the game began. But with two out in the last of the ninth and a Dodger on, Gibbie was called on to hit against Oakland's Dennis Eckersley (who was on his way to a Hall of Fame spot). Gibson looked bad on the first two pitches, but he coaxed the count to 3–2 before reaching out on a backdoor slider and yanking the ball into the right-field seats. Then he

limped around the bases as the crowd went wild. In his only at-bat of the Series, Gibson gave the Dodgers a win over the favored A's, propelling them to a 4–1 Series win.

Japan: Crazy for Baseball

America's pastime has become the most popular game in Japan, producing some of today's top North American major-leaguers.

It was a question John McLaren had never been asked before. In fact, it was a question the Seattle Mariners bench coach had never *heard* before. It came from members of the enormous Japanese media contingent covering Ichiro Suzuki in their native son's first major-league spring training in 2001.

"I threw Ichiro a lot of batting practice early," McLaren said, referring to the scene before an exhibition game in Arizona. "One day they came up to me and said, 'Yesterday, Ichiro took 214 swings. Today, he took 196. What's wrong?'

"What's wrong? Nothing. I've never known anyone to count batting-practice swings. But they watch absolutely everything he does."

Ichiro arrived in America as Japan's greatest hitter. The same media mayhem took place when that nation's top home run hitter, Hideki Matsui, debuted in the major leagues with the New York Yankees two years later. And when the two squared off in a game for the first time on April 29, 2003, at Yankee Stadium, millions of fans in Japan tuned in at 8 A.M. to witness what Fuji announcer Yoshi Fukushima described in the telecast as "the biggest moment in Japanese baseball history, especially [since it occurred] at Yankee Stadium, the House that Ruth Built."

Baseball Fever Begins

In the early part of the 20th century, such a scene would have been difficult to imagine. It was not Japanese players in America who captured headlines in the Far East but rather the American stars who made trips to Japan in an effort to globalize the game. Eleven years after Japan's first pro team, the Nihon Undo Kyokai, was formed in 1920, a group of major-leaguers that included Lou Gehrig and Lefty Grove arrived for a tour. In 1934, the great Babe Ruth joined Gehrig, Al Simmons, Jimmie Foxx, Charlie Gehringer, and Lefty Gomez for a 17-game swing that enthralled Japanese fans. Though the Americans easily won all of the exhibitions, Ruth's 14 home runs and antics in right field—including a memorable inning played while holding an umbrella—won over a growing nation of baseball enthusiasts.

Superstars of Japanese Ball

Once the game took hold on Japanese soil, it would rarely be as easy for major-leaguers to dominate such meetings. The Japan Pro-Baseball League launched in 1936, and by the 1950s the country was churning out some impressive talent. Tetsuharu Kawakami, known as the "God of Batting" or "Japan's Lou Gehrig," hit .364 in a 1956 exhibition series against the Dodgers that saw the Japanese claim four games. Shigeo Nagashima won five Japanese MVP Awards, and in 1966 his torrid hitting helped Japan take nine of 17 games against the Dodgers in another major-league exhibition tour.

And perhaps the biggest name of all was Sadaharu Oh, the world's all-time home run king. Oh slugged 868 professional home runs, topping major-league home run champion Hank Aaron by more than 100.

Central vs. Pacific

As Japan's love affair with baseball began to produce such stars on the diamond, the sport grew in much the same way it did in North America. In 1950, two major leagues were formed—the Central and the Pacific. Large stadiums were built, most notably the massive Tokyo Dome in 1988. Salaries soared, and competition for top players became intense. Dynasties emerged, led by the Yomiuri Giants, a team that has captivated fans and earned the unofficial nickname "Japan's Team." Some liken the following the Giants have in Japan to that of the Yankees on U.S. soil, and their championship legacy follows a similar pattern as well. The Giants have won more pennants and Japanese Series Championships than any other team, including nine in a row beginning in 1965. Like the Yankees, they also draw the biggest stars to their lineup, including the likes of Oh and Matsui.

The Silent Treatment

While the Japanese have embraced America's favorite pastime, they have also put their own spin on the game. This is particularly noticeable in the stands. Led by "oendan," or cheerleaders, Japanese fans are known to sing, chant, and make noise using drums, horns, and whistles to root for their team. They do not boo the opposition, so when the visiting team bats, the stadium goes nearly silent. When the Yankees were in Tokyo playing the Hanshin Tigers in an exhibition series in 2004, Jack Curry of *The New York Times* described it as transforming "from a Metallica concert to a library in seconds." That silence, however, does not mean Japanese fans are not "into" the games. Quite the contrary. Baseball has far outpaced sumo wrestling as the most popular sport in the country, and now it is Japanese players who are helping to raise the caliber of play in North America.

Success in the U.S.

In 1995, Hideo Nomo became the first Japanese-born major-leaguer in 30 years when he took the mound for the Los Angeles Dodgers. Since then, he has won more than 100 games, while position players like Ichiro and Matsui have followed with great success of their own. Ichiro shattered George Sisler's 84-year-old major-league record for hits in a season when he smacked 262 in 2004, and he is the only player in history to start his big-league career with a run of six successive 200-hit campaigns. Matsui played in 1,768 consecutive games spanning his career with Yomiuri and New York, and he was just the second player since 1940 to begin his major-league career with three straight 100-RBI seasons. Is it any wonder these guys have a global following?

All-Time Great

Willie Mays

No player ever combined such high levels of skill in every category along with a natural exuberance for the game.

Born: May 6, 1931; Westfield, AL
MLB Career: New York/San Francisco Giants, 1951–52, 1954–72; New York Mets, 1972–73
Hall of Fame Resume: 660 home runs (fourth all time) * 63 games with two or more homers (NL record) * 22 extra-inning homers (first all time) * All-time leader in outfield putouts and chances * 12 Gold Gloves
Inside Pitch: Mays was batting .477 for AAA Minneapolis when he was called up to the bigs in May 1951. But after 12 at-bats he was hitless, and he asked to be sent back down. Manager Leo Durocher refused. The next day Willie got his first hit—a home run off Warren Spahn.

The number of people who saw Babe Ruth play are lessening each year, as are those who saw Ty Cobb perform. It is becoming increasingly difficult to judge players of days gone by against those of more recent vintage, but among careers still remembered by a great many fans, no ballplayer has been more glowingly praised than Willie Mays. Mickey Mantle may have represented pure power, Ted Williams precision at the plate, and Roberto Clemente grace in the field. But for overall ability the vote usually goes to the "Say Hey Kid."

Mays, among the last Negro Leaguers to make the majors, was a strapping young Alabaman who could hit with power, run with style and speed, and catch anything struck in the direction of center field when he emerged as a 20-year-old New York Giant in 1951. Rookie of the Year (.274, 20 homers) on the National League champions, he missed most of the next two years fulfilling service obligations and returned in '54 rippling with new muscle and ready to wreak havoc on NL pitching. He didn't disappoint, hitting a career-high .345 to win his only batting title and ranking among league leaders with MVP totals of 41 homers, 119 runs, and 110 RBI.

In coming years, those types of numbers would seem almost commonplace, as from 1954 to '66 Mays accomplished the following for the Giants in New York and San Francisco: slugged at least 29 homers each season, averaging 40 a year; scored 100 or more runs 12 times, averaging 117; and notched 100 or more RBI on ten occasions, averaging 109. He won four stolen-base titles, and he once swiped 58 of 68 over a two-year span.

Willie's over-the-shoulder catch of Vic Wertz's 430-foot smash to deep center in the '54 World Series has been called the greatest grab of all time, and it brought into national focus another key aspect of Mays's game: his defense. He won a Gold Glove each of the first 12 years the trophy for fielding excellence was awarded, routinely turning in fantastic plays. He patented a flashy, one-handed basket catch, and—even with runners weary of testing his arm—he recorded 12 or more assists on nine occasions.

For most of his career, Mays was viewed alongside Mantle as one of the two men most likely to break Ruth's all-time record of 714 home runs. After Willie slugged 52 to take home his second MVP Award in 1965, he had 505 and at age 34 appeared within striking distance. But by 1967, the man named Player of the Decade for the '60s had seemingly aged overnight. His flashes of brilliance grew increasingly less frequent, and by 1973 he was a slow-moving bench-warmer for the Mets. He never caught the Babe and was eventually passed by Hank Aaron, but no one would question that his 660 home runs, 2,062 runs, 1,903 RBI, .302 average, and 338 steals qualify him as an all-time great.

Baseball Lingo

Sprechen sie baseball?

Angler: A ballplayer who looks for endorsement opportunities.
Origin: Descriptive, from fishing.

Aspirin: A baseball, particularly when thrown hard. Also: *pill, pea.*
Origin: Descriptive. A ball resembles an aspirin when it's thrown
so fast it appears to the batter to shrink.

Bag: Base. **Origin:** From 19th-century equipment guides describing a base as a sack of sand or sawdust.

Balloon: A pitch that's easy to hit. **Origin:** Descriptive of a sphere
that's larger than a baseball.

Blue: An umpire. **Origin:** Historically, the color of their uniform.

Brass: Team management. **Origin:** Military. Refers to insignias on
the uniforms of officers.

Bush: Unprofessional. **Origin:** Refers to "bush league."

Bush leagues: Minor leagues. **Origin:** Bushes indicate remoteness, as in, "Out there, where the bushes grow."

Can of corn: An easy basket catch. **Origin:** Refers to a grocer
retrieving canned goods from high shelves by pushing them with a
stick and allowing them to drop into his smock.

Cheese: A fastball, usually the pitcher's best pitch. Also "cheddar."
Origin: British expression meaning "top quality."

Daisy cutter: A low line drive. **Origin:** Descriptive.

Fungo: Fielding practice retrieving hit balls, and the special bat used to hit those practice balls. **Origin:** Numerous theories, ranging from a combination of the words "fun" and "go," to the cricket expression "fun goes," to the German word "fungen," or catch.

Goose egg: Zero. **Origin:** Descriptive of the numeral. A pitcher who is throwing a shutout is said to be "throwing goose eggs."

Hose: An arm, usually a pitcher's. **Origin:** Descriptive.

Irregular: A bench player. **Origin:** Opposite of "regulars," or everyday players.

Junk: Pitches with movement but not velocity. **Origin:** Descriptive of the repertoire of a pitcher who doesn't have a good fastball.

Moneyball: An economic approach to team-building that exploits market inefficiencies revealed by advanced statistical analysis. **Origin:** The title of Michael Lewis's bestseller about the Oakland A's and Billy Beane, their general manager.

Payoff pitch: A pitch delivered on a 3-and-2 count. **Origin:** Descriptive in that the pitch has potential to "pay off" for the batter (a walk) or the pitcher (a strikeout).

Stepping in the bucket: When a batter pulls away from a pitch with his front foot. **Origin:** Probably refers to the dugout, which often contained a bucket of water.

Texas Leaguer: A bloop single, similar to a dying quail or duck-snort. **Origin:** Named for the Texas League, where minor-leaguers of dubious skill might play.

Uncle Charley: A curveball. **Origin:** Unknown, but "uncle" suggests warm familiarity. An especially good curveball can be referred to as "Lord Charles." Occasionally called "Aunt Susie."

Two Thumbs Down

Some baseball movies have as much entertainment value as a pop-up. Here are a few of the worst.

Bad News Bears (2005): Billy Bob Thornton is too crass to be likable in a film that fails to capture hearts like the 1976 original.

The Bad News Bears Go to Japan (1978): The original was a classic. *Breaking Training*, the 1977 follow-up, was tolerable. But a pickup game against Japanese kids in a parking lot? Please, no.

The Benchwarmers (2006): Potty humor that doesn't elicit a chuckle. This nonsensical flick deserves a lifetime ban.

Ed (1996): Baseball plus monkeys plus Matt LeBlanc equals flop. This was a Razzie Award nominee for worst picture, worst screen couple, and worst screenplay.

Major League II (1994): The original, in 1989, was hilarious. The sequel tried too hard, and it missed the mark by a home run.

Mr. 3,000 (2004): Bernie Mac is a 47-year-old coming out of retirement to try for his 3,000th hit in a movie that features one clichéd scene after another.

The Scout (1994): A scout who keeps his job despite finding psychotic pitchers? And even less believable: George Steinbrenner's Yankees as underdogs?

The Slugger's Wife (1985): Neil Simon's screenplay has the trappings of a light romantic comedy, but gloom and neurosis make this a "must-not-rent."

Summer Catch (2001): There's little chemistry between Freddie Prinze, Jr., and Jessica Biel in a movie that's not sure if it wants to be a comedy or a drama.

Battlefields of Dreams

During the country's darkest days, baseball was a welcome respite.

By 1860, baseball's popularity had swelled throughout the northeastern United States and into the South, and the New York *Mercury* declared it "The National Pastime." But while many Americans agreed on their favorite sport, they were deeply divided on the much weightier issue of slavery. The rift resulted in 11 southern states seceding from the Union early the next year, and in April 1861 the Civil War began.

During the four years that followed, more than 600,000 people died, cities burned, and families mourned, but a simple pleasure shone through the madness: baseball. The game was played by Union and Confederate soldiers on both sides of the Mason-Dixon Line, from training camps to prison camps and everywhere in between. In some cases, games would spontaneously spring up between battles as a way of combating fear and boredom, and even jailers would allow their captured charges to play a few innings. When soldiers died, charity contests back in their hometowns helped generate funds for their families.

Soldiers told their loved ones about the game and what a significant distraction it was from the war. One private from Virginia wrote: "It is astonishing how indifferent a person can become to danger. The report of musketry is heard but a very little distance from us... yet over there on the other side of the road most of our company, playing bat ball and perhaps in less than half an hour, they may be called to play a Ball game of a more serious nature."

It wasn't just the men on the battlefields who were fans of the game. President Abraham Lincoln was said to enjoy watching baseball games played on fields behind the White House.

At war's end in 1865, soldiers who had been introduced to or comforted by the game returned to their farms, factories, and college campuses to further spread its virtues. Countless teams popped up north and south, and by 1871 the first professional league emerged. For helping the nation get through its darkest hours, baseball's status was secured.

Casey at the Bat

This famous poem always hits a home run with fans.

The outlook wasn't brilliant when, in 1888,
A man named Ernest Thayer penned a poem blessed by fate.
Its printed form drew little praise but when performed aloud,
"Casey at the Bat" brought forth great cheering from its crowd.

Then all around this favored land his words gained new steam,
They turned up in the papers and were learned by every team.
And somewhere Thayer's smiling now—you can be sure of that,
For decades later we're still cheering "Casey at the Bat."

"Casey at the Bat" is much more than a poem about a baseball team from Mudville, whose star player strikes out with the game on the line. It has become part of the very fabric of American culture, a fun-to-read—or, better yet, fun-to-hear—story about not only baseball, but hope.

Rhymes and Recitations

When former *Harvard Lampoon* editor William Randolph Hearst took over the *San Francisco Examiner* from his father, he brought three former *Lampoon* staffers on board with him. Ernest Lawrence Thayer was one of them. Thayer wrote "Casey at the Bat" under the pen name "Phin" on June 3, 1888. He was reportedly paid $5 for his efforts. It rhymed well and told a wonderful story under the heading, "Casey at the Bat, a Ballad of the Republic," but it did not hold great significance for many readers. Fortunately, it did make an impression on one of them.

Novelist Archibald Gunter kept a clipping of the poem from the *Examiner* as possible subject matter for a novel. Months later, when he learned that members of the New York Giants and Chicago White Stockings would be attending a comedy show in New York, he suggested to a comedian friend of his that he recite the poem for the players. DeWolf Hopper did just that, and the entire audience—not only the ballplayers—responded loudly.

Hopper later wrote in his memoir, *Once a Clown, Always a Clown,* "When I dropped my voice to B flat, below low C, at 'But one scornful look from Casey, and the audience was awed,' I remember seeing [Giants standout] Buck Ewing's gallant mustachios give a single nervous twitch."

Something for Everyone

The rest, one might say, is history—more than 119 years of it. The poem grew to such popularity that several people tried to take credit for writing it under the name "Phin." When Thayer came forward years later, he signed over the ballad's rights to Hopper, feeling it was not one of his greatest writings. Audiences felt differently, as Hopper went on to recite "Casey at the Bat" an estimated 10,000 times.

The poem has been performed by countless others in theaters, ballparks, classrooms, and stages everywhere. Comic magicians Penn and Teller have performed it. It has graced the airwaves of *Saturday Night Live* and entertained crowds waiting to see their heroes inducted into the Baseball Hall of Fame. It was performed by Disney cartoon characters in a 1946 production, as well as by legendary radio personality Garrison Keillor, actor/comedian Jackie Gleason, horror-film master Vincent Price, and baseball announcer Bob Costas.

Magic in Mudville

Legend has it that Casey was modeled after a Stockton, California, player named John Cahill, whom Thayer had reportedly watched play. To honor that story, and presumably to drum up a little publicity, the Stockton Ports changed their name to the Mudville Nine during the 2000 and 2001 seasons. Others speculate that the name Mudville represents an area in Boston where Thayer grew up before going to Harvard.

This much is certain: In every true recital of one of the most recognized poems in American history, Flynn and Blake set the table for the Mighty Casey with two-out hits for Mudville. And with runners on second and third base and two outs, poor Casey always—as he did in 1888—strikes out.

"Casey at the Bat"
by Ernest L. Thayer

The outlook wasn't brilliant for the Mudville nine that day:
The score stood four to two, with but one inning more to play.
And then when Cooney died at first, and Barrows did the same,
A sickly silence fell upon the patrons of the game.

A straggling few got up to go in deep despair. The rest
Clung to that hope which springs eternal in the human breast.
They thought, "If only Casey could but get a whack at that.
We'd put up even money now, with Casey at the bat."

But Flynn preceded Casey, as did also Jimmy Blake,
And the former was a lulu, while the latter was a cake.
So upon that stricken multitude, grim melancholy sat;
For there seemed but little chance of Casey getting to the bat.

But Flynn let drive a single, to the wonderment of all.
And Blake, the much despised, tore the cover off the ball.
And when the dust had lifted, and men saw what had occurred,
There was Jimmy safe at second, and Flynn a-hugging third.

Then from 5,000 throats and more there rose a lusty yell;
It rumbled through the valley, it rattled in the dell;
It knocked upon the mountain and recoiled upon the flat,
For Casey, mighty Casey, was advancing to the bat.

There was ease in Casey's manner as he stepped into his place,
There was pride in Casey's bearing and a smile lit Casey's face.
And when, responding to the cheers, he lightly doffed his hat,
No stranger in the crowd could doubt 'twas Casey at the bat.

Ten thousand eyes were on him as he rubbed his hands with dirt;
Five thousand tongues applauded when he wiped them on his
    shirt.

Then, while the writhing pitcher ground the ball into his hip,
Defiance flashed in Casey's eye, a sneer curled Casey's lip.

And now the leather-covered sphere came hurtling through
    the air,
And Casey stood a-watching it in haughty grandeur there.
Close by the sturdy batsman the ball unheeded sped—
"That ain't my style," said Casey. "Strike one!" the umpire said.

From the benches, black with people, there went up a muffled
    roar,
Like the beating of the storm waves on a stern and distant shore.
"Kill him! Kill the umpire!" shouted someone on the stand;
And it's likely they'd a-killed him had not Casey raised his hand.

With a smile of Christian charity, great Casey's visage shone;
He stilled the rising tumult; he bade the game go on.
He signaled to the pitcher, and once more the spheroid flew;
But Casey still ignored it, and the umpire said, "Strike two!"

"Fraud!" cried the maddened thousands, and echo answered
    "Fraud!"
But one scornful look from Casey and the audience was awed.
They saw his face grow stern and cold, they saw his muscles strain,
And they knew that Casey wouldn't let that ball go by again.

The sneer has fled from Casey's lip, his teeth are clenched in hate;
He pounds, with cruel violence, his bat upon the plate.
And now the pitcher holds the ball, and now he lets it go,
And now the air is shattered by the force of Casey's blow.

Oh, somewhere in this favored land the sun is shining bright.
The band is playing somewhere, and somewhere hearts are light.
And somewhere men are laughing, and somewhere children shout,
But there is no joy in Mudville—mighty Casey has struck out.

The No Spin Zone

The wobbly history, and mystery, of the knuckleball.

The knuckleball is delivered softly so as to limit spin, exposing the ball and its seams to vagaries of aerodynamics and wind resistance that physicists have labeled "Bernoulli's principle" and "the Magnus effect." Batters just see the pitch as an unpredictable series of whirls, flutters, and drops.

The pitch has been thrown in various forms since the 19th century but owes its name to infamous junkballer Eddie Cicotte, who unveiled the pitch as a member of the Red Sox in 1908.

Cicotte gripped his pitch by steadying his knuckles against the surface of the ball, a style that is rarely used today. Practitioners of the pitch contend there is no "correct" way to grip a knuckleball: Limiting the ball's rotation is all that matters, which is why there are as many different knuckleball grips as there are knuckleball pitchers. "There are no patents on this delivery," said Cicotte.

Knuckleballers come around at a rate of only a few per generation, in part because the pitch is so difficult to master. "It takes a fanatical dedication that most people don't have," knuckleballer Charlie Hough told *The New York Times.*

The same dedication is required of catchers, who find that receiving a knuckeball is often more difficult than hitting one. Bob Uecker, the former catcher and broadcaster, is fond of saying the best way to catch a knuckleball is to "wait'll it stops rolling, and go to the backstop and pick it up."

Baseball's process of natural selection works against knuckleballers, too: Few teams have the patience or inclination to develop them, and scouts tend to search for attributes in amateur talent—the ability to light up a radar gun, for example—that simply aren't useful skills when delivering a pitch that rarely exceeds 70 miles per hour.

As a result, many prominent knuckleballers are accidental pitchers. Tim Wakefield was a low-ceiling infield prospect in the Pirates system when a coach caught him fooling around with a knuckleball and subsequently convinced him to give pitching a try.

Others, like Hough and Tom Candiotti, developed knuckleballs only after they were forced to abandon their other pitches due to arm injuries or ineffectiveness. And occasionally, a position player called in to pitch in a blowout—Todd Zeile and Jose Canseco are two examples—uses the opportunity to experiment with his own knuckler, frequently with disastrous results.

In its purest form, the knuckleball is thrown completely without spin—pushed rather than flung. Its slow flight to home plate is marked by massive turbulence caused by the ball's raised stitches disrupting the flow of air around the sphere. Willie Stargell described it as "a butterfly with hiccups."

Hoyt Wilhelm, who debuted at age 28 and provided relief work until he was 49, and Phil Niekro, who threw knuckleballs almost exclusively throughout his 318-win career, are recognized as baseball's greatest flutterballers. Both are in the Hall of Fame. Several major-league knuckleballers, including Candiotti and Wakefield, have since worn uniform number 49 as a tribute to Wilhelm.

In 2006, Wakefield completed his 15th year as a big-league pitcher and was the only practicing knuckleballer working regularly. Several were waiting turns in the minors. When the next arrives, he'll join an exclusive club that includes Wilbur Wood, Steve Sparks, Eddie Fisher, and Jim Bouton.

🄒 🄒 🄒

"You don't save a pitcher for tomorrow. Tomorrow it might rain."

—Leo Durocher

🄒 🄒 🄒

"Only if she were digging in."

—Early Wynn, notorious brushback pitcher, on whether he would use such tactics on his own mother

Greatest Games of All Time

1986 World Series, Game 6

Mets 6, Red Sox 5

The Setting: Shea Stadium, New York

The Drama: It looked like "The Curse of the Bambino" had finally been put to rest—but then the Mets kicked it up a notch, and the Sox imploded.

For a game ending that moves past improbability into the realm of science fiction, Game 6 of the 1986 World Series is unsurpassed. Both the Mets and the Red Sox had been through debilitating League Championship Series. Both had fought back from near-certain defeat with near-miraculous effort. What nobody could have predicted was how much fight was still left in these two teams. The Sox won the first two games; the Mets the next two. The 4–0 Red Sox lead after five innings of Game 5 was whittled in half before the Mets came up short in the ninth inning.

Leading three games to two, the Red Sox had their chance to avenge both the "Curse of Babe Ruth" as well as ugly comments about their character and guts. They needed a good pitching performance, and they had their best, Roger Clemens, starting. Clemens had a 24–4 record that season and the lowest ERA in the American League. The Mets countered with Bob Ojeda, who had pitched an effective seven innings in winning Game 3.

The Sox scored in the first, on a single by bat champ Wade Boggs and a Dwight Evans double. Then they scored again in the second, on singles by Spike Owen, Boggs, and Marty Barrett. Clemens set down six of the first nine Mets he faced on strikes. Darryl Strawberry walked to open the fifth, however, and after a stolen base, a single, and an error, the Mets were able to plate the tying run when Danny Heep grounded into a double play.

Boston reclaimed the lead in the top of the seventh. Barrett walked to lead off and moved to second on Bill Buckner's ground-out. Ray Knight gloved a smash by Jim Rice but threw poorly to first. Rice was safe; Barrett went to third. Then the Mets botched an Evans double-play grounder, and Barrett scored. Rich Gedman singled to left, but Mookie Wilson made a huge throw, nailing Rice trying to score. The Sox held on to a 3–2 lead.

The Mets tied things up in the eighth. Lee Mazzilli hit a pinch single, and Lenny Dykstra was safe when Sox hurler Calvin Schiraldi (who had replaced blister-fingered Clemens) tried to turn his bunt into a force at second but made a bad throw. When next hitter Wally Backman bunted, too, Schiraldi made the wise play. Both runners advanced. After an intentional walk, Gary Carter's fly to left was deep enough for Mazzilli to tag and score. The first two Mets reached in the last of the ninth, but Schiraldi hung tough.

The tenth inning was almost too much to believe. Dave Henderson yanked a Rick Aguilera pitch over the left-field wall. The Sox were in business. Two outs later, the Boggs/Barrett tandem struck again: a double, a single, and Boston had a two-run lead heading into the bottom of the tenth.

Schiraldi got both Backman and Keith Hernandez to fly out, and some of the Mets faithful began to leave the ballpark. Red Sox fans prepared to celebrate after 68 years of waiting. But the game wasn't over yet. Carter lofted a soft single to left field. Kevin Mitchell rapped a pinch single up the middle. Knight's bloop to center barely fell in for a single, scoring Carter and moving Mitchell to third. It was now 5–4 Boston.

Schiraldi was replaced by Bob Stanley to pitch to Wilson. The result was one of the greatest at-bats in Series history. With the count 2–2, Mookie fouled off consecutive Stanley offerings. The seventh pitch was wild inside; Wilson bent himself in half to avoid the pitch, and Mitchell roared home, with Knight heading to second. The game was tied.

After two more foul balls, Wilson topped the tenth pitch down the first base line. There stood Bill Buckner, long a solid defensive first sacker. The ball rolled under his glove, between his legs, and into short right. The Mets had pushed home three runs to stave off World Series defeat in spectacular—and bizarre—fashion. The Mets took the title two days later, winning 8–5.

Big Dudes

The big and tall who made the other guys look small.

Monsters

Walter "Jumbo" Brown: 6′4″, 295 lbs.
He led the National League in saves in 1940 and '41. Enos Slaughter called him the toughest pitcher he ever faced.

Garland Buckeye: 6′0″, 260 lbs.
In the 1920s, "Gar" wasn't just a threat on the baseball field—he played professional football, too.

Frank Howard: 6′7″, 275 lbs.
In 1968, a year known for dominant pitching, "The Capital Punisher" slugged ten home runs in a 20–at-bat stretch.

Ted Kluszewski: 6′2″, 225 lbs.
He cut the sleeves off his Reds uniform because they were so tight on his massive arms that they impeded his swing.

Boog Powell: 6′4″, 270 lbs.
He won the 1970 AL MVP Award and formed a powerhouse pennant-winning duo with Orioles teammate Frank Robinson.

Dick Radatz: 6′5″, 235 lbs.
Known as "The Monster," this powerhouse holds the single-season record for most strikeouts by a relief pitcher: 181 in 1964.

Stocky Guys

Steve Bilko: 6′1″, 240 lbs.
While in the minors in 1956 and '57, "Stout Steve" hit 55 or more home runs per season.

Tony Gwynn: 5′11″, 199 lbs.
In 1997, this lifelong Padre tied Honus Wagner's record of eight NL batting titles.

Harry Lumley: 5′10″, 183 lbs.

He led the National League in both triples and homers as a rookie for the Brooklyn Superbas in 1904.

Kirby Puckett: 5′8″, 210 lbs.

This career-long Twin was the first player born in the 1960s to be elected to the Hall of Fame.

Tall Pitchers

John Candelaria: 6′7″

The "Candy Man" was a quality pitcher, winning 177 games in 19 big-league seasons.

Randy Johnson: 6′10″

"The Big Unit's" size (and glare) has kept batters in line for nearly two decades.

Jon Rauch: 6′11″

When he debuted with the Chicago White Sox in 2002, he surpassed Randy Johnson as major-league baseball's tallest player ever.

Rick Sutcliffe: 6′7″

One of the greatest midseason pickups ever. In June 1984, he hurled the Cubs to the NL East Division pennant.

Bob Veale: 6′6″

In 1965, he had a career-high 276 strikeouts.

Tallest Non-Pitcher

Richie Sexson: 6′8″, 237 lbs.

"Big Sexy" has hit 29 homers or more in seven seasons of major-league play.

Tallest Champs

The 1979 world championship Pittsburgh Pirates had five pitchers who stood 6′4″ or taller: Bruce Kison (6′4″), Don Robinson (6′4″), Kent Tekulve (6′4″), Jim Bibby (6′5″), and John Candelaria (6′7″).

Fast Facts

- *On September 14, 1990, Ken Griffey, Sr., and Ken Griffey, Jr., hit back-to-back home runs for the Seattle Mariners.*

- *Some players who went straight to the majors without ever playing in the minor leagues are Catfish Hunter, Al Kaline, Mel Ott, Bob Feller, Sandy Koufax, Ernie Banks, George Sisler, Dave Winfield, Robin Yount, and Jim Abbott.*

- *In the early days of baseball, runners could be called out by hitting them with the ball. Ouch!*

- *The player with the most hits in the 1990s was Chicago Cub Mark Grace, with 1,754.*

- *The movie* The Babe Ruth Story *premiered in New York City on July 26, 1948, and Babe Ruth himself attended. He died three weeks later.*

- *John Smoltz of the Atlanta Braves once burned himself accidentally on his chest. He decided it would be faster to iron his shirt while he was still wearing it.*

- *In 1885, home plate could be made of marble.*

- *Dale Long of the 1956 Pirates, Don Mattingly of the 1987 Yankees, and Ken Griffey, Jr., of the 1993 Mariners share the major-league record of hitting home runs in eight consecutive games.*

- *Walter Alston managed the Dodgers in Brooklyn and Los Angeles for 23 years, always on a one-year contract.*

- *During the 1935 season, only 80,922 fans turned out to watch the St. Louis Browns. That's only about 1,000 fans per game.*

Magical Moments

Mac outslugs Sammy in the Great Home Run Chase.

The Setting: Busch Stadium, St. Louis; September 8, 1998
The Magic: Mark McGwire breaks Roger Maris's home run record, set in 1961.

Mark McGwire was a big home run hitter while he was still in college, and in his first full big-league season (1987) he broke the record for homers by a rookie (49)—a record, set by Boston Brave Wally Berger, that had stood for 57 years. McGwire and fellow Oakland A's power hitter Jose Canseco were dubbed "The Bash Brothers." Together they led Oakland to three consecutive World Series, and McGwire slugged 52 homers in 1996, making him just the second man to top 50 in nearly 20 seasons. Dealt to St. Louis in July 1997, McGwire finished the season with 58 homers, thereby setting the record for most homers hit without winning a homer title (he hit 34 in the AL and 24 in the NL). The following season he and Cub Sammy Sosa put on a summer-long homer fest that kept the nation enthralled.

McGwire started by homering in March (the season started early), then kept rolling with ten in April, 16 in May, and ten more in June. That month Sosa swatted a record-setting 20, and the race was on. It seemed that every fan in America chose one of the two affable giants to root for. McGwire slugged his 60th on September 5, his 61st two days later, and on the night of September 8, with a national TV audience watching, Big Mac lined a Steve Trachsel fastball barely over the left-field fence (it was his shortest homer of the year, but no one cared). Maris's record, which had stood for 37 years (three years longer than Babe Ruth's), had bitten the dust. McGwire finished the season with 70 homers; Sosa, 66.

⚾ ⚾ ⚾

An official major-league bat cannot be more than 2.75 inches in diameter or 42 inches in length.

Baseball's Clown Princes

Cracking up the fans by being goofy, wacky, and zany—such was the job of the baseball clown.

Before there were stadium video screens, T-shirt launches, and PA systems that blared rock, rap, and reggae between pitches, there was the baseball clown. Forerunners of Mr. Met, the San Diego Chicken, the Phillie Phanatic, and every other major-league mascot, clowns used a brand of slapstick and pantomime that was sometimes more entertaining than the game.

Nick Altrock

Nick Altrock was the star pitcher of the "Hitless Wonder" White Sox in the 1906 World Series and was instrumental in the team's championship title. But an arm injury essentially ruined his career, and he was traded to the Washington Senators, where he became a coach in 1912. There he started a clown act with infielder Germany Schaefer, until Schaefer defected to the Federal League. Altrock then teamed up with Al Schacht, the "Clown Prince of Baseball." Their antics kept Altrock in a Senators uniform for more than 40 years. He played up his oversized ears and mouth with exaggerated gestures, and he goofed around with a huge, oversized baseball glove. The fans also loved Altrock's one-man shadowboxing routine. He even made a joke of the record book, batting randomly in games for years and pinch-hitting at the age of 57.

Al Schacht

Born on the site that eventually became Yankee Stadium, Al Schacht once fanned Babe Ruth three times in a game in 1920. Schacht found his calling the following year, working with Nick Altrock in a clown act in the World Series. Schacht worked 25 World Series and 18 All-Star Games. Like Altrock, Schacht was hired by the Senators as a coach, but he gained fame for his signature tattered frock coat and crumpled top hat. He toured with the USO on three continents during World War II, opened a restaurant, and penned the cleverly titled tome *G.I. Had Fun.*

Jackie Price

Jackie Price showed potential as a ballplayer, but when his career seemed to be languishing, he incorporated his playing skills into entertaining performances as a way to stay in the game. Indians owner—and a master showman himself—Bill Veeck hired Price in 1946 to perform for the crowd before games. Price even ended up playing in seven games that year. But mostly he kept the fans amazed and delighted by antics such as taking batting practice while hanging upside down. As part of his act, Price would sometimes wrap himself in live snakes. Unfortunately, during a train ride with the team in 1947, Price let some of the snakes loose, and they frightened female passengers to the point that the conductor had to stop the train. Manager Lou Boudreau ordered him off the train, and that was the end of Price's career with the Indians. However, he did appear in short films and continued to travel around with his act.

Max Patkin

Another player-turned-clown was Max Patkin, whose athletic skill petered out at the minor-league level. But when he served up a home run to Joe DiMaggio in a 1944 military exhibition and then chased DiMaggio around the bases, imitating his every move, a hilariously goofy star was born. Patkin was blessed with a rubber face, which he contorted in countless ways. He wore a patchwork of different uniforms with a question mark on the back. Unlike Nick Altrock and Al Schacht, Patkin did most of his work in the minors. He was beloved in small towns throughout America, even playing himself in the film *Bull Durham.* He never missed a scheduled appearance, performing more than 4,000 times until he finally retired in 1993.

◖ ◖ ◖

Manager Charlie Dressen had an ingenious way of catching curfew violators. At 1:00 A.M., he'd give the hotel elevator operator a new baseball and tell him to collect as many autographs as he could.

Bob Sheppard: The Voice of God

With a voice as familiar to fans as any player in Yankees history, Bob Sheppard has become a baseball legend in his own right.

Reggie Jackson called announcer Bob Sheppard's vocals "The Voice of God." A plaque in Yankee Stadium's Monument Park displayed next to those of Jackson, Ruth, DiMaggio, and other pin-striped legends deems him "The Voice of Yankee Stadium."

Whatever one calls the incomparable Sheppard is inconsequential compared to the way *he* calls batters to the plate in the Bronx, in a job he has held since April 17, 1951. His first lineups included Joe DiMaggio, Mickey Mantle, and Yogi Berra for the Yankees and Ted Williams for the visiting Red Sox.

The words flow, as always, and sound something like this: "Now batting for the Yankees, the shortstop, Derek Jeter...number 2." Sheppard's perfect diction, deliberate pace, and classy style are impossible to convey on paper, but those who have heard him would not have a hard time believing he once taught speech at St. John's University or that he serves as a lector at his church.

Since his debut, when he first boomed the words, "Ladies and gentlemen, welcome to Yankee Stadium," Sheppard has delighted crowds at more than 4,000 major-league games. He also served for nearly 50 years as the voice of the New York Giants football team. Yet today, well into his 90s, he can still roam the corridors of Yankee Stadium and only be recognized occasionally.

His voice, however, is a different story—few lovers of America's pastime would have a hard time placing that deep, distinguished tone. It belongs to a man who prefers unique names like Melky Cabrera to easy ones like Steve Sax; who has gone about his job in the same hardworking manner for more than 55 years; and who is so irreplaceable that the Yankees are considering a digital recording of Sheppard as his only viable replacement. Not that Sheppard is contemplating retirement just yet. "Most men go to work," he noted. "I go to a game. Not a bad life, is it?"

Can of Corn

"This should prove the leather is mightier than the wood."

—White Sox manager Fielder Allison Jones
after his 1906 "Hitless Wonders" won the
World Series with a .228 club batting average

"I never questioned the integrity of an umpire. Their eyesight, yes."

—Leo Durocher, *Nice Guys Finish Last*

"Allen Sutton Sothoron pitched his initials off today."

—Lead in St. Louis newspaper, 1920s, quoted in *The Pitcher*

"It was so wonderful, Joe. You never heard such cheering."
"Yes, I have."

—Exchange between newlyweds Marilyn Monroe and
Joe DiMaggio on Monroe's return from Korea,
where she had entertained some 100,000 Army troops

*"I never had to be lonely behind the plate, where I could talk to
hitters. I also learned that by engaging them in conversation, I
could sometimes distract them."*

—Catcher Roy Campanella, *It's Good to Be Alive*

*"With this batting slump I'm in, I was so happy to hit a double that
I did a tap dance on second base. They tagged me between taps."*

—Frenchy Bordagaray of the Dodgers

*"Age is a question of mind over matter. If you don't mind, it doesn't
matter."*

—Satchel Paige

Greatest Teams of All Time

1975-76 Cincinnati Reds

Record: 108–54 (1975)
Manager: Sparky Anderson
Hall of Famers: Anderson, Johnny Bench, Joe Morgan, Tony Perez
The Season: The Reds won their division in 1975 by 20 games, then steamrolled the powerful Pirates in three straight in the LCS to advance to the Series.
The Legacy: Will be best remembered for their incredible 1975 World Series victory against the Red Sox, followed by their four-game sweep of the Yankees in the 1976 Series.

They called them the "Big Red Machine" because they rolled over their opponents like a bulldozer in knickers, taking National League West titles in 1970, '72, '73, '75, and '76 and four times advancing to the World Series.

But of all those great Reds teams, it was the back-to-back world champions of 1975 and '76 that stand the tallest. Manager Sparky Anderson and the boys won their division by 20 in '75 and ten in '76, swept through two League Championship Series undefeated, played heroically to win one of the greatest World Series ever, and then stopped the famous Yankees in four straight in the next fall classic.

These were complete teams. The Reds featured exceptional defense in the infield, in the outfield, and behind the dish. Their pitching lacked star quality, but it was sturdy, workmanlike, and quietly effective. A lefty/righty bullpen duo could be counted on to snuff out most fires. They were a marvelous scoring machine, combining power, speed, and intelligent hitting. They could steal bases to change the complexion of a key inning. And they were driven by two of the most engaging personalities in major-league history.

The 1975 Reds didn't have a single starting pitcher win 16 games, but three won 15 and seven won ten or more. In the bullpen, lefty Will McEnaney posted 15 saves and five wins, while right-hander

Rawly Eastwick led the league with 22 saves. In 1976, only Gary Nolan could muster 15 victories, but six others won 11 or more, and Eastwick added 26 saves, again leading the NL. The starting eight for the two seasons was identical: RBI machine Tony Perez at first, back-to-back MVP (and now Hall of Famer) Joe Morgan on second, slick fielder Dave Concepcion at short, all-time hit leader Pete Rose at third, and an outfield of slugging George Foster, ball hawk Cesar Geronimo, and speedster Ken Griffey. Behind the plate was arguably the best catcher in baseball history, Johnny Bench, both an offensive and defensive superstar who's now in the Hall of Fame.

The 1975 team led the National League in runs scored and stolen bases. The 1976 team led in everything: runs, hits, doubles, triples, homers, walks received, batting average, slugging average, on-base percentage, and stolen bases.

The core of the team lay in the uniquely paired duo of Rose and Morgan. Both men were passionately driven to excellence, and they had the numbers to show for it. In 1975, Morgan batted .327, hit 17 homers, drove in 94 runs, and led the league in on-base percentage. He was named Most Valuable Player. Then in 1976, he hit 27 home runs, drove in 111, and led the league in both on-base percentage and slugging average. The MVP Award could also have gone to Rose, who batted .317 and .323 those two years and led the league in doubles both times.

In the 1975 World Series, the Reds took on the Boston Red Sox. The two played the Series at a level of breathtaking excellence, overcoming deficits, making brilliant clutch plays, and providing one of the greatest Series ever. Game 6 was the all-time classic tied by Bernie Carbo's three-run homer in the eighth and won by Carlton Fisk's dinger for the Sox in the 12th. The Reds came back to win Game 7.

The 1976 World Series was anticlimactic, as the Yankees scored just eight runs in the four games. After the sweep, Reds president Bob Howsam was congratulated for having "a truly great team." "Yes," Howsam answered, "and it's probably the last great team." The specter of free agency was on the doorstep, and building and keeping a team long enough to make it a dynasty was passing from baseball forever.

Fast Facts

- *According to legend, the Cleveland Indians took their nickname from a brilliant but short-lived Native American baseball player named Louis Sockalexis, from the Penobscot nation.*

- *The only pitcher with more than 3,000 strikeouts and fewer than 1,000 walks is Ferguson Jenkins.*

- *The 1991 World Series between the Minnesota Twins and the Atlanta Braves is considered one of the toughest and tightest ever. To some, this Series was the greatest in history. Three games went into extra innings, four games ended with the winning run scoring on the final pitch, and five games were decided by one run. Best of all, the Series brought together the previous season's last-place teams, the first time in modern major-league history that a team had gone from worst to first.*

- *Until 1920, if a player drove in the winning run with a home run and a man on third, he would be credited only with a single.*

- *Carl Yastrzemski holds the record for the most games played with one team: 3,308 for the Boston Red Sox from 1961 to 1983.*

- *President Truman was the first U.S. president to throw two first pitches, one left-handed and one right-handed, on April 18, 1950.*

- *In 1981, Fernando Valenzuela became the only player to win the Rookie of the Year and the Cy Young Award in the same season.*

- *Only one no-hitter has ever been pitched on Opening Day: a 1–0 win by Cleveland's Bob Feller against the Chicago White Sox on April 16, 1940.*

The King Bows Out

*Both entertaining and amazing on the mound, softball pitcher
Eddie Feigner was in a league all his own.*

Fastpitch softball lost a legendary showman and its greatest
pitcher of all time when Eddie Feigner died on February 9, 2007,
at the age of 81. A meticulous record-keeper, his final statistics
read 9,743 wins, 141,517 strikeouts, 930 no-hitters, and 238 perfect games—Hall of Fame numbers by anyone's standard.

Feigner, who gained fame for his "Feigner fast pitch" in the
1940s, struck out opponents and made crowds laugh for more than
60 years. He took his four-man team to more than 100 countries
and played in 10,000-plus games, winning about 90 percent of
them while raising money for local charities. *Sports Illustrated*
once dubbed Feigner "the most underrated athlete of his time."

During his heyday, the King and His Court were the Harlem
Globetrotters of the diamond. And Feigner, the marquee attraction, was Meadowlark Lemon and Curly Neal rolled into one.
Long after age and a stroke (which he suffered in 2000) prevented
him from flaunting his legendary "Feigner fast pitch," which
exceeded 100 mph, he remained a star emcee and straight man as
the team took "Feigner's Farewell Tour" on the road in 2006.

Feigner once struck out big-league stars Willie Mays, Maury
Wills, Harmon Killebrew, Brooks Robinson, Willie McCovey,
Roberto Clemente, and Pete Rose (twice) in a 1967 exhibition
game. Imagine how amateur softballers across the land fared when
they came up against him! And, to top it off, many of Feigner's
strikeouts came while he was blindfolded, throwing between his
legs, or pitching from second base.

"Eddie Feigner was a genuine Jekyll and Hyde," former teammate Jack Knight told the Associated Press. "On the field, a master
showman, brilliant pitcher, creator of the most popular softball
attraction in history. And off the field, one tough son of a gun. He
was a former Marine, everything was by the numbers. He made
millions and was generous to a fault."

All-Time Great

Roger Clemens

Only the Rocket has won seven Cy Young Awards (two more than anyone else), with four different teams, in both leagues.

Born: August 4, 1962; Dayton, OH
MLB Career: Boston Red Sox, 1984–96; Toronto Blue Jays, 1997–98; New York Yankees, 1999–2003, 2007–present; Houston Astros, 2004–2006
Hall of Fame Resume: 348 career wins (eighth all time) * 4,604 strikeouts (second all-time) * 46 career shutouts
Inside Pitch: Clemens was chosen by a panel of baseball experts as one of the six best pitchers of all time.

Teams keep giving up on Roger Clemens, but the burly right-hander doesn't let it faze him. He just moves on, dusts himself off, and wins another Cy Young Award.

Clemens first showed he was something special in college, where he sported a 25–7 record in two All-American seasons with the Texas Longhorns. His first two big-league years were pretty average, but his talent exploded in 1986, and Clemens became the dominant pitcher in the American League. On April 29, 1986, he struck out 20 Mariners, the first pitcher ever to fan that many in a nine-inning game. His 24–4 record resulted in a winning percentage of .857, and he also led the league in earned run average and opposing batting average. He took home both the Cy Young and MVP Awards and helped put his team in the World Series. That would become typical of the Clemens style—not just to be one of the best, but to dominate.

After that sensational 1986 season, Clemens followed up with another 20-win year that included 18 complete games and seven shutouts, and he put another Cy Young Award on his mantel. The next five seasons he won 18, 17, 21, 18, and 18 games, respectively; won two strikeout crowns; and piled up 24 shutouts.

But something slipped out of gear for Clemens after that; he had four seasons with no more than 11 wins each. When Clemens became eligible for free agency, the Red Sox let him go, with the team's general manager uttering the now-notorious quote that Roger was "in the twilight of his career." Clemens signed with the Toronto Blue Jays and kicked things back into high gear, winning 21 and 20 games and earning back-to-back pitching "Triple Crowns" (league leadership in wins, strikeouts, and ERA).

After two years with the Blue Jays, Clemens wanted out, so the Jays traded him to the Yankees in 1999. With New York, Clemens landed his first World Series victory as the Yanks swept Atlanta. In 2001, he started the season 20–1, the first pitcher ever to do that, and finished 20–3, which earned him his sixth Cy Young Award. That year he also won his 300th game and netted his 4,000th strikeout (both on the same night—Friday, June 13). Clemens announced his retirement and was feted by teams around the league during the 2003 season, but then the Houston Astros made him an offer he couldn't refuse, and he signed with them for the 2004 season. Clemens and longtime pal Andy Pettitte formed a dangerous pitching duo that helped secure the NL wild card for the Astros. That season Clemens went 18–4, with an ERA under 3.00, and he brought home his seventh Cy Young Award.

In 2005, Clemens won 13 games and two in the postseason as he helped the Astros reach the World Series. He didn't sign for the 2006 season until late, and then he appeared in just 113 innings, the second fewest of his career. In 2007, 44-year-old Clemens signed a $28 million deal with the Yankees that lets him go home between starts. Once again, the Rocket can't be counted out.

◎ ◎ ◎

"As I took the position, I felt a strange relationship between myself and that pitcher's mound . . . It seemed to be the most natural thing in the world to start pitching—and to start striking out batters."

—Babe Ruth on his first time pitching at St. Mary's Industrial School for Boys, *The Babe Ruth Story*

Chatter

"I was not able to understand how it could be right to pay an actor, or a singer, or an instrumentalist for entertaining the public, and wrong to pay a ball player for doing exactly the same thing."

—Albert Spalding, circa 1900

"My favorite umpire is a dead one."

—Johnny Evers

"We owe a great deal to Base Ball.... It is one of the reasons why American soldiers are the best in the world—quick witted, swift to act, ready of judgment, capable of going into action without officers.... It is one of the reasons why as a nation we impress visitors as quick, alert, confident and trained for independent action."

—Chicago American, 1906

"Sometimes in this game it's as good to be lucky as it is to be good."

—Vida Blue, Vida: His Own Story

"I hope so, just as I hope someone will come along and break all my records. I wouldn't want my records to just stay in the books all the time. I'd like to see someone break them. It means there's improvement."

—Hank Aaron, when asked in 1971 if he felt he could
break Babe Ruth's career home run record,
Hammerin' Hank of the Braves

"If you're not having fun [in baseball], you miss the point of everything."

—Chris Chambliss

So Long, Farewell

Most players leave baseball because they are no longer capable of producing like they once did. Then there are those few who depart while still at the top of their game.

Baseball careers can come to an end for any number of reasons. Sometimes a player decides the wear and tear of a long season has become too much for an aging body and mind. For others, a major injury or a severe illness leaves a player with no choice but to step aside. And then there are those awful times when tragedy brings both a career and a life to end.

Ted Williams: A Measurable Good-Bye

In the waning days of the 1960 season, longtime Boston Red Sox legend Ted Williams contemplated his future in the game. Although he was still a competent ballplayer and a dangerous hitter, the 42-year-old realized that his skills had declined to the point where he was no longer willing to subject his body to the rigors of a long season. Williams came to the conclusion that he would retire at season's end.

On September 28, he prepared to play in the final Red Sox home game. The team still had three more road games to play, but Williams had decided he would not travel with the team and would instead take his final at-bats at Fenway Park. He said nothing publicly about his intentions, but word filtered out and was soon common knowledge throughout Boston and the baseball world. Aware of his intentions, the Red Sox staged a simple ceremony to honor Williams prior to the game.

Williams did little of consequence in his first three turns at bat. He walked in his first plate appearance of the afternoon and then flied out twice, with the second fly ball falling just short of home run distance because of the cold, damp Boston air. Given the weather conditions, Williams felt he had no chance of reaching the seats in his finale.

In the bottom of the eighth inning, he faced Baltimore Orioles pitcher Jack Fisher, who had retired him the two previous at-bats.

For a third straight time, Williams hit a fly ball against Fisher. This one, a long line drive, carried farther than the previous two, however. Traveling on a low trajectory toward the right-center-field bleachers, the ball landed in the bullpen, some 450 feet away. This was no routine fly ball, but a tape-measure home run! It was Williams's 29th home run of the season and the 521st of his career, placing him third on the all-time home run list, behind only Hall of Famers Babe Ruth and Jimmie Foxx. (He's currently 15th.)

Sandy Koufax: Pitching Through Pain

Six years after Williams bowed out, another future Hall of Famer faced a less certain future in his career. On October 2, 1966, Sandy Koufax of the Los Angeles Dodgers won his 27th game of the season. The 6–3 win clinched the NL pennant for the Dodgers, which meant Koufax was slated to pitch in the World Series. With the Dodgers down 1–0, Koufax started Game 2 against the Baltimore Orioles. He pitched scoreless ball until the fifth, when Dodgers center fielder Willie Davis committed three errors while battling a harsh outfield sun, leading to three unearned runs. In the meantime, the Dodgers could muster nothing offensively, saddling Koufax with a 6–0 loss. (The Orioles swept the Series in four.)

Koufax pondered his future over the next month and a half. Despite his remarkable season, which saw him lead the league in wins, strikeouts, and ERA, he had endured extreme pain caused by an arthritic elbow. He was told it was a permanent condition, one that would only worsen the more he pitched, with the possibility of permanent damage to his arm. For Koufax, who was just 30 years old, the benefits of pitching did not outweigh the risks of such damage. On November 18, he announced his retirement. Unlike Williams, Koufax didn't get to savor a final encore in front of appreciative fans, who respected him for stoically pitching through pain and performing at his peak.

Roberto Clemente: A Career Cut Short

The 1971 Pittsburgh Pirates came back from being down 2–0 to win the World Series, thanks in part to 37-year-old Roberto Clemente's amazing .414 batting average and great defense. In fact, his efforts earned him that year's World Series MVP Award. Yet in 1972, Clemente played in only 102 games because of a series of injuries and a recurring viral infection. On the days that he did play, however, he performed like an athlete in his prime. On September 30, in what would turn out to be his final regular-season at-bat, Clemente collected the 3,000th hit of his major-league career—a double against Jon Matlack of the New York Mets. He would finish the season at .312 and win his 12th consecutive Gold Glove Award.

Clemente's contributions helped Pittsburgh clinch a third consecutive National League East title. Playing the Cincinnati Reds in the playoffs, the Pirates lost a decisive fifth game on a wild pitch. No one could have realized it at that moment, but as the Reds celebrated, Clemente walked off a major-league field for the final time.

Two and a half months later, Clemente stepped onto an airplane as part of an effort to send relief supplies to the earthquake-ravaged country of Nicaragua. Shortly after takeoff, the plane crashed into the Atlantic Ocean. In one of the sport's most terrible tragedies, baseball lost not just a great player but a humanitarian and a hero.

⚾ ⚾ ⚾

"Sure, I believe [Sandy Koufax] has arthritis. But it doesn't hurt from the first to the ninth inning. I know that."

—Roberto Clemente, *The Baseball Life of Sandy Koufax*

⚾ ⚾ ⚾

"It is not so dignified as some of the learned professions, but I would rather be a good baseball player and win the pennant for my club than be a poor, dishonest merchant, constantly failing and swindling my creditors, or a briefless lawyer hunting up divorce scandals for a livelihood."

—Rev. Thomas E. Green, October 4, 1885, as quoted in *The Sporting News*, September 26, 1967

Greatest Games of All Time

1975 World Series, Game 6

Red Sox 7, Reds 6

The Setting: Fenway Park, Boston

The Drama: The seemingly down-and-out Red Sox engineer a comeback for the ages that ends on one of the game's indelible images—Carlton Fisk waving the ball fair.

When it comes to exciting comebacks and thrilling plays, there have been more great sixth games in World Series history than seventh games. But this one in 1975 earned itself the honorific title, now and forever, as "Game 6."

The Reds and Red Sox seemed almost destined to meet there, as neither had much trouble disposing of their LCS foes. And even though no one knew it at the time, when the Series was done these two teams had changed baseball forever.

Cincinnati was the "Big Red Machine," a high-scoring attack supported by a brilliant defense, excellent team speed, and a manager (Sparky "Captain Hook" Anderson) willing to deal for a pitching advantage on a moment's notice. Three of its starters, Joe Morgan, Tony Perez, and Johnny Bench, are in the Hall of Fame. A fourth starter, Pete Rose, is considered by many to deserve a spot there, too.

The Red Sox, on the other hand, seemed stitched together. Their great rookie tandem of Fred Lynn and Jim Rice was only half there for the Series; Rice was out hurt. Elder statesman Carl Yastrzemski was now a first baseman, but the whole team played Yaz-style. They made heady plays when they had to: sometimes a great catch, sometimes a great throw, sometimes a key hit or homer. The issue was timing, and the 1975 Red Sox had it in spades.

Game 6 was delayed three days by a steady Boston rain. It was as if the gods were mercifully forestalling the inevitable; Boston had reached the World Series only twice since 1918 and had lost both times. They trailed in this Series 3–2.

But soon after the game began on October 21, Lynn pounded a two-out Gary Nolan pitch into Fenway's center-field bleachers, and the Sox had a delightful 3–0 lead. Pitching magician Luis Tiant lost the lead to the Reds in the fifth, with the key hit being a two-run triple by Ken Griffey on which Lynn banged hard against the wall in pursuit and crumpled against the fence.

In the seventh, a two-out double by George Foster sent Griffey and Morgan home, and the Reds' lead rose to 5–3. Cesar Geronimo's homer added the sixth run in the top of the eighth. The spirits of Bostonians were flagging.

Lynn opened up the last of the eighth with a single off the leg of relief pitcher Pedro Borbon, and Rico Petrocelli worked the pitcher for a walk. Anderson called for his bullpen ace, Rawly Eastwick. Two outs later, Bernie Carbo was sent to hit for pitcher Roger Moret. Carbo had belted a pinch homer in Game 3, but Eastwick seemed to have his number. Carbo barely stayed alive by getting the slightest amount of bat on a 2–2 pitch to send it foul.

But then Eastwick made a mistake, and Carbo crushed it into the center-field stands, a hit one sportswriter described as "a giant electric jolt." Fenway Park was rocking. The Red Sox had miraculously tied the game. The Sox seemed seconds away from winning it when they loaded the bases with none out in the last of the ninth. But a fly ball down the left-field line by Lynn was grabbed by Foster, and the outfielder made a perfect throw home to double up Denny Doyle on a risky dash home. At the top of the 11th, Rose was hit by a pitch and forced at second. Morgan then smacked a ball into right field that looked like a sure home run. But Sox outfielder Dwight Evans went dashing back, made a sensational twisting, turning catch, and doubled off the runner who had left first and not returned.

All of America was breathless when Fisk led off the bottom of the 12th. "Pudge" got under Pat Darcy's sinker and lifted it down the foul line, over the "Green Monster." The Red Sox had won one of the most thrilling games in history.

Perhaps even more important was the impact this game had on baseball. Experts of the time who had written off baseball as too slow and dull were proven wrong. Game 6 was watched by 62 million people; 75 million tuned in to Game 7.

Fast Facts

- Because of a dispute with team owners regarding salary caps, major-league ballplayers went on strike from August 12, 1994, through April 2, 1995. During that time, 938 games were canceled, including all postseason games and the World Series. This was the eighth work stoppage in baseball history.

- In 1867, Candy Cummings was credited with throwing the first curveball.

- Former Yankees center fielder Mickey Mantle holds the record for most career home runs (18) and RBI (40) in World Series history.

- On July 8, 1947, Spec Shea became the first rookie pitcher to win an All-Star Game.

- Night games were banned by the Pacific Coast League in 1943 because of wartime blackout restrictions.

- Many people believe Ernie Banks won the MVP Award while playing for a last-place team, but during both of Banks's winning years (1958 and 1959), his Cubs finished in fifth place. The first MVP to play for a cellar dweller was Andre Dawson for the Cubs in 1987.

- Only two major-league players under the age of 18 have ever received an intentional walk: Wayne Causey and Mike Ivie.

- On September 30, 1971, unruly fans, unhappy that owner Bob Short was moving their Washington Senators to Texas, stormed onto the field in the last inning of the final game, causing the Senators to forfeit a game they were winning. The Washington Senators became the Texas Rangers the following year.

Lenny Harris: Pinch Hitter Extraordinaire

There's no doubt that pinch hitting is a high-pressure job. Lenny Harris took the pressure and ran with it.

Longtime manager Ralph Houk called pinch hitting "one of the toughest pressure jobs in baseball.... [You have] to walk up there cold... [and] most of the time it means the ballgame." Few people have been able to excel in this area, much less do it for more than a year or two. Jerry Lynch, Manny Mota, Dave Philley, Greg Gross, and Gates Brown have all been pinch-hitting standouts.

But one player—Lenny Harris—stands head and shoulders above the rest for successfully pinch hitting for a long time. Harris was dependable defensively and was also a serious singles hitter. He even pitched once; *The Cincinnati Post* reported, "Harris, who hadn't pitched since... high school... proved to be effective when working on 14 years of rest."

But it was his stickmanship off the bench that earned him the chance to play for eight different National League teams, including the Cincinnati Reds and Los Angeles Dodgers, during his 18-year career.

Harris was a true pinch-batting specialist. For instance, one season (2005) he played in 83 games and had only 70 at-bats. His 212 pinch hits are 62 more than the major league's second-place finisher. He batted 804 times in the pinch, nearly 400 times more than the American League record holder, Gates Brown. He also holds the title for most pinch-hit at-bats (83) and appearances (95) in a season.

Harris appeared in four postseasons—with the Reds in 1995, the Diamondbacks in 1999, the Mets in 2000, and the Marlins in 2003. He had a total of three hits and one RBI in his 15 postseason at-bats. The RBI was a crucial one: For the Marlins he delivered a clutch pinch single in Game 2 of the division series against the Giants, which played a vital role in the inning that earned the Marlins the lead on the way to their Series win.

The MVS (Most Valuable Sod)

A soft mound, a swampy outfield, a puddle surrounding first base. These are just some of the tricks groundskeepers have used to help their team walk away with a victory.

"A good groundskeeper can be as valuable as a .300 hitter," owner Bill Veeck once said. He would have known. Veeck's head groundskeeper was Emil Bossard, who spawned a legacy that has helped keep the "home" in home field advantage.

Bossard had a big job in Cleveland from the 1930s to the 1950s as caretaker for League Park and Municipal Stadium, the two fields used by the Indians at the time. He built the mound tall when fireballer Bob Feller pitched, and he kept the grass on the left side thick, as player-manager Lou Boudreau requested. When slugging clubs like the Yankees came in, the outfield grass was left especially long and wet to turn their doubles into singles. And that's not all. Years later, Roger Bossard confessed that his grandfather used to move the portable fence back 10 to 15 feet against the Yankees to diminish their power. Interestingly enough, Cleveland was the only American League team to win multiple pennants during the Yankees' run from 1941 to '64.

The Bossards branched out. Harold and Marshall took over in Cleveland for their father. Brother Gene went to Chicago's Comiskey Park, where the club won its only pennant in 88 years with Veeck and Bossard having a hand in things. Gene watered down the field—earning Comiskey the nickname of "Camp Swampy"—and kept baseballs in a freezer to cut down on

home runs by slugging opponents. Grandson Roger maintains Comiskey's successor (U.S. Cellular Field) and claims to be one of the last groundskeepers to know the special maneuvers used by previous generations. "I won't let the tricks die," he told the Sports Turf Managers Association. ESPN listed the Bossard family as number seven on the all-time list of baseball cheaters.

Other groundskeepers took to drowning the field to help ensure victory. During the 1962 best-of-three playoff between the San Francisco Giants and Los Angeles Dodgers, Candlestick Park groundskeeper Matty Schwab stepped in to give his players an edge. At the behest of Giants manager Alvin Dark, the ground was soaked around first base to slow Dodgers speedster Maury Wills. While umpire Jocko Conlan made Schwab work to dry out the right side of the infield, the left side went untouched and remained a sponge to slow down grounders. The Giants won the game (Wills never reached base), and shortstop Joe Pagan fielded eight chances flawlessly. The Giants went on to win the pennant. Schwab, who'd been lured from the Dodgers to the Giants back when the teams were in New York, received a full World Series share. Dark would forever retain the nickname "Swamp Fox."

But Schwab was not alone in his tactics. The Tigers grounds crew regularly drenched the area around home plate so Ty Cobb's bunts would stay fair. The Indians watered down third base to protect Al Rosen, who broke his nose nine times while fielding ground balls. Kansas City groundskeeper George Toma, among others, wet the mound and then let it bake in the sun when the opposing pitcher was Catfish Hunter, who preferred a soft mound. If a team wants to use every possible advantage, they might as well start with the foundation beneath their feet.

◐ ◐ ◐

"Fenway Park in Boston is a lyric little bandbox of a ballpark. Everything is painted green and seems in curiously sharp focus, like the inside of an old-fashioned peeping-type Easter egg."

—John Updike, *The New Yorker*

Magical Moments

Dodgers belt four straight homers in the ninth.

The Setting: Dodger Stadium; September 18, 2006
The Magic: In the midst of an eye-to-eye pennant race, the Dodgers hit four consecutive homers to tie the game in the last of the ninth, then win on another homer in the tenth.

The San Diego Padres had just moved past the Dodgers into first place in the NL West with a tense 2–1 win on Sunday, September 17, and they had been dominating the Dodgers all year. But on Monday night, the men from Los Angeles felt the heat of the pennant race and conjured up a powerful jolt of baseball magic. The Padres' four-run lead had disappeared by the end of the third, but two scores by the Pads in the eighth and three more in the ninth put them in charge, 9–5. Before the game, Dodger pitcher Derek Lowe, the previous night's loser, had said, "We need to play [this] game as if it's a must-win." Apparently the Dodgers batsmen felt the same way.

The first L.A. hitter in the last of the ninth, Jeff Kent, faced Jon Adkins and homered to center on a 1–0 pitch. Next up was J. D. Drew, who slammed his homer to right on a 2–1 count. With the Dodgers now only two runs back, Padre ace reliever Trevor Hoffman—who had just netted his 475th save the day before to put him three behind the all-time leader—served up two pitches, both of which left the park, to Russell Martin and Marlon Anderson. Tie game. It was the first time a team had tied up a game with four consecutive homers in the last of the ninth—especially important with the pennant on the line.

The Padres eked a run across in the top of the tenth and handed the ball to Rudy Seanez to seal the deal in the last half. But Dodger Kenny Lofton walked, and five pitches later teammate Nomar Garciaparra homered to left. The Dodgers had escaped with an impossible—and vital—victory. For the season the two teams finished with identical records, and the Padres' better percentage against the Dodgers earned them the division title, with the Dodgers landing the wild card.

The Bad and the Ugly

The integrity of the game is of utmost importance in baseball.
Unfortunately, that honor has not always been upheld.

Money to Be Made? You Bet

Game-fixing didn't start with the 1919 White Sox, although the Black Sox scandal has come to define this crime. It actually began when the National League was barely a year old.

The first-place 1877 Louisville Grays made a number of suspicious errors during an Eastern road trip that caused them to lose seven games and tie one. This prompted speculation that players dumped games—and the pennant—intentionally. It turned out they did. Western Union telegrams linked players with a known gambler, and four men—Bill Craver, Jim Devlin, Al Nichols, and George Hall (who confessed)—were banned from baseball for life.

The first two decades of the 20th century were also filled with baseball corruption. First baseman Hal Chase served as its poster boy, having been linked to several "thrown" games before earning a ban for his role in the Black Sox scandal. There were attempts to bribe umpires (Bill Klem in 1908) and even official scorers (a 1910 attempt to get Cleveland's Nap Lajoie a batting title over the unpopular Ty Cobb). Suspicions that the 1914, 1917, and 1918 World Series were fixed were never proven, or perhaps the drama of 1919 would have been avoided. As it was, the eight White Sox players banned for life served notice that baseball was serious about keeping its games on the up-and-up.

Charlie "Hustle"

If the 1919 White Sox are Exhibit A in the argument against game-fixing, Pete Rose holds the same distinction when it comes to the dangers of gambling. In 1989, the all-time major-league hits king was banned from baseball (and subsequently from becoming eligible for Hall of Fame election) for bets he made while managing the Cincinnati Reds.

Initially, Rose vehemently denied having bet on the game. In his 2003 book *My Prison Without Bars*, however, he admitted to placing wagers with bookmakers as many as five times per week on Reds games while serving as the team's manager. He insists he never bet *against* the Reds as he continues to plead his case for reinstatement, but thus far the commissioner's office has held its ground.

Rose wrote: "I've consistently heard the statement: 'If Pete Rose came clean, all would be forgiven.' Well, I've done what you've asked. The rest is up to the commissioner and the big umpire in the sky."

Colluding with the "Enemy"

Collusion is defined as a secret agreement, particularly one used for treacherous purposes. Baseball fans learned the word in the 1980s, when owners apparently worked together to keep player salaries down at a time when the game was thriving financially.

From 1984 to 1987, baseball attendance soared, as did licensing revenues and profit margins, yet free-agent salaries did not keep pace. For example, in 1985 more than half of all players who filed for free agency wound up signing with other clubs. The following year, however, only four of 33 signed deals with new teams. The rest re-signed with their old clubs—some for less money than they'd made before. Furthermore, most were only offered one-year contracts.

The players union filed a grievance in February 1986 called Collusion I, and 19 months later an arbitrator ruled in their favor. Team owners were forced to pay damages for their decision not to outbid one another for players, thus stifling salary growth. Collusion grievances were brought twice more against owners during this period. An arbitrator sided with players on those occasions, too. In all, owners were found to owe more than $100 million in the 1980s collusion cases.

Cocaine Crackdown

Celebrating wins or drowning the sorrow of a loss into the early morning hours can be traced back to baseball's inception. And some of the game's greatest players were also among its legendary carousers. Somewhere along the line, however, instances of illegal and dangerous off-field behavior became no innocent matter.

Texas pitcher Fergie Jenkins was arrested in 1980 and charged with possession of marijuana, hashish, and cocaine. What followed was a rapid-fire succession of drug-related incidents. Padres rookie Alan Wiggins was arrested for cocaine possession in 1982. That year also marked the first of several rehab attempts by Dodgers pitcher Steve Howe, who was also repeatedly suspended. Kansas City teammates Willie Aikens, Vida Blue, Jerry Martin, and Willie Wilson pleaded guilty in 1983 to attempting to purchase cocaine.

In 1985, a federal grand jury in Pittsburgh heard testimony from 11 active big-leaguers. The result: An indictment of seven drug dealers who were linked to players between 1979 and '85. During the "Pittsburgh Drug Trials," Mets first baseman Keith Hernandez estimated that 40 percent of players had used cocaine by 1980. Soon after, some of his teammates—most notably Dwight Gooden and Darryl Strawberry—could be counted among that number.

Steroid Scandals

During the last decade, the game's longstanding home run records have fallen in rapid succession as several players have made enormous gains in strength and stature. Few would argue that some of those gains have not been natural ones. In fact, in his 2004 State of the Union address, President George W. Bush called for "strong steps" to be taken to rid baseball of performance-enhancing drugs.

While the "steroid scandal" has been highlighted by far more speculation than fact, grand jury testimony in a highly publicized case against the San Francisco–area laboratory BALCO did produce some compelling testimony about the use of these drugs. As a result of the same case, Barry Bonds admitted to using two types of performance enhancers—the "clear" and the "cream"—but said it was without knowledge of what those substances contained.

As President Bush (a former part-owner of the Texas Rangers) said in his State of the Union address, "The use of performance-enhancing drugs like steroids in baseball, football, and other sports is dangerous and sends the wrong message—that there are short-cuts to accomplishment."

Hit Me with Your Best Shot

Get ready for some eye-bulging stats! These are the greatest season-long hitting performances in MLB history.

Baseball is a numbers game, and over the course of a long season those numbers tend to even out. A batter might hit over .400 for a month or even two, but in the course of a 162-game schedule, that average is bound to drop. A great hitter might slump for a few weeks, but eventually that average creeps back where it belongs.

Every now and then, however, something special happens: pure magic at the plate. Fans expect greatness from their stars, but over the years some ballmen have reached dizzying heights at the plate, defying all expectations.

Nap Lajoie, 1901, Philadelphia Athletics
The Numbers: .426 BA, 14 HR, 125 RBI, 145 R, 232 H, 350 TB, .463 OBP, .643 SLG
The Dominance: The average Lajoie posted in the American League's inaugural season remains the league's best ever—more than a century later. The batting race wasn't much of a race. Second-place Mike Donlin hit .340. Nap took home the Triple Crown, leading the AL in—among other categories—home runs, RBI, hits, total bases, slugging average, and on-base percentage. His addition to the AL helped legitimize the junior circuit.

Ty Cobb, 1911, Detroit Tigers
The Numbers: .420 BA, 8 HR, 127 RBI, 147 R, 248 H, .467 OBP, .621 SLG, 83 SB
The Dominance: In the midst of the "dead-ball era," the Georgia Peach found all kinds of ways to create offense. His average was the best in the major leagues, and he stole 25 more bases than his nearest AL pursuer. He paced the league in singles, doubles, triples, runs, RBI, and slugging, and his eight home runs ranked second. The result was perhaps the greatest offensive campaign since Nap Lajoie's a decade earlier.

Babe Ruth, 1920, New York Yankees

The Numbers: .376 BA, 54 HR, 137 RBI, 158 R, .532 OBP, .847 SLG, 150 BB

The Dominance: Ruth enjoyed several colossal seasons, but none greater than this. He had set the major-league home run record a year before, socking 29 in his final season in Boston. In 1920, he hit that many in his home stadium. The Babe's total topped that of every other *team* in the AL. He outslugged every NL club save Philadelphia. The Browns' George Sisler, with 19 homers, was baseball's second-leading long-ball hitter.

Babe Ruth, 1921, New York Yankees

The Numbers: .378 BA, 59 HR, 171 RBI, 177 R, 457 TB, .512 OBP, .846 SLG

The Dominance: Yes, Ruth broke his own home run record, and that garnered the headlines of the day. Looking back, however, it was his remarkable total base standard that set this season apart. It was 92 sacks superior to his nearest AL competitor, and to this day it remains a major-league record. Ruth also won the league RBI and runs crowns by 32 and 45, respectively, posting career-high totals in each.

Rogers Hornsby, 1922, St. Louis Cardinals

The Numbers: .401 BA, 42 HR, 152 RBI, 141 R, 250 H, 450 TB, .722 SLG

The Dominance: Hornsby's batting average was 47 points higher than his nearest NL pursuer. His home run and RBI totals also led the league, giving him the first of his two Triple Crowns. He racked up 136 more bases than anyone else in the NL with a total that has not been matched by any major-leaguer since. And Hornsby shattered the previous NL season home run record of 27.

Lou Gehrig, 1927, New York Yankees

The Numbers: .373 BA, 47 HR, 175 RBI, 447 TB, .765 SLG, 52 2B, 18 3B

The Dominance: Not content playing in Ruth's shadow, Gehrig emerged from it in his breakout season. The result was a 110-win championship year for the Yankees. The Iron Horse beat out the Babe for the AL MVP Award by breaking his teammate's season RBI record and also leading the league in doubles, extra-base hits, and total bases. He was 30 bases ahead of Ruth in the latter category.

Hack Wilson, 1930, Chicago Cubs
The Numbers: .356 BA, 56 HR, 191 RBI, 146 R, 208 H, 423 TB, .723 SLG
The Dominance: In one remarkable season, Wilson put two marks in the record books that stood for decades. His major-league RBI record still stands, and his National League home run mark of 56 held up until Mark McGwire and Sammy Sosa came along in '98. Even 51 years after his death, Hack's RBI total grew: In 1999, the commissioner's office officially raised it from 190 to 191.

Jimmie Foxx, 1932, Philadelphia Athletics
The Numbers: .364 BA, 58 HR, 169 RBI, 151 R, 438 TB, .749 SLG, 116 BB
The Dominance: Foxx hammered 17 more homers than Ruth and led the AL in RBI, runs, total bases, and slugging—all by comfortable margins. However, it was his run at the legendary Ruth that set this season apart. He fell two short of the Babe's homer mark but was a victim of circumstance. Five times he hit St. Louis's right-field screen, which did not exist when Ruth set the mark.

Ted Williams, 1941, Boston Red Sox
The Numbers: .406 BA, 37 HR, 120 RBI, 135 R, .553 OBP, .735 SLG, 147 BB
The Dominance: Given the chance to sit out a season-ending twin bill with a .39955 average that would have been rounded up to the vaulted .400 mark, baseball's best hitter refused. Instead, he went 6-for-8, becoming the last man in major-league history to eclipse the .400 mark. And his on-base percentage stood as a major-league record until Barry Bonds broke it in 2002. Williams missed the Triple Crown by just five RBI.

Mickey Mantle, 1956, New York Yankees

The Numbers: .353 BA, 52 HR, 130 RBI, 130 R, 376 TB, .705 SLG, 112 BB

The Dominance: New Yorkers were in love with Mantle even before he won a Triple Crown at age 24. This summer elevated him to legend status. The Mick led the AL in almost every major offensive category. He launched 20 more homers than his nearest AL competitor. His slugging average was 100 points higher than that of second-place Ted Williams and was bettered just once—by Williams—between '56 and the '90s.

Carl Yastrzemski, 1967, Boston Red Sox

The Numbers: .326 BA, 44 HR, 121 RBI, 360 TB, .418 OBP, .622 SLG, 91 BB

The Dominance: On his way to an MVP Award and the most recent Triple Crown in the major leagues, Yaz carried the Red Sox to a pennant. He hit .523 with five home runs and 16 RBI in the last 12 games to help Boston emerge from a four-team AL pack. He went 4-for-4 with a key outfield assist in the clinching victory, then hit .400 with three homers in the World Series.

Mark McGwire, 1998, St. Louis Cardinals

The Numbers: .299 BA, 70 HR, 147 RBI, 130 R, .470 OBP, .752 SLG, 162 BB

The Dominance: One by one, records tumbled as McGwire and Sammy Sosa dueled for the home run title. First, Hack Wilson's 68-year-old NL record of 56 homers fell. Then came the biggie: Roger Maris's major-league-record 61 home runs from 1961. "Big Mac" swatted two in the final game of the season to become base-ball's first 70-homer man. Five of his '98 blasts landed more than 500 feet from home plate.

Sammy Sosa, 2001, Chicago Cubs

The Numbers: .328 BA, 64 HR, 160 RBI, 146 R, 425 TB, .437 OBP, .737 SLG, 116 BB

The Dominance: Sosa's 2001 did not command the attention that his '98 home run title chase had. However, it was not only his best all-around season, but one of history's best. The one-time free swinger finished among the NL's batting leaders and paced the league in RBI, runs, total bases, and intentional walks (37). And Slammin' Sammy's total base figure was the best in the majors since Stan Musial's 429 in '48.

Barry Bonds, 2001, San Francisco Giants

The Numbers: .328 BA, 73 HR, 137 RBI, 129 R, 411 TB, .863 SLG, 177 BB

The Dominance: Fans were diving into McCovey Cove all season to retrieve Bonds's colossal, history-making home runs. Topping Mark McGwire's single-season home run record by three was an amazing and well-documented feat, but that was merely part of the story of this milestone campaign. Barry also broke Babe Ruth's 81-year-old major-league mark for season slugging average and Ruth's 78-year-old record for walks in a season.

⚾ ⚾ ⚾

"He seems to have an obligation to hit."

—Lou Brock on Pete Rose, *Late Innings*

⚾ ⚾ ⚾

"He says hello on opening day and good-bye on closing day, and in between he hits .350."

—Mickey Cochrane on Charlie Gehringer

⚾ ⚾ ⚾

"Heck, if I'd a known it was going to be a famous record, I'd a stuck it in his ear."

—Tom Zachary, after allowing Babe Ruth's 60th homer of the 1927 season

Chatter

"If he's played that many games without an error, he isn't going after the hard ones. The fellow who never makes a mistake is the fellow who never does anything."

—Tigers manager Hugh Jennings upon being told a minor-league prospect had played 87 straight errorless games

"Baseball gives every American boy the chance to excel. I hope that some day Satchel Paige and Josh Gibson will be voted into the Hall of Fame as symbols of the great Negro players who are not here only because they weren't given the chance."

—Ted Williams, in his 1966 Hall of Fame induction speech

"The power of the team blinded onlookers to the skill and smoothness of its fielding. Enemy teams cracked and broke wide open before their assaults."

—Frank Graham on the 1927 Yankees, *The New York Yankees*

"Players have hurts and fears and anxieties. As an announcer, I'm strictly for the underdog."

—Catcher-turned-broadcaster Joe Garagiola, *The Sporting News*, April 4, 1962

"Hitting is timing. Pitching is upsetting timing."

—Warren Spahn

"This is really more fun than being president. I really do love baseball, and I wish we could do this out on the lawn every day."

—Ronald Reagan on playing ball with old-timers during National Baseball Month, 1983

Animal Acts

Rarely do animals and baseball go hand-in-hand, but some key moments on the field have made animals the stars of the show.

Ballplayers know to expect the unexpected, to try to be prepared for whatever pitches, hits, or plays they might encounter. But sometimes the unexpected arrives in a different package—a furry or feathered one—when an animal makes a surprise appearance on the field.

Fowl Balls

Even the best batters admit that hitting Randy Johnson's fastball isn't easy, but a dove flying a bit too close to the action at a 2001 spring-training game certainly made solid, if not tragic, contact. Johnson's seventh-inning delivery, intended for Giants outfielder Calvin Murray, hit the bird instead. Feathers erupted, and the ball—and what was left of the bird—ricocheted into foul territory behind the first base line. The delivery was ruled a non-pitch.

On August 4, 1983, Dave Winfield of the Yankees had a similar "fowl" incident, but with more dramatic consequences. Between innings of a game against the Blue Jays in Exhibition Stadium, Winfield struck and killed a seagull while throwing in the outfield. He was arrested after the game on a charge of cruelty to animals. He posted $500 bail and was scheduled for a court date the next time the Yankees visited Toronto, but the charges were later dropped. If convicted, Winfield could have faced up to six months in jail. "They say he hit the gull on purpose," remarked Yankees manager Billy Martin. "They wouldn't say that if they'd seen the throws he'd been making all year."

The Curse of the Cat?

Occasionally in player-animal matchups, it's the players who fall victim. A stray black cat made an eerie appearance in a critical Mets–Cubs game on September 9, 1969. Just as Billy Williams dug into the batter's box in the first inning, the cat darted out from beneath the Shea Stadium stands, stopped briefly to consider

Williams, slinked past Ron Santo in the on-deck circle, then headed for the visiting dugout, where Mets fans believe he hissed at manager Leo Durocher.

Was it an omen? It marked the last night of the season that the Cubs went to bed in first place. Despite holding a lead as large as ten games over the Mets on August 13, the Cubs' 7–1 loss the night the cat appeared reduced their lead to a half-game, which the surging Mets erased the next night. Like the cat, the Cubs weren't heard from again.

Her Dogs Called the Schotts

Marge Schott, the brash one-time owner of the Reds, was known for her inappropriate behavior and comments and also for her love of animals. Her beloved St. Bernards, Schottzie and Schottzie 02, like several of her struggling Reds teams, were known to leave a mess on the Riverfront Stadium field. However, it was the dogs, not the players, who graced the cover of the team's media guides.

In September 1998, Mark McGwire arrived in Cincinnati fresh from breaking Roger Maris's home run record, only to be humiliated when Schott forced him to pet Schottzie and rub the dog's hair on his Cardinals jersey for good luck. Unfortunately, McGwire was not so lucky. He's allergic to dogs.

Fleeing the Bees

In March 2005, a spring-training game between the Rockies and the Diamondbacks was called after a swarm of bees invaded the field. Darren Oliver, pitching for Colorado, was literally chased off the mound by the swarm. He suspected coconut-scented gel in his hair was to blame. However, after he fled, the bees chased shortstop Sergio Santos out to deep center field before umpires stepped in. "I guess we've got to call that a 'bee' game," said Arizona manager Bob Melvin.

Greatest Teams of All Time

1998 New York Yankees

Record: 114–48
Manager: Joe Torre
All-Stars: Scott Brosius, Derek Jeter, Paul O'Neill, David Wells, Bernie Williams
The Season: Their 114-win season was the second best in major-league history. And if you add their 11 postseason victories, it becomes a mighty impressive 125, the most wins by any team ever.
The Legacy: The first of three consecutive World Series victories.

In 1998, baseball's love for the big bang was hitting second gear. After 21 seasons in which the 50-homer mark was reached only six times, it happened four times in 1998 alone, with National Leaguers Mark McGwire, Sammy Sosa, and Greg Vaughn hitting 70, 66, and 50, respectively. Ken Griffey, Jr., bopped 56 in the junior circuit. But the team that ran away with baseball that year was not a noisy band of behemoths; rather, it was one of the most balanced and disciplined teams the game had ever seen.

The 1998 AL East race was never in doubt. In fact, the Bronxmen had a 7½-game lead after two months and finished the year 114–48. Then they powered through the postseason, losing only two of 13 games to top the year with 125 wins, the most by any team in baseball since it had begun 123 seasons before.

The New York Yankees of 1998 had eight players who hit at least 15 homers. But not one hit 30. They led the league in runs but with a balanced attack: Four starters batted over .300; four had slugging percentages better than .500. Six players stole more than ten bases. If you looked up and down their lineup, you saw one potential all-time great in shortstop Derek Jeter, but the rest were just a crew of highly competent professionals. They were led by manager Joe Torre, who knew how to balance the off-field pressures of New York City with on-field dedication.

Paul O'Neill and Bernie Williams in the outfield were batting title winners (O'Neill in 1994, Williams in 1998). Joining them were dependable Scott Brosius at third, consistent Chuck Knoblauch at second, and ever-reliable Tino Martinez at first. Their catching tandem of Jorge Posada and Joe Girardi was unspectacular but got the job done.

The team's greatest asset was its sensational pitching staff. Andy Pettitte, David Cone, and David Wells each started 30 games; Hideki Irabu started 28; and swingman Ramiro Mendoza added 14 starts as well as 27 relief appearances. The Yank hurlers led the AL with 22 complete games and 16 shutouts, with Wells throwing five himself. Lefties Mike Stanton and Graeme Lloyd were superb setup men for the remarkably efficient Mariano Rivera, who finished with 36 saves and an ERA under 2.00. The staff as a whole allowed the fewest hits, homers, and walks per nine innings in the league.

After the season ended, *The Sporting News* columnist Michael Knisley attempted to ascertain this team's place in history. He decided they ranked as the fifth-best team of all time, behind the 1927 Yanks, 1929 Philadelphia A's, 1961 Yanks, and 1976 Cincinnati Reds. His reason: "The Yankees' ability to play well in nearly every aspect of [the game]."

In the World Series, the team continued to display their all-around prowess. Down three runs in the seventh inning of Game 1 against Padre ace Kevin Brown, two men got on base, and Chuck Knoblauch cracked a tying homer off Brown's successor in a flash. With two outs, Martinez sent a grand slam out of the park. Then in Game 3, Padres ace reliever Trevor Hoffman allowed a three-run homer to Brosius to turn the tide. That's how the Yankees played all year: efficiently.

In 1999, the Yanks swept the Atlanta Braves in the Series, and in 2000 they disposed of the Mets in just five games, becoming world champs for the third time in a row. From 1998 to 2000, this highly efficient Yankee team had a 33–8 record in postseason games. They may not have been the flashiest team around, but they were certainly one of the most effective.

Fast Facts

- A player has hit 20 or more triples in a single season 112 times in major-league history. However, it's only been done three times since 1979: by Willie Wilson in 1985, Lance Johnson in 1996, and Cristian Guzman in 2000.

- New York Yankees pitcher Whitey Ford has the most World Series wins (ten).

- Only 29 National League pitchers have struck out four men in one inning. On September 2, 2002, Kerry Wood of the Chicago Cubs became the first to do so and also hit a home run in the same game.

- The first major-league player to hit four home runs in one game was Bobby Lowe for the Boston Beaneaters on May 30, 1894.

- President George W. Bush is the first U.S. president to have once been a general partner in a major-league team (the Texas Rangers).

- On March 29, 1954, Phil Cavarretta became the first manager fired during spring training.

- The first major-leaguer to be paid $100,000 was Hank Greenberg in 1947. The first to be paid $10 million was Albert Belle in 1997.

- During a game on July 15, 1973, California Angels pitcher Nolan Ryan was working on his second career no-hitter. Detroit Tigers first baseman Norm Cash, who was already a strike victim twice that night, went to the plate in the bottom of the ninth with two outs using a sawed-off leg of an old table from the clubhouse instead of a bat. Although the fans loved it, the stunt drew immediate action by the umpire, who ordered Cash to use a legal bat.

All-Star Quiz

1) When Whitey Ford pitched 33⅓ consecutive scoreless World Series innings, whose 43-year-old record of 29⅔ did he break?

A: Babe Ruth's

2) Who captured more league strikeout crowns than any other pitcher?

A: Walter Johnson (12)

3) Who became the first former major-league non-pitcher to play professionally in Japan?

A: Larry Doby, with Chunichi in 1962

4) Which Hall of Famers comprised two-ninths of baseball's first all-black starting lineup on September 1, 1971?

A: Roberto Clemente and Willie Stargell of the Pirates

5) Who pitched no-hitters during the terms of three different U.S. presidents?

A: Cy Young

6) Who are the only two players in history to steal a base in four different decades?

A: Ted Williams and Rickey Henderson

7) Which player graced the cover of the first edition of *Sports Illustrated*?

A: Eddie Mathews, on August 16, 1954

8) Which Hall of Famer is the only grandfather ever to hit a major-league home run?

A: Stan Musial, at age 42, hours after the birth of his grandson

9) Who hit his first home run inside the park and the remaining 510 of his career over the wall?

A: Mel Ott

Baseball's Craziest

It was always a laugh when any of these characters were around.

People complain that today's game, with its stratospheric payrolls and second-by-second analysis, has lost the sense of good fun and genuine silliness it once had. No one did more to keep things humorous than this gaggle of goofies.

Yogi Berra
This popular Hall of Fame catcher had a unique way with words. His marvelous, sometimes uproarious, nearly Zen (but not quite) "Berra-isms" are inextricably intertwined with baseball lore, and they often show off a mind with a keen understanding of the game. His malapropisms made people scratch their heads, but they also coaxed a chuckle.

Dizzy Dean
No ballplayer ever had a more accurate nickname. Horrible English ("there is a lot of people in the United States who say 'isn't,' and they ain't eating") and a genuine boyish love of the game characterized Dizzy's personality. After a short but highly successful pitching career in the 1930s, he was a broadcaster for more than 20 years.

Arlie Latham
A song written about Latham called him the "freshest man on Earth," and the fans of the late 1800s loved him for his roaring enthusiasm. Latham would lead the fans in cheers and heckle the opposition without mercy. Then, just to show them all how much fun he was having, he'd somersault his way out to his position. In the off-season, fans would turn out around the country for his stage act.

Bill Lee
"The Ace from Outer Space," Bill Lee marched to the beat of a different drummer—or two or three. Saying outrageous things was

as natural to him as breathing. The first time he saw Fenway Park's Green Monster, he asked, "Do they leave it up during games?" After Game 4 of the 1975 World Series, a reporter asked his impression of the Series so far. Lee answered, "Tied."

Rabbit Maranville

It may be that no one had more fun playing baseball than the Rabbit—the eternal puckish clown, the one with the funniest faces, the loudest pratfalls, and the highest consumption of gold-fish. As a defensive player in the 1910s, '20s, and '30s, this long-time Brave was a superstar. As an on-the-field entertainer and practical joker, he was a genius. The fans couldn't take their eyes off him.

Germany Schaefer

Schaefer's famous steal of first base—from second—was not a joke. He was trying to get a run home from third by drawing a throw from the catcher. When the catcher didn't bite (and the umpire ruled there was nothing illegal about the act), Schaefer set out from first to re-steal second. The catcher threw; the run scored. It worked.

Casey Stengel

"Stengelese" was the way this colorful manager dealt with the pestering questions of the press. "Best thing wrong with Jack Fisher is nothing," said Case. But Stengel was a beloved, fun-loving player long before he became a manager. Traded from Brooklyn to Pittsburgh in 1918, he returned to Ebbets Field by tipping his cap to the crowd and having a bird fly out.

Rube Waddell

A colorful oddball, Waddell possessed a childlike sense of life and baseball—an endearing trait attached to a sensational left arm. He loved fire trucks and fishing trips, he wrestled alligators, and his roommate had it written in his contract that Rube was forbidden to eat crackers in bed.

Remember These Dingers? Probably Not

Some of baseball's most crucial home runs were overshadowed by a moment that proved even more magical.

Memorable home run: Bill Mazeroski's ninth-inning solo home run off Ralph Terry, Game 7 of the 1960 World Series
Forgotten dinger: Hal Smith's eighth-inning three-run home run off Jim Coates

Mazeroski's shot, the first ever to end a World Series, put a stunning cap on a wild victory for the Pirates that would have been impossible were it not for Hal Smith's one and only plate appearance in the game. Smith, a reserve catcher, entered the game in the eighth inning after the Pirates starting catcher, Smoky Burgess, was removed for a pinch runner. Smith's two-out, three-run homer off Jim Coates capped a five-run rally, giving Pittsburgh a 9–7 lead that the Yankees erased with two runs of their own in the ninth.

Mazeroski led off the ninth by depositing Ralph Terry's second pitch over the left-field wall at Forbes Field, winning the World Series for the Pirates despite having been outscored 55–27.

Memorable home run: Carlton Fisk's 12th-inning solo home run off Pat Darcy, Game 6 of the 1975 World Series
Forgotten dinger: Bernie Carbo's eighth-inning three-run home run off Rawly Eastwick

If Carlton Fisk provided the dramatic climax, Bernie Carbo supplied the surprise plot twist.

Batting for Rogelio Moret with two on and two out in the eighth and the Red Sox trailing 6–3, Carbo faced the Reds' Rawly Eastwick in what looked like a mismatch. Eastwick had already won two games and saved a third in the Series, and Carbo, some believed, was sent up to hit merely to tempt manager Sparky Anderson's famous hook. However, after working the count to 2–2, Carbo hacked at a waist-high inside fastball and sent it over the center-field fence. The shot set the stage for Fisk's 12th-inning shot off the foul pole, tying the 1975 World Series at three games apiece. (The Reds won Game 7.)

Memorable home run: Kirk Gibson's ninth-inning two-run homer off Dennis Eckersley, Game 1 of the 1988 World Series
Forgotten dinger: Mickey Hatcher's first-inning two-run homer off Dave Stewart

The Dodgers' status as heavy underdogs to the mighty Oakland A's in the 1988 World Series was made more acute due to an injury to left fielder and NL MVP Kirk Gibson. His replacement was lumpy veteran Mickey Hatcher, who had hit only a single home run all year but connected for a two-run shot against A's ace Dave Stewart to open the scoring. Gibson eventually limped into action and hit the decisive shot off closer Dennis Eckersley in his only appearance of the Series. But Hatcher wasn't finished. He hit another home run in the Dodgers' five-game Series upset and finished with a .368 average.

Memorable home run: Aaron Boone's 11th-inning solo home run off Tim Wakefield, Game 7 of the 2003 ALCS
Forgotten dingers: Jason Giambi's fifth- and seventh-inning solo home runs off Pedro Martinez

Grady Little's lazy trigger finger and Aaron Boone's game-ending home run are the lasting images of one of the cruelest heartbreakers in Red Sox history. Boston starter Pedro Martinez was magnificent through the first seven innings but faltered in the eighth. Red Sox manager Little waited to lift Martinez until after the Yankees erased a three-run lead on four straight hits. To that point, the only blemishes on Martinez's game were solo home runs by Jason Giambi in the fifth and seventh innings that put the previously scoreless Yankees on the board and kept them alive. By the eighth, the game was an even 5–5.

In the bottom of the 11th, with the game still tied, Boone launched Tim Wakefield's first delivery into the left-field stands at Yankee Stadium, ending the game and the Series in favor of New York—and also ending Little's employment with the crestfallen Red Sox.

All-Time Great

Barry Bonds

*He leaped from excellence to true greatness at an age
when many others are hanging it up.*

Born: July 24, 1964; Riverside, CA
MLB Career: Pittsburgh Pirates, 1986–1992; San Francisco
Giants, 1992–present
Hall of Fame Resume: 73 homers, 2001 * Seven other seasons
of 40+ homers * Seven-time league MVP * Three-time MLB
Player of the Year * 734 home runs, lifetime (through 2006)
Inside Pitch: Barry and his father, Bobby, are the only players
who've each had five 30-homer/30-steal seasons.

If you're looking for truly dramatic proof of what a sensational
hitter Barry Bonds is, you won't find it in the hit totals, but in the
stats for walks received. No hitter ever intimidated pitchers and
managers into giving him a free base like Barry. Take a look: Babe
Ruth was walked 170 times in 1923. For the next 77 years, no one
came close to that figure. Then Barry Bonds garnered 177 walks in
2001. Three years later he was passed an unbelievable 232 times.
A record that had stood for three-quarters of a century was
leapfrogged by 36 percent. It's the equivalent of someone breaking
Hack Wilson's RBI record by knocking in 260 runs!

With his dad being a highly talented star, Barry Bonds grew up
in major-league locker rooms. His godfather was Willie Mays. So
he was never cowed by the atmosphere or the attention of the big
leagues. When he began his career with the Pirates in 1986, his
cocky attitude showed that he knew he belonged. Bonds was at the
center of a developing team that canny GM Syd Thrift was building slowly but surely. In 1990, it all came together. Bonds led the
way with a .301 average, 33 homers, and a league-leading slugging
average. He also drove in 114 runs and stole 52 bases. The Pirates
took their division each of the next three years, with Bonds win-

ning his first of two MVP Awards as a Pirate. The brash Bonds made it clear he was looking for big money, and if Pittsburgh couldn't deliver, he'd move on.

He made good on his promise when he signed with the San Francisco Giants in December 1992 for $43 million over six years. San Fran fans were pleased, and Bonds won his third MVP Award, belting 46 home runs. For the next three years, Bonds put up big numbers, but his team couldn't take the flag. He routinely hit 30 to 45 home runs and drove home more than 100 RBI. But the postseason, in which Bonds always faltered, continued to be a struggle. When his Giants took their division in 1997 and 2000, they lost in the first round both times, with Barry collecting just six hits in those seven games.

Meanwhile Bonds was undertaking an intensive strength-building program. He'd always had a quick bat, but the combination of eye surgery and newly bulked-up muscles (perhaps because of steroid use) turned him into an incredibly disciplined home run hitter, the likes of which the game had never seen before. The result was that Bonds blew past the three-year-old record of 70 home runs set by Mark McGwire in 1998, pounding out a total of 73 in 2001. That, along with his .863 slugging percentage (breaking Ruth's 81-year-old record), firmly established Bonds as one of the most elite sluggers in baseball history.

His performance in the 2002 postseason finally knocked that monkey off his back, as he batted .471 in the World Series and hit eight home runs in 17 postseason games. In 2006, he moved past Babe Ruth for second most homers lifetime. A year later, he took aim at Hank Aaron's all-time record.

Best Closers

When the game is on the line, these are the guys to call.

Dennis Eckersley
Eck was a starter during his first 12 years in the majors, but alcohol problems kept him from stardom. He put his demons behind him when he moved into the bullpen, where he can lay claim to being the greatest closer ever. From 1988 to '92, his record was 24–9 with 220 saves, and he struck out 378 while walking only 38. In 1989–90, he had more saves (81) than hits (73) and walks allowed (seven). He was inducted into the Hall of Fame in 2004.

Rollie Fingers
In 1972, Oakland owner Charlie Finley asked his players to grow mustaches. Fingers's handlebar became his trademark, along with his deadly efficiency. One of the first pitchers to refuse to pitch more than two innings (so he could be effective several days in a row), Rollie's regimen earned him AL MVP and Cy Young Awards, the ML record for saves upon his retirement (341), six World Series saves, and a spot in the Hall of Fame.

Goose Gossage
No one ever said Gossage was "sneaky fast." He looked every inch the flamethrower, firing the ball with his powerful build and appearing as if every bone in his body would pop out of his skin. He was the captain of the Yankee bullpen during their 1978 world championship season, and he helped the Padres into the Series in 1984. He notched 310 saves.

Trevor Hoffman
Hoffman took over the all-time saves leadership in 2006, moving past Lee Smith and ending the season with 482 career saves. You don't get to that level without being consistent, but Hoffman has had truly spectacular seasons as well. In 1998, he converted 53 of 54 save opportunities, with a teeny ERA of 1.48. Not surprisingly, his Padres played in the World Series that year.

Mariano Rivera

Every closer thrives on pressure; Rivera thrives on the most intense pressure—postseason, when championships are on the line. He has appeared in 25 postseason games and has an 8–1 record, with 34 saves and an ERA of 0.80. He is fourth on the all-time saves leaderboard. And he does it all with an impossibly calm demeanor, never getting flustered on the mound, no matter what.

Lee Smith

Like 1960s closer Dick Radatz, Smith was one big dude. But unlike "The Monster," Smith compiled a long and productive career. He threw hard and stared at the batter even harder. But for some reason, GMs kept trading him; he pitched for eight different clubs. Smith retired in 1997 as the all-time saves leader, with 478. (He's now in second.)

Bruce Sutter

When Sutter began throwing his split-fingered fastball, every opposing manager was sure he was loading up. It just dropped too far too fast to be anything but a spitter, they reasoned. Sutter used it to dominate National League batters for nearly a decade. He led the Cardinals to the World Series in 1982 and rang up two saves there. He won one Cy Young Award and four Fireman of the Year Awards. He was elected to the Hall of Fame in 2006.

Hoyt Wilhelm

Wilhelm turned 29 the first year he pitched in the big leagues, but he stuck around long enough after that to appear in more ML games than any pitcher ever (1,070) at the time of his retirement. (He is currently fifth.) The secret was the dazzling dance of his knuckleball, so daunting that catchers turned to extra-large gloves to snag it. He had an ERA under 2.00 each year from 1964 to '68 and earned a spot in the Hall of Fame.

Can of Corn

"You're only as smart as your ERA."

> —Jim Bouton, *I'm Glad You Didn't Take It Personally*

"When Steve and I die, we're going to be buried 60 feet, six inches apart."

> —Tim McCarver, Steve Carlton's "personal" catcher
> for much of his career, *The Pitcher*

"It took eight hours... seven and a half to find the heart."

> —Oakland pitcher Steve McCatty on hearing of A's owner
> Charlie O. Finley's heart surgery, *Temporary Insanity*

"On turf the ball comes to me and says, 'Catch me.' On grass it says, 'Look out, sucker.'"

> —Greg Pryor, *Playing the Field*

"I have trouble remembering my wedding anniversary, but I remember those four pitches. I remember I got a big hand from the crowd when I left."

> —Angels pitcher Paul Foytack, recalling the four straight home
> runs he allowed in a game at Cleveland on July 31, 1963

"... jumped about like colts, stamped their feet, clapped their hands, threw their hats in the air, slapped their companions on the back, winked knowingly... and from a baseball standpoint, enjoyed themselves tremendously."

> —*New York Times* account of fans at a Giants game, May 31, 1888

"You do things my way, or meet me after the game."

> —Manager Frank Chance's supposed warning to his Cubs players

Babe Ruth's Called Shot: Did He or Didn't He?

Whether Ruth called a home run in the 1932 World Series remains one of baseball's greatest mysteries.

This much is known. The Yankees had already won the first two games of the '32 fall classic when they met the Cubs at Wrigley Field for Game 3. Although Chicago players were understandably frustrated, there was bad blood between the teams that extended beyond the norm. In August, the Cubs had picked up former Yankee shortstop Mark Koenig from the Pacific Coast League to replace injured starter Billy Jurges, and Koenig hit .353 the rest of the season. Despite these heroics, his new teammates had only voted him a half-share of their World Series bonus money—a slight that enraged his old colleagues. The Yanks engaged in furious bench-jockeying with their "cheapskate" opponents the entire series, and Chicago players and fans shouted back, jeering that Ruth was old, fat, and washed-up.

Up to bat. When Ruth stepped up to bat in the fifth inning of Game 3, the taunts started as usual. A few people threw lemons at Babe from the stands, and he gestured toward the crowd before settling in at the plate. Charlie Root's first pitch was a called strike, and Ruth, looking over at the Chicago dugout, appeared to hold up one finger—as if to say, "That's only one." He did the same thing with two fingers after taking the second pitch, another strike. Then, some eyewitnesses recalled, he pointed toward dead center field. Others didn't remember this act, but there was no mistaking what happened next: Ruth slammed Root's third offering deep into the edge of the right-field bleachers. Onlookers recalled him laughing as he rounded the bases. And, as shown in a much-published photo, he and on-deck batter Lou Gehrig laughed and shook hands back at home plate.

What really happened? Here is where the facts end and speculation begins. Those among the 49,986 fans on hand who noticed Ruth's display likely assumed it was just another round in the ongoing feud between the two clubs, and most sportswriters made nothing out of it in their accounts of New York's 7–5 victory. The homer was not a game-winner; it was just one (in fact, the last) of 15 home runs Ruth hit in World Series play during his career. He had already taken Root deep earlier in the same contest, and Gehrig also had two in the game. The Yanks finished their four-game sweep the next day.

This being Babe Ruth, however, it only took a few speculative accounts from among the many reporters present to get the ball rolling. "Ruth Calls Shot" read the headline in the next day's *New York World Telegram,* and soon sports fans everywhere were wondering. Gehrig claimed he heard Ruth yell to Root, "I'm going to knock the next one down your goddamned throat" before the fateful pitch, while Cubs catcher Gabby Hartnett recalled the remark as "It only takes one to hit." Root and Cubs second baseman Billy Herman denied any gesture to the outfield, and grainy film footage that surfaced in 1999 was unclear either way. Ever the diplomat, Ruth himself granted some interviews in which he substantiated the claim, and others in which he denied it.

So did he or didn't he? We may never know for sure, but perhaps it's better that way. When the subject is Babe Ruth, facts are only half the fun.

⚾ ⚾ ⚾

"I figured if I wasn't a good ballplayer, it wouldn't make any difference where I played; but if I was a good ballplayer, then I wanted to be with the Yankees."

—Tommy Henrich, *Baseball Between the Lines*

Index

465

Be sure to check out
www.armchairreader.com.

Contributing Writers

Paul Adomites has authored or coauthored six books, including *October's Game, The Golden Age of Baseball,* and *Babe Ruth: His Life and Times.* A former publications director for the Society for American Baseball Research (SABR), Paul founded the SABR *Review of Books* and published its successor, *The Cooperstown Review.* He is currently the book review editor for *Base Ball: A Journal of the Early Game.*

Bruce Markusen is the author of eight books, including *A Baseball Dynasty: Charlie Finley's Swingin' A's,* which was awarded the Seymour Medal from the Society for American Baseball Research. He has also written *The Team That Changed Baseball: Roberto Clemente and the 1971 Pittsburgh Pirates, Tales From the Mets Dugout,* and *The Orlando Cepeda Story.* An employee of the National Baseball Hall of Fame and Museum from 1995 to 2004, Markusen currently authors MLB.com's "Cooperstown Confidential," found at www.bruce.mlblogs.com.

Matthew Silverman is the author of *Mets Essential,* the coauthor of *Meet the Mets,* and he cowrote (with Jon Springer) the forthcoming *Mets by the Numbers.* He has been an associate editor for *The ESPN Baseball Encyclopedia* since 2004. He served as principal editor for *Baseball: The Biographical Encyclopedia* and was managing editor for the sixth and seventh editions of *Total Baseball.* He has edited many other books, including *The Ultimate Red Sox Companion, Ted Williams: My Life in Pictures,* and two versions of *Total Mets.*

Jon Springer is an editor at a business publication in New York. He is a member of the Society for American Baseball Research and the creator and author of the "Mets by the Numbers" project at www.mbtn.net.

Marty Strasen is an editor at www.TBO.com/*The Tampa Tribune* in Tampa, Florida. He has authored or been a contributing writer on several sports books, including *Dark Horses & Underdogs* and *Reel Baseball: Baseball's Golden Era.*

Saul Wisnia is the author or coauthor of numerous books about baseball and other subjects, including *Prime Time Baseball Stars, Wit & Wisdom of Baseball, Babe Ruth: His Life and Times,* and *Best of Baseball.* A former sports and features correspondent for *The Washington Post,* Wisnia has also written for *The Boston Globe, Sports Illustrated,* the *Boston Herald, Red Sox Magazine,* and many other publications. He is a founding member of the Boston Braves Historical Association.